Responsible Leadership

With a range of well-respected voices from across the business, political, third sector and research spectrum, this important book provides an accessible insight into responsible leadership. It represents the most comprehensive and informed work on responsible leadership linked to the United Nations (UN) Sustainable Development Goals (SDGs) produced to date.

This carefully edited volume, based on a collaborative partnership between the Institute for Responsible Leadership (IRL) and the United Nations Institute for Training and Research (UNITAR), contains twenty chapters in seven parts which address the relationship between responsible leadership and the UN Sustainable Development Goals. These original and accessible contributions discuss progress in a variety of areas relevant to the goals, including climate change and biodiversity, global health, cybercrime, human trafficking, corporate social responsibility, gender, education and social cohesion. The world-leading expert contributors are drawn from a wide range of societies and continents and cover key aspects of responsible leadership in a lively and impactful fashion.

This book is for leaders at every level in the public, private and third sectors, students concerned with responsible leadership, academics and researchers studying leadership in different disciplinary fields, and all those committed to sustainable development and progressing the UN SDGs.

Mike Saks is Emeritus Professor at the University of Suffolk and Visiting Professor at the University of Lincoln and the University of Westminster, UK, and the University of Toronto, Canada. He is also Chair of the United Nations-endorsed Institute for Responsible Leadership. He has published extensively on health, professions, regulation and research methods.

Responsible Leadership

Essential to the Achievement of the UN Sustainable Development Goals

Edited by
Mike Saks

Routledge
Taylor & Francis Group
LONDON AND NEW YORK

Cover image: Getty Images/anaion

First published 2023
by Routledge
4 Park Square, Milton Park, Abingdon, Oxon OX14 4RN

and by Routledge
605 Third Avenue, New York, NY 10158

Routledge is an imprint of the Taylor & Francis Group, an informa business

British Library Cataloguing-in-Publication Data
A catalogue record for this book is available from the British Library

Library of Congress Cataloging-in-Publication Data
Names: Saks, Mike, editor.
Title: Responsible leadership : essential to the achievement of the UN sustainable development goals / edited by Mike Saks.
Description: Abingdon, Oxon ; New York, NY : Routledge, 2023. | Includes bibliographical references and index.
Subjects: LCSH: Leadership. | Sustainable development. | Environmental responsibility.
Classification: LCC HD57.7 .R4635 2023 (print) | LCC HD57.7 (ebook) | DDC 658.4/092—dc23/eng/20220610
LC record available at https://lccn.loc.gov/2022023985
LC ebook record available at https://lccn.loc.gov/2022023986

ISBN: 978-0-367-65372-9 (hbk)
ISBN: 978-0-367-65378-1 (pbk)
ISBN: 978-1-003-12918-9 (ebk)

DOI: 10.4324/9781003129189

Typeset in Adobe Garamond Pro
by Apex CoVantage, LLC

A collaboration between the United Nations-endorsed Institute for Responsible Leadership and the United Nations Institute for Training and Research

IRL
INSTITUTE for RESPONSIBLE LEADERSHIP

unitar
United Nations Institute for Training and Research

Contents

Permissions

Grateful thanks are expressed for permissions for the following:

The United Nations-sponsored Institute for Responsible Leadership (IRL) for the IRL logo displayed in this book.

The United Nations Institute for Training and Research (UNITAR) for:

- The UNITAR logo displayed in this book
- Figure 1.1 on the United Nations Sustainable Development Goals
- Box 20.1 on the ten principles of the UN Global Compact.

PYXIS Culture Technologies for Figure 5.1 on Primary Causal Factors for the Sustainable Development Goals.

The copyright for all the other Figures and Tables in this book lies with the authors of the chapters concerned.

About the Editor

Professor Mike Saks is Emeritus Professor at the University of Suffolk and Visiting Professor at the University of Lincoln, the University of Westminster, United Kingdom (UK) and the University of Toronto, Canada. He was previously Visiting Professor at the Royal Veterinary College, University of London, Plymouth Marjon University and the University of Essex, UK. In 2018, he became Honorary Senior Adviser on Leadership to the United Nations (UN) and co-founder of the UN-endorsed Institute for Responsible Leadership (IRL). He is at present an appointed member of, and only UK representative on, the World Health Organization (WHO) Technical Expert Group on global Health Practitioner Regulation – a crucial agenda for both the WHO and the UN. He is a current Fellow of the Institute of Directors, the Institute of Knowledge Exchange, the Research Council for Complementary Medicine and the Royal Society of Arts. Internationally, he was until recently President of the International Sociological Association (ISA) Research Committee on Professional Groups and is the present Vice President of the ISA Research Committee on Health and a Board member of several top international journals, including the *Journal of Professions and Organization* (Oxford University Press). He also has a strong enterprise profile as a member of the Innovation Council, along with Chief Executives of major multinational corporations. In addition, he has been a chair/member of many National Health Service and health committees at all levels – covering areas from the changing healthcare workforce to research and development. He has frequently advised both professions and governments internationally on health and other matters – most recently producing the commissioned *Saks Report* in 2021, charting a strategic direction for the Royal College of Podiatry in the UK.

Mike Saks received his PhD in Sociology from the London School of Economics in 1986, where he also taught. He has held a university Chair since 1992. He was previously Provost and Chief Executive at University Campus Suffolk, Deputy Vice Chancellor at the University of Lincoln and Dean of Faculty of Health and Community Studies at De Montfort University – after contributing extensively to the Schools of Business, Law, Public Administration and Social Sciences there. He is a current Board member at Rose Bruford College of Theatre and Performance in London, having earlier served on the Executive of the University of Essex and University of East Anglia in the UK. His successful career in universities has included receiving *Times Higher Education* awards for Widening Participation University of the Year and Outstanding Leadership and Management Team of the Year. During his career, he has published over one hundred high-profile journal articles/chapters on health, professions, regulation and research methods, as well as more than twenty edited and single authored books on these subjects with top publishers including Routledge. He has given keynote presentations at conferences in dozens of countries, ranging from Argentina, Australia and Azerbaijan to Italy, Japan and South Africa, as well as addressing diplomats and ambassadors at the UN in Geneva. He has participated in funded research with partners spanning from the Russian Academy of Sciences in Moscow to the University of Toronto in Canada, where he received the Best Brains Exchange Award in 2014 from Health Canada and the Canadian Institutes of Health Research. Recent invited global activities include visiting roles at the University of California in the United States and Wuhan University in China, as well as being a Member of the Advisory Council of the School of Creative Arts in Ghana.

Mike Saks as Editor has pulled this collection together, but grateful thanks are due to Professor Michael Hopkins, Mike Eldon and Julie Search-Whittaker, co-founders of the IRL, and Alex Mejía, Director of Division for People and Social Inclusion, United Nations Institute for Training and Research, for their support in reading and feeding back to myself on the final version of this book.

Contributors

Dr Andromachi Athanasopoulou Senior Lecturer/Associate Professor in Organisational Behaviour and Head of the Department of People and Organisations in the School of Business and Management at Queen Mary University of London, and Associate Fellow at the Saïd Business School, Oxford University, United Kingdom

Professor Brigid Carroll Fletcher Building Employee Educational Fund Professor of Leadership in the Department of Management and International Business, University of Auckland, New Zealand

Professor Martin Cortazzi Visiting Professor of Applied Linguistics in the Department of Applied Linguistics at the University of Warwick, United Kingdom, and at City University of Macau, China

Professor Colin Coulson-Thomas Honorary Professor, Aston University, and Visiting Professor, Lincoln International Business School, United Kingdom, Distinguished Professor, Sri Sharada Institute of Indian Management, President of the Institute of Management Services, Leader, OSLJ International Governance Initiative, Director-General, UK and Europe, Institute of Directors, India, and Fellow of the Institute for Responsible Leadership

Professor Sue Dopson Rhodes Trust Professor of Organisational Behaviour and Associate Dean of Faculty at the Saïd Business School, Oxford University, and Fellow of Green Templeton College, Oxford University, United Kingdom, and Visiting Professor at the University of Alberta, Canada

James M. Durant III Retired United States Air Force Judge Advocate Colonel, Chief Counsel for the Office of Science, US Department of Energy, Fellow of the American Bar Foundation, former Senior NATO Legal Advisor, and Chair of the Senior Executives Association, United States

Mike Eldon Director of the Institute for Responsible Leadership, management consultant, newspaper columnist, Chair/Director of various companies, and until recently Chair of Council of KCA University, Kenya

Sebastian Hofbauer Programme Manager at the Global Surgery Foundation, former United Nations Fellow, Geneva, Switzerland, and Associate of the Institute for Responsible Leadership

Professor Michael Hopkins Director of the Institute for Responsible Leadership and former Senior Economist at the United Nations International Labour Organization, Geneva, Switzerland

Professor Miwako Hosoda Professor in the Faculty of Life Network Science and former Vice-President at Seisa University and President of Inclusive Action for All, Japan

Professor Lixian Jin Chair/Professor of Applied Linguistics and Dean of Faculty of Humanities and Social Sciences at City University of Macau, China

Dr Rhiannon Lloyd Professional Teaching Fellow in the Department of Management and International Business, University of Auckland, New Zealand

Professor Sa'ad Sam Medhat Chief Executive of the Institute of Innovation and Knowledge Exchange and Chief Executive STEM Foundation, Visiting Professor at the University of Westminster, United Kingdom, and Fellow of the Institute for Responsible Leadership

Alex Mejía Director of Division for People and Social Inclusion, United Nations Institute for Training and Research, Geneva, Switzerland, former Minister of Finance and Planning, Ecuador, and Fellow of the Institute for Responsible Leadership

Edward Milner Visiting Professor at the Sustainability Research Institute, University of East London, former BBC producer, and independent environmental consultant, United Kingdom

Dr Mahima Mitra Research Fellow at the Saïd Business School and Academic Associate of Brasenose College, Oxford University, United Kingdom

Professor Mike Saks Chair of the Institute for Responsible Leadership, Emeritus Professor at the University of Suffolk, Visiting Professor at the University of Lincoln and the University of Westminster, United Kingdom, and Visiting Professor at the University of Toronto, Canada

Professor Guy Standing Professorial Research Associate at the School of Oriental and African Studies, University of London, United Kingdom, and Fellow of the Institute for Responsible Leadership

Julie Search-Whittaker Chief Executive of the Institute for Responsible Leadership, co-Director of StorytellingPlus and experienced educationalist, United Kingdom

Professor Louise Shelley Omer L. and Nancy Hirst Endowed Professor at the Schar School of Policy and Government and Director of the Terrorism, Transnational Crime and Corruption Center at George Mason University, United States

Adrian Sladdin Educational consultant and Managing Director of Seventh Wave Education Group, United Kingdom

Professor Michael Smets Professor of Management at the Saïd Business School, Oxford University, and Fellow of Green Templeton College, Oxford University, United Kingdom

Christiane Wuillamie OBE Chief Executive of Pyxis Culture Technologies, United Kingdom, and Fellow of the Institute for Responsible Leadership

Enver Yücel President of BAU Global, Bahçeşehir Uğur Education Foundation, and the UNITAR CIFAL Centre in Istanbul, Turkey

Professor David Zakus Adjunct Professor in the Dalla Lana School of Public Health at the University of Toronto, Editor and Publisher of *Planetary Health Weekly*, and Principal of D&D Education Services Inc, Canada

About the Institute for Responsible Leadership

Mike Saks's profile underlines his wide-ranging and high-level experience in editing this exciting collaborative book on responsible leadership with the United Nations (UN), making special reference to the achievement of the Sustainable Development Goals (SDGs). His global experience, combined with a range of expert contributors from several different countries and continents covering many facets of responsible leadership, makes for a timely volume based on a collaboration between the Institute for Responsible Leadership (IRL), of which he is now the Chair, and the United Nations Institute for Responsible Leadership (UNITAR). As such, this book is intended to have a high impact in making the world a better place. Half of the proceeds will go towards the activities of the UN-endorsed IRL, a not-for-profit organization based in London, United Kingdom, to fulfill its primary aim of advancing responsible leadership across the globe. Its principles include:

- Promoting leadership integrity resonant with Corporate Social Responsibility/ Sustainability in the public and private sector
- Offering courses/seminars, accreditation, mentoring, coaching and research support in responsible leadership
- Providing high-quality input and facilitation through founding members and key examples of responsible leadership through Associates
- Publicizing our Fellowships as examples of good practice
- Promoting a charter on responsible leadership for companies and other organizations.

Those interested in the IRL should consult its website (https://www.responsibleleadership.org), which also provides further information on its activities and how to become a member.

About the United Nations Institute for Training and Research

The United Nations Institute for Training and Research (UNITAR) provides innovative learning solutions to individuals, organizations and institutions to enhance global decision-making and support country-level action for shaping a better future. UNITAR was created over fifty years ago to train and equip young diplomats from newly independent United Nations (UN) Member States with the knowledge and skills needed to navigate through the diplomatic environment. Over the years, UNITAR has acquired unique expertise and experience in designing and delivering a variety of training activities. It has become a leading institute in the provision of customized and creative learning solutions to institutions and individuals from both public and private sectors. With a strategy fully focused on achieving the Sustainable Development Goals (SDGs), UNITAR supports governments to implement the agenda for 2030. Its main functions are:

- Providing high-quality learning solutions to address the capacity development needs of individuals, organizations and institutions
- Advising and supporting governments, the UN and other partners with knowledge services, including those that are technology based
- Facilitating knowledge and experience sharing through networked and innovative processes
- Integrating innovative strategies, approaches and methodologies into our learning and related knowledge products and services.

These all accord with its mission of developing the individual, institutional and organizational capacities of countries and other UN stakeholders through high-quality learning solutions and related knowledge products and services to enhance decision-making and to support country-level action for overcoming global challenges. More details are given on the UNITAR website (https://www.unitar.org).

Part I

Challenges of Responsible Leadership in a National and International Context

Chapter 1

Responsible Leadership

Following the Spirit of Nelson Mandela

Mike Saks

Introduction

The world is currently in crisis on a number of fronts, and this book endeavors to analyze the situation – past, present and future – covering a broad range of perspectives and areas related to responsible leadership. The importance of this volume is highlighted by a recent speech by the Secretary-General of the United Nations (UN), Antonio Guterres (2020), who reflected from a UN perspective that: "From health to the economy to the climate and beyond, we are confronting the biggest set of global challenges in generations." However, he optimistically argued that we "have the opportunity to not simply reset the world but to transform it" – not least in a more sustainable, inclusive and resilient manner with respect to human rights on a healthy planet. As he indicated, this will require responsible leadership including coordination, cooperation and action in both lower- and middle-income countries and richer societies that will affect the lives of generations to come.

The need for this transition and the central role of the UN in the process is highlighted in a recent book by Barack Obama (2020), ex-President of the United States. He has claimed that, for all its understandable shortcomings in a complex

DOI: 10.4324/9781003129189-2

world, the UN has served a vital function in shaming countries into better behavior and strengthening international norms. As a result of

> the UN's work in mediation and peacekeeping, cease-fires had been brokered, conflicts had been averted, and lives had been saved. The UN played a role in more than eighty former colonies becoming sovereign nations. Its agencies helped lift tens of millions of people out of poverty, eradicated smallpox, and very nearly wiped out polio and Guinea worm.
> (Obama, 2020: 469–70)

For him, this wide span of activities – also encapsulated in actions ranging from the building of schools to combatting sex trafficking – has been strongly driven by the responsible leadership of the UN from its headquarters in New York City and elsewhere.

Parallel sentiments have been expressed by other key thought leaders of the twenty-first century around climate change. Thus, Sir David Attenborough (2020) has reinforced the need for a sustainable lifestyle in which the modern human world is brought back into balance with nature. As the renowned broadcaster says: "Only then will the biodiversity loss we have caused begin to turn to biodiversity gain. Only then can the world rewild, and stability return" (Attenborough, 2020: 126). He too positively believes that, if we choose to follow it, we already have a compass for this journey, which tells us that "we must immediately halt and preferably start to reverse climate change by attending to greenhouse gas emissions whenever they occur, the chief measure by which we judge our actions is the revival of the natural world". Similar thoughts have been expressed by Greta Thunberg, the environmental activist, who has spoken at the UN and mobilized millions of young people from Melbourne to San Francisco to protest about the lack of actions by governments on climate change. She has also emphasized the word 'responsibility' in endeavoring to inspire those in power, as well as individual citizens, to more fervently address this issue (Giannella, 2019).

The objectives of the book

These thoughts by young and older opinion leaders represent at least some of the insightful wisdom of the greats on leadership (Davis, 2016). In so doing, they reinforce the main objective of this book, which is to provide an accessible work on leading-edge thinking on responsible leadership. The need for responsible leadership has been underlined by the recent conflict in Ukraine. This unfortunate situation has destabilized the world economically and militarily – and has caused suffering to the Ukrainian civilian population, leading to the biggest refugee crisis since the Second World War. It has therefore been roundly condemned by almost all countries of the world. In this respect, the UN General Assembly in the first part of 2022 voted to demand the end of the conflict, with 141 states in favor and only five against, with 35 abstentions (Borger, 2022). Although the resolution is not legally binding, its strong language is a litmus test of global opinion about responsible leadership.

This condemnation by the UN General Assembly of the violation of the territory of a sovereign nation is very relevant because this edited volume is intended to offer leaders at all organizational levels in the public, private and third sector a critical, academically informed guide to the essential role of responsible leadership in achieving sustainable development in line with the Sustainable Development Goals (SDGs) of the UN (2015). In the case of the conflict in Ukraine, this flies in face of the UN SDGs promoting just, peaceful and inclusive societies, and the need for global partnership in fostering sustainable development. More broadly in terms of the extensive range of SDGs that will be outlined shortly in this chapter, there is increasing interest in a wider range of issues surrounding responsible leadership in a highly turbulent world plagued by the effects of divisive political leadership and damaging leadership scandals in private, public and third sector organizations (Saks and Search-Whittaker, 2018). This book accordingly brings together in one volume a broad span of extremely topical work on responsible leadership linked to the UN SDGs.

The book takes its lead from the co-founders of the UN-sponsored Institute for Responsible Leadership (IRL) and draws on its world-leading network of Fellows and Associates. It is based on a unique partnership between the United Nations Institute for Training and Research (UNITAR) and the IRL. It is significant that the logo of the UN-endorsed IRL – which appears on the cover of this volume along with that of UNITAR – is based on an image of Nelson Mandela. He is considered a universally acknowledged and iconic responsible leader. He had every right to feel bitter as a result of his lengthy prison experience of over twenty-five years on Robben Island and elsewhere for conspiracy to overthrow the state in South Africa. Instead, on release, he set aside prejudice to lead the country in partnership with both the previously oppressive government and the African National Congress into the period beyond apartheid (Mandela, 1994). Following his election as President through South Africa's first truly democratic election, he rightly became seen globally as a role model of an exemplary leader (Stengel, 2018).

In the spirit of Mandela, responsible leaders in both the public and private sector, as defined by the IRL, treat stakeholders with integrity to ensure that issues of sustainability, ethics and the wider public interest are best addressed. In referring to the public and private sector, there may be different conceptions of what constitutes responsible leadership. In the latter, there tend to be shareholder notions of such leadership centered on delivering the highest dividends to shareholders. Although there is increasing appreciation of the financial and other value of a wider corporate social responsibility approach (Hopkins, 2016), good governance is frequently seen as focused on the efficient and effective running of companies with due attention given to areas such as risk management, shareholder relations, remuneration and succession planning. Here value is typically defined in terms of the generation of profits, selling products/services, the generation of cashflow, increasing shareholder returns, the ability to pay off debts and resilience to operational failure (Grant Thornton, 2019).

While there are intersections, this concept of value is given a slightly different spin by wider concepts of good governance for holders of public office. These include the seven Nolan Principles, addressed to a more generic span of stakeholders, which were established at the direction of a British Prime Minister concerned at ensuring high standards of conduct at a time of growing scrutiny, through the Committee on Standards in Public Life (1995). These Principles for leaders can be set out as follows:

- Selflessness: Holders of public office should act solely in terms of the public interest.
- Integrity: They must avoid placing themselves under any obligation to people or organizations that might try inappropriately to influence them in their work. They should not act or take decisions in order to gain financial or other material benefits for themselves, their family, or their friends. They must declare and resolve any interests and relationships.
- Objectivity: They must act and take decisions impartially, fairly and on merit, using the best evidence and without discrimination or bias.
- Accountability: They are accountable to the public for their decisions and actions and must submit themselves to the scrutiny necessary to ensure this.
- Openness: They should act and take decisions in an open and transparent manner. Information should not be withheld from the public unless there are clear and lawful reasons for so doing.
- Honesty: They should be truthful at all times.
- Leadership: They should exhibit these principles in their own behavior and treat others with respect. They should actively promote and robustly support the principles and challenge poor behavior wherever it occurs.

Of course, such Principles are subject to debate in terms of how they are articulated in practice – for example, the notion of the 'public interest' is inevitably contentious depending on how it is defined, as economic, legal, political, sociological and other interpretations tend to vary every which way (Saks, 1995). However, these broader Principles, which were established in the United Kingdom, have international resonance. They are also extended and made more specific in this book, where responsible leadership is regarded as being inextricably tied to the broad-ranging global SDGs of the UN that apply to both the private and public sectors. These goals will now be presented in a little more detail.

Responsible leadership and the Sustainable Development Goals of the United Nations

This book argues that the concept of responsible leadership as set out above centrally encompasses the SDGs of the UN. The SDGs represent a call for action for poor, middle-income and rich countries aimed at promoting prosperity, while protecting the planet (United Nations, 2015). They are based on the tenet that ending poverty and social injustices must go hand in hand with strategies building economic growth and addressing social needs from education and health, to creating job opportunities, as well as tackling climate change and environmental protection. The 17 composite goals also provide a framework to enable the world's recovery from the recent ravages of COVID-19 – in which no one is fine until everyone reaches at least a satisfactory level of existence.

Further details of the SDGs and their subsidiary targets are to be found on the UN website (https://sdgs.un.org), but their content can be conveniently summarized for the purposes of this book in Figure 1.1 below:

Figure 1.1 The United Nations Sustainable Development Goals

Source: United Nations (2015) *Transforming Our World: The 2030 Agenda for Sustainable Development*, Geneva: UN.

Here the various SDGs in the chart can be elaborated as follows:

Goal 1: End poverty in all its forms everywhere
Goal 2: End hunger and ensure access by all to safe, nutritious and sufficient food all year round
Goal 3: Ensure healthy lives and promote well-being for all at all ages
Goal 4: Ensure all people have access to free, equitable and quality education
Goal 5: Achieve gender equality and empower all women and girls
Goal 6: Ensure access to water and sanitation for all
Goal 7: Ensure access to affordable, reliable, sustainable and modern energy
Goal 8: Promote inclusive and sustainable economic growth, employment and decent work for all
Goal 9: Build resilient infrastructure, promote sustainable industrialization and foster innovation
Goal 10: Reduce inequality within and among countries
Goal 11: Make cities inclusive, safe, resilient and sustainable
Goal 12: Ensure sustainable consumption and production patterns
Goal 13: Take urgent action to combat climate change and its impact
Goal 14: Conserve and sustainably use the oceans, seas and marine resources
Goal 15: Sustainably manage forests, combat desertification, reverse land degradation and halt the loss of biodiversity
Goal 16: Promote just, peaceful and inclusive societies
Goal 17: Revitalize the global partnership for sustainable development.

Sustainability is a key underlying concept in the SDGs, which have been adopted by all member states of the UN as a universal call to action to end poverty, protect the planet and ensure that all people enjoy peace and prosperity by 2030. Sustainable development requires an integrated approach that takes into consideration everything from environmental concerns and health to economic development. The publication on *Our Common Future* by the World Commission on Environment and Development (1987), now known as the Brundtland Report, which was debated at the UN General Assembly, classically defined sustainability as "meeting the needs of the present without compromising the ability of future generations to meet their own needs". As will be seen, this concept is implicit in many of the contributions to this book.

The contents of the book

This carefully curated volume contains twenty specially commissioned chapters which address in various ways responsible leadership and the UN SDGs from a global perspective. Its original, well-referenced and coherently structured offerings discuss progress in a myriad of areas relevant to these UN goals in lively, and yet impactful, fashion. An important strength of this book is that its expert contributors are drawn from a wide range of societies and several continents – with voices covering a variety of key aspects of responsible leadership in the context of global endeavors to achieve the UN SDGs in many regions of the world, from Europe and the Americas to Africa and Asia. This gives this book great international traction.

Following this overarching introduction, which forms Chapter 1 of Part I 'Challenges of responsible leadership in a national and international context', Chapter 2 contains a personal statement on this central theme from Alex Mejía, a longstanding Director at UNITAR. From his high-level position of global oversight, he is well placed to explore developments in responsible leadership primarily in the public sector in relation to the SDGs, to which there has been widespread buy in from civil society. His comments underline the challenges that have been posed in advancing these in the 'left field' but devastating period of the COVID-19 pandemic, which is referred to in many of the subsequent contributions. Having set the tone for the volume more generally, the further ensuing analytical, engaging and interdisciplinary chapters are organized into six further parts.

Part II 'Leadership and social responsibility' starts with Chapter 3 by James M. Durant III, a highly experienced international lawyer, who gives his personal view unrelated to his other official roles of notions of human rights, ethics and justice in relation to responsible leadership from an historical and a contemporary constitutional perspective, including responsibilities to stakeholders. Drawing on a range of examples, Sa'ad Sam Medhat in Chapter 4 then examines in the context of business and industry the topical issue of responsible leadership and innovation, the latter of which is one of the core UN SDGs and is becoming ever more important in modern societies. This is followed in Chapter 5 by Christiane Wuillamie, whose contribution covers responsible leadership and the increasing partnership imperative to protect against ever more organized digital crime, including data scamming, which is escalating under the impetus of the digital revolution in a global context. Pleasingly, she points to a number of steps that can give greater organizational cybersecurity.

There are debates as to whether the definition of responsible leadership is more limited in private, as opposed to public, domains. In Part III 'Responsible leadership in the private and public sector', Colin Coulson-Thomas, from a highly-informed international base, highlights in Chapter 6 that there can be good governance in both of these domains and sets out some key markers in face of the challenges and opportunities presented to boards. However, Guy Standing emphasizes in his more politicized Chapter 7 that the growing spread of privatization and rentier capitalism has increasingly impacted on responsible leadership, with highly detrimental implications – not least in neo-liberal societies in relation to poverty, the alleviation of which lies at the heart of the UN SDGs. Nonetheless, as Michael Hopkins persuasively argues in Chapter 8, corporate social responsibility can still bring broader benefit in the private, as well as the public, sector – especially since it has its own financial rewards for the companies concerned, along with sustainability and other vital gains.

Part IV 'Communication and responsible leadership' focuses on the role of empowering interaction and responsible leadership in the context of the UN SDGs. It incorporates Chapter 9 by Mike Eldon on the crucial part played by emotional intelligence, as opposed to simply technical expertise, in responsible leadership and its central role in increasing social cohesion – arguably one of the most challenging tasks for government. Chapter 10 by Lixian Jin and Martin Cortazzi then addresses intercultural communication and responsible leadership, with reference to two case studies on university teacher-leaders and senior leaders in international companies based on their own research linked to the advancement of the UN SDGs. Part IV of the book also includes Chapter 11 by Rhiannon Lloyd and Brigid Carroll again on a theme central to achieving the SDGs – namely, the need for co-responsible leadership and partnership, involving communication, shared responsibility and collective problem solving, as illustrated by the field-breaking case of the 2015 Paris Agreement on climate change.

Part V 'Education, professions and responsible leadership' begins with Chapter 12 by Julie Search-Whittaker and Adrian Sladdin on the role of responsible leadership in school and college education, which underlines the significance of revitalization in this area if such goals as advancing equality and quality are to be achieved as human rights. In Chapter 13, Enver Yücel, himself heavily engaged as the head of a major international university, considers higher education as a key fulcrum for responsible leadership and central to the realization of the UN SDGs – at a time when many global universities have aligned their mission with these goals. Higher education also typically now underpins the qualifying route to the professions. Chapter 14 by Mike Saks accordingly charts the past, present and future of such intermediary groups, in terms of the responsible leadership they can potentially provide in the future betterment of society by translating their longstanding codes of ethics into practice.

One central task of responsible leadership is to avoid a global apocalypse, which is discussed in Part VI 'Responsible leadership, the environment and global health'. In Chapter 15 Miwako Hosoda examines the relationship between COVID-19 and global human health – with particular reference to the problems the pandemic has posed for health resources, education, socio-economic status, and discrimination and stigma and how the international community might address these. Meanwhile in Chapter 16 David Zakus examines the depressing global response to climate change and preserving planetary health – highlighting the devastating effects of global warming and the need for urgent action, given the hard-edged scientific evidence for impending disaster. This part of the book finishes with Chapter 17 by Edward Milner on the no less disturbing associated theme of biodiversity – relating to the millions of life forms on Earth and their interdependencies – in which humanity has again not covered itself in glory. All these chapters represent a clarion call for responsible leadership in the achievement of the associated UN SDGs, which we ignore at our peril.

Finally, Part VII 'Diversity, challenge and change' covers various high-profile issues of inclusivity in exercising responsible leadership in fulfilling the SDGs. In Chapter 18, Mahima Mitra, Andromachi Athanasopoulou, Sue Dopson and Michael Smets focus on gender and ethnicity and the route to the top – examining institutional and individual barriers to a more diverse and responsible leadership and how these might be overcome in future. Louise Shelley in Chapter 19 then explores the sensitive subject of human trafficking, including sex trafficking and labor trafficking, by employing a similar lens – albeit highlighting the invidious and often hidden role that even legitimate companies have played in this criminal activity, despite efforts by government legislators and enforcement authorities. Sebastian Hofbauer in Chapter 20 concludes the book by analyzing the challenges of youth leadership, which is so pivotal to the future achievement of the UN SDGs; he particularly explores how young influencers can find a stronger responsible voice through social media with the support of tighter but proportionate regulation in moving forward global agendas in the public interest.

The benefits of the book

There is no shortage of literature on leadership, including many articles in journals related to this subject, from the *Journal of Leadership and Organizational Studies* to the more simply titled publication *Leadership*. There are also very many books on leadership – far too many to mention in detail here – spanning from compilations of classic insights (for example, Thomas, 2021), to distillations of best practice based on experience (for instance, Blakey, 2021). Moreover, both Oxford University Press (Day, 2014) and Routledge (Storey et al., 2016) have produced handbooks and companions which provide edited academic overviews of the leadership field. Other well-regarded evidence-based books include those covering general aspects of leadership (as illustrated by Kouzes and Posner, 2017). Some of these are more specific in their focus, such as the refreshing volume by Østergaard (2018) titled *The Responsive Leader*, even if this calls for lateral expansion, as responsiveness is an important subset of responsible leadership.

Within this literature, responsible leadership is a niche area all too rarely directly addressed, despite its critical significance. Here recent books include that by Badaracco (2013) and Piroti and Venzin (2017), who respectively write about the dilemmas of responsible leadership in an unforgiving world and the associated question of resilience in organizations in times of uncertainty. The edited collections by Kempster and Carroll (2016) and Kempster, Maak and Parry (2020) helpfully discuss the broader relevance of responsible leadership too, not least in a business context. This is also where the relationship with corporate social responsibility is forged (Hopkins, 2016). All this sits alongside other volumes on the more detailed links of responsible leadership to areas ranging from ethics (Moody-Stuart, 2014) to project management (Clarke et al., 2017).

What marks out this particular book, though, is its accessibility, scope and global reach – going beyond the limits of many other texts in this field. Its breadth is underlined by its focus on the UN SDGs, which – together with its evidence-driven approach – makes it the most comprehensive, up-to-date and informed work on responsible leadership to date. Its further benefits lie in the integrated style and top-level international expertise in dealing with a broad span of areas in a single volume – and the close partnership between the IRL and UNITAR on which this volume is founded. As such, the main readership of the book will be members of the public with an interest in responsible leadership, leaders at every level in the public, private and third sectors aiming to act responsibly, students concerned with the implementation of responsible leadership, academics/researchers studying leadership in a wide span of disciplinary fields, and all those concerned with sustainable development and progressing the UN's crucial SDGs.

References

Attenborough, D. (2020) *A Life on Our Planet: My Witness Statement and a Vision for the Future*, London: Witness Books.

Badaracco, J. (2013) *The Good Struggle: Responsible Leadership in an Unforgiving World*, Brighton, MA: Harvard Business Review Press.

Blakey, J. (2021) *Trusted Executive: Nine Leadership Habits that Inspire Results, Relationships and Reputation*, 2nd edition, London: Kogan Page.

Borger, J. (2022) 'UN votes to condemn Russia's invasion of Ukraine and calls for withdrawal', *The Guardian*, 2 March.

Clarke, N., Damato, A., Higgs, M. and Vahidi, R. (2017) *Responsible Management in Projects*, Philadelphia: Project Management Institute.

Committee on Standards in Public Life (1995) *The Seven Principles of Public Life*, London: Cabinet Office.

Davis, J. (2016) *The Greats on Leadership: Classic Wisdom for Modern Managers*, Boston, MA: Nicholas Brearley Publishing.

Day, D. V. (ed) (2014) *The Oxford Handbook of Leadership and Organizations*, Oxford: Oxford University Press.

Giannella, V. (ed) (2019) *We Are All Greta: Be Inspired to Save the World*, London: Laurence King Publishing.

Grant Thornton (2019) *Corporate Governance and Company Performance*, London: GT.

Hopkins, M. (2016) *CSR Sustainability: From the Margins to the Mainstream*, London: Routledge.

Kempster, S. and Carroll, B. (eds) (2016) *Responsible Leadership: Realism and Romanticism*, London: Routledge.

Kempster, S., Maak, T. and Parry, K. (eds) (2020) *Good Dividends: Responsible Leadership of Business Purpose*, London: Routledge.

Kouzes, J. M. and Posner, B. Z. (2017) *The Leadership Challenge*, Hoboken, NJ: John Wiley & Sons.

Mandela, N. (1994) *Long Walk to Freedom*, London: Little, Brown and Company.

Moody-Stuart, M. (2014) *Responsible Leadership: Lessons from the Front Line of Sustainability and Ethics*, London: Routledge.

Obama, B. (2020) *A Promised Land*, New York: Penguin Books.

Østergaard, E. K. (2018) *The Responsive Leader*, London: Lid Publications.

Piroti, G. B. and Venzin, M. (2017) *Resilient Organizations: Responsible Leadership in Times of Uncertainty*, Cambridge: Cambridge University Press.

Saks, M. (1995) *Professions and the Public Interest*, London: Routledge.

Saks, M. and Search-Whittaker, J. (2018) 'Responsible leadership in challenging times', *Brite Innovation Review*, December.

Stengel, R. (2018) *Mandela's Way: Lessons for an Uncertain Age*, New York: Crown Publishing Group.

Storey, J., Hartley, J., Denis, J-L., Hart, P. and Ulrich, D. (eds) (2016) *The Routledge Companion to Leadership*, London: Routledge.

Thomas, M. (ed) (2021) *Gurus on Leadership: A Guide to the World's Thought-Leaders in Leadership*, Reprinted edition, London: Thorogood Publishing.

United Nations (2015) *Transforming Our World: The 2030 Agenda for Sustainable Development*, Geneva: UN.

United Nations (2020) UN Secretary-General's opening press message to the G20 leaders on 20 November.

World Commission on Environment and Development (1987) *Our Common Future: From One Earth to One World*, Geneva: UN.

Chapter 2

Responsible Leadership and the Sustainable Development Goals of the United Nations

Alex Mejía

Introduction

The analysis of responsible leadership can be rather different depending on which field we examine. The easiest way to dissect what constitutes responsible leadership could be to separate it into two fields or spheres of influence: the private sector and the public sector. Here both areas present similar challenges and can have a great impact on society. My own experience most heavily lies in the public sector domain, where successes or failures of leaders can often be very critical. After all, when a political leader or public figure demonstrates the right type of leadership, the results of decisions and behavior not only make a society more virtuous and progressive but also create inspiration, lifting the morale of a community. However, when that leader is flawed or corrupt, the consequences are suffered by the whole of society. And those consequences are not only the obvious negative results that the media covers in following a crisis or a scandal but also invisible consequences that damage a society in ways that are less conspicuous, like the lessons or the examples the next

DOI: 10.4324/9781003129189-3

generation receives. Great leaders inspire and make us better. Poor leaders demotivate us all and create the wrong role models.

From my perspective as a former government official from a middle-income country, and after working for many years at a United Nations (UN) agency, I would postulate that responsible leadership has been strengthened in recent decades by the advent of the information age. Now it is more difficult to ignore the scrutiny and the demands of the people we serve, as information flows in a microsecond and accountability is ever-present in the minds of political leaders. We no longer live in a society where public opinion is controlled by the media moguls or shaped by titans of industry, as social media has upset the powers that be and instead provides real information in real time to real people with real access to the Internet. But if that is the case, why do we see a rise in corruption and populism in recent years? Why does it seem that many societies show apathy towards the big issues facing a nation?

Many experts will point to manipulation of the narrative through disinformation of fake news but also to an excess of information that is overwhelming all of us (see, for instance, Rusbridger, 2021). It seems that in this era of hyperconnectedness, even in democratic systems, access to information and the ability to scrutinize our leaders in real time has not necessarily improved the quality of their decision-making, or shown a tangible improvement in the responsibility and integrity evidenced by their behavior (Klaas, 2022). For some leaders of the current generation, things in the public sector simply appear to have changed pace, and everything now goes at viral speeds. This could show that changes in the environment in which a leader operates indeed affect them but that they simply adapt to the new reality. They adapt, but their identity and essence does not necessarily change. Who they are is what counts. And if they lack integrity, their behavior will show it. No matter how much scrutiny we subject them to, no matter how much information flows covering their actions, no matter how fast the result of their decisions reaches the public, the quality of their principles and commitments is an integral part of who they are and not a factor of how we constantly peer over them.

My grandfather was a public servant for many decades, and he used to say that integrity is to do the right thing when nobody is watching. I grew up listening to his stories and to the narrative of his generation, which reaffirmed that integrity was expected of everyone but particularly of civil servants. He used to correct me when I had just joined our government and would tell my friends that I was 'working' in the public sector. He would consistently tell me that to belong to the civil service was 'to serve' society and not just 'work' for society. This differentiation has stayed with me for many decades, and when I train young government officials as part of my job at the UN, I make the point that we not only have a 'job' but a 'duty' and that we 'serve' as opposed to just 'work'. And why is this important? It is critical if we expect people in the public sector to become leaders that actually 'serve' society and carry with them a sense of 'duty' and purpose that goes beyond receiving a paycheck at the end of every month.

A few years after joining my government, I became a deputy minister at the age of 34. I was catapulted into the ever-present turmoil and disarray of the pinnacle of the public sector and to the tip of the totem pole of decision-making. I started intuitively observing how things work in a Cabinet of Ministers or at the Presidency. I remember from my classes in university the theory about risk analysis and making decisions with imperfect information but would have never imagined how high the risk or how imperfect the data or the evidence would be in real life. I became an acting minister when my boss was no longer around, and I served the President in a closer type of relationship that taught me life lessons that I still cherish. I understood early on that the type of person a leader is makes the whole difference in government, as simplistic, pragmatic or superficial persons tend to choose the easy way forward and to make every decision in a way that maintains or enhances political capital. I served a President who depleted his political capital for the right causes and who – contrary to the norm – frequently ignored what the media said about him. One of the first things that I remember of my interaction with him is that he frequently overrode the pressure of the moment to open an urgent meeting in which he shared with several senior members of his Cabinet the real meaning of the word 'minister' in Latin, which is 'servant', and the fact that it was derived from the word 'minus', which means 'less'.

I use this episode in my career to assert that the right type of leadership comes from humility and from the ability to understand that leadership should be grounded in service. This is directly opposed to what we see sometimes when interacting with senior politicians or government officials. The concept of humility goes directly against seeing yourself as a dignitary who has reached the top of society and is entitled to privileges and admiration. The concept of service means that you are where you are to serve others, not to serve yourself. And that seems to be obvious for every person working in the public sector; however, it is not necessarily the case, as we have seen in recent years, at the highest levels of government. This points directly to the need to better understand what responsible leadership is in order to prevent the consequences of failed leadership. This is an urgent and permanent task that seems to be forgotten when you perform under constant and relentless pressure. I invoke as real-life examples decision-makers who fail to remember what responsible leadership is – the numerous cases of harsh populism and blatant corruption we are witnessing around us today. Without using particular examples of politicians who are ushering their nations towards radical political positions and populist solutions, there is a high correlation between those behaviors and the personal traits of those leaders. The same goes for cases of systemic corruption that have rocked entire societies and that have been managed directly from presidents' offices with the silent concordance of hundreds of top officials with shared poor integrity and the wrong values.

On the other side of the spectrum, we should be glad to see that the vast majority of world leaders are committed democrats who respect human rights and care for their populous. This implies that even if they were tempted to follow irresponsible and easier paths they went back to their senses and remembered their principles and the reason why they were there in the first place. Now, there is the eternal tension between the 'urgent' and the 'important'. I argue that responsible leaders focus as much on the 'urgent' as on the 'important' and actually manage to strike a balance between the two. What I have seen during more than two decades interacting at the highest levels of government is that the whirlwind of events forces you to focus almost entirely on extinguishing fires and not necessarily on the substantive and more long-term issues that society requires to see better days. This is why I am a firm believer in long-term development programs, and particularly in the UN (2015) Agenda 2030 for Sustainable Development. It persuades political leaders and invites senior government officials to maintain as a permanent priority a holistic approach towards development and a long-term vision on the path to progress for their nations.

Responsible leadership and sustainable development

When the Agenda 2030 for Sustainable Development was adopted in New York at the UN General Assembly in September 2015, the world celebrated, and all member states embraced this new roadmap. The implementation of the Sustainable Development Goals (SDGs) started at the beginning of 2016 with renewed optimism, after the limited success of the UN (2001) Millennium Development Goals (MDGs) pursued during the previous decade and a half. I remember the initial discussions on the SDGs and everyone's focus on monitoring and evaluating new goals and the need to develop and adopt indicators to measure progress. There was some reflection about what could be the biggest risks or challenges that the implementation of the Sustainable Development Agenda could face from that moment until its expected completion in the year 2030.

The UN and its member states gave priority to policy coherence and the need to fund governments' plans to achieve the SDGs, and we at the UN in Geneva joined forces with the UN Department of Economic and Social Affairs (DESA) in New York and with all UN Regional Commissions around the world to build capacity and engage senior government officials from developing nations through a series of regional capacity-building events under the name 'A2030 Learning Conferences'. This was conceived by UN Assistant Secretary-General Nikhil Seth, the Executive Director of the United Nations Institute for Training and Research (UNITAR). That strategy was opportune and productive, generating serious policy analysis and deep conversations with senior politicians and bureaucrats in many countries while we co-hosted these conferences in 2017 and 2018 with colleagues from New York and from every UN Regional Commission.

We discussed at length the what, why, how, who, where and when of the SDGs, but I have to say that we failed to forecast possible risks that could disrupt their implementation. We all understood that war and conflict could indeed become an insurmountable challenge, as peace and proper governance are pre-requisites for any virtuous policy cycle or for the implementation of a global campaign like Agenda 2030. We also discussed how natural or man-made disasters could become a serious challenge in the global fight against poverty and the quest for sustainable development, but none of us saw issues of global health as a potential disruptor. Who would have conceived at that moment that a global pandemic would arrive and create such havoc around the world, bringing entire countries to their knees and halting global progress almost to zero. Nobody in those dialogues saw it coming, and the few that may have seen it were not there.

We must remember this failure to anticipate and learn from our mistakes. It is understandable that we had no precedent to believe that something like a health pandemic would create a global crisis of such magnitude. But if we look closer, we have a precedent in the Spanish Flu pandemic, which was endured from February 1918 until April 1921 and infected a third of the global population (Abdo, 2020). If you extrapolate those numbers to our present-day population of 7.7 billion people, we could panic, thinking that we are only beginning with this global health crisis and that the worse is still to come. But things are different now, and we have vaccinations and medical advances that were not seen in the late 1920s. That is good news, but one of the lessons learnt is that we could have drafted plans to ensure that the SDGs continued under crisis scenarios. Pursuing the SDGs in conflict zones is almost impossible, but pursuing them during a health pandemic is possible by, for example, creating global funds for education that insulate poor boys and girls from losing access to teachers. A simple idea, during the pandemic, would have been the acceleration and enhancement of already existing programs for the provision of computers and ICTs for primary education in developing nations. Another idea could have been the creation of a harmonized response to the pandemic by enacting multilateral agreements. Here a global treaty could have facilitated coordination and decision-making in vaccination campaigns and in the travel restrictions and lockdowns that halted economies and exacerbated unemployment beyond what experts believed was necessary (Petrosky-Nadeau and Valletta, 2020).

On the whole, we still have time to analyze and discuss how global leadership could have worked better at the beginning of the pandemic, perhaps in the early months of 2020, so next time we are more resilient and better prepared. And that introspection should lead us to a better understanding of the reasons that led to the dissimilar behavior of political leaders that we have witnessed. We have all seen how every country had a different reaction and a particular way to manage the crisis. And some of those reactions were perhaps too political or calculated in terms of government stakeholders. Many critics believe that partisan reactions in the middle of a pandemic that affects everyone are not desirable and are not the type of leadership needed when the whole of society is suffering. After all, responsible leadership is the ability to serve all, a permanent attitude of responsibility towards the whole of society, and a set of principles that says a leader should serve with humility and listen to constructive criticism. If a leader is indeed a person of integrity, he or she can publicly accept mistakes and make corrections in time. Responsible leadership implies possessing emotional intelligence and empathy for the most vulnerable populations. That type of leadership is perfectly aligned with Agenda 2030.

Inclusivity and civil participation in global decision-making processes: A first in the history of multilateral architecture

I have always believed that the key factor in achieving the level of acceptance the SDGs enjoy around the world today was the involvement of Civil Society in its conceptualization and adoption. History would recognize UN Secretary-General Ban Ki-Moon for his visionary role in creating something different from the MDGs, which could be considered as one of the first global development policies. But first, let us go back in time and remember how this all started. During Ban's tenure, his team envisioned a global consultation that would end up engaging more than one million people. They provided their perspectives on what the future should bring, answering questions and submitting comments on the 'world we want'. There were 88 national consultations organized by the UN Development Group (UNDG) in as many countries. The UN also organized 11 thematic dialogues with the full involvement of Civil Society organizations and gave voice to the common citizen through a survey on the Internet. The decision to listen to these voices certainly contributed to reaching a global consensus on what was needed to move towards a common sustainable future. Secretary-General Ban launched the report *A Million Voices: The World We Want* in 2013 in New York (United Nations News, 2013).

The report was well received and praised as a critical tool to make the adoption of the 'post-2015 agenda' (as it was called at the time) a legitimate process. The UN (2012) outcome document *The Future We Want* forms the link between the agreement at the 2012 UN Rio De Janeiro Conference on Sustainable Development (Rio+20) and the MDGs. In paragraph 246 and 249 it states that:

> We recognize that the development of goals could also be useful for pursuing focused and coherent action on sustainable development. The goals should address and incorporate in a balanced way all three dimensions of sustainable development (environment, economics, and society) and their interlinkages. The development of these goals should not divert focus or effort from the achievement of the Millennium Development Goals.

Moreover, "the process needs to be coordinated and coherent with the processes to consider the post-2015 development agenda" (United Nations, 2013).

During the years preceding the adoption of the 2030 Agenda, beginning in 2012, an important role was played by the Special Advisor to the UN Secretary-General on Post-2015 Development Planning. Amina Mohammed of Nigeria, the current UN Deputy Secretary-General, ensured that non-governmental organizations had a space in the process to adopt the SDGs and gave them a voice at the High-Level Panel of Eminent Persons (HLP), and the General Assembly's Open Working Group, which ultimately shaped Agenda 2030. Another important actor during this time was Kenya's ambassador to the UN, Macharia Kamau. He was the co-chair of the General Assembly Working Group on the SDGs from 2012 to 2014 and served as co-facilitator of the post-2015 Development Agenda in 2014 and 2015. In addition, Nikhil Seth (at the time with UN DESA) was also instrumental in integrating stakeholders in this historic global consultation and including their inputs in the drafting of the document that would become the UN Resolution adopting Agenda 2030. This was a first in the history of multilateral architecture and an example of inclusivity and civil participation in global decision-making processes. All these protagonists are mentioned because many see them as unique leaders that made the SDGs legitimate in a way that the MDGs never were.

The Sustainable Development Goals and the road to 2030

Moving on to the years after 2015, the world really embraced the adoption of Agenda 2030 at the highest levels of government, with adaptation to the local realities (what we call 'localization' in UN jargon) of the SDGs in every nation, developed or developing, rich or poor, from the Global North to the Global South. I am a witness to the commitment every government made towards Agenda 2030 and to the level of energy that every actor involved with the SDGs brought to the table, as I travelled from country to country during 2018 and 2019 'preaching' on the new goals and the need to build capacity to ensure we achieve them by the year 2030. Here I must comment on the increasing quality and level of the country reports presented at the High-Level Political Forum in New York every July, as part the Voluntary National Review (VNRs) that are organized at the UN Secretariat. This was very evident to me because I was a senior government official during the MDGs implementation more than a decade before, and I can attest to the low importance that developing nations like my country in Latin America assigned to this UN policy recommendation. It was different now. It was really something that had achieved traction and went beyond governments, as the media, academia, private sector and even every citizen seemed to be interested. It went beyond the halls of the UN and of public sector institutions. The SDGs were really advancing. They were succeeding where the MDGs had failed and finally were galvanizing our societies. And their implementation accelerated, having become top priorities for governments around the world.

However, at the end of 2019 we saw the news about a strange virus called Corona, which had recently appeared in China. In Geneva, our colleagues at the World Health Organization (WHO) started global monitoring of the spread of the Coronavirus disease (COVID-19) from the beginning of 2020. As most of you know, COVID-19 is a highly contagious disease caused by severe acute respiratory syndrome coronavirus 2 (SARS-CoV-2). This virus belongs to the SARS family and is easily transmitted amongst humans by proximity via airways and respiration. It can kill and it did so. In a few months, COVID-19 was present in almost all countries of the world, and on 11 March 2020 the Director-General of WHO, Dr. Tedros Adhanom Ghebreyesus (2020), declared COVID-19 a global pandemic. In the following weeks, this declaration and the rapidly advancing rate of contagion mobilized the vast majority of UN member states' governments to declare the fight against COVID-19 a matter of national emergency and of the utmost priority. And when this happens, every level and lever of a government is dedicated to the task. Presidents, Prime Ministers, Cabinet members – with all their authority, institutions, budgets, personnel, infrastructure and policy – are concentrated on saving lives. Nothing was more important and media outlets maintained the pressure, as it should be in any democracy. The numbers of citizens infected by COVID-19, and the number of deaths, became a permanent fixture in the news.

The COVID-19 conundrum: Are the Sustainable Development Goals important but not urgent?

The global fight against COVID-19 has taken resources away from other government tasks non-related to the crisis. This meant that the commitment and priority assigned to Agenda 2030 and the accomplishment of the SDGs had to some degree be put to one side. National budgets and personnel assigned to the 17 goals became secondary – still somehow important but definitely not as urgent. The continuation of the global fight against poverty and all our common efforts to safeguard vulnerable populations, to protect the environment, to improve education and social standards, was no longer possible, as the first priority was to ensure that the citizens of our countries were still alive and well. That is itself the *raison d'être* of every government and the core mandate of every public servant. Most efforts related to Agenda 2030 and its SDGs were therefore unfortunately put on hold during the initial months of the pandemic.

As time has gone by, the level of urgency assigned to the pandemic has allowed the world to develop several vaccines in record time and to implement vaccination campaigns in every country that are slowly producing results. However, the pandemic is not yet over, as hundreds of millions of people have been infected, and the number of dead is still rising. What was initially a global health crisis became a global social crisis with dire consequences, a by-product of the harsh measures introduced by governments to lockdown entire cities, regions and countries to stop the spread of the virus. This in turn created a global economic crisis not seen in decades, as most productive systems were halted or slowed, affecting services and industry alike, with transportation networks entirely grounded for months on end. The global economy decelerated, and global Gross Domestic Product (GDP) decreased 3.5 percent in 2020 with a cumulative loss of approximately 9 trillion dollars, similar to the size of the economies of Germany and Japan combined (Gopinath, 2020). Who would have thought that this could be on the horizon back in 2017 when we were discussing potential disruptors to the SDGs? No one.

On 28 September 2019, the UN Secretary-General issued a statement when the pandemic reached the one millionth death from the COVID-19 virus. He invoked responsible leadership as one of the things needed to deal with this global crisis. He said:

> And still there is no end in sight to the spread of the virus, the loss of jobs, the disruption of education, the upheaval to our lives. Still, we can overcome this challenge. But we must learn from the mistakes. Responsible leadership matters. Science matters. Cooperation matters – and misinformation kills.
>
> (United Nations News, 2020)

The perpetual fight between the important and the urgent impacts responsible leadership. It does so because of the relentless pressure leaders face day after day; it makes them lose their appetite to deal with the important things that our society needs. There is no time. There is no money. There is no political imperative. And during this pandemic, there is only the urgent need to save lives and keep people from getting infected. That means that sustainable development needs to go on the backburner. But, does it? Not really. The backburner should be for things that are optional or secondary in nature. The global fight against poverty is definitely not one of those optional or secondary matters. The need to protect the environment is also not secondary. As it is not in the case of peace, disarmament, democracy, universal primary education and the like. Responsible leadership dictates that anyone in a position of leadership should keep one eye on the urgent and the other on the important; and one hand on the immediate and another on the longer term. That is why being a responsible leader is difficult, but it is not impossible.

Conclusion: What is next?

When I talk to my daughters and their young university friends about what we should expect in the years ahead, I am imbued with the optimism of their generation; but at the same time, I remain aware of a certain realism that my generation cannot easily evade. Things are increasingly returning to a new 'normal', with COVID-19 vaccination campaigns delivering the results we expect, with the virus becoming part of our lives but under control, with our societies regaining the freedom we have always enjoyed in recent decades, and with the economy getting back on track, growing and creating much needed employment. But how long will it take for all governments to say: back to the important, back to the quest for sustainable development?

Most importantly, we do not know how many years of achievements will be 'erased' in the process towards 2030. Imagine how much terrain we have lost in terms of global poverty and social advancement that our societies need to ensure the improvement of the lives of their citizens. Due to the COVID-19 pandemic, for the first time in a generation, the global quest to end poverty has suffered a setback. The World Bank (2020) reports that in 2019 about 120 million additional people started living in poverty as a result of the pandemic, with several million more going under the poverty line in 2021 and 2022.

What we know is that as of the end of 2019 approximately 10 percent of the global population lived on $1.90 a day or less, meaning 770 million people out of a total population of 7.7 billion. Even worse, the Global Multidimensional Poverty Index (MPI) 2019 reported that across 101 countries, 1.3 billion people are multidimensionally poor (United Nations Development Programme, 2019). However, we have to remember that we had indeed advanced relentlessly in the fight against poverty, as more than a third of the world lived in extreme poverty 30 years ago. The World Bank (2015) had also reported that between 2000 and 2015, 15 countries lifted 802.1 million people out of extreme poverty. Seven of these 15 countries were in Sub-Saharan Africa. Indeed, the MDGs, and subsequently the SDGs, were part of the roadmap they followed, with the support of international organizations and Official Development Assistance from developed nations.

Being aware that we have lost so much during the pandemic and that we will still see more people becoming poor, we must focus on the post-COVID-19 era – on what policies are needed to create recovery and what priorities a resurgence period should have. The UN Secretary-General has become the global preacher on the need to 'build-back-better', meaning that – whatever the new 'normal' – we should avoid the mistakes of the past. This sounds reasonable but requires that every government, every member of our societies agrees on the need to avoid 'leaving anyone behind' as the seminal document on Agenda 2030 and the SDGs postulates. That concept remains vital today, several years after its conception. We must protect the vulnerable and include the disenfranchised in the recovery (United Nations Sustainable Development Group, n.d.).

One of the best ways to legitimize the post-COVID-19 recovery process is to follow the example of the SDGs' global consultation before their adoption. Can we have again one million (or several million) voices telling us what they think? Can we open the gates of the highest level in government or of the international organizations so they can ensure inclusivity and civil participation in the decision-making processes? Can we leverage the power of social media to involve every citizen in a global discussion about the future? The answer is yes, we can – but not only governments and international organizations. We all should play our part. I invite you to think about this; there will always be a need to hear everyone, everywhere, every time. And you can help.

References

Abdo, K. (2020) *Spanish Flu*, Oxford: Blackwell.

Ghebreyesus, T. A. (2020) 'Opening remarks at the media briefing on COVID-19', 11 March. Available at: https://www.who.int/director-general/speeches/detail/who-director-general-s-opening-remarks-at-the-media-briefing-on-covid-19–11-march-2020

Gopinath, G. (2020) 'The great lockdown: Worst economic downturn since the Great Depression'. Available at: https://blogs.imf.org/2020/04/14/the-great-lockdown-worst-economic-downturn-since-the-great-depression/

Klaas, B. (2022) 'Why we always get the wrong leaders and how to get the right ones', *The Sunday Times*, 16 January.

Petrosky-Nadeau, N. and Valletta, R. G. (2020) 'An unemployment crisis after the onset of Covid-19', *Federal Reserve Bank of San Francisco*, Economic Letters, 18 May. Available at: frbsf.org

Rusbridger, A. (2021) *News and How to Use It: What to Believe in a Fake News World*, Edinburgh: Canongate.

United Nations (2001) *Millennium Development Goals*. Available at: https://www.un.org/millenniumgoals

United Nations (2012) *The Future We Want*. Available at: https://sustainabledevelopment.un.org/futurewewant.html

United Nations (2013) 'Resolution adopted by the General Assembly on 27 July 2012'. Available at: https://www.un.org/ga/search/view_doc.asp?symbol=A/RES/66/288&Lang=E

United Nations Development Programme (2019) *Global Multidimensional Poverty Index 2019: Illuminating Inequalities. United Nations Development Programme*. Available at: http://hdr.undp.org/en/content/2019-global-multidimensional-poverty-index-mpi

United Nations News (2013) 'New UN report reflects voices of more than 1 million people on development issues'. Available at: https://news.un.org/en/story/2013/09/448542

United Nations News (2020) 'Millionth death from COVID-19 "an agonizing milestone", UN Secretary-General'. Available at: https://news.un.org/en/story/2020/09/1074102

United Nations Sustainable Development Group (n.d.) 'Universal Values Principle Two: Leave No One Behind'. Available at: https://unsdg.un.org/2030-agenda/universal-values/leave-no-one-behind

World Bank (2015) *Annual Report*. Available at: https://www.worldbank.org/en/about/annual-report-2015

World Bank (2020) 'COVID-19 to add as many as 150 million extreme poor by 2021'. Available at: https://www.worldbank.org/en/news/press-release/2020/10/07/covid-19-to-add-as-many-as-150-million-extreme-poor-by-2021

Part II

Leadership and Social Responsibility

Chapter 3

Constitutional Ethics, Human Rights and Responsible Leadership

James M. Durant III

Introduction: Understanding responsible leadership

Leadership is the art and science of influencing behavior. Responsible governmental leadership is accountability for the ethical administration of a sovereign's sworn duties to effectively manage matters of state, including health, education, environment, human rights, economic prosperity, justice, diplomacy, energy, transportation, infrastructure and defense. As such, accountability is the genesis, or primary driver, for the ethically responsible leader. Through this understanding, the responsible-ethical leader is held to the highest standards of accountability to the state and its people. But for the sovereign person in particular, these concepts first demand a clear and comprehensive understanding as well as ethical appreciation of all matters under the sovereign's aegis. Thus, the basic expectation of a responsible-ethical governmental leader is that they will govern fairly by law, custom and practice and that they will be held to the highest standards of accountability to the people and across governmental agencies, ministries, departments and so on. These concepts are best expressed in the preamble to the United States (US) constitution, which states that government is established for the people and by the people. These words articulate

DOI: 10.4324/9781003129189-5

the fundamental purpose of government, which naturally includes implied checks and balances on basic governmental power.

In the United Nations (UN) and on a diplomatic global scale, the concept of accountability in governmental leadership is uniquely evidenced by the UN Security Council and the collective Veto Power authority possessed by UN representatives from the five permanent members: China, France, the Russian Federation, the United Kingdom (UK), and the US. As such, there is a distinct notion that these sovereign countries will behave responsibly and will be accountable to constituent UN member nations and the world in general in maintaining international peace and security in accord with the principles and purposes of the UN Security Council (2021).

The celebrated architect of an enhanced and more effective UN Security Council, the late Secretary-General Dag Hjalmar Agne Carl Hammarskjöld, envisioned this level of responsible and accountable leadership when he developed the scope and charter of the UN Security Council (Fofack, 2021). Through its successful reformation, he ensured responsible collective leadership on a global scale. And to his credit, the words of Hammarskjöld in a classic UN speech in 1953 are exceptionally relevant today on responsible leadership:

> Our work for peace must begin within the private world of each one of us. To build . . . a world without fear, we must be without fear. To build a world of justice, we must be just. And how can we fight for liberty if we are not free in our own minds? How can we ask others to sacrifice if we are not ready to do so? . . . Only in true surrender to the interest of all can we reach that strength and independence, that unity of purpose, that equity of judgment which are necessary if we are to measure up to our duty to the future, as men of a generation to whom the chance was given to build in time a world of peace.
>
> (United Nations, 1953)

Nonetheless, the definition of 'responsible leadership' should not be confused with 'responsible government', such as the Westminster system of responsible government in the UK, where ministers of government must be Members of Parliament. In comparison, US Presidents are responsible to those who elected them but are not responsible to Congress. However, as part of a checks and balances system for governmental accountability, the US Congress can remove a sitting President through impeachment and conviction for treason, bribery or other high crimes and misdemeanors, which may in some cases be the by-products of unethical governance.

The opposite of this narrative is the abdication or irresponsible action by a state leader in deflecting or eschewing accountability to the state for matters under their domain and control – such as when a state leader does not take responsibility in face of a pandemic threatening the lives of millions. This is the abdication of leadership, and clearly not responsible leadership. Responsible leaders are expected to put the needs of their state first. A responsible leader sees the state's interests as the primary duty without regard to self-preservation, monetary aggrandizement, or political power. Furthermore, responsible leadership is also ethical leadership based in law, custom and practice. In the US, implicit in the oath of office for public servants are the words, "I swear to support and defend the US Constitution . . . and I take this oath without any mental reservation, or purposes of evasion" (US Code of Federal Regulations 3331, 1966). These words embody the expectations of constitutional ethics for a responsible state leader or public servant before they assume an elected or appointed office, thus serving the people of the state.

As such, constitutional ethics are how government officials rule, and they encapsulate how a leader manages their sovereign duties, state-accumulated wealth and property, temporal constraints and political boundaries, based upon principles of fairness and interest. According to Omoregi (2015), these principles are often found in general management by objectives – that is, a basic business model focused on responsible-ethical management of the state using such principles. Often these principles become law by acts of legislatures. Arguably, however, this 'how' in defining constitutional ethics speaks specifically to statecraft, an action of the state leader in the deliberative task of balancing competing interests – including diplomatic concerns, information management, industrial production and defense forces. In sum, be it a code of ethics or universal equity, constitutional ethics are *how* the state leader manages state affairs.

The annals of history therefore record not the event but *how* the state leader acted to resolve the matter. This was evident, for example, when a state leader used deadly chemical agents against citizens alleged to be rebelling against the state (White House, 2013). In this case, the action of the state leader breached ethical expectations and boundaries. When Dr Reverend Martin Luther King (1968) remarked that "We shall overcome because the arc of the moral universe is long but it bends toward justice," he spoke to constitutional ethics. In his case, the Alabama legislature enacted unethical laws in direct discord with the 14th Amendment of the US Constitution, specifically the Equal Protection Clause. These unethical laws, or Jim Crow Laws (Howard University, 2021), were normative rules in the US for over 70 years.

During Dr. King's illegal incarceration in Birmingham, Alabama, for exercising a constitutionally-sanctioned speech, he wrote about just laws and unjust laws:

> An unjust law is a human law that is not rooted in eternal law and natural law. Any law that uplifts human personality is just. Any law that degrades human personality is unjust. All segregation statutes are unjust because segregation distorts the soul and damages the personality. It gives the segregator a false sense of superiority and the segregated

> a false sense of inferiority. Segregation, to use the terminology of the Jewish philosopher Martin Buber, substitutes an 'I it' relationship for an 'I thou' relationship and ends up relegating persons to the status of things. Hence segregation is not only politically, economically and sociologically unsound, it is morally wrong and sinful. Paul Tillich has said that sin is separation. Is not segregation an existential expression of man's tragic separation, his awful estrangement, his terrible sinfulness? Thus it is that I can urge men to obey the 1954 decision of the Supreme Court, for it is morally right; and I can urge them to disobey segregation ordinances, for they are morally wrong.
>
> (King, 1963)

In his address, Dr. King articulated God-given rights of humanity, and as such he informs us of the indispensable need for governmental purveyance of basic human rights; focused imperatives by a sovereign over matters such as health, sustenance, justice and habitat – which are implicitly tied to our universally agreed upon conceptual theory of responsible leadership. Further, these human rights are based largely upon the concept of agreeing to be the subject of a sovereign government as described by the English philosopher John Locke (1689). As Locke professed in social contract theory, a legitimate form of government is one where the governed explicitly agree to be governed and the governed freely give to the sovereign their natural law rights. These natural law rights are life, liberty, health and property, which existed equally in a state of nature well before the institution of modern civil government. For example, in the US, a Human Rights pronouncement can be seen in the Declaration of Independence by Thomas Jefferson (1776), the third US President and an enslaver of hundreds of Africans, who wrote: "We hold these truths to be self-evident, that all men are created equal, that they are endowed by their creator with certain unalienable rights, that among these are life, liberty and the pursuit of happiness."

This is paralleled by the Marquis de Lafayette (1789) in the French Revolution who proclaimed that: "Men are born and remain free and equal in rights." Although sadly he was known to have professed disdain for people from Africa, Mahatma Gandhi (1930) commented on human rights: "We believe that it is the inalienable right of the Indian people, as of any other people, to have freedom and to enjoy the fruits of their toil." We now tend to use the phrase human rights in general to further define natural law rights. According to the UN (2021):

> Human rights are rights inherent to all human beings, regardless of race, sex, nationality, ethnicity, language, religion, or any other status. Human rights include the right to life and liberty, freedom from slavery and torture, freedom of opinion and expression, the right to work and education, and many more. Everyone is entitled to these rights, without discrimination.

What followed were the thirty articles of the International Declaration on Human Rights (UN, 2021). These and the Bill of Rights in the American constitution go back over 800 years to the Magna Carta – attested by the rebel Barons and signed by King John – which also spoke of the 'rights of man' (Rathbone, 2014). The Magna Carta in turn was informed by the Justinian Code, which originated around 550 BC in the Roman Empire. It specifically informed government and people about human rights (Human Rights Evolution, 2009). In the US constitution, human rights can also be traced to the concept of due process – an opportunity to be heard before judgment is rendered and life, liberty or property is taken by the state. With this historical understanding of constitutional ethics, human rights and responsible leadership, we now examine these three elements of government and how they intertwine in the current age.

Constitutional ethics

The Rule of Law

According to the American Bar Association (2021):

> The rule of law is a set of principles, or ideals, for ensuring an orderly and just society. Many countries throughout the world strive to uphold the rule of law where no one is above the law, everyone is treated equally under the law, everyone is held accountable to the same laws, there are clear and fair processes for enforcing laws, there is an independent judiciary, and human rights are guaranteed for all.

However, from a UN (2021) perspective, the Rule of Law is further defined as

> a principle of governance in which all persons, institutions and entities, public and private, including the State itself, are accountable to laws that are publicly promulgated, equally enforced and independently adjudicated, and which are consistent with international human rights norms and standards. It requires measures to ensure adherence to the principles of supremacy of the law, equality before the law, accountability to the law, fairness in the application of the law, separation of powers, participation in decision-making, legal certainty, avoidance of arbitrariness, and procedural and legal transparency.

There are six definitive sources of the Rule of Law, including international treaties, state constitutions, state legislatures, judicial orders (precedent), executive orders by chief executives or prime ministers, and the regulations and orders of state administrative agencies. These sources of law inform leaders on *how* they govern, and how society communes – essentially, how we exist as an advanced civilization. Similarly, the Magna Carta of 1215, seen by many as the mother of all democratic constitutions, informed King John on *how* he was to govern. Yet all too often we hear the phrase 'no one is above the law', but sadly some public servants believe they are immune to the rule of law. The idea of being above the law was recently elucidated by the murder of American citizen George Floyd at the hands of the state police. However, when former police officer Derek Chauvin was found guilty of his murder, it was clear that law enforcement is not above the law and that police officers should rightfully be held to a higher standard since they are sworn to protect and serve whilst enforcing the law.

Ethical checks and balances supporting constitutional ethics

Essential to constitutional ethics is self-governance. As such, a focused inquiry is often the action used to ensure regulatory accountability. As mentioned previously, the US government has a checks and balances approach to accountability between the legislative branch, the executive branch, and the judicial branch of US government (Cornell University, 2021). This power was witnessed for the first time in US history when the legislative branch impeached a sitting US President twice during his first and only term in office. This was a quintessentially ethical accountability check on government backed by a written constitution authorizing such action. This can be tracked back to the checks and balances system in ancient Rome.

Furthermore, through such a system, a responsible state leader ensures ethical governance by embracing transparency, inquiry and criticism while demanding the same from other branches of government. As an example, with the case *Marbury v. Madison* (1803), the US Supreme Court developed the principle of Judicial Review, which gave it the power to rule a newly enacted law unconstitutional, null and void (Cook et al., 2016). Similarly, and according to the Institute for Government (2019), in the British Parliament a vote of no confidence can immediately unseat the Prime Minister. However, such checks and balances have to be judiciously used to avoid setting a dangerous precedent. Abuse of the power of checks and balances may lead to systemic governmental mistrust, thus dissolving essential ligaments that hold branches of government together as a whole.

Constitutions departing from ethics

In 1964, the Republic of South Africa incarcerated South African citizen and attorney-at-law Nelson Mandela for speaking out against the state for deprivation of life, liberty and the pursuit of happiness for some 90 percent of South Africa's citizenry. At his sentencing, Mandela (1994: 368) stated,

> During my lifetime I have dedicated myself to this struggle of the African people. I have fought against white domination, and I have fought

> against black domination. I have cherished the ideal of a democratic and free society in which all persons live together in harmony and with equal opportunities. It is an ideal which I hope to live for and to achieve. But if needs be, it is an ideal for which I am prepared to die.

Was the President and legislature of the new Republic of South Africa ethically following the 1961 second constitution, or was their constitution ethically flawed? The latter question can be answered in the affirmative. South Africa's apartheid system allowed for pervasive and insidious discrimination that objectively benefited those of European descent, who represent less than 10 percent of the total population:

> Coloured voters were finally removed from the common voters' roll and were placed on a separate list in 1956. They became entitled to vote for a small number of white Members of Parliament to represent their interests. In 1968, even these indirect representatives were abolished, leaving both the Senate and the House of Assembly to represent white voters only. Instead, a Coloured Persons' Representative Council (CPRC) consisting of 40 elected coloured representatives and 20 nominated white members was instituted. The council would be able to pass laws about parochial matters affecting coloured people. The CPRC proved largely ineffectual and was but a prelude to the equally ineffectual Tricameral Parliament, created in 1983.
>
> (Constitutionhill, 2017)

The US too shares this stain on its constitution but in a far worse way – through slavery. Although the original US Constitution does not mention the term 'slave', in Article 1, Section 2, Clause 3, better known as the 3/5th Clause of the US Constitution (Simba, 2014), it arguably characterizes millions of Africans as non-humans. Of note, 10 of the first 12 presidents of the US enslaved hundreds of humans in perpetuity (Morris, 2020). And the laws that flowed down from the US Constitution, the 'Black Codes' (Middleton, 2020), and thereafter social incarceration in the form of 'Jim Crow Laws' (Howard University, 2021), fortified a pernicious caste system that allowed seemingly ethically responsible leaders to deny and eschew humanity and basic citizenry to Americans of African descent for decades.

Arguably, the South African Constitution followed this maleficent ideology by allowing state-sanctioned apartheid to deny indigenous South African citizens basic human rights, as compared to South Africans of European descent. The same might also be said of the Third Reich, in which the 1919 Weimar Constitution and the 1933 Enabling Act and other laws allowed the new National Socialist President to break away from constitutional ethics (Lowenstein, 1937) – thereby paving the way for Adolph Hitler to commit and inflict mass genocide upon ten million human beings.

Thus, the question remains, when the essential Rule of Law is unethical, are those leaders who follow and enforce it ethical? Change-agent leaders who first recognize a flawed rule of law and second take affirmative responsibility to amend and correct the wrong are rightly revered as honored leaders. They include US President Abraham Lincoln, who moved a group of legislators to end slavery and grant citizenry to over two million Africans dehumanized as slaves. He did this with the passage of the 13th Amendment to the US Constitution in 1865. Although, like Gandhi, Lincoln believed Caucasians were superior to Africans, he was morally against slavery – even if he only moved to end it to preserve the Union as a military tactic through the Emancipation Proclamation (Erath, 2015), which allowed loyal as opposed to disloyal states to keep Africans enslaved. Understandably, given the subsequent equal protections under law for these new American citizens with the passage of the 14th and 15th Amendments (Donald, 2018), he is acclaimed for freeing slaves.

As a leader, Lincoln therefore recognized a flawed rule of law and took affirmative responsibility to correct the wrong. Similarly, in South Africa, Nelson Mandela followed up President De Klerk's actions in 1993 to take responsibility for change to a flawed rule of law. Together they changed South Africa's rule of law and thus liberated millions of oppressed indigenous South African citizens, thereby ensuring and protecting their human rights – including equal access to such areas as justice, medical care, sustenance, education, housing and employment.

Cross-cultural and international comparisons

How does a society arrive at a flawed rule of law upon which a seemingly responsible leader follows or does not follow? Sometimes this occurs through outside influencers imposing a foreign nation's rule of law following armed conflict. As Hasegawa (2021) says:

> In the immediate aftermath of conflict, the critical task for national leaders is to balance the need for securing political stability, if necessary, with force, with governing their countries by influencing the thought and behavior of opponents, as well as their followers. It requires both resolute leadership and the willingness to share and accommodate divergent interests and aspirations. The surest way to establish a society based on the rule of law is for leaders to act virtuously, exercising discipline in their personal conduct and behavior, rather than using power and force to strengthen their position.

In this circumstance, caution must govern the day. An ethically-responsible leader can change the socio-economic and other constructs in a region by order of law, or *fiat*, but cannot immediately change the culture of that region, although this may happen over time.

The danger in reconstructing a foreign country's rule of law is in eschewing or denigrating a country's culture. This often occurs when foreign entities rely on their own interpretations and cultural biases to reach decisions regarding new rules and laws for the subject region. Although international law and the UN Security Council forbids annexing another sovereign state (Abasa, 2020), normally a new governmental system and leader is put in place in that state following the stabilization of operations, thus paving the way for new indigenous leaders (US State Department, 2021). Rule-making then occurs – namely, treaties and agreements on the essential Rule of Law governing the country, as most recently seen in Bosnia with the Dayton Agreement (1995). The ensuing implementation, however, is fraught with practical dilemmas (Roberts, 1995). Ideally, the new rule of law governing the defeated nation should be culturally consistent, adequate, appropriate and not flawed in any reconstruction, as most recently illustrated in Somalia and Rwanda. But before all of this occurs, and during the proceeding armed conflict, many nations have subscribed to a waring rule of law, the Laws of Armed Conflict, which include the Geneva Conventions of 1949, the Hague Conventions of 1899/1907 and the like.

However, where a culture is inimical to human rights, the new rule of law may be justified even if it is not resonant with the defeated nation's culture. This is most relevant in the discussion of the Sharia legal system (Saliba, 2011), which for many Western jurisprudence experts has fundamental equity disparities. Here a Western rule of law may appear appealing and inviting, even if based on a biased Western perspective. However, although Sharia has adapted to 'modern times', it is simply different from the principles of Western jurisprudence. For example, in the US, the death penalty is used in 29 states – and sometimes on the grounds of circumstantial evidence (Duran, 2021). Many Western industrialized countries consider this to be barbaric. And while under Sharia law in some Islamic countries people can be put to death for crimes such as adultery, blasphemy, publishing pornography and sorcery, the burden of proof is exceedingly high, and circumstantial evidence is usually not admitted (Asif, 2021). Therefore, evaluating or judging a foreign entity's laws is difficult, especially from a myopic perspective.

The ethically responsible leader normally respects these boundaries when engaged in multilateral rule-making. Nonetheless, some seemingly responsible-ethical leaders have chosen not to follow the Geneva Conventions or the human rights principles under the Conventions in their state's best interest. For instance, Dörmann and Colassis (2004: 332) note that:

> Prisoners of war enjoy fundamental guarantees requiring that they be treated in a humane manner at all times (the right to respect for their lives and their physical integrity, protection from insults, etc.). An example that made the headlines in the early days of the war in Iraq was the issue of the photographs of Iraqi prisoners of war published in the media, as well as US prisoners of war being shown on Iraqi television and the re-transmission of these images by various international television channels.

Here the Iraqi government was obviously acquainted with the essential principles articulated in the Geneva Conventions regarding treatment of prisoners of war but failed to abide by them on occasion – resulting in allegations of breaches. By the same token, however, but in accordance with Geneva as it pertained to enemy combatants, the US chose more recently not to accord Geneva rights to non-state actors detained in Guantanamo Bay (*Hamdi v. Rumsfeld*, 2004). However, the US did grant to these detainees rights articulated under Common Article III, which basically afforded them cognizant protections under Geneva (International Committee of the Red Cross, 2010). Nevertheless, ethically responsible leaders who elect not to follow Geneva and other internationally agreed upon measures to lessen the severity of war risk similar treatment to their own citizens captured by opposing factions as well as diplomatic ridicule from the international community. And when that occurs, moral imperatives demand accountability to the state and the international community by the responsible leader concerned.

Human rights

As discussed earlier, human rights are rights shared and respected by every person on this planet. And as defined earlier by the UN (2021), "human rights [include] . . . the right to life and liberty, freedom from slavery and torture, freedom of opinion and expression, the right to work and education, and many more". The ethically responsible leader understands human rights and ensures citizens are afforded sufficient protections to guard against domestic violations of human rights. The estimated potential ire from the international community for alleged breaches of human rights is damning in and of itself and can carry long-lasting repercussions, both political and diplomatic. Moreover, such breaches of human rights often result in actions only marginally short of armed conflict and armed conflict itself, including wars based on humanitarian interventions.

In this regard, the Icelandic Human Rights Centre (2021: Paragraph 3) points out that:

> Humanitarian intervention refers to the use of force against one state by another state or states with the declared objective of ending or reducing suffering within the first state. That suffering may be the result of civil war, humanitarian crisis, or crimes by the first state including genocide. Humanitarian intervention is traditionally justified for instances of massive human rights violations – when put in motion by an international body, such as the UN Security Council.

Recent examples of humanitarian interventions include Iraq, Sierra Leone and the former Yugoslavia. Sometimes, however, international collective wisdom plays a significant role in limiting the employment of force, such as in 2013 when the UN Security Council did not authorize this to enable the US and its allies to protect civilians from the use of chemical weapons by President Bashar al-Assad's regime in Syria (Stokes, 2013). Nevertheless, the Security Council did authorize the destruction of Assad's chemical arsenal after hundreds of people were killed in a sarin gas attack in the outskirts of the capital, Damascus (Irish and Nichols, 2013).

The greatest crime and assault on human rights in history lasted for almost 250 years – Afro-American slavery (Ferris State University, 2021). While several world leaders condoned it, many benefited from and perpetuated this tragically dark episode in the evolution of humankind. Some ethically responsible leaders moved their countries to end slavery, but only after over two centuries of this practice. As previously noted, following the US Civil War, ethically responsible leaders protected human rights by amending the US Constitution, granting civil rights to over two million new citizens. These essential amendments changed the course of a nation for these new Americans, who were considered (by European Americans) chattels, on par with chickens, goats, or mules – as opposed to human beings (Finkelman, 2012).

However, thereafter, apparently ethically responsible leaders abandoned their oath to uphold and support the US Constitution in practice – resulting in ongoing segregation, social abandonment, xenophobic hate, and notions of racial superiority among Caucasians against Americans of African descent. This included disproportionate rates of homicide, as well as lack of access to justice, medical services, education, housing and employment, in which Americans of African descent were found to be 3.23 times more likely than Americans of European descent to be killed by police, according to researchers from Harvard T. H. Chan School of Public Health (2020):

> The researchers examined 5,494 police-related deaths in the US between 2013 and 2017. Rates of deadly police encounters were higher in the West and South than in the Midwest and Northeast, according to the study. Racial disparities in killings by police varied widely across the country, with some metropolitan areas showing very high differences between treatment by race. Black Chicagoans, for example, were found to be over 650% more likely to be killed by police than white Chicagoans.

Fortunately, some ethically responsible leaders in the US have made great strides to ensure human rights protections with subsequent specific acts of legislation, such as the Civil Rights Acts of 1861 (Franklyn, 1989) and 1964/68 (Georgetown Law, 2021). The George Floyd Justice in Policing Act will hopefully stem the systemic-egregious human rights abuse by state law enforcement officers of the law against Americans of African descent and others (Bass, 2020). And from a global perspective, with the murder of George Floyd by an agent of the state, the world came together in the summer of 2020, embracing human life under the ubiquitous phrase Black Lives Matter. As such, human rights abuse is an ever-evolving focal point upon which ethically responsible leaders must be informed, educated and inspired to be positive change agents in their environments as well as exemplars for others who lead governments across the globe.

This includes international human trafficking, which is arguably the next major global frontier for ethically responsible leaders in addressing systemic violations of human rights. As the US State Department (2021) notes:

> Human trafficking, also called modern slavery or trafficking in persons, has no place in our world. As both a grave crime and a human rights abuse, it compromises national and economic security, undermines the rule of law, and harms the well-being of individuals and communities everywhere. It is a crime of exploitation; traffickers profit at the expense of their victims by compelling them to perform labor or to engage in commercial sex in every region of the United States and around the world. With an estimated 24.9 million victims worldwide at any given time, human traffickers prey on adults and children of all ages, backgrounds, and nationalities, exploiting them for their own profit.

Expectations of ethical and responsible leaders in sovereign states

What are reasonable expectations of ethical and responsible leaders? We are uniformly similar as members of the human race. Where we part in our humanity is a factor of pernicious contrived caste systems, political subdivisions, cultural awareness and socio-economic development. We each have a homeland, a place we are willing to defend, that we call home. We regard our homeland as our primary identity, our state. And it is human to identify with a state, a culture, a homeland. It is also human to have great admiration, love and longing for one's homeland. But, where this falls apart is when this love and longing breaks away from mutual respect for another state's culture, religion and love of their homeland – as warlike motivations then take over.

According to the Prussian military theorist Carl von Clausewitz (1989), the idea of compelling another to do your will is the object of war. This objective, moreover, is fueled by the ill-conceived notion that one nation and its way of life is better than another nation. On the international stage, this ideological concept of greatness must not be part of an ethically responsible leader's DNA. The greatness of a state is not defined by its accumulated wealth or economic prosperity, or even its weaponry or military might; on the contrary, it is marked by its peaceful interactions with fellow sovereign nations, its benevolence, kindness and mutual support in times of crisis or national emergency, and its sharing of technology, science, arts and medicine that benefits humankind. The ethically responsible leader who understands this is also able to forge sustainable and mutually beneficial relationships with other nations and is a revered leader.

As a classic example, in the first free republic in the Caribbean, the country of Haiti, formerly Saint-Domingue, General Toussaint Louverture is internationally regarded as an ethically responsible leader whose work ultimately liberated thousands of Africans who were enslaved in Haiti (Morris, 2020). Influenced by Locke and Rousseau's philosophy on human equality, General Louverture successfully led a massive slave revolt, which began 1791, and decided, against France's wishes, to invade the Spanish-controlled Santo Domingo to free the Africans enslaved there. He successfully contained the British troops who were sent to Hatti to challenge France's hold in 1801. General Louverture masterfully understood the relationship between his new homeland, France, Great Britain and Spain. Despite being tricked into going to France, where he was incarcerated, his work is indelibly ingrained in many minds as that of a great leader.

Another ethically responsible great leader who truly understood the interactive global communal construct, and who shone brilliantly during the failed invasion of Hitler's war machine – not least in forming an indispensable relationship with the US and other nations to defeat Hitler – was Sir Winston Spencer Churchill, former Prime Minister of the UK. As Nicholas (2021) said:

> As prime minister (1940–45) during most of World War II, Winston Churchill rallied the British people and led the country from the brink of defeat to victory. He shaped Allied strategy in the war, and in the war's later stages he alerted the West to the expansionist threat of the Soviet Union.

As such, he and General Louverture exceeded the expectations of ethically responsible leadership through their selfless acts of courage and perseverance in face of lethal conflict. They are both therefore great leaders revered in the annals of history. They put the needs of their state first against mounting odds and incalculable difficulties while embodying their nation's character and preserving the promise of humanity.

The national character of an ethically responsible leader

In addressing the national character of an ethically responsible leader, President Nelson Mandela deserves the most honorable mention. In 1962, during his final trial in South Africa, Mandela entered the court room with his nation's cry for justice and human rights upon his shoulders and with a deep understanding of his homeland's character. This is best expressed by Mandela (1994: 372) as follows:

> I entered the court that Monday morning wearing a traditional Zhosa leopard-skin kaross instead of a suit and tie. The crowd of supporters rose as one and with raised, clenched fists shouted "Amadela!" and "Ngawethu!" The kaross electrified the spectators . . . Winnie also wore a traditional beaded headdress and an ankle-length Xhosa skirt. I had chosen traditional dress to emphasize the symbolism that I was a black African walking into a white man's court. I was literally carrying on my back the history, culture, and heritage of my people. That day, I felt myself to be the embodiment of African nationalism, the inheritor of Africa's difficult but noble past and her uncertain future.

In this sense, Mandela socially articulated, adopted and embraced his country, and after serving 27 years in prison promoting justice and human rights, he emerged as the leader of a land he loved. South Africa now records President Mandela as the embodiment of its national identity. The same applies to the Great Spirit Mahatma Gandhi, who professed peaceful resistance in not raising a single sword or shooting a single bullet in liberating his country from Great Britain (Parker, 2014). In his later years, he too discarded his European dress for his national cloth. And, like President Mandela, the national identity of India is inextricably tied to Gandhi, an ethically responsible leader of the highest character.

Speaking of character, the ethically responsible leader is a diplomat from a rudimentary to a highly theoretical perspective involving multiple layers of understanding of international behavioral norms and culture. Moreover, as a diplomat, such a leader must appreciate that no nation is an island in itself; nations rise and succeed through carefully calculated alliances with other nations for a myriad of needs, from energy, water, food and medicine to national defense. This relationship ensures a state's mutual growth and sustainability within a global context. According to Nye (2002): "Globalism, at its core, seeks to describe and explain nothing more than a world which is characterized by networks of connections that span multi-continental distances."

A good example of a form of globalism comes from US President Bill Clinton, Mexico's President Enrique Peña Nieto, and Canada's Prime Minister Jean Chrétien's efforts to secure a free trade zone in North America. During the early 1990s, these three sovereign ethical leaders produced an astounding tri-national trade accord. Together, they entered their respective countries into the North American Free Trade Agreement (NAFTA). NAFTA was essentially an agreement between three sovereign nations to engage in free trade, thereby lessening the impediments of most tariffs and border regulations to enable successful international commerce.

Clinton, Nieto and Chrétien, three ostensibly ethical leaders, therefore developed a crown jewel in their diplomacy to peacefully engage on common ground between nations, mutually supporting the free exchange of trillions of dollars in goods and services. NAFTA represented a diplomatic imperative that benefited three sovereign nations with almost 500 million people. History now records them as celebrated leaders who comprehended international trade reliance serving the needs of three separate sovereign nations in the purveyance of goods and services. Similarly, ethically responsible diplomatic leaders understand and support global climate imperatives, to which we finally turn.

Domestic and international environmental responsibility

With global climate imperatives, ethically responsible diplomatic leaders embrace the scientifically agreed notion that our planet is an inextricably connected biosphere whereupon any harm or neglect to one system detrimentally impacts other systems. Similar to a quilt, pulling one thread impacts several threads and thereby damages the whole. This example is best elucidated with atmospheric emissions. We have learned over decades of polluting the atmosphere that the effects are not localized to one zone or region and that – together with increasing concentrations of greenhouse gases and particulate matter in the atmosphere (American Chemical Society, 2021) – the effects of human pollution are indeed maleficent, resulting in global warming. And with manifest respect for and appreciation of the protection of the environment beyond the political boundaries of the state, the ethically responsible leader stands at center stage on matters of global accountability.

With global environmental accountability, the ethically responsible diplomatic leader must initiate or engage in honest international dialogue on environment. They also need to sufficiently engage in lessening the negative environmental effects of human production in their own and neighboring nations. An example of this is the Paris Agreement, which was adopted by 106 party nations at COP21 in Paris on 12 December 2015. Pleasingly, prior to the subsequent Glasgow Agreement struck at COP26 in November 2021, US President Joseph R. Biden re-entered the US following the withdrawal by former US President Donald J. Trump – thus exhibiting resolute diplomacy and indeed responsible leadership.

As Antony J. Blinken (2021), the US Secretary of State, observed:

> On January 20, on his first day in office, President Biden signed the instrument to bring the United States back into the Paris Agreement. Per the terms of the Agreement, the United States officially becomes a Party again today. The Paris Agreement is an unprecedented framework for global action. We know because we helped design it and make it a

reality. Its purpose is both simple and expansive: to help us all avoid catastrophic planetary warming and to build resilience around the world to the impacts from climate change we already see. Climate change and science diplomacy can never again be 'add-ons' in our foreign policy discussions. Addressing the real threats from climate change and listening to our scientists is at the center of our domestic and foreign policy priorities. It is vital in our discussions of national security, migration, international health efforts, and in our economic diplomacy and trade talks.

Conclusion

In considering ethically responsible leadership, it is important that we also consider failed responsible leadership. Leaders held in the lowest esteem for governing without character, without veracity and without the best interests of their nations and the wider world share a common denominator – individual self-aggrandizement accented with greed, dishonesty, avarice, chauvinism and narcissism. Somewhere along their political paths, these unethical, irresponsible leaders made ill-advised decisions, gaining pyrrhic victories amounting to little in the grand equation. Cumulatively, their transgressions color their offices and personalities in ways that cannot easily be recovered. These unethical leaders thus slip into the abyss of treachery, debauchery and crime. Failed leaders, whatever their apparent success in the tasks they carry out, are ethically failed leaders based on their personality and character and *how* they have deleteriously led and managed resources.

In sum, ethically responsible diplomatic leaders fully understand, appreciate and honor their distinct duties to the state and to the global community as a whole. Moreover, ethically responsible diplomatic leaders are accountable and answerable to their state and its national interests, placing such interests above all other interests, including personal preservation and survival. Such leaders are of the highest character and follow duly established rules of law. Their practices and measures support fairness in law, policy and administration among people in the state and the global community – and, in doing so, they ensure, protect and enforce the fundamental natural rights of humankind.

References

Abasa, R. (2020) 'Rights experts call for global opposition to Israel's annexation plans', *United Nations News*, 16 June 2020.

American Bar Association (2021), *The Rule of Law*. Available at: https://www.americanbar.org/groups/public_education/resources/rule-of-law/

American Chemical Society (2021) 'Global climate change'. Available at: www.acs.org/content/acs/en/policy/publicpolicies/sustainability/globalclimatechange.html#

Asif, N. (2021) 'An introduction to Sharia law and the death penalty', Faculty of Law, University of Oxford.

Bass, K. (2020) *H.R. 7120-George Floyd Justice in Policing Act of 2020, Representative Karen Bass (D-CA- 37)*, Washington, DC: Library of Congress.

Blinken, A. (2021) 'The United States officially re-joins the Paris Agreement', Washington DC: US Department of State press statement, 19 February. Available at: https://www.state.gov/the-united-states-officially-rejoins-the-paris-agreement/

Constitutionhill (2017) *South Africa's Second Constitution*. Available at: constitutionhill.org.za

Cook, A., Kennedy M., Spangler R. and Wilt M. (2016) *Marbury v. Maddison 1803*. Available at: U.S. Conlawpedia (gsu.edu)

Dayton Agreement (1995) *Dayton Peace Accords*, Vienna: Organization for Security and Co-operation in Europe.

De Lafayette (1789) *The Declaration of the Rights of Man and of the Citizen*, Paris: Jefferson Monticello.

Donald, B. (2018) 'When the rule of law breaks down: Implications of the 1866 Memphis massacre for the passage of the Fourteenth Amendment', *Boston University Law Review* 98: 1673–75.

Dörmann, K. and Colassis, L. (2004) 'International humanitarian law in the Iraq conflict', *German Yearbook of International Law* 47: 293–342.

Duran, G. (2021) 'Florida Supreme Court reverses course on death penalty', *Florida Political Review*, 20 January.

Erath, J. (2015) 'Union success in the Civil War and lessons for strategic leaders', *Joint Force Quarterly: National Defense University Press*, 1 April.

Ferris State University (2021) *Slavery in America*, Ferris State University, Jim Crow Museum of Racist Memorabilia.

Finkelman, P. (2012) 'Slavery in the United States: Persons or property?', in Allain, J. (ed) *The Legal Understanding of Slavery: From the Historical to the Contemporary*, Oxford: Oxford University Press.

Fofack, H. (2021) Chief Economist and Director of Research and International Co-operation Department at the African Export-Import Bank: Telephonic Interview with Colonel James M. Durant III and Dr Hippolyte Fofack on 17 March.

Franklyn, J. H. (1989) 'Civil Rights Act of 1866 revisited'. Available at: http://repository.uchastings.edu/tobriner/15

Gandhi, M. (1930) *Declaration of Sovereignty and Self-Rule*, Lahore: Indian National Congress.

Georgetown Law (2021) 'A brief history of Civil Rights in the United States', *Georgetown Law*, 3 June.

Hamdi v. Rumsfeld (2004) 542 US 507, 124 S. Ct. 2633. Available at: Hamdi v. Rumsfeld, Case Brief for Law School, LexisNexis.

Harvard T. H. Chan School of Public Health (2020) 'Black people more than three times as likely as white people to be killed during a police encounter', School of Public Health, 24 June.

Hasegawa, S. (2016) 'Post-conflict leadership: Key to sustainable peace and development', *UN Chronicle*, April.

Howard University (2021) *Jim Crow Era – A Brief History of Civil Rights in the United States*, Washington, DC: Howard University School of Law Library.

Human Rights Evolution (2009) *The Justinian Code*. Available at: https://sites.google.com/site/humanrightsevolution/justinian-code

Icelandic Human Rights Centre (2021) *Human Rights and Armed Conflict*, Reykjavik: IHRC.

Institute for Government (2019) 'Confidence motions and Parliament', *Institute for Government*, 13 September.

International Committee of the Red Cross (2010) *The Geneva Conventions of 1949 and Their Additional Protocols*, Geneva: ICRC.

Irish, J. and Nichols, M. (2013) 'UN Security Council demands elimination of Syria chemical arms', *Reuters Editor's Picks*, 27 September.

Jefferson, T. (1776) *The Declaration of Independence*, Second Continental Congress, Philadelphia, Pennsylvania.

King, M. L. (1963) *Letter from a Birmingham Jail*, African Studies Centre, University of Pennsylvania, Philadelphia.

King, M. L. (1968) 'Remaining awake through a great revolution', Speech given at the National Cathedral, 31 March Washington, DC: National Museum of African American History. Available at: https://www.si.edu/spotlight/mlk?page=4&iframe=true

Locke, J. (1689) *An Essay Concerning Human Understanding*, London: Thomas Basset.

Lowenstein, K. (1937) 'Dictatorship and the German Constitution: 1933–1937', *University of Chicago Law Review* 4(4): 537–74.

Mandela, N. (1994) *Long Walk to Freedom*, London: Little, Brown & Co.

Marbury v. Madison (1803) 5 US 137.

Middleton, S. (2020) 'Repressive legislation: Slave Codes, Northern Black Laws, and Southern Black Codes', *Oxford Research Encyclopedia of American History*, Oxford: Oxford University Press.

Morris, T. (2020) *Raped and Robbed: Time for 21st Century Reparations*, New York: Different Day Publishing.

Nicholas, H. G. (2021) 'Winston Churchill: Prime Minister of United Kingdom, during World War', *Encyclopaedia Britannica*.

Nye, J. (2002) 'Globalism versus Globalization', *The Globalist*, 15 April.

Omoregi, H. (2015) *The 5 Ms of Business Management: Organizing Them Effectively*, LinkedIn.

Parker, C. (2014) 'Gandhi's nonviolent approach offers lessons for peace movements', *Stanford Scholar Says*, 29 October.

Rathbone, M. (2014) *The Human Rights Act: A Magna Carta for the Twenty-First Century?* London: Political Studies Association.

Roberts, A. (1995) 'The laws of war: Problems of implementation in contemporary conflicts', *Duke Journal of Comparative and International Law* 6(1): 11–78.

Saliba, I. (2011) What is Sharia Law? Washington, DC: Law Library of Congress.

Simba, M. (2014) 'The Three-Fifths Clause of the United States Constitution (1787)', *Blackpast*, 3 October. Available at: https://blackpast.org/african-american-history/events-african-american-history/three-fifts-clause-united-states-constitution-1787/

Stokes, B. (2013) 'UN approval before using military force lacks widespread global agreement', Washington, DC: Pew Research Center.

United Nations (1953) Press Release SG/360, 22 December.

United Nations (2021) *What is the Rule of Law: United Nations and The Rule of Law*, Geneva: UN.

United Nations Security Council (2021) *Current Members, Permanent and Non-Permanent*. Available at: https://www.un.org/securitycouncil/content/current-members

United States Code of Federal Regulations 3331 (1966) *Oath of Office*, Public Law 89–554, Statute 424.

US State Department (2021) *About Human Trafficking*, Washington DC: USSD.

Von Clausewitz, C. (1989) *On War*, Princeton, NJ: Princeton University Press.

White House (2013) *Government Assessment of the Syrian Government's Use of Chemical Weapons on August 21, 2013*, Washington, DC: Office of the Press Secretary. Available at: https://obamawhitehouse.archives.gov/the-press-office/2013/08/30/government-assessment-syrian-government-s-use-chemical-weapons-august-21

Chapter 4

Innovation and Responsible Leadership in Business and Industry

Sa'ad Sam Medhat

Introduction

The combination of innovation and responsible leadership presents a very powerful mandate that touches every part of the 17 Strategic Development Goals (SDGs) of the United Nations (UN) (2015), as it activates the critical behaviors of citizens, public and private business leaders, and policy makers. This chapter highlights the inextricable but underplayed relationship between innovation and responsible leadership in business and industry and its influencing role in shaping the realization of the UN SDGs. It attempts to define the characteristics of innovative responsible business leaders. In doing so, it underscores the role of responsible leadership in relation to industrial innovations, particularly when considering aspects of innovation that have positive local, national and global effects, as well as those carrying possible unintended consequences.

Influencing a change in approach to the way innovations are managed rests on the prevalent culture inherent within the management of enterprises – and the way in which their business models are configured – which is often an exclusively profit-oriented culture driven by the need to maximize shareholder value. Unfortunately, the adoption of a more balanced approach is not common in business cultures,

DOI: 10.4324/9781003129189-6

although it has started to grow more noticeably in recent years, as at least exemplified in the statements of intent and the associated reports of corporate organizations (Grant Thornton, 2019).

Therefore, the objective here is how to accelerate this more balanced cultural approach in every industrial sector. Clearly, this can only be achieved initially by legislation, and eventually by self-regulation, with incentives to demonstrate negative effect mitigation. This chapter argues how organizations can create the conditions for innovative responsible leadership without producing a dichotomous outcome, and thus accelerate implementation of the UN SDGs. It also suggests the application of instruments and interventions that might entice public and private sector organizations to apply the SDGs as part and parcel of their innovation processes to support sustainable, responsible value creation.

Innovation: A shared understanding

Innovation was initially supported by the famous German economist Joseph Schumpeter (1934) – an early champion of entrepreneurial profit. Social economist John Elliott (1983: xix) classically defined innovation in Schumpeter's work as "the commercial or industrial application of something new – a new product, process, or method of production; a new market or source of supply; a new form of commercial, business, or financial organization". Schumpeter's theories on how firms search for new opportunities and competitive advantage over current or potential competitors have been a major influence on the notion of capitalist society. Schumpeter introduced the concept of 'creative destruction' to describe the disruption of an existing economic activity by innovations that create new ways of producing goods or services, or entirely new industries (McCraw, 2007).

The Technical Committee of the International Standards Organization (ISO) (2021: 1) defined innovation as "a new or changed entity creating or redistributing value". The ISO advocates that innovation is a discipline and not a management fad or a popular cliché. However, many scholars and governmental organizations have given their own definition of innovation. The basic premise is that having just a good idea is not innovation without acting on it, and executing it, to demonstrate results. This therefore calls for an iterative process of experimentation, execution, evaluation and adaptation to manage uncertainty and mitigate risk.

The late Harvard Professor Clayton Christensen favored three categories of innovation: *efficiency*, which is about doing the same thing faster or cheaper; *sustaining*, which is about making current solutions better; and *disruptive*, a phrase he coined in the early 1990s, which is about transforming complicated solutions into simple, accessible and affordable ones (Christensen, 1997). In this light, it is helpful to think about different 'levers' for innovation. These can range from introducing a new internal process to a new business model. When managed effectively, innovation can have a world-changing impact. For example, in a recent interview with the editor of *Harvard Business Review*, Microsoft's co-founder and philanthropist Bill Gates said the following on the need to reduce carbon emissions to zero by 2050, recognizing the difficulty of such an undertaking: "it will need to be the most amazing thing humankind has ever done" (Ignatius, 2021).

Making such leaps requires new government policies, changes in corporate and individual behaviors and, above all, more Research and Development (R&D) funding and larger innovation budgets to create cleaner technologies and green products to combat future planetary climate crisis. Examples that could benefit from more innovations include, amongst many others:

- The development and deployment of green hydrogen for process heat, shipping and heavy vehicles, as well as in the production of ammonia, the starting point for nitrogen fertilizers (Ludwig et al., 2021; Oliveira, Beswick and Yan, 2021)
- The handling of CO_2 emissions inherent in the current processes of cement and steel making (Hoffmann, Van Hoey and Zeumer, 2020)
- The decommissioning of capital plants (including power generation and manufacturing) that use hydrocarbon fuel and shifting them towards renewables, at pace (United Kingdom Government, 2021)
- The identification of more effective and efficient methods to improve biodiversity to protect our natural assets (United Nations, 2021b).

Such a new generation of low and zero carbon innovations and their practical adaptations are normally referred to as 'green innovations' (Tietze, Schiederig and Herstatt, 2011). They will undoubtedly have a profound impact on the realization of the UN's 17 SDGs and their associated targets. However, these green innovations should be pursued responsibly and supported by sustainable mainstream investments to prevent any potential collapse of industrial sectors and businesses (Carney, 2021).

Innovation and the United Nations Sustainable Development Goals

Innovation appears as one of the 17 SDGs adopted by the 193 UN Member States in 2015 as a universal call to action to end poverty, protect the planet and ensure that all people enjoy peace and prosperity by 2030. Innovation is located within the SDG on Industry, Innovation and Infrastructure. Whilst innovation has provided a good start to delivering global sustainable infrastructure, the concept of innovation as used by the UN needs to be expanded to allow for speed and scale in the delivery of the SDGs, which are to be met by 2030. However, the current view of innovation within the UN SDGs is primarily linked to research, thus presenting a narrow view of innovation that inadvertently may result in limiting the scope of the business leaders' responsibility when they set objectives and key results for their strategy (Doerr, 2018). As such, the current indicators used to monitor innovation within the SDGs are determined by measuring the R&D spend per capita and the number of researchers within the R&D population per million people.

The nearest international definition of innovation comes from the Oslo Manual on the Measurement of Innovation from the Organization for Economic Co-operation and Development (2018). It defines innovation as "a new or improved product or process (or a combination thereof) that differs significantly from the unit's previous products or processes, and that has been made available to potential users (as products) or brought into use by the unit (as a process)". The Oslo definition of innovation carries a number of implications, including, amongst others, that innovation is more about adoption than just invention, and that innovation is as much about new processes, new business practices and new techniques as it is about new products or new technologies. Beyond having more workers working harder, innovation can boost production and profits, and as such innovation can drive productivity growth, and this in turn creates new jobs and improves the quality of jobs. So, the need to deliver societal and social change to allow for better sustainable outcomes – in line with the intended value creation of the SDGs and timeline – requires a broadening of the current limited scope of the definition of innovation.

Drivers of innovation adoption

Adoption of innovation, either in the form of new technologies or new approaches, is often driven by the expectation of increased future profits and the development of differentiated capabilities. Such an undertaking is predicated on the availability of the necessary capital, a willingness to take risks and having a capable workforce. These concepts are often referred to as *adaptive capacity*. Analysis suggests a growing workforce with good qualifications is the critical factor. Today, the frontier technologies and approaches are usually geared toward tertiary qualified individuals of 15 years and older. Here the share of the population with completed tertiary education remains patchy and heavily lopsided in favor of Western countries, according to the World Bank (2010).

Investment in new technologies, processes and products has multiple benefits. Generally, such benefits include:

- Productivity gains, which help to meet the targets of the SDG on Decent Work and Economic Growth

- Efficiency gains, which help to meet the targets of the SDG on Industry, Innovation and Infrastructure
- Carbon intensity reductions, which help to meet the targets of the SDG on Responsible Consumption and Production and also help to meet the targets of the SDG on Climate Action
- Reduction of polluting emissions, which helps to meet the targets of the SDG on Good Health and Well-Being.

A critical part of meeting the targets for the SDG on Affordable and Clean Energy, and the SDG on Industry, Innovation and Infrastructure, as well as the SDG on Climate Action, is the decarbonization of electricity supply. This involves the replacement of fossil-fueled generation through increasing the capacity of energy generated by renewables. It also requires providing a comprehensive electricity supply to many countries, particularly Africa, where this is likely to involve renewable microgrids for cost and speed of diffusion reasons. This is taken as an illustrative case linked to the theme of responsible leadership.

Scaling and cost reduction of renewable electricity technologies from offshore or onshore wind and solar photovoltaic sources to ensure that they are offered at below that of fossil-fueled electricity supply prices remains a critical aspect in driving up the acceptance of renewables under these terms. Generally, new products have a cost-reduction pattern that is propelled by an increase in market size. This, in part, is due to a combination of technical improvements in product development and deployment within an expanding market and also the availability of investments in new capital plants, making the product introductions much quicker and cheaper.

Analysis from the International Renewable Energy Agency (IRENA) (2019) indicates that the onshore wind started off in 2010 with the lowest lifetime cost for producing a kilowatt hour of electricity. This initial advantage meant that despite a relatively slow cost reduction, this first renewable technology became cheaper than operating even the cheapest existing fossil-fueled electric power stations. Solar photovoltaics, despite in 2010 producing electricity at about four times the cost of the average fossil fuel plant, saw a sustained and significant reduction in costs, making them cheaper than fossil fuel plants in late 2019, just after onshore wind.

The offshore wind cost was initially maintained relative to fossil fuel plants but with a more recent scaling up has started to reduce and is on track to produce electricity for less than fossil fuel plants in the near future (International Renewable Energy Agency, 2021). A recent report from Bond and colleagues (2021) at Carbon Tracker shows that wind and solar renewables could easily supply more than the current levels of energy demand. This finding could unlock energy reserves one hundred times our present demand. It could also create new possibilities for cheaper energy and more local jobs in a more equitable world with far less environmental stress.

However, despite these cost reductions and increasing cost competitiveness for renewables, coal and natural gas remain responsible for a growing proportion of energy supply. Solar photovoltaic, solar thermal, wind and tide represent a small part of the overall picture. Encouragingly, energy supply from hydro has roughly doubled over the 1990 to 2018 period. An important consideration here is that Africa, especially central Africa, has very low levels of access to electricity. This presents an opportunity for developing renewable-based microgrids rather than the large-scale centralized fossil fuel-led models used elsewhere.

Government support in various forms for renewables and low carbon measures based on responsible leadership allows the market size to grow and the costs to reduce. Support has taken many forms including grants for basic and developmental research, feed-in tariffs and other forms of subsidies. All of these measures grew the size of the low carbon renewables market, allowing manufacturers to benefit from economies of scale. Solar photovoltaics, with lower unit costs and higher governmental support, benefited the most. Growing markets also meant that the average age of manufacturing plants stayed low, ensuring that more plants were up to date. Newer plants are also benefiting from the 'learning by doing', and as experience has been accumulated, better cost efficiencies in reducing greenhouse gas emissions have been yielded.

Responsible innovation

While the concept of 'responsible innovation' is increasingly common amongst researchers and policy makers at all levels, including globally (Voegtlin and Patzer, 2020), its true meaning is still emerging within the leadership of businesses. Responsible innovation is defined as

> the careful consideration of, and action to address, the potential impacts of introducing a new product, service, process or business model. It considers the benefits that are derived from innovation and seeks to eliminate, minimize or mitigate any potential downsides from the perspectives of the company, its employees, suppliers and customers and stakeholders.
>
> (British Standards Institution, 2020: 8)

As a relational concept, responsible innovation is the result of the intersection of three main contexts: the Governance Context, which includes the rules, regulations and policies within which innovation occurs; the Innovation Context, which includes the feasibility of technical possibilities, and the social responsibility priorities set by governments including those of the UN SDGs; and Stakeholder Engagement, which includes transparency about the business direction of innovation travel and its accountability towards likely outcomes. This is illustrated through Figure 4.1 below based on a personal visual representation of PAS 440 of the British Standards Institution (2020: 5).

Responsible innovation – that is, ensuring scientific research and technological development processes take into account the environment and society – was originally said to be a grand challenge by the European Union's Framework Programs (Stilgoe and Guston, 2017). The responsible innovation approach was recently formalized by the British Standards Institution (2020) as part of a guide introduced by the United Kingdom (UK) government's innovation agency, Innovate UK. It emphasizes the role of the state in solving grand challenges like the UN's 17 SDGs. Such a role can be manifested through different means such as providing patient investments, introducing regulatory frameworks and setting agendas that embrace the context and principles of responsible innovation.

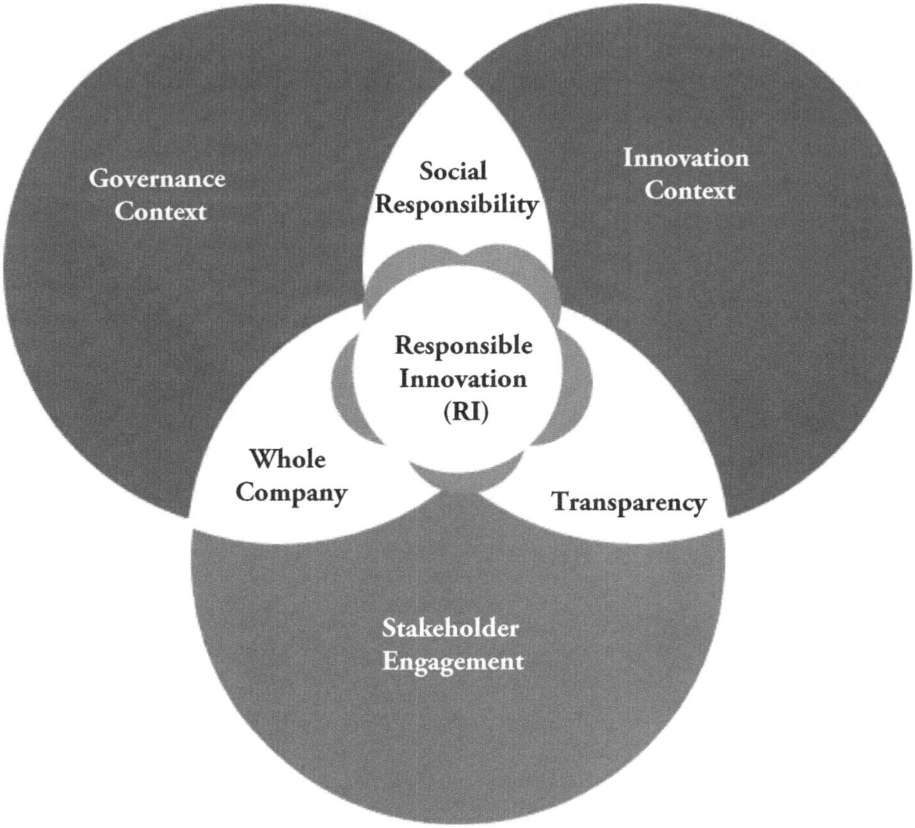

Figure 4.1 Responsible innovation

In her book *Mission Economy: A Moonshot Guide to Changing Capitalism*, the economist Professor Mariana Mazzucato (2021: xxiv) said:

> we need to ask ourselves again what sort of role governments should play in the economy, and consequently the instruments, structures and capabilities it requires – both within public organizations but also to foster collaborations between public and private organizations that work together symbiotically – sharing both risks and rewards – to solve the most pressing problems of our time.

Mazzucato advocated that government-led targeted Mission Projects can drive innovation forward to address grand challenges, resulting in much better outcomes for societies. For example, achieving plastic-free oceans can be a governmental-led challenge that galvanizes cross-sector innovations to generate a series of targeted missions that enable bottom-up experimentation and are directed to drive innovation processes to generate portfolios of desired outcomes (Miedzinski, Mazzucato and Ekins, 2019).

Undoubtedly, there are common features that synergistically bind the concepts of responsible innovation and mission economics. While the concept of responsible innovation focuses on the role of companies, the concept of mission economics focuses on the role of governments. Both concepts seek to address grand global and societal challenges, and as such they consider innovation as the means to deliver transformative outcomes that do no economic or societal harm. They emphasize the role of government in de-risking innovation as critical and recognize the importance of the precautionary principle of protecting human health, safety and the environment.

Responsible leadership

Both responsible Innovation and Mission Economics rely on the foundational element of 'responsible leadership'. In business, responsible innovation demands responsible leadership to coordinate all the contexts and pressures of its intersecting circles, as previously outlined in Figure 4.1. Similarly, mission economics calls for informed and engaged responsible leadership from within government to coordinate and lead the missions as well as determine what these missions should be.

In an attempt to shed some light on the role of leadership in business, this chapter examines an early definition of leadership as stated by the distinguished academic William Prentice (2004), who defined leadership as "the accomplishment of a goal through the direction of human assistants". Within this notion, Prentice argued that leadership is a human and social achievement that stems from the leader's understanding of his or her fellow workers and the relationship of their individual goals to that of the overall group's purpose. Prentice rejected the notion that leadership is about popularity, power, showmanship, or wisdom in long-range planning, but instead linked good leadership to responsible and ethical behavior. While his language is somewhat dated, Prentice's observations on how leaders can motivate their employees to support their business goals are timeless in their construct and are remarkably prescient, reflecting today's business world.

A more recent view of ethical leadership was presented by Professor Max Bazerman (2020), who postulated that today's leaders should seek to create the most 'value for society'. He said that

> for centuries, philosophers have argued over what constitutes moral action, theorizing about what people *should* do. More recently, behavioral ethicists in the social sciences have offered research-based accounts of what people *actually* do when confronted with ethical dilemmas. These scientists have shown that environmental and psychological processes can lead us to engage in ethically questionable behavior even if it violates our own values.
>
> (Bazerman, 2020: 93)

In maximizing value for society and aiming to improve ethical decision-making, Bazerman advocates the need to blend philosophical thought with business-school pragmatism. He subscribes to the tenets of utilitarianism, a philosophy initially offered by the British philosopher and economist Jeremy Bentham (1789), who argued that ethical behavior maximizes utility in the world, which Bazerman called value. Bazerman (2020) thus suggests that the notion of utilitarianism underlies the most ethical choice, as it produces the greatest good for the greatest number of people. He thereby postulates ethical leadership as a value that includes maximizing aggregate wellbeing and minimizing aggregate pain, goals that are helped by pursuing efficiency in decision-making, reaching moral decisions without regard for self-interest, and avoiding tribal behavior such as nationalism or in-group favoritism.

Thomas Maak and Nicola Pless (2006) have picked up on the importance of relationships to leadership and have thus laid out a relational approach toward responsible leadership in business. They defined responsible leadership as a relational and ethical phenomenon which occurs in social processes of interaction with those who affect, or are affected by, leadership and have a stake in the purpose and vision of the leadership relationship. They therefore shifted the leadership focus to the responsibilities that leaders have in relation to the various stakeholder groups and accordingly asserted that relationships are at the center of leadership (Pless and Maak, 2011). Furthermore, Maak and Pless argued that "building and cultivating . . . ethically-sound relations toward different stakeholders is an important responsibility of leaders in an interconnected stakeholder society" (Maak and Pless, 2006: 101). In this case, responsible leadership recognizes effectiveness as an outcome and captures the relational nature of the leader-stakeholder and its implications for responsibility. In turn, it acknowledges the tension between ethics and effectiveness and is cautious about exploiting ethics as a tool to enhance leader effectiveness.

In this chapter, we shall adopt the Maak and Pless understanding of responsible leadership as being that of a values-based and thorough ethical, principle-driven relationship between leaders and stakeholders, who are connected through a shared sense of meaning and purpose through which they raise one another to higher levels of motivation and commitment for achieving sustainable values creation and social change (Pless, 2007). In other words, a responsible leader is a person of character, with *ethical literacy* (moral reasoning, moral imagination), who makes moral and principled decisions by considering their impact on others while also using their influence and power to pursue moral and legitimate ends through justifiable means (Poech and Potter, 2020).

Therefore, a common feature of responsible leadership is one of coordination and guidance when responding to sectoral, national or global economic and social needs. Exercising sensitivity when navigating the fault lines of nationalistic and global demands is needed to ensure that any growth in economic value creation is reasonably well balanced with that of societal and social needs. Interestingly, a research study conducted by the Young Global Leaders and the Global Shapers Community (World Economic Forum, 2020), in partnership with Accenture, demonstrated that whilst business leaders often value remaining at the forefront of technology and innovation, their stakeholders – such as customers, employees and community representatives – value more long-term vision, strong ethics and inspiring authenticity. The study also showed that these stakeholders worry significantly more about the negative side effects of technology than business leaders, and, as such, they are one-third more likely to force their business leader's hand to embrace and enforce 'do no harm' in tech strategies and policies.

Innovation and responsible leadership

An inextricable link starts to emerge between responsible leadership and innovation, in that innovative leadership is defined in terms of the ability to both think and influence others to create 'new and better' ideas and to move toward positive results (Couros, 2015). Katarzyna Kozioł-Nadolna (2020) identified five dimensions of innovative leadership, which are:

- creative thinking
- holding the willpower to be innovative
- being tolerant of different opinions and various risks
- establishing mechanisms for innovation
- implementing innovative ideas.

Her research highlighted the inextricable relationship between leadership and innovation in an organization. For example, how leaders stimulate and motivate their employees, how clearly they communicate with them, and how leaders create the conditions for employees to take action, such as by giving them the autonomy to facilitate their abilities and triggering their willingness to develop and implement innovations.

The relationship between innovation and responsible leadership presented thus far serves to highlight the characteristics of responsible leadership when creating value for a business. However, cascading these characteristics beyond the realms of a business might have a broader economic, social and ecological impact. In the UK, for example, the BSI (2020) guide on responsible innovation lays down that a business should consider wider positive and negative impacts when pursuing transformative innovations, as these may lead to:

- The creation of new modes of production and new markets
- Sectoral transformations and/or the displacement of incumbent products, or even companies
- The creation of entirely new sectors with significant societal and economic benefits.

Used as a self-regulatory instrument, this guide is relevant where significantly new types of innovations in business are being considered. It could be used in any market, based on new developments, in any frontier technology including, but not limited to, artificial intelligence (AI), big data, biotechnology, robotics, smart materials, photonics, quantum and sensors. It is intended to help companies to manage the process of responsible innovation across all their development stages up to and beyond market launch. Essentially, it gives guidance on how to chart a path through potentially conflicting aspirations and demands of a broad range of different stakeholders. Many companies have already gone down the route of specifying their ethical and social responsibility pledges and are committed to observing these as part of their basic corporate governance.

The United Nations Sustainable Development Goals and the responsible leader in business and industry

The UN SDG on Industry, Innovation and Infrastructure has far-reaching and specific direct interactions and influences on several other of the SDGs. Direct interactions here include those with the SDGs on gender equality, decent work and growth, reducing inequality, sustainable cities and communities, responsible consumption and production, climate action, and partnerships to achieve these goals. Due to this far-reaching influence, responsible leadership in business and industry – coupled with the need to continuously innovate to compete and adapt – increasingly requires sophisticated skills and capabilities that leaders must develop in order to contribute positively to the multi-component UN SDG matrix.

Previous examples of single innovations that have not considered the multi-component goals and consequently produced negative side effects include, amongst others:

- Plastics proliferation across all industries, continents and environments with uncertain long-term consequences for species' survival and environmental stability
- The expansion of social media platforms leading to uncontrolled, disguised agenda promotions, misinformation and disinformation campaigns and fake news
- Low-cost mobile communications exposing individuals to fraud, abuse and misrepresentation
- Low-cost manufacturing migration and its negative, unplanned and unmanaged societal change
- Low budget airlines and tourism proliferation resulting in an explosion of air travel, and built infrastructure, generating pollution in air and sea, and on land.

All of these innovations have, of course, brought positive local and global changes to their spheres of influence, but responsible leadership needs to consider all aspects of innovations, thus ensuring negative effects are anticipated and countered.

The cultural lever to transform business innovation

Influencing a change in approach to these issues eventually rests on the prevalent culture inherent in the management of innovative change. For example, if the culture in building social media platforms had been about expansion of their customer base but with control of content to police and exclude as an essential feature at their inception, their consequential negative influences arguably could have been reduced. Similarly, if the business models that generated low-cost airlines, low-cost manufacturing migration and other similar examples were hatched within a culture that considered and reviewed consequences, rather than a culture that was exclusively profit-orientated, perhaps some of the negative societal and environmental impacts could have been mitigated, if not totally avoided.

Unfortunately, this balanced approach is not common in Western cultures, although it is growing more strongly in the Eastern world, at least as exemplified in Company Statements of Intent. The objective of an innovative responsible leader has to be about accelerating and maturing this balanced cultural approach throughout every industrial sector, demonstrated through well-defined cases of desired outcomes. Clearly, this can only be achieved by a combination of legislation and self-regulation, with incentives to demonstrate negative effect mitigation. Generating cultural change is usually more difficult than that of changing organizational structure. And some of the reasons for this are embedded in the mix of personalities involved in industrial management and the difficulty of ensuring that key competencies of all influential individuals are aligned with a common desirable culture.

Leadership choices made by Executive Boards in business rarely concentrate primarily on cultural styles. Although the processes and assessments in human resources have evolved considerably over the last two decades, final selection processes of senior leadership candidates tend to focus on required deliverables in the West, often excluding any detailed discussion on methodologies or cultural objectives. In the East, the selection processes are more subtle and are often preordained from within the company or industry sector to ensure continuity rather than innovative change, and cultural change, which historically takes place more slowly. Professor Hiroshi Ono (2021), a specialist in Japan's work culture, has gone so far as to call the COVID-19 pandemic a 'blessing in disguise', since it has exposed many aspects of excessive overwork and bureaucracy within Japan's business culture (Heck, 2020).

Fundamentally, if we believe cultural change is increasingly necessary for world improvement, and the minimization of damage to societies and the planet, then the selection processes of senior business and industry leaders need to change to combine management competence and results orientation with that of a balanced desirable culture of innovation that recognizes additional components to the business model that formally mandates 'do no harm'. Reviewing an organization's business model, with this in mind, may produce greater visibility at an early stage of many global innovations.

Operationally within a business, if the innovation governance review procedure of producing a minimum viable product included a consequence assessment – not only on the business growth, revenue and profit parameters but on assessment and mitigation of negative effects and possible related influences across the UN goals – then the innovative responsible leadership agenda will at a minimum gain visibility and at best accelerate the 'do no harm' concept of mitigation across all of the UN's SDG touchpoints that impact on the SDG relating to Industry, Innovation and Infrastructure. This could become the new normal for innovation assessment, integrated within the innovation process, and its associated governance and authorization.

Activating Sustainable Development Goals in business

With 193 governments coming together to agree a common framework to tackle 17 major world issues by 2030, business engagement is critical to achieving the SDGs.

Indeed, Diepenmaat, Kemp and Velter (2020) have argued that sustainable development positively requires societal innovation. National governments therefore hope to see business develop new solutions as well as apply skills and specialist knowledge to innovate and create new materials, products and processes. Utilizing this new thinking within, for example, the energy space by using climate-smart agriculture coupled with the use of advanced analytics and new materials and the like will go some way to achieving these goals.

However, there is a direct consequence for the corporate governance structure of organizations if they are going to comply with activities culturally, in line with the UN SDGs. Embracing and complying with the SDGs will inevitably add cost and complexity to businesses. So, how can incentives be generated that are linked to governance to compel senior business leaders – particularly those of large industrial businesses together with their global supply chains and ecosystems – to work in a responsible manner within an overarching UN directive? In simply terms, this urgent question can be rephrased – what is in it for them? This was a poignant argument that was strongly put by many business and world leaders at the latest Climate Change Conference COP26 in Glasgow (United Nations, 2021a). Here, the following suggestions could be offered:

- National governments could consider awarding funding support to innovation projects examining new technology developments (at Technology Readiness Levels 1–4) that support the realization and acceleration of the SDGs. This incentive mechanism would emphasize compliancy requirements of applications with SDG requisites. The UN and national governments would publicize the benefits to maximize global take-up and interest. This would encourage the participation of small and medium-sized enterprises, particularly Original Equipment Manufacturers.
- The UN could offer a resource to identify and target prioritized markets and regions with links to innovation initiatives at Technology Readiness Levels 5 and above that aim to deliver maximum impact against the SDGs, based on regional operations and resources.
- Innovative programs could be introduced to challenge the *status quo*, both in a region and industry sector. Identifying potential areas of interest for sponsored innovation activity will need to be prioritized by various criteria such as potential impact, problems to solve and current irresponsible behavior. Identifying key SDG activities and priority programs will be an essential driver to prevent an overly diffused approach. Spreading success stories across UN member states will also increase the adoption of SDG-informed programs.

Business leaders and their Boards of Directors should also anticipate a groundswell of interest and pressure from a range of stakeholders, such as their own employees, customers and investors. Therefore, mandating the UN's 17 SDGs as part of corporate governance would be a smart step, as corporate governance is "a system by which the whole organization is directed, controlled and held accountable to achieve its core purpose over the long term" (British Standards Institution, 2013: 2). After all, a business often profits from solving social problems. So, when it makes a profit whilst benefiting society, the business has the potential to create solutions that can become widely scalable and attractive.

Most industries will be able to identify the specific SDGs that are core to their operating space and that they can incorporate into their innovation programs so that mistakes of the past within their industries are not repeated or magnified. From their point of view, this recognition will attract like-minded personnel to their businesses, forming the cultural change agents needed to create and cohere value in their markets and customer bases. Embracing the mantra of 'do no harm' will become a feature of the next two to three decades, particularly in environmental climate action and affordable and clean energy domains. Such an authenticity in approach will also strike a chord in many other areas, like collaborative research into, and applications of, biodegradable plastics and different forms of packaging – for example, avoiding Single Use Plastics. Businesses need to actively prepare by reflecting on what they are doing for the greater good. And that is what customers and stakeholders are ultimately going to expect.

Conclusion: The innovative responsible leader

The global pandemic crisis and its resulting business dislocations have unlocked change at a pace and magnitude that has made even the boldest and most progressive of leaders question their assumptions. Responsible leadership involves formally establishing multi-faceted reviews that act as a brake on purely money-making schemes or those with just a nationalistic focus operated at all costs. Clearly, establishing Code of Practice recognition for UN-inspired responsible innovation leaders would be an effective step forward. Responsible leadership of innovation is a collective act that includes the following actors and influencers:

- Policy makers in governments, who can support the mission of addressing climate change and addressing the SDGs
- Scientists, whose research can address the critical issues of providing a sustainable infrastructure
- Entrepreneurs, who can ensure that technologies are adopted and delivered at scale to produce sustainable infrastructure
- Financiers, who can provide the needed innovative financial structures that deliver this sustainable infrastructure
- Individuals, who can choose more sustainable products, services and lifestyles.

Orchestrating partnerships amongst all these actors and influencers to achieve the global goals by 2030 requires better knowledge. Knowledge is the common denominator. It refers to an understanding of information and the ability to use information for different purposes. Knowledge is used to develop new ideas, models, methods and prototypes that can form the basis for responsible innovations. Promulgating and assimilating the UN's 17 SDGs and their targets will provide the foundational knowledge base needed to rebalance profit against purpose responsibly. The COVID-19 inflection point has galvanized many nations to reimagine our potential together by kick-starting or accelerating new innovations and increasing scientific knowledge through collaborative research – not least as developing countries upgrade their technological capabilities, thus ensuring the target date for meeting the UN global goals becomes closer to reality.

The power to reimagine the possible to recalibrate what can be achieved is now profoundly critical. Questioning where we should be and aspiring to get there ten times faster and therefore determining what we say no to, or stop doing, to create the additional space to 'do no harm' should be a key attribute of the innovative responsible leader of the future. A final thought to guide moral decision-making is highlighted in the words of the influential medieval Persian poet Saadi that are inscribed on the entrance to the UN building in New York City:

> Human beings are members of a whole; since in their creation they are of one essence and soul. If one member is afflicted with pain; other members uneasy will remain. If you have no sympathy for human pain; the name of human, you cannot retain!

References

Bazerman, M. H. (2020) 'A new model for ethical leadership: Create more value for society', *Harvard Business Review*, September/October: 91–97.

Bentham, J. (1789) *An Introduction to the Principles of Morals and Legislation*, London: T. Payne & Sons.

Bond, K., Benham, H., Vaughan, E. and Butler-Sloss, S. (2021) *The Sky's the Limit: Solar and Wind Energy Potential is 100 Times as much as Global Energy Demand*, London: Carbon Tracker.

British Standards Institution (2013) *BS 13500: Effective Governance Management Systems*, London: BSI.

British Standards Institution (2020) *PAS 440: Responsible Innovation Guide*, London: BSI.

Carney, M. (2021) *Value(s): Building a Better World for All*, London: Harper Collins.

Christensen, C. M. (1997) *The Innovator's Dilemma: When New Technologies Cause Great Firms to Fail*, Boston, MA: Harvard Business School Press.

Couros, G. (2015) *The Innovator's Mindset: Empower Learning, Unleash Talent, and Lead a Culture of Creativity*, San Diego, CA: Dave Burgess Consulting.

Diepenmaat, H., Kemp, K. and Velter, M. (2020) 'Why sustainable development requires societal innovation and cannot be achieved without this', *Sustainable Innovation and Transformation*, 10 February.

Doerr, J. (2018) *Measure What Matters: OKRs: The Simple Idea that Drives 10x Growth*, London: Penguin Books.

Elliott, J. E. (1983) 'Introduction', in Schumpeter, J. A. *The Theory of Economic Development: An Inquiry into Profits, Capital, Credit, Interest and the Business Cycle*, Piscataway, NJ: Transaction Publishers.
Grant Thornton (2019) *Corporate Governance and Company Performance*, London: GT.
Heck, L. (2020) *Stamping Out Tradition: A Rethink of Japan's Work Culture Post COVID*, Washington, DC: Institute for Security and Development Policy. Available at: https://isdp.eu/stamping-out-tradition-japan-work-culture/
Hoffmann, C., Van Hoey, M. and Zeumer, B. (2020) *Decarbonization Challenge for Steel*, McKinsey & Company.
Ignatius, A. (2021) '"It will need to be the most amazing thing humankind has ever done": A conversation with Microsoft cofounder and philanthropist Bill Gates', *Harvard Business Review*, March/April.
International Organization for Standardization (2021) *ISO 37000 Guidance for the Governance of Organizations*, Geneva: ISO.
International Renewable Energy Agency (2019) *Renewable Energy Statistics Report July 2019*, Abu Dhabi: IRENA.
International Renewable Energy Agency (2021) *Offshore Renewables: An Action Agenda for Deployment: A Contribution to the G20 Presidency*, Abu Dhabi: IRENA.
Kozioł-Nadolna, K. (2020) 'The role of a leader in stimulating innovation in an organization', *Administrative Science* 10(3). Available at: http://dx.doi.org/10.3390/admsci10030059
Lubberink, R., Blok, V., Van Ophem, J. and Omta, O. (2017) 'A framework for responsible innovation in the business context: Lessons from responsible-, social- and sustainable innovation', in Asveld, L., Van Dam-Mieras, R., Swierstra, T., Lavrijssen, S., Linse, K. and van den Hoven, J. (eds) *Responsible Innovation 3: A European Agenda?* London: Springer.
Ludwig, M., Lüers, M., Lorenz, M., Hegnsholt, E., Kim, M., Pieper, C. and Meidert, K. (2021) *The Green Tech Opportunity in Hydrogen*, Boston, MA: Boston Consulting Group. Available at: https://www.bcg.com/publications/2021/capturing-value-in-the-low-carbon-hydrogen-market
Maak, T. and Pless, N. M. (2006) 'Responsible leadership in a stakeholder society: A relational perspective', *Journal of Business Ethics* 66(1): 99–115.
Mazzucato, M. (2021) *Mission Economy: A Moonshot Guide to Changing Capitalism*, Dublin: Allen Lane.
McCraw, K. (2007) *Prophet of Innovation: Joseph Schumpeter and Creative Destruction*, Cambridge, MA: Harvard University Press.
Miedzinski, M., Mazzucato, M. and Ekins, P. (2019) 'A framework for mission-oriented innovation policy road mapping for the SDGs: The case of plastic-free oceans', UCL Institute for Innovation and Public Purpose, Working Paper Series (IIPP WP 2019–03). Available at: https://www.ucl.ac.uk/bartlett/publicpurpose/wp2019-03
Oliveira, A. R., Beswick, R. and Yan, Y. (2021) 'A green hydrogen economy for a renewable energy society', *Current Opinion in Chemical Engineering* 33, September 2021.
Ono, H. (2021) 'How COVID-19 has transformed Japan's culture of (over-)work', Hitotsubashi University Webinar, 23 February 2021.
Organization for Economic Co-operation and Development (2018) *"Oslo Manual" Guidelines for Collecting, Reporting and Using Data on Innovation*, 4th Edition, Paris: OECD.
Pless, N. M. (2007) 'Understanding responsible leadership: Role identity and motivational drivers', *Journal of Business Ethics* 74(4): 437–56.
Pless, N. M. and Maak, T. (2011) 'Responsible leadership: Pathways to the future', *Journal of Business Ethics* 98: 3–13.

Poech, A. and Potter, C. (2020) 'Ethical literacy: Design thinking as a pathway to teach and acquire ethical Competencies', Neuro Psycho Economics Conference, Amsterdam, June.
Prentice, W. C. H. (2004) 'Understanding leadership', *Harvard Business Review*, January.
Schumpeter, J. A. (1934) *The Theory of Economic Development: An Inquiry into Profits, Capital, Credit, Interest, and the Business Cycle*, Piscataway, NJ: Transaction Publishers.
Stilgoe, J. and Guston, D. H. (2017) 'Responsible research and innovation', in Felt, U., Fouché, R., Miller, C. A. and Smith-Doerr, L. (eds) *The Handbook of Science and Technology Studies*, 4th edition, Cambridge, MA: MIT Press.
Tietze, F., Schiederig, T. and Herstatt C. (2011) 'What is green innovation? A quantitative literature review', paper presented at the ISPIM Conference. Available at: https://ssrn.com/abstract=1846882
United Kingdom Government (2021) 'Guidance publication: Aligning UK international support for the clean energy transition', 31 March.
United Nations (2015) *Transforming Our World: The 2030 Agenda for Sustainable Development*, Geneva: UN.
United Nations (2021a) 'Climate change conference outcomes', World Leaders Summit COP26, Glasgow, November. Available at: https://ukcop26.org/the-conference/cop26-outcomes/
United Nations (2021b) 'Tackling biodiversity and climate crises together and their combined social impacts', UN Secretariat of the Intergovernmental Science-Policy Platform on Biodiversity and Ecosystem Services, June 2021.
Voegtlin, C. and Patzer, M. (2020) 'Responsible global leaders as drivers of responsible innovation', in Mendenhall, M. E., Žilinskaite, M., Stahl, G. K. and Clapp-Smith, G. K. (eds) *Responsible Global Leadership: Dilemmas, Paradoxes, and Opportunities*, London: Routledge.
World Bank (2010) *The World Bank Annual Report 2010: Year in Review*, Washington, DC: World Bank. Available at: https://openknowledge.worldbank.org/handle/10986/5906
World Economic Forum (2020) 'Seeking New Leadership: Responsible leadership for a sustainable and equitable world', Young Global Leaders and the Global Shapers Community, WEF Annual Meeting, Davos, Switzerland, January.

Chapter 5

Cybercrime, Digital Technology and Responsible Leadership

Christiane Wuillamie

Introduction: Digital technology and cybercrime

Digital technology is central to the aptly named Fourth Industrial Revolution (Skilton and Hovsepian, 2018). The application of digital innovations has already transformed lives and livelihoods around the globe and will continue to do so with increasing speed. However, new digital products are often developed in haste without security being part of the design process. Together with a lack of discipline in information technology (IT) management and cyber hygiene, digital transformation has resulted in increased vulnerabilities and the rapid escalation of cybercrime. It is a leapfrog race that companies and governments acting alone cannot win in terms of governance – hence it is a fit subject for discussing how this might best be addressed in terms of responsible leadership.

IT, like the industrial revolution before, is the platform for global economic growth. The world runs on technology, which powers digital applications, the Internet, Internet of Things devices, cloud platforms and almost every other element of modern society. Hackers, criminal cyber gangs and nation state actors are eager to exploit any vulnerabilities in this global network of interconnections, both legacy and digital, for profit and political gain. It is estimated that in 2020 cybercriminals pocketed $1.5 trillion (Greig, 2020). Cybercrime not only creates monetary losses

DOI: 10.4324/9781003129189-7

through ransomware, shutdowns and data theft but in an increasing number of incidents threatens human life (Abrams, 2021). Cybercrime fosters distrust in our global financial institutions, disillusion with governments who cannot stop it and frustration with a judicial system which is slow to prosecute and punish those few cybercriminals that are caught. Being opportunists as well as professional criminals, they also target those easily exploited, such as the elderly and undereducated.

While cybercrime has been steadily growing over the past twenty years, it exploded during the COVID global pandemic as large numbers of employees moved to working from home, where computers, networks and mobile phones have much weaker security protocols than in the office. The result is an increase in the number of cyber vulnerabilities, which are easily exploitable by cybercriminals (Interpol, 2020). In addition, global competition has driven many businesses to deploy emerging technologies and outsource their technology needs to third parties to lower costs, improve customer service and drive innovation. Adopting new technological innovations and capabilities can deliver positive returns but also greatly increases cyber risk.

Cybersecurity is not just a technology issue. Over 90 percent of breaches, successful cyber scams and phishing emails are the result of human activities, often caused by stressful work conditions or lack of adequate training. Cyber security and data privacy are intrinsically linked, as cybercrime's many aspects include the theft of data through data leakages and human errors. This stolen data is then sold on the Dark Web and used in conjunction with ransomware, fraud and extortion. The battle can only be won with changes in human behavior and organizational culture, and greater collaboration between countries, governments and public and private businesses. Cybersecurity has moved from breaches through technology to exploiting human mistakes and lack of cyber awareness training. Vulnerabilities at home have added to this growing set of vulnerabilities.

Cybersecurity is a global human issue. Since every individual is at risk, we must engage and equip every citizen, employee and student with the skills and capabilities to take responsibility for their own cybersecurity and understand how to protect their family members as well. The mobilization of this shift in accountability from technology to people is the responsibility of leadership in all sectors.

The impact of cybercrime on the United Nations Sustainable Development Goals

Information security is crucial to social, economic and political growth, and development. If digital systems are insufficiently secured or if employees and users are not well trained, cyber-attacks can destabilize governments, electoral systems, economic systems, media spheres and public debate. Global cybercrime is an immediate and growing threat that undermines the foundations of global institutions and societies, which in turn negatively impacts the entire 17 UN Sustainable Development Goals (SDGs) (United Nations, 2015).

Not all the SDGs are impacted by cybercrime in the same way. If we look at the SDGs as an interconnected ecosystem instead of individual issues, we discover that several of the SDGs determine the fate of most of the remaining goals. We can classify them as *Primary Causal Factors*, which work together to impact a series of *Enabling SDGs*, which in turn ultimately drive the three important global *SDG Outcomes*: No Poverty, Zero Hunger, and Good Health and Wellbeing. Using a system mapping methodology developed by PYXIS Culture Technologies (2021), we can see the various interconnections between the 17 UN SDGs and determine the Primary Causal Factors that are most at risk from cybercrime. This is set out in Figure 5.1 below:

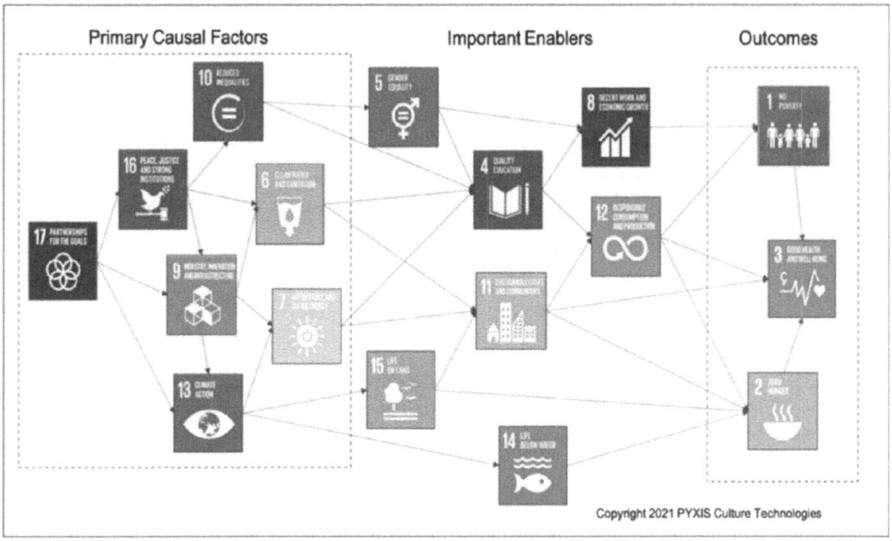

Figure 5.1 Primary Causal Factors for the Sustainable Development Goals

This ecosystem map of the UN SDGs shows how the individual goals are interconnected and how the 7 Primary Causal Factors together impact the remaining 10 SDGs. Unless the world unites to work in coordination in securing and delivering these Primary Causal Factors, little actual progress can be made on the overall goal of global sustainability. It is these Primary Causal Factors that are most susceptible and negatively impacted by cybercrime. The following comments can be made on each of these:

Partnerships for the goals

The single most critical driver for the successful delivery of global sustainability is for governments, businesses and social organizations to work together in partnership. With an effective partnership, shared objectives can be developed, and joined-up efforts can take advantage of collective knowledge, skills, technologies and approaches. A global solution requires a joined-up global effort. While many countries are determined to fight cybercrime, forming national cyber security taskforces and working with other like-minded countries, not all have the investment, the skills and capabilities to defend against cybercrime. There are several countries such as Russia, China, Iran and North Korea that either turn a blind eye to cybercriminals operating inside their boundaries or in a few cases actively sponsor cybercriminal activities (Robinson, 2021). It is the disjointed nature of the global cyber security effort that enables cybercriminals to operate with relative impunity.

Peace, justice and strong institutions

Cybercrime weakens and even destroys the fabric of national and global institutions. The massive amounts of money collected by cybercriminal organizations are often used to destabilize governments by purchasing weapons for terrorists and other anti-government organizations (United Nations, 2012). Peace, justice and strong institutions are thus negatively impacted by cybercrime in many ways:

- Use of the Internet for terrorist purposes
- Fake news that sows fear and mistrust among citizens and weakens trust in governments
- Cyber-enabled financial crimes siphon off large amounts of money
- Disruption of national security organizations
- Taking a police or government website offline by overloading it with data.

Industry, innovation and infrastructure

Modern industry has inadvertently created the current sustainability crisis the world is facing today. And it is through industry, innovation and infrastructure that we can bring about more sustainable development. Technology can connect people and institutions, enable sharing of information, and promote the dissemination of ideas and innovation across industries and nations. The global infrastructure of airports, ports and highways powers our global economy and relies heavily on technology, cloud platforms and the Internet. In many ways, cybercrime is a direct threat to these critical elements. The cost of defending against a tsunami of cyber-attacks drains a company's human and financial resources, slowing down efforts on research and development and innovation. Attacks on critical national infrastructure are growing, such as the recent cyber takeover of a power plant by an organized crime group – or the recent ransomware attack on the Colonial Pipeline Company, shutting off fuel to hospitals, emergency medical services, law enforcement agencies, fire departments, airports, truck drivers and travelers and negatively impacting millions of customers (Eaton and Volz, 2021).

Climate action

Due to decades of no action on climate change, natural disasters such as hurricanes, droughts and wildfires are becoming more frequent and intense. Polar ice is melting faster than predicted, resulting in rising sea levels and risks for coastal population centers. Around 10 percent of the world's population live in coastal areas that are less than 10 meters above sea level (United Nations, 2017). The global disruption caused by climate change can easily lead to geopolitical disruption, with nation states and organized crime stepping up hacking, data theft and cyber-attacks on critical institutions and infrastructure. Cybercrime has both a direct and indirect impact on our ability to make significant progress on climate change (Allen, 2014).

Reduced inequalities

Hackers and cybercriminals are opportunists, seeking the easiest path to their objectives. As a result, cyber bullying and cyber sexual exploitation of women and children has grown to epidemic proportions – thereby centrally impacting on the UN SDG to reduce inequalities. European Union estimates show that 10 percent of women have experienced some form of cyber violence (European Institute for Gender Equality, 2017). In a similar vein, a Dark Web platform, known as 'Boystown', recently taken down by the German Federal Criminal Police, focused on the sexual abuse of children and had nearly half a million registered users (Coble, 2021).

Clean water and sanitation

As recognized in the UN SDGs, clean water and sanitation are the foundations for human health and wellbeing. They are especially important in underdeveloped countries as the first line of defense against disease and infections. In the developed nations, clean water and sanitation services are part of modern healthy living. Cyber-attacks against water and sanitation plants are not uncommon and have been steadily growing as hackers realize that most water and sanitation utilities have vulnerable legacy software systems and unsophisticated cyber defenses (Mathews, 2021).

Affordable and clean energy

Clean and affordable energy relies heavily on technology for the capture and storage from non-fossil energy sources. This new industry of clean energy requires a new, technology-enabled power grid, distributed generation, renewable energy sources, energy storage, advanced metering and controls. All of these depend on technology and have increasingly become the targets of cybercriminals. As cyber-attacks burden this new and developing industry, it slows down development and implementation (Cabinet Office, 2011). While cybercrime can negatively impact all of the 17 SDGs, of critical concern are affordable and clean energy and the other 6 Primary Causal

Factors, which together have a significant impact on our ability to deliver on the SDGs by 2030. Cybercrime is divisive, growing and will continue to negatively impact global sustainability unless we band together in a global partnership with coordinated actions to eradicate this growing global cancer.

The critical role of responsible leadership

According to Juhan Lepassaar, the Executive Director of the European Union Agency for Cybersecurity (2017):

> It's important that company leaders take cybersecurity seriously. I would encourage policy makers to think about the liability of a company CEO to ensure that the systems or services are cyber secure because the worst-case scenario might have consequences on human life.

As of yet, there is no international consensus to limit cybercrime or state-sponsored hacking. It is time for responsible leadership to step up and step in. To develop a cyber safe world and deliver on the UN SDGs by 2030, it must be understood that cybercrime has become a global business. The days of lone wolf hackers are largely gone. We need a coordinated global response led by responsible leaders from all sectors.

It is imperative that leaders of nations, corporations, social agencies and government bodies recognize the linkages between cybercrime and sustainable global development. The cybersecurity arsenal is vast and growing, but these tools are disparate and often overlap each other, contributing to the already unmanageable legacy technology environment. Furthermore, cybercriminals are always one step ahead. The rise of cybercrime can only be mitigated through a collective, joined-up approach, where leaders and experts apply their efforts collectively in focused programs, rather than separately. Just as cybersecurity inside a company is the collective responsibility of all employees and not just the cybersecurity department, so must reducing and stopping global cybercrime be the collective responsibility of all governments and public and private organizations.

What should responsible leaders do to create an effective global response to cybercrime? After speaking with numerous Chief Information Security Officers (CISOs) and cyber industry experts, including senior members of law enforcement, the military and government agencies, we find there are several important ingredients in a global cybersecurity initiative. These are:

- Accountability and a strong cybersecurity culture
- Data, privacy and cyber hygiene
- Design for security
- Education and collaboration
- Globally binding regulations and enforcement.

Accountability and a strong cybersecurity culture

Cybersecurity is no longer just an IT issue. Cybercrime impacts everyone, and everyone must step up and assume accountability for cyber safety. However, it is up to the Board, senior executives and leaders everywhere to lead the way. Nonetheless, such cybersecurity leadership at the top is not always the case. At one global consumer goods company researched by PYXIS Culture Technologies (2021), cybersecurity was found to be rarely mentioned in company annual reports and internal documents. The Board and senior leaders focused most of their communications and decisions on how to increase profits and brand value. In addition, this lack of accountability at the top for cybersecurity has resulted in year-on-year cuts to the IT and cybersecurity budgets, while cyber-attacks across their global enterprise have increased exponentially. Until this Board, like many others, raises their cyber awareness and understanding, and diligently works with management to understand the company's cyber vulnerabilities, there is a major breach waiting to happen.

The Board must ensure that cybersecurity is part of the company strategy and risk management framework, and then hold management accountable for the effectiveness of cybersecurity planning and execution. The Board and senior leaders must develop a set of enterprise cybersecurity objectives that are built into the company strategy and business plan and regularly review the state of cybersecurity. Together with senior managers, the Board should participate in tabletop exercises to understand the company response approach in the event of a cyber-attack. When the Board understands and embraces their accountability for cybersecurity, only then will they understand the importance of recruiting a CISO with the leadership and business communication skills to engage the entire enterprise, people, process and technology.

In the words of Stéphane Nappo, CISO of the Year in 2018, in an interview with the author: "CISOs must have the courage to speak up and be open to management and the Board and be able to present the case for cybersecurity in business language and not just technical-speak." To give cybersecurity even more importance, regulators are requiring proof of adequate Board oversight and management focus on cybersecurity. Insurance companies are also refusing to write cybersecurity insurance for those companies that lack adequate cybersecurity protections, protocols and recovery plans.

According to Johan Boije, CISO of KONE Corporation, in another interview with the author in May 2021: "Embed cybersecurity activities in the processes and the tasks performed by the organization and support the organization in consistent execution and you create the patterns and behaviors that build a strong culture of cybersecurity." A strong cyber safe culture is therefore more than improving Cyber Training and Employee Engagement. There are many more cyber culture causal factors, all of which form the cybersecurity culture ecosystem.

To establish a strong cyber safe culture, the Board and Senior Leadership must develop values and behavioral standards that are operationalized into company policies, work processes, goals and objectives for managers and supervisors, performance reviews, promotion criteria, hiring profiles and on-boarding programs. In many companies with a strong cyber safe culture, a cadre of specially trained cyber champions support employees with cyber concerns. A focus on building a cyber safe culture has proven to improve employee safety and engagement. In a weak cyber culture, fear of speaking up and retribution for mistakes are key risk factors. Building a global culture of cyber awareness and safety should in fact begin early in schools. In the United States (US) in the 1950s, the Smokey the Bear fire awareness campaign taught school children at a very young age to be fire aware and fire safe. It is time for a cyber safety campaign of similar magnitude and effectiveness. In addition, we must engage the elderly and the vulnerable in cyber safety since they are particularly susceptible to cyber scams.

Data, privacy and cyber hygiene

The speed of digitalization has resulted in a huge amount of data. Alignment and collaboration between the business areas, the Chief Information Officer (CIO), the CISO and the Legal Department on data and privacy is critical. The European Union spearheaded more stringent data regulations through the General Data Protection Regulation (GDPR) compliance guidelines. Most countries have now adopted some form of regulation modelled after GDPR.

Keeping data safe is now a legal responsibility, yet the understanding of data classification, data usage and storage is still a challenge for most organizations (see, for example, Taane, Solanki and Dey, 2017). Keeping data safe is even more important with the speed of data migration to the cloud during the COVID pandemic. It is vital for organizations to ensure that the CIO, who is responsible for the storage of the data, the Chief Legal Officer, who ensures that the company has fulfilled its legal obligations, and the CISO, who is responsible for information security, collaborate with the business heads who collect and use the data. All must work together to ensure the correct processes are in place and training is up to date to keep the data safe.

Every organization has multiple cyber-attack vulnerabilities, yet few take the time to identify and prioritize them. Most organizations try to identify their technology vulnerabilities but overlook vulnerabilities associated with business process and people. It is impossible to improve cybersecurity until the broad range of vulnerabilities are identified. Once vulnerabilities are known, the next step in blunting cybercrime is for every organization to apply basic cyber hygiene to strengthen their internal cybersecurity ecosystem. Research by PYXIS Culture Technologies (2021) has found that IT management is often slow or does not have the right processes in place to perform regular cyber hygiene, such as timely software patches and recommended updates. In addition, most CIOs at best have an incomplete list of their technology assets, leaving many devices open for attack.

Undocumented laptops and digital devices create significant cybersecurity vulnerabilities. If an organization does not know what assets are on their network (such as workstations, servers, network devices), who owns and manages them, what business process they are part of and what data is stored or processed on them, it is impossible to drive good cyber hygiene, respond swiftly to incidents or understand the potential impact of an incident. When functions or employees purchase technology equipment and software applications on their own, without going through proper IT and cybersecurity purchasing protocols, these shadow IT devices and applications become easy entry points for cyber attackers.

Access management – that is, monitoring who can and does connect to internal systems – is often relegated to lower-level technical staff or outsourced altogether. Every individual, whether full-time employee, external contractor or third-party provider, must be known, logged and audited by Information Security. In organizations with weak access management, it is not uncommon for external contractors to walk away with company laptops and key cards at the end of their assignment without the company knowing.

Working from home has also opened new avenues for cybercriminals. Many organizations allow employees to use their own devices for work purposes (BYOD – Bring your own device) to save money, increase productivity or just for convenience. This exposes the organization to both cybersecurity and privacy issues, yet many organizations are lax at providing cyber training and appropriate safeguards for home workers. A growing cyber risk also comes from outsourcing and supply chain partners. Many recent breaches and ransomware attacks have infiltrated companies through their supply chain and outsourcing partners (Gaudenzi and Siciliano, 2018). Many companies too are lax in reviewing and auditing their supply chain and outsourcing partners for cybersecurity.

Secure by design

In the rush to introduce new digital products, applications and Internet of Things (IoT) devices, which connect wirelessly to a network and have the ability to transmit data, to gain competitive advantage, companies often fail to adequately design security. They then sometimes find that attackers have entered their system through the air conditioning controller or other equipment attached to the network. In one case, hackers stole 10 gigabytes of customer records and data from a North American casino by accessing a large, digitally monitored fish tank (Mathews, 2017). Such IoT devices are proliferating across all types of industry. One of the most vulnerable, and life-threatening, situations is in hospitals (Batsford, 2021). Digital records, patient monitoring systems and even operating rooms are awash with digital technologies and IoT devices, with little up-front design for security. There are currently between 10 and 15 connected devices for each hospital bed in the US, many of which are vulnerable to attack (Alpine Security, n.d.).

Design for security is the best way to make devices and applications safe. As a good historical example of design for safety, the automobile industry has done an excellent job, with seatbelts, airbags, turn indicators, rear-view and side mirrors, crash-resistant frames, parking radar and a host of other built-in safety elements. Responsible leaders should turn security from a cost to an opportunity. More and more companies and hopefully consumers demand evidence of cybersecure digital solutions and products. Thus, cybersecurity is no longer only optional for businesses but necessary to be able to do business. This will improve cyber safety for all.

Educate and collaborate

With 90 percent of successful cyber breaches the result of human error (Muncaster, 2014), it is past time to double down on cybersecurity education. Responsible leaders must commit to educating everyone in their organization, including ensuring that third party and supply chain partners do the same. Cybersecurity training and education should be seen as an investment, and not as a line-item cost. During hard times, many organizations cut back on training (Krow, 2020). Responsible leaders invest more.

Since organizations are shadows of their leaders, cyber education and training must begin with the Board and senior leadership. All Board members are required to be financially literate, but most Board members have a limited understanding of cybersecurity and as such are not well prepared to guide the company against the growing onslaught of sophisticated cyber-attacks (Grant Thornton, 2019). By mandating annual cybersecurity training for every Board member and securing their home and family digital environment, Board members gain a personal understanding and respect for the importance of cybersecurity. We need to make cybersecurity personal for everyone.

Training in cybersecurity and data protection must become mandatory, interesting and engaging, with special, customized training for employees in sensitive roles. In the military, superior tactics with mediocre soldier training is a design to fail. Expensive cyber technology without mandatory cyber training for all employees unlocks the front door for cybercriminals. In addition, internal company communications about internal cybersecurity attacks and breaches must go out to all employees on a real-time basis so they can understand the magnitude and importance of this ongoing and escalating threat level.

Rick McElroy, Principal Cybersecurity Strategist at VMware, in an interview with the author in 2021, said: “It amazes me how often we are not talking to each other. Within the same industry Information Security teams are still not working together to solve shared security problems. It’s time we got wise together.” If it takes a village to raise a child, then it will take collaboration on a global scale to blunt the negative impact of cybercrime. It is up to responsible leaders in business to share information about cybersecurity threats and defenses. However, collaboration and transparency are behavioral aspects that are not ingrained in most businesses, where information about the inner workings, and vulnerabilities, of a business are kept secret, especially from competitors, who are eager to seize on any competitive advantage.

When it comes to cybersecurity, cybercriminals are our common enemy, not each other. The benefit of global collaboration and consistent sharing of cyber information is that we can incorporate new cyber learnings quickly and proactively, as opposed to each company discovering the same problems separately. When business and government leaders reach out and develop partnerships, it goes a long way to building trust and making it safe for everyone to open up and share cyber vulnerabilities. In the US, the Cybersecurity and Infrastructure Security Agency has recently launched the National Risk Management Dialogue, a series of high-level conversations with chief risk officers and risk management executives at critical infrastructure organizations, with the goal of building cooperation and cyber threat information sharing.

The public sector must begin to create cooperative relationships with the business community, meaning information sharing that is two-way. Government must provide effective cybersecurity guidelines and guidance that are unambiguous and where necessary apply regulations in terms of better practices of information sharing and security breach sharing. Government needs the cooperation of companies experienced in cyber-attacks to help develop effective cybercrime laws. If a global cybercriminal gang or nation state targets a business or government entity, given time they will find a way of breaching that organization's defenses. How do you protect yourself? We all think we will not be the next one, but there are no guarantees. In fact, everyone is a target for opportunistic cybercriminals. A unified global culture of collaboration is required to ensure that we are sharing information and warning each other.

The commercial benefit is huge, since companies will no longer be dealing with attack approaches blind. Collaboration and information sharing gives us the ability to learn from a recent attack and prepare our defenses accordingly. To translate the value of global collaboration on cybercrime to customers, value could be safety, superior products at a superior price, and more trust in our global businesses and institutions. And collaboration is beginning, even among competing companies. Recently, leading cyber insurers AIG, Axis Capital, Beazley, Chubb, The Hartford, Liberty Mutual Insurance and Travelers formed a company to pool their data and expertise to enhance cyber risk mitigation efforts across the insurance industry (Insurance Journal, 2021).

Globally binding regulations and enforcement

In the very near future, technology and everyday life around the globe will be intertwined and everyone will be faced with cybercrime, unless all nations get together to develop a set of global cyber conventions. The future is already here. The cybercrime threat continues to grow, and governments are largely failing to work together and to bring perpetrators to justice. Large cybercriminal gangs and nation states are mounting more and more sophisticated cyber-attacks daily. The lack of globally agreed cybersecurity standards and regulations allows them to act with relative impunity. Like the outcomes of the Geneva Convention (American Red Cross, 2011), the world needs new international standards, regulations and product guidelines to protect our interconnected global society from cybercriminal gangs and nation state threats.

Currently, 154 countries have enacted some form of cybercrime legislation and established enforcement agencies. The problem is that they are not joined up. As a result, a great deal of money and brainpower is wasted through lack of information sharing and cooperation. It is time for a Cybersecurity 'Geneva' Convention where nations come together to establish global standards for a cyber safe world and put cybercriminals on notice that they can no longer act, wherever they are domiciled, with impunity. Establishing effective global cybersecurity standards will take responsible leadership from all corners of the globe.

A case study: The SolarWinds cyberattack

In early 2020, SolarWinds, a technology company whose network application, Orion, is used by 33,000 customers to manage their IT resources, was the subject of a cybersecurity attack that installed malware and a malicious code into its software. SolarWinds unknowingly sent out software updates to its customers that included the rogue code. The code created a backdoor to its customers' IT systems, which hackers then used to install even more malware that helped them spy on companies and organizations, as well as download sensitive information and data. US agencies – including parts of the Pentagon, the Department of Homeland Security, the State Department, the Department of Energy, the National Nuclear Security Administration, and the Treasury – were attacked. So were private companies, like Microsoft, Cisco, Intel and Deloitte. Sensitive data was stolen and exposed. The attack went undetected for months.

Once discovered, Sudhakar Ramakrishna, the new SolarWinds CEO, a cybersecurity expert and former CEO of Pulse Secure, quickly focused on internal cyber hygiene and then stepped up sharing and collaborating with others in the industry. He said in a recent interview with the author that:

> Although I accepted the position to become CEO before SolarWinds was notified of the cyberattack, I feel an even greater commitment now to taking action, ensuring we learn from this experience, collaborating and sharing information, and continuing to deliver for our customers and society.

Transparency, investment in cyber hygiene, a religious focus on software quality, design for security, customer cyber safety and collaboration are the foundations of Ramakrishna's philosophy of responsible leadership. As he related:

> Our customers will be using software from different vendors, so the more proactively we share threat information with our customers and other vendors, everyone can learn and collectively we can protect our global cyber environment, our customers and society. There is an opportunity for every company, large or small, to learn from every incident that happens to others, but only if we collaborate and share information.

Conclusion

To protect against the onslaught of global cybercrime from a governance viewpoint, we must have well trained people, well-designed cyber policies, meaningful regulation and technology applications that are designed-for-quality and frequently updated. But, above all, we must have responsible leadership across the globe willing to come together to do the heavy lifting. Responsible leadership is not a position of authority but one of influence, commitment and courage. Business and government leaders already have a full plate of initiatives and constituent demands from all sides. Their time is limited. Yet we do not need one person to take full responsibility. Rather, we need many individual leaders working together to start the process of global responsibility. To do this effectively, we must shift from blame and fault finding to generating sustainable solutions. We are all to blame for the current unsustainable planet and the unchecked rise of cybercrime. And we are all the solution. The UN is the place where global conventions, laws and regulations are forged. It should know that responsible leaders will step up and step in to support a global initiative to defeat cybercrime and remove this large impediment to building a sustainable planet and the delivery of the 17 UN Sustainable Development Goals.

References

Abrams, L. (2021) 'Ireland's health services hit with 20 million ransomware demands', *Bleeping Computer*, 15 May. Available at: https://www.bleepingcomputer.com/news/security/irelands-health-services-hit-with-20-million-ransomware-demand/

Allen, D. (2014) 'Climate change and cyber threats: Acknowledging the links', Washington DC: The Center for Climate and Security. Available at: https://climateandsecurity.org/2014/09/climate-change-and-cyber-threats-acknowledging-the-links/

Alpine Security (n.d.) 'Most dangerous hacked medical devices', Alpine Security blog. Available at: https://alpinesecurity.com/blog/most-dangerous-hacked-medical-devices/

American Red Cross (2011) *Summary of the Geneva Conventions of 1949 and Their Additional Protocols*, Washington, DC: American Red Cross.

Batsford, T. L. (2021) 'How do cyber attacks happen in hospitals and healthcare clinics?', *Hello Health*, 15 April. Available at: https://hellohealth.com/blog/how-do-cyber-attacks-happen-in-hospitals-and-healthcare-clinics/

Cabinet Office (2011) *The Cost of Cyber Crime*, London: Detica Ltd and UK Government.

Center for Strategic and International Studies (2021) 'Significant cyber incidents', Washington, DC: CSIS. Available at: https://www.csis.org/programs/strategic-technologies-program/significant-cyber-incidents

Coble, S. (2021) 'Online child abuse platform with 400k users taken down', *InfoSecurity Magazine*, 3 May. Available at: https://www.infosecurity-magazine.com/news/boystown-taken-down/

Eaton, C. and Volz, D. (2021) 'Colonial pipeline CEO tells why he paid hackers a $4.4 million ransom', *Wall Street Journal*, 19 May. Available at: https://www.wsj.com/articles/colonial-pipeline-ceo-tells-why-he-paid-hackers-a-4-4-million-ransom-11621435636

European Institute for Gender Equality (2017) *Cyber violence is a growing threat, especially for women and girls*, European Institute for Gender Equality. Available at: https://eige.europa.eu/news/cyber-violence-growing-threat-especially-women-and-girls

European Union Agency for Cybersecurity (2017) 'Cyber hygiene'. Available at: https://www.enisa.europa.eu/publications/cyber-hygiene

Gaudenzi, B. and Siciliano, G. (2018) 'Managing IT and cyber risks in supply chains', in Khojasteh, Y. (ed) *Supply Chain Risk Management: Advanced Tools, Models and Developments*, Singapore: Springer.

Grant Thornton (2019) *Corporate Governance Review*, London: GT. Available at: https://www.grantthornton.co.uk/globalassets/1.-member-firms/united-kingdom/pdf/publication/2019/corporate-governance-review-2019.pdf

Greig, J. (2020) 'Cybercriminals raking in $1.5 trillion every year', *Tech Republic*, 12 March. Available at: https://www.techrepublic.com/article/cybercriminals-raking-in-1-5-trillion-every-year/

Insurance Journal (2021) '7 Major cyber insurers form company to coordinate cyber analysis, risk mitigation', *Insurance Journal*, 21 June. Available at: https://www.insurancejournal.com/news/national/2021/06/21/619446.htm

Interpol (2020) 'INTERPOL report shows alarming rate of cyberattacks during COVID-19', Lyon: Interpol. Available at: https://www.interpol.int/en/News-and-Events/News/2020/INTERPOL-report-shows-alarming-rate-of-cyberattacks-during-COVID-19

Krow, E. (2020) 'Why now is not the time to reduce training budgets', *Forbes Magazine*, 11 June. Available at: https://www.forbes.com/sites/forbescoachescouncil/2020/06/11/why-now-is-not-the-time-to-reduce-training-budgets/?sh=4a63723d2818

Mathews, L. (2017) 'Criminals hacked a fish tank to steal data from a casino', *Forbes Magazine*, 27 July. Available at: https://www.forbes.com/sites/leemathews/2017/07/27/criminals-hacked-a-fish-tank-to-steal-data-from-a-casino/?sh=48c88ab632b9

Matthews, L. (2021) 'Florida water plant hackers exploited old software and poor password habits', *Forbes Magazine*, 15 February. Available at: https://www.forbes.com/sites/leemathews/2021/02/15/florida-water-plant-hackers-exploited-old-software-and-poor-password-habits/

Muncaster, P. (2014) 'Human error blamed for most UK data breaches', *InfoSecurity Magazine*, 5 December. Available at: https://www.infosecurity-magazine.com/news/90-data-breaches-human-error/

PYXIS Culture Technologies (2021) 'What's blocking performance?' Available at: https://www.pyxisculture.com

Robinson, J. (2021) 'Cyberwarfare statistics: A decade of geopolitical attacks', *Privacy Affairs*, 21 November. Available at: https://www.privacyaffairs.com/geopolitical-attacks/

Skilton, M. and Hovsepian, F. (2018) *The 4th Industrial Revolution: Responding to the Impact of Artificial Intelligence on Business*, Basingstoke: Palgrave Macmillan.

Taane, S., Solanki, V. K. and Dey, N. (eds) (2017) *Privacy and Security in Big Data*, Hershey, PA: IGI Global.

United Nations (2012) *The Use of the Internet for Terrorist Purposes*, New York: UN Office on Drugs and Crime.

United Nations (2015) *Transforming Our World: The 2030 Agenda for Sustainable Development*, Geneva: UN.

United Nations (2017) 'Ocean fact sheet', paper presented at the United Nations Sustainable Development Ocean Conference, June. Available at: https://www.un.org/sustainabledevelopment/wp-content/uploads/2017/05/Ocean-fact-sheet-package.pdf

Part III

Responsible Leadership in the Private and Public Sector

Chapter 6

Responsible Leadership and Good Governance

Colin Coulson-Thomas

Introduction

There are many different kinds of leadership, whether individual or of a particular team, group, community or organization. The extent to which leadership can be regarded as responsible depends on how it is exercised and the criteria used for deciding the degree to which aims, activities, behaviors or decisions are responsible. Forms of leadership that are desirable or should be avoided can vary depending on the arena, context or sector, the situation and circumstances, aspirations and priorities, and also perspective (Coulson-Thomas, 2021b; 2021c). Community, corporate and team leadership, and business, social, political, scientific, intellectual and moral thought and other forms of leadership, can also overlap and combine in different ways according to challenge, opportunity and requirements.

What is acceptable in terms of activity, conduct or outcomes in one arena or context might be viewed as irresponsible in another. The responsibilities and relative influence of different stakeholders and the sanctions at their disposal can vary by sector and organization. This chapter will examine what might represent 'good governance' in relation to corporate governance arrangements and how they are used. It will focus primarily on private sector companies, recognizing that these can vary in type, size, activities, ownership and control, but certain comparisons will also be made with the public sector. Particular attention will be paid to the roles of directors and boards and the achievement of responsible outcomes in relation to challenges

DOI: 10.4324/9781003129189-9

facing entities in all jurisdictions and the achievement of the United Nations (UN) Sustainable Development Goals (SDGs) (United Nations, 2015b).

The roles and responsibilities of directors and boards might encompass those set out in applicable company and other legislation, regulations, rules and requirements, a company's own constitution, relevant codes of practice and a board's own decisions, or enabling legislation for public sector bodies. External expectations and requirements can vary by jurisdiction and company type (for instance, public or private). Ideally, all those in a position to influence or make changes should consider how a particular company should be governed. They should look beyond compliance with mandatory requirements or simply explaining considerations on what would be most appropriate in the situation and circumstances for achieving responsible conduct and outcomes.

In the context of current challenges, opportunities and requirements, and available timescales for change, transition and transformation, how entities are and should be governed is more than ensuring that board structures in terms of committees and relationships accord with relevant and applicable laws, requirements and corporate governance codes. It should also be about behaviors, individual and collective decisions, and the conduct of directors and boards.

In endeavoring to comply with legal and other requirements and relevant codes, many boards do not regularly review their governance arrangements in light of significant developments and fast-moving situations. They remain tied to monthly meetings and annual calendars of business. They operate a cycle of strategy analysis, formulation and implementation that does not reflect the reality and uncertainty of the contemporary business environment. While the governance of a public sector body might have to comply with a standard or mandated model, corporate boards may have greater freedom to initiate the development of more bespoke business and governance models that reflect their particular situation and context and can intelligently adapt, and which they can steer to accommodate changing circumstances and address issues as they arise.

While governance arrangements may create the potential for accountability and challenge, what directors do, the purpose and priorities they establish and the decisions they take will determine the extent to which their actions and corporate activities can be regarded as appropriate and responsible. Given existential challenges such as climate change, in this chapter the acid test of corporate governance and whether or not it and the actions and decisions of a board are responsible is whether they are conducive towards addressing and supporting the UN SDGs (United Nations, 2015b).

Contemporary challenges and future requirements

Company directors and boards are confronted with multiple, inter-related challenges and opportunities. In the case of many company boards, diverse possibilities, testing developments, uncertain trends and unexpected events face a relatively small group of similar people whose experience might relate to a previous era and who may meet for a relatively short time, perhaps once a month or quarterly, to consider agenda items set out in an annual calendar of meetings, about which they may have limited knowledge. Can such a board presiding over a large enterprise cope with contemporary challenges (Coates, 2019)? Within the public sector, a body's departmental remit may only cover some aspects of a multifaceted issue. A public sector board may also be subject to Ministerial intervention, may need to refer certain matters for Ministerial decision and additionally have to ensure that what is done complies with government policy and Manifesto commitments.

If our current approaches to corporate governance are to better meet stakeholder requirements, new models and practices may need to be adopted and better support provided. Applications of artificial intelligence and digital technologies might help some directors to better handle information. In relation to the organizational, governance and decision-making possibilities created by digital technologies, what should the role of directors and other humans be (Tenner, 2018)? Legal, regulatory and governance frameworks need to be aligned with growing diversity, changing operational requirements and new business models. They should not inhibit innovation.

Recent business practices and contemporary lifestyles have damaged the environment, reduced biodiversity and destabilized eco-systems (Dasgupta, 2021). Human activities contribute to global warming, climate change and the spread of respiratory diseases. Environmental and sustainability concerns and growing negative impacts of climate change create an unprecedented opportunity for innovation, entrepreneurship, risk mitigation, beneficial change and value creation. In the face of multiple challenges and opportunities, and greater uncertainty, governance arrangements may need to become more capable, flexible, representative and resilient. The focus of governance might need to switch from structures to behavior and conduct. Culture change has been identified as a route to desired changes of behavior (Financial Reporting Council, 2016). Alternatively, given the diversity of cultures that can exist across different functions and within stakeholder groups, there are easier and less distracting ways of achieving shifts in behavior when required (Coulson-Thomas, 2015a; 2015b).

Current governance arrangements are already under pressure, without the challenge of preparing for an even more complex future. The nature and reach of organizations are changing. As they become networks of relationships, board leadership and governance arrangements may increasingly have to span boundaries. They may need to move from leveraging corporate capabilities to embracing those of wider value chains, co-operating collaborators and public-private partnerships. The traditional governance arrangements of many companies are more suited to relative stability and continuity rather than modern disruptive technologies, insecurity and exclusion, and climate, pandemic and other crises. Where Ministers have powers to intervene, legislation can be quickly passed and/or delegated powers may permit some public sector bodies to move quickly in crisis situations.

Crisis situations can test governance resilience, and crisis leadership presents particular challenges (James and Wooten, 2009). When under pressure, some decision-makers limit their aspirations, narrow their objectives or pursue fewer aims (Allison and Zelikow, 1999). During crises, directors should concentrate on their rationale for existence. Forgetting their wider ambitions, goals and objectives might lead them to being unprepared for future situations and requirements. A crisis may be an opportunity to progress a longer-term agenda or tackle another issue that could be overlooked or lost under the pressure of events.

At the height of a crisis, some decision-makers may find themselves largely alone with a few loyal and trusted supporters. A combination of increasing reliance on a small group of decision-makers and their advisers, a shortage of time and a desire to reduce inputs and simplify can lead to the risk of significant and informed viewpoints being ignored or excluded (Allison and Zelikow, 1999). As a consequence, valid and desirable options might be missed. A lack of diversity of perspectives and viewpoints, limited challenge and/or an absence or shortage of counter-argument and contrary opinions can also increase the risk of groupthink (Janis, 1972).

Many companies opt for familiar models of governance, and public sector bodies are often required to adopt a standard governance model, resulting in a lack of diversity and innovation in governance arrangements (Coulson-Thomas, 2017a). Despite possibilities for bespoke approaches that better reflect the aspirations, context, situation and stage of development of individual companies, many boards are reluctant to adopt new models of business, governance, operation and organization. They cling to traditional practices and often adhere to standard models derived from listed companies whose numbers have declined in some jurisdictions. Sadly, successive crises and economic downturns or recessions regularly reveal that in a changed environment some businesses have the flexibility and resilience of a beached whale (Coulson-Thomas, 2021a). Furthermore, innovation in the governance arrangements of a public sector body may require Ministerial approval and/or legislative change.

Addressing arenas of growing importance

Many contemporary challenges are global in their impacts and implications (Dasgupta, 2021; Stern, 2007; United Nations Environment Programme, 2019). This is because addressing them may require collective effort, as more companies may need to coordinate and align their responses with supply chain partners and other entities and consider arrangements for collaborative governance. More governments may also need to form coalitions of countries and international organizations with similar objectives. While the likelihood of a global pandemic appeared on many risk registers, many national responses of varying effectiveness to COVID-19 have been inadequate. Even with international cooperation, governments may not be able to deliver without the active engagement and contribution of businesses with decision-making and income-generation processes different from their own.

Directors have particular duties and responsibilities, but they are not alone. Burdens can be shared. Greater involvement and wider participation can speed up implementation when people are willing to adopt, advocate and promote what they have influenced or played a part in creating. Boards should think through the implications of having to negotiate, cooperate and form alliances and public-private partnerships (Coulson-Thomas, 2021d). They may need to both govern and ensure the effective management of collaborations with public bodies and companies from different countries and business sectors, with varying technologies, infrastructure and constitutions – and subject to diverse laws, regulations and other pressures. For public sector boards, certain collaborations may involve issues that have policy implications.

Traditional, single and largely standard approaches to corporate governance are struggling to cope with multiple challenges and opportunities and the diversity of possibilities offered by disruptive technologies and new businesses and organizational models. Different arrangements may be required according to the situation, context, nature and scale of an entity. More than one governance model might be required across a diverse enterprise and/or network. What form should an overall umbrella take? Sustainability against a background of environmental pressure, climate change and commitment to the UN SDGs (United Nations, 2015b) might provide a unifying theme that could embrace monitoring, compliance and risk frameworks, hold a network of relationships together and help to align organizational goals and ethical practices. This could provide the responsible leadership that might start to rebuild trust with stakeholders. More ethical, inclusive and principle-based forms of corporate governance may emerge focused on sustainable development.

Could more effective and responsible corporate governance become the cornerstone of sustainability? More boards focus on and exercise their legal responsibilities. In several jurisdictions, these reflect a concern for sustainability and may further a company's long-term interests or promote its success, rather than the frequent pre-occupation with short-term performance. Not to do so favors the interests of traders and speculators, rather than those with a longer-term perspective. The exercise of corporate governance involves board decisions (Useem, 2003), and directors may need to view more matters through a sustainability lens – not least whether wider, downstream, upstream, life-time and decommissioning costs are overlooked when decisions are taken.

More attention may need to be devoted to collective responses, collaboration and the alignment and co-evolution of corporate and political strategies (Bleischwitz, 2004). Responsible board leadership should go beyond strategy and policy to include a review of a company's rationale, mission and purpose (Handy, 2002; Kempster, Maak and Parry, 2020; Mayer, 2018). Boards could give a lead in relation to sustainability by redefining corporate purpose, excellence, quality, performance, productivity and success in terms of sustainability considerations such as reducing environmental and resource footprints and addressing climate change. Responsible boards champion the adoption of more sustainable approaches, paradigms, lifestyles and business models.

The evolution of humanity and human civilizations has been shaped by our relationship with the natural world and the availability of its resources (Dartnell, 2019). Awareness and concern about biodiversity risk within many boards and the financial services sector is still at an extremely low level, despite its potentially catastrophic impacts on financial and infrastructure asset values, the economy and the planet. Human activity is transforming natural capital into outputs that do not renew – much of which ends up as difficult to recycle and environmentally damaging waste (Dasgupta, 2021).

Governance arrangements and board decisions should reflect the reality of a company's role within eco-systems, take account of impacts on them and ensure that the use of natural capital is sustainable. Boards should also ensure appropriate strategies for automation, robotics and the adoption of new business and operating models. Digital developments could transform some aspects of corporate governance. New forms of governance and management may be required for the digital era (Dunleavy et al., 2005). Many current organizational and governance models are expensive compared with digitally enabled alternatives. Could a community or network of relationships grow organically and be largely self-governing, with stakeholders exercising voting rights as appropriate? There are relationships between and within actors to consider (Daily et al., 2003). Governance arrangements and our understanding and regulation of them may need to take more account of interactions among the members of value networks.

Many boards appear resistant to some scientific advice, particularly if it impacts negatively on growth and profits. Fossil fuel consumption has grown fastest since scientists confirmed it is the main cause of global warming. Science and technology governance should address challenges and mega risks such as the consequences of the loss of the Internet and new opportunities for collaboration and co-creation with universities and others. Technology can address sustainability issues and widen participation. Digital and other disruptive technologies such as robotics and 3D printing can have multiple impacts and create challenges and opportunities. They can enable transformation and better business models but also open doors to new forms of hacking. Boards that are proactive and move quickly can use them to support new ways of working, learning, operating and building relationships. Those failing to react can suffer from alert competition or become victims of malevolent cyber activities.

Reviewing purpose, priorities and practices

Within contemporary boardrooms, some directors may wish to return quickly to pre-pandemic activities and plans. Others may want to take stock of what has changed and what new possibilities have emerged and question whether a reset is required to make up for lost time in tackling challenges such as climate change. Goalposts may have moved and long-established rules replaced by new imperatives. Different games may need to be invented and played. Perhaps the focus should now be on radical change, innovation and re-invention to create a different and more inclusive and sustainable future.

Directors should encourage questioning and challenge and the development of alternatives. Rather than impose standardization, which can be a requirement in the public sector, company boards could encourage parallel developments to create multiple options and widen choice. Corporate or central services could be encouraged to become more engaged with creative spirits. Previously challenging personnel might have the potential to become business partners and co-creators of new income streams. Where damaging existing activities have to cease, key stakeholders could be involved in corporate re-purposing and the prioritization of innovation.

Boards that act responsibly and are proactive might be surprised by the support they receive. Taking the initiative can lead to first-mover advantage and reputational benefit (Dasgupta, 2021). When change seems inevitable, those most likely to be directly and adversely affected might appreciate being respectfully given an honest account of realities and consequences. Rather than being surprised by events, many investors and other stakeholders prefer fair and balanced reporting of damaging activities needing to be reduced or discontinued. Uncertainty can be more debilitating than knowledge of shut down and the reasons why. Coming clean may improve reputation whereas concealment and deceit may destroy it.

While the purpose of a public sector body might be established by enabling legislation, the question has been raised of for what purpose does a company exist (Handy, 2002; Mayer, 2018). Maybe the purpose of board and corporate leadership and how business value and social outcomes can be better aligned could be reviewed (Kempster, Maak and Parry, 2020). Where directors have a duty and/or accept a responsibility to have regard for the longer-term and the interests of a wider range of stakeholders, responsible purpose could embrace producing beneficial practical solutions to challenges facing people and the planet when their externalities, consequences and implications are taken into account (Mayer, 2018).

The purpose of many public sector organizations is relatively specific and limited by the remit of the responsible government department. Significant change may require legislative amendment or a restructuring of responsibilities. Policies and priorities may be set by Ministers, and strategies might have to be constrained by a government rather than a particular board's agenda. Conformity with norms and standards may also be needed (Committee on Standards in Public Life, 1995). Where a particular body has a monopoly, consumer choice may be limited, and there is often a requirement for a public body to offer all citizens/areas the same service. This can limit the scope for experimentation, diversity and innovation.

Objects or purpose clauses in private sector company constitutions frequently give directors and boards more freedom to decide their focus and priorities, and greater flexibility in responding to evolving and emerging challenges and collaborations.

They may also have more scope for trying alternatives and doing things differently. Diversity, innovation and progress might only be limited by regulatory and legal constraints and the ambition and imagination of directors. Where there are many players, more options can be kept open and pursued and minds can be involved in activities leading to a breakthrough.

Corporate objectives could and should be aligned with the UN SDGs and the Paris Agreement target of 'net zero' greenhouse gas emissions by 2050 (United Nations, 2015a). Areas in which a company might contribute could be a basis for discussion with stakeholders about the prioritization of activities making the best use of corporate capabilities. The challenge is often to ensure that each stage of the journey and the destination are responsible. Objectives could be set in areas such as recycling, recovery, repair and reuse and reinvention, rebalancing and reforestation. Teams drawn from different parts of an organization and its network could scope new ways of addressing pressing issues. Companies could work with public bodies and cities to develop mechanisms to rebalance the supply of natural capital and demand for it.

Corporate and shared objectives could focus on particular vulnerabilities and win-win situations. For example, greater biodiversity also increases our resilience. Aspirations, visions and goals can be aligned with changing stakeholder objectives, such as those of Environmental, Social and Governance (ESG) investors seeking more emphasis within their portfolios on safeguarding natural capital. Insurers might wish to support activities reducing their exposure to climate change-related risks. As well as satisfying moral criteria, environmental and social responsibility might also have a positive impact on innovation as well as reputation, legitimacy and sustainability (Asongu, 2007). It may take courage to reject government subsidies for carbon-producing activities, but to do so and lobby for their removal may be the responsible action to take. It might also avoid loss and damage claims following the Glasgow COP26 meeting in 2021 and court action in cases brought by climate activists.

Balancing contending and shared interests

As well as beneficial and profitable activities when externalities are taken into account, the overriding duty of directors to a company and its long-term success should be to embrace protecting its reputation and avoidance of penalties resulting from causing harm to others and the environment – not least by contributing to climate change. Too often directors have tried to balance perceived contending interests of different groups of stakeholders with their own requirement for investment in renewal, transition or transformation, when focusing on responses to challenges facing all people and organizations could increase awareness of shared interests. This could encourage engagement, involvement and collaboration.

Some checklist-type approaches to corporate governance result in so many issues to track, risks to mitigate and factors and interests to balance that a board can lose sight of what is important. Boards should focus on what is material and avoid becoming excessively preoccupied with modest risks (Rabin, 2019). They should prioritize and ensure responsible decision-making. A public sector board may have the powers to collect required information. A longstanding criticism of corporate boards is that directors lack the information and time to be more effective and to challenge executive teams (Lorsch, 1989). Many boards face a mass of data continually being refreshed in 'real time'. However, a growing variety of tools are available to analyze, interrogate and present data for those with questions to ask. Here intelligent scanning, AI and cognitive systems could be combined and harnessed to enhance analysis, increase understanding, identify areas to probe and improve decision-making.

Some public sector bodies have required mechanisms for obtaining user views of services or the general public. Relationships with certain company stakeholders are usually based on legal frameworks, including company law. However, directors and boards can go beyond activities such as Annual General Meetings (Coulson-Thomas, 2021a). Other ways could be used to engage with stakeholders and cooperate with organizations with shared interests. In relation to coping, diversity and innovation, more 'outsiders' could be brought inside the tent (Stevenson, 2017). Relationships with a wider range of stakeholders rather than legislation and/or imposed structures could be the key to innovation (Freeman and Reed, 1983). The Financial Reporting Council (2018), for example, has consulted on proposed revisions to the UK Stewardship Code, which is focused on how effective stewardship could deliver sustainable value for beneficiaries, the economy and society.

Enlightened boards assume responsibilities for a wider range of stakeholders and more explicitly take material ESG factors into account. Political skills may be required to navigate between contending interests as balances of power, relevance, significance, costs and benefits quickly change with unfolding events (Coulson-Thomas, 2021d). Some stakeholders are more engaged than others, but directors should not favor particular interests. Activists may or may not be representative of stakeholders in general, but boards may need to better understand their opinions. Sometimes a confidential discussion can result in a more open and less defensive dialogue and build mutual understanding. Listening leadership is therefore recommended (Coulson-Thomas, 2014). Those ignored might otherwise be tempted to pursue avenues such as initiating legal challenges.

More democratic mechanisms could be explored. Should certain board committees be opened up to stakeholder participation? A dedicated committee could be established to better engage stakeholders and enable them to express their views. Should there be votes on important issues and choices as the need arises, either in addition to or at Annual General Meetings? The emphasis may shift in governance debates from the notion of a company as a single hierarchy to network governance (Pirson and Turnbull, 2015). How could certain stakeholder groups be better involved and perhaps consulted on certain issues? The case has been put for the bottom-up participation of communities as the 'third pillar' of a democratic society in addition to markets and the state (Rajan, 2019). Certain communities are heavily dependent on particular local enterprises. How they and their city authorities, municipal bodies and others might best be engaged and involved with corporations could be explored.

Corporate governance codes may advocate certain types of committees (Financial Reporting Council, 2018). Boards should consider whether they correspond with current requirements and deal with issues such as sustainability and climate change that may impact more than one committee and require board involvement, direction and oversight. What role should board and/or joint committees play in contemporary corporate governance? Factors such as firm size and the proportion of independent directors can influence committee activity (Chen and Wu, 2016). Sometimes issues are delegated to a committee that should be addressed by the whole membership of a board. Committees can also result in unnecessary delay without adding much value. Perhaps some committees should be temporary or *ad hoc* in advance of wider board involvement.

Compliance and risk

Many public sector boards and some company boards are risk averse. Given current challenges, the emphasis in company boards may need to switch from monitoring and compliance to inspiring creativity, encouraging and enabling innovation and supporting entrepreneurship (Coulson-Thomas, 2017a; 2017b). Some boards need to review their strategies, policies and practices for managing risk and preventing frauds, and to establish the role of risk managers in an uncertain world (Coulson-Thomas, 2017c). This raises the question, though, of whether they are equipped to assess the risks identified by the World Economic Forum (2018) and take steps to monitor related trends, consider and mitigate their impacts, address their root causes and seize related opportunities. Better strategies may be required for managing risk and monitoring performance. Boards should recognize that the collective activities of companies can represent a major risk for directors, external parties, including stakeholders, and life on our planet (Dauvergne, 2018). Individually and collaboratively, directors and boards should try to mitigate such risks. Helping others to understand and cope with them might represent a business opportunity.

Embracing uncertainty has been described as the essence of leadership (Clampitt and DeKoch, 2015). However, corporate networks may have so many connections and generate so much data for central teams that hierarchical control of many activities becomes almost impossible unless sub-networks are given greater autonomy. In relation to cyber exposure and cyber fraud, changes may be needed here too (Leech and Hanlon, 2017). We cannot afford cyber risks evolving such that digitally enabled and Blockchain and AI based networks and their governance are taken over by hackers. Corporate internal and external arrangements, processes and systems need to be sufficiently dynamic and resilient to cope. Collaborative arrangements, law enforcement agencies, and corporate, national and international laws and regulations must also keep pace with the diversity of new applications and models.

Some corporate reporting could better represent risk and performance. The 'International Integrated Reporting System' and practice must keep pace with that of emerging sustainability and other risks. In the latter case, it needs to provide the integrated global approach required by company stakeholders for performance monitoring and reporting, including dealing with climate change and other threats. Directors should also be clear about their responsibilities for financial reporting (Association of Chartered Certified Accountants, 2017). This could inhibit or enable new forms of corporate governance at a time when greater diversity of access to financial information is needed, not least through individualized searches and personalized information alerts.

Accepting wider responsibilities

Certain challenges facing humankind result from the fact that when individuals and organizations make decisions the factors taken into account tend to include the costs and benefits directly affecting them. Indirect and external costs and benefits experienced by others and the environment are often ignored (Coulson-Thomas, 2019; Dasgupta, 2021). Many externalities, especially those which are difficult to compute, are usually ignored. Consequences include degradation of the environment, the erosion of biodiversity, the excessive over-exploitation of natural capital and global warming and climate change. A consensus on market mechanisms such as carbon pricing is yet to be achieved.

Economists, governments, regulators and concerned citizens need to find ways of internalizing externalities when individual and corporate decisions are made. Many corporate boards and governments are currently overlooking the human, social and environmental impacts of current approaches to growth and development (Dasgupta, 2021; Raworth, 2017; United Nations Environment Programme, 2019). The challenge for designers and reviewers of governance arrangements is that ownership – whether by leading families, institutions or other companies and interests – is often highly concentrated. Relatively few people may benefit from irresponsible activities, while a great many people may suffer their costs, many of which might be externalities not taken into account when board and corporate decisions are made.

Various criteria could be used to assess company board performance and consider what constitutes a high-performance board. It could depend on a company's mission, vision, situation, context, opportunities, stage of development and the aspirations of its stakeholders. Particular consequences of activities, such as impacts on global warming or SDGs, could be used as a litmus test. An increasing range of disclosure and reporting requirements relating to ESG factors may impact the investment and lending appetites of European Union financial institutions, and new rules and investor demands may constrain the ability of some companies to raise capital (KPMG, 2019).

As well as thinking and acting differently, boards need to redefine success and rethink how they measure it (Dasgupta, 2021). Environmentally damaging activities still contribute to traditional measures of output such as Gross National Product (GNP) (Coulson-Thomas, 2019; 2021a). Striving for economic growth may increase the harm that is done. Intangibles that contribute to the quality of life are often overlooked. The natural world is largely treated as a free good. As it is increasingly plundered, the value of what remains ought to be increasing. This is especially true as resources become scarcer and the survival of species is threatened. The depletion of natural assets and depreciation of natural capital could therefore be accounted for as deductions from estimates of wealth creation.

Governance, financial and public and private sector risk management processes and practices need to address climate, environmental, eco-system and natural asset related risks and their avoidance and mitigation. Success could be defined in relation to adequacy and sufficiency of action while it is still possible to halt and reverse particularly dangerous situations and/or trends. Urgency and speed are important. Recovery opportunities are being lost. Reports could include assessments of impacts to stabilize and improve, and when these are likely to occur in relation to available time before it is too late.

Sustainable development can be a source of competitive advantage (Pop, Hahn and Radulescu, 2018). A sustainable approach to corporate governance, with a board addressing ESG expectations, might be a source of competitive advantage and a long-term success factor for more boards (Salvioni, Gennari and Bosetti, 2016). More directors should ensure that strategies for longer-term sustainable value creation are developed, adopted and implemented. A wider range of interests may need to be involved in their formulation. Boards should determine and pursue the collective responses and collaborative action required to address global challenges such as climate change. Stern (2019) believes the pursuit of a zero-carbon economy will generate strong and inclusive growth that might result in a more acceptable climate and assist the delivery of the UN SDGs (United Nations, 2015b).

Achieving required transitions

Delay in changing direction can increase the damage, erosion of reputation and crawl out costs caused by corporate activities. A governance practice such as a calendar of meetings may need to change if director time is to be front-ended (Coulson-Thomas, 2021a). Hitherto, many directors have mainly operated within the confines of boardrooms, where their discussions have been confidential, leading to collective decisions. The nature and timescale of the required transition to more sustainable lifestyles and business and operating models, and the engagement needed with stakeholders, may demand greater openness and dialogue rather than prepared comments from a spokesperson. More directors may have to explain, justify, listen and learn if they are to build trust and gain support.

Business and consumption activities are converting the world's stock of natural capital into harmful emissions that endanger health and ever larger quantities of waste. Turning precious resources needed by future generations into forms that will be less useful to them is being counted as a contribution to output, growth and GNP. Ascribing prices to elements of natural capital highlights the destruction of value for which many directors are responsible. Guidance is available on the requirements for building an effective boardroom team and what higher performing directors do differently in key areas for corporate success (Coulson-Thomas, 2007a; 2007b). Some directors might need to acquire, develop or secure access to diplomatic and scientific awareness and skills to intelligently steer through transitions and transformations while contributing to addressing shared challenges and collaborating in the pursuit of shared opportunities (Coulson-Thomas, 2021d).

Some company boards may also need to become more engaged with government-business relations. Self-serving ones may slow change and protect existing operations. Hitherto, some government subsidies and support, together with their aspirations for higher growth, are increasing the exploitation of the natural world and compounding the threats faced. While competitor initiatives might force a company board to respond, many public sector organizations remain monopolies with boards, and employees are happy with the *status quo*. Weak governments may be reluctant to adopt policies to slow damaging growth and development opposed by vocal elements among their supporters and/or electorates. More responsible boards may need to call for a change of direction.

Reviews have suggested that the transformations required to address climate change and the loss of biodiversity are possible (Dasgupta, 2021; Stern, 2007; Stern 2015). Questions to consider are:

- who should be involved in the discussion of future corporate governance arrangements
- whether the aim should be refinement or reinvention
- who might best articulate and/or represent sustainability concerns and options
- the role company secretaries, chief officers, auditors, consultants, stakeholders and regulators could play in future.

We certainly need to better understand a range of external individuals and groups who exert influence over directors and boards and their decisions and corporate governance arrangements (Hambrick, Werder and Zajac, 2008). And if recruitment issues continue the trend towards smaller boards, who will be the powers behind the thrones? In particular, how will additional and more varied conflicts of interest be handled?

Conclusion

There are so many questions and uncertainties to address and possibilities to explore that current inflexible approaches to corporate governance and sustainability may need to give way to more agile, diverse and fast-moving alternatives that can evolve and mutate to benefit from innovation and accommodate changing responsibilities and new options. Might general guidance and principles governing conduct, rights, responsibilities and relationships replace detailed codes and rules? Whether or not this unleashes the creativity and innovation required in the time available to avert the worst consequences of climate change will depend on today's directors. Are they too cynical, jaded and distracted to respond, or will they be sufficiently alert, open and determined to provide inspired and responsible leadership?

Within both the private and public sectors, directors may require courage to challenge a powerful and strongminded Chief Executive. They may not be helped by a weak and/or colluding board chair. In both arenas, all bodies should be subject to applicable laws and have appropriate recourse to the legal system. Failures in either sphere may be subject to external investigation. Whether or not checks and balances work and applicable remedies are effective will depend on the integrity of political, administrative and judicial systems in the jurisdiction concerned. In various countries, corruption, favoritism and nepotism are perceived as widespread (Transparency International, 2021). Within the public sector, abuses may range from Ministers awarding appointments and contracts to cronies, family members and friends, to junior officials expecting businesses and citizens to pay them bribes.

Here, in more dictatorial, exploitative and secretive leadership regimes, open and fair competition for public appointments and contracts, with independent members on selection committees, may seem a remote possibility. For change to occur and basic principles of good governance to apply, particularly within the public sector, responsible leadership at the highest level is required. Stereotypes should be avoided, recognizing the differing pressures facing private and public sector organizations and their relative strengths and weaknesses in relation to the collaboration needed to address shared challenges. In the public sector, policy, direction and priorities may be set by a Minister or sponsoring department. Private sector directors may have greater freedom to explore alternatives and create the diversity needed for creativity and innovation. Companies may be essential for implementation, but a public sector collaborator may be able to ensure a national roll out.

Turning the potential of boardroom decisions into reality will depend on the extent to which people with integrity apply for, and are appointed to, directorships. Many people like to serve a cause greater than their own self-interests and to feel they are on the right side of history – benefiting future generations. In both the private and public sectors, governance arrangements should open doors for those who are intent on becoming directors for responsible reasons, such as enabling more sustainable and inclusive lifestyles. Becoming a director creates an opportunity to make a difference. Determined action to reduce the emission of pollutants, the use of fossil fuels and the production of greenhouse gasses, rewild to increase biodiversity and/or achieve broader UN SDGs could galvanize concerned people in an organization and give them a new sense of meaning and purpose.

References

Allison, G. T. and Zelikow, P. (1999) *Essence of Decision: Explaining the Cuban Missile Crisis*, 2nd edition, London: Longman.

Asongu, J. J. (2007) 'Innovation as an argument for corporate social responsibility', *Journal of Business and Public Policy* 1(3): 1–21.

Association of Chartered Certified Accountants (2017) *Directors Responsibilities for Financial Reporting: What You Need to Know*, London: ACCA with Chartered Accountants Australia and New Zealand, November.

Bleischwitz, R. (2004) 'Governance of sustainable development: Co-evolution of corporate and political strategies', *International Journal of Sustainable Development* 7(1): 27–43.

Chen, K. D. and Wu, A. (2016) *The Structure of Board Committees*, Working Paper 17–032, Cambridge, MA: Harvard Business School.

Clampitt, P. G. and DeKoch, R. J. (2015) *Embracing Uncertainty: The Essence of Leadership*, London: Routledge.

Coates, J. C. (2019) *The Future of Corporate Governance Part I: The Problem of Twelve*, Harvard Public Law Working Paper No. 19–07, Cambridge, MA, Harvard Law School.

Committee on Standards in Public Life (1995) *The Seven Principles of Public Life*, London: Cabinet Office.

Coulson-Thomas, C. (2007a) *Developing Directors: A Handbook for Building an Effective Boardroom Team*, Peterborough: Policy Publications.

Coulson-Thomas, C. (2007b) *Winning Companies; Winning People: Making it Easy for Average Performers to Adopt Winning Behaviours*, Peterborough: Policy Publications.

Coulson-Thomas, C. (2014) 'Listening leadership', *Effective Executive* 17(3): 11–18.

Coulson-Thomas, C. (2015a) 'Learning and behaviour, addressing the culture change conundrum: Part One', *Industrial and Commercial Training* 47(3): 109–15.

Coulson-Thomas, C. (2015b) 'Learning and behaviour, addressing the culture change conundrum: Part Two', *Industrial and Commercial Training* 47(4): 182–89.

Coulson-Thomas, C. (2017a) 'Leadership for creativity, innovation and entrepreneurship', *Effective Executive* 10(2): 12–30.

Coulson-Thomas, C. (2017b) 'Stimulating creativity, enabling innovation and supporting entrepreneurship', *Management Services* 61(2): 26–29.

Coulson-Thomas, C. (2017c) *The Future of Risk Management in an Uncertain World*, New York: Risk and Insurance Management Society.

Coulson-Thomas, C. (2019) 'Revisiting performance assessment', *Management Services* 63(2): 13–17.

Coulson-Thomas, C. (2021a) 'Critical decisions and existential choices for future strategic direction', *Director Today* 7(3): 21–24.

Coulson-Thomas, C. (2021b) 'Relevant, responsible and professional leadership', *Management Services* 65(2): 26–32.

Coulson-Thomas, C. (2021c) 'Reviewing and rethinking board and corporate leadership', *Director Today* 7(2): 31–34.

Coulson-Thomas, C. (2021d) 'Strategic foresight in the boardroom', *Director Today* 7(4): 46–49.

Daily, C. M., Dalton, D. R. and Cannella, A. A. (2003) 'Corporate governance: Decades of dialogue and data', *Academy of Management Review* 28(3): 371–82.

Dartnell, L. (2019) *Origins: How the Earth Made Us*, London: Bodley Head.

Dasgupta, P. (2021) *The Economics of Biodiversity: The Dasgupta Review*, London: HM Treasury.

Dauvergne, P. (2018) *Will Big Business Destroy Our Planet?* Cambridge: Polity Press.

Dunleavy, P., Margetts, H., Bastow, S. and Tinkler, J. (2005) 'New Public Management is dead – Long live digital-era governance', *Journal of Public Administration Research and Theory* 16(3): 467–94.

Financial Reporting Council (2016) *Corporate Culture and the Role of Boards: Report of Observations*, London: FRC.

Financial Reporting Council (2018) *The UK Corporate Governance Code*, London: FRC.

Freeman, R. E. and Reed, D. L. (1983) 'Stockholders and stakeholders: A new perspective on corporate governance', *California Management Review* 25(3): 88–107.

Hambrick, D. C., Werder, A. V. and Zajac, E. J. (2008) 'New directions in corporate governance research', *Organization Science* 19(3): 381–85.

Handy, C. (2002) 'What's a business for?', *Harvard Business Review*, December. Available at: https://hbr.org/2002/12/whats-a-business-for

James, E. H. and Wooten, L. P. (2009) 'Leading teams in crisis situations: From chaos to extraordinary performance', *Effective Executive* 12(5): 14–19.

Janis, I. L. (1972) *Victims of Groupthink: A Psychological Study of Foreign-Policy Decisions and Fiascos*, New York: Houghton Mifflin.

Kempster, S., Maak, T. and Parry, K. (eds) (2020) *Good Dividends: Responsible Leadership of Business Purpose*, London: Routledge.

KPMG (2019) *Impact of ESG Disclosures: Embracing the Future*, London: KPMG.

Leech, T. J. and Hanlon, L. C. (2017) 'Board cyber risk oversight: What needs to change?', in Antonucci, D. (ed) *The Cyber Risk Handbook: Creating and Measuring Effective Cybersecurity Capabilities*, Hoboken, NJ: John Wiley & Sons.

Lorsch, J. W. (1989) *Pawns or Potentates: The Realities of America's Corporate Boards*, Cambridge, MA: Harvard Business Review Press.

Mayer, C. (2018) *Prosperity: Better Business Makes the Greater Good*, Oxford: Oxford University Press.

Pirson, M. and Turnbull, S. (2015) 'The future of corporate governance: Network governance – A lesson from the financial crisis', *Human Systems Management* 34(1): 81–89.

Pop, I. L., Hahn, R. F. and Radulescu, C. M. (2018) 'Sustainable development as a source of competitive advantage: An empirical research study', *UTMS Journal of Economics* 9(1): 73–83.

Rabin, M. (2019) 'Fretting about modest risks is a big mistake', *California Management Review* 61(3): 34–48.

Rajan, R. (2019) *The Third Pillar*, New York: Penguin Books.

Raworth, K. (2017) *Doughnut Economics: Seven Ways to Think Like a 21st-Century Economist*, London: Penguin Books.

Salvioni, D. M., Gennari, F. and Bosetti, L. (2016) 'Sustainability and convergence: The future of corporate governance systems?', *Sustainability* 8(11). Available at: https://doi.org/10.3390/su8111203

Stern, N. (2007) *The Economics of Climate Change: The Stern Review*, Cambridge: Cambridge University Press.

Stern, N. (2015) *Why Are We Waiting? The Logic, Urgency and Promise of Tackling Climate Change*, Cambridge, MA: MIT Press.

Stern, N. (2019) *Sustainability and Internationalism: Driving Development in the 21st Century*, London: Grantham Research Institute and Centre for Climate Change Economics and Policy, LSE.

Stevenson, M. (2017) *We Do Things Differently: The Outsiders Rebooting Our World*, London: Profile Books.

Tenner, E. (2018) *The Efficiency Paradox: What Big Data Can't Do*, New York: Alfred A Knopf.

Transparency International (2021) *Corruption Perceptions Index 2020*, Berlin: Transparency International.

United Nations (2015a) *The Paris Agreement*, New York: UN.

United Nations (2015b) *Transforming Our World: The 2030 Agenda for Sustainable Development*, New York: UN.

United Nations Environment Programme (2019) *Global Environment Outlook*, Cambridge: Cambridge University Press.

Useem, M. (2003) 'Corporate governance is directors making decisions: Reforming the outward foundations for inside decision making', *Journal of Management and Governance* 7(3): 241–53.

World Economic Forum (2018) *Global Risks 2018*, 13th edition, Geneva: WEF.

Chapter 7

Privatization, Poverty and Responsible Leadership

Guy Standing

Introduction

In terms of responsible leadership, we are at a critical point in the global transformation. Those of you familiar with the writings of Karl Polanyi (1957) about the great transformation will understand this. He argued that the great transformation was begun by the powerful modern state, which allowed a competitive capitalist economy to emerge, following the destruction of the pre-modern social order. Thereafter factors of production, such as land and labor, came to be sold on the market at market-determined prices instead of being allocated according to tradition, redistribution or reciprocity. There was a certain phase of embeddedness when the economic system was out of control by society, and gradually a crisis emerged, characterized by growing inequality and insecurities until a moment was arrived at where there was a threat of the annihilation of civilization.

In my view, the threat of the annihilation of civilization is now as real it was in the 1930s. And in the 1930s, of course, you had the emergence of leaders who inspired the confidence of people. But unfortunately, they were fascist leaders, leading us into the Holocaust and the Second World War. It is not beyond the realm of possibility that that could be the direction this crisis takes now. It is a frightening scenario, but when you have the likes of Donald Trump as world leaders, we have to say that it is a real possibility (Schmidt, 2020). On the other side of the coin, it is also an opportunity for a great transformation globally, where we usher in a new and more convivial, more egalitarian, freer type of society. And one form of leadership that

DOI: 10.4324/9781003129189-10

has not been mentioned so far, which is absolutely crucial, is intellectual leadership. Intellectual leadership is the type of leadership that the Institute for Responsible Leadership and other cognate multilateral organizations can foster.

It is extremely important in the years coming up that we have brave, courageous intellectuals in institutions that are bold enough to abandon old ideologies and paradigms and forge a new paradigm because there is one thing that any scientist or social scientist understands. This is that you will only replace an old paradigm when a new model exists, ready to take its place. But at the moment, it appears this is absent in international discourse. The danger is that new leaders in government will try to restore the *status quo ante*, which would be disastrous, and attempt to deal with the crisis in the way they dealt with the financial crash in 2008. Then, within a year, they spent the equivalent of the world's general domestic product trying to put back a system that was in terminal decline. This will merely increase inequality and has created the conditions for the current crisis, to which we shall return shortly.

The current economic model

I want to begin by recalling the economic model that has emerged over the past 40 years. It began in the 1970s with the Mont Pelerin Society – a group of liberal economists, philosophers and historians who believe in minimal and dispersed government – suddenly becoming hegemonic intellectually. And of course, they were represented by political leaders like Ronald Reagan and Margaret Thatcher, who gleefully took hold of the new economics, the ideology of the Mont Pelerin Society, to implement their model (Wapshott, 2008). No fewer than 8 of the 36 original members of the Mont Pelerin Society went on to receive Nobel prizes in economics, since they became so strong, and so dominant, in determining what happened in the 1980s.

The essence of their neo-liberalism was that they wanted financial liberalization, open economies, the so-called Washington Consensus, and the dismantling of institutions of social solidarity standing against market forces. Their policies were distortions in the eyes of many neo-liberals, and the very institutions which give us our Commons and our social support systems were actively, systematically and deliberately dismantled at a time of crisis. Instead, they were led by international financial institutions, as well as the new dominant political class or political leaders, who led the revolution through the 1980s and the 1990s.

What we saw was, first of all, an incredible financialization and, as I have argued previously (Standing, 2020b), financial capital has become the tail that wags the dog. So much so that just before the pandemic, in countries like the United Kingdom, financial assets equaled over 1,000 percent of Gross Domestic Product (GDP). That is incredible by any standards, but in Japan it is 739 percent, in France it is 649 percent, in Germany it is 480 percent, in Italy it is 400 percent and in the United States (US) it is 500 percent. So, finance has become the dominant force in the global economic system. And it was accompanied by the fact that after the Big Bang, which opened up the world economy, what effectively happened was that the world's labor supply trebled in an instant, and all the two billion people who became part of the global labor market were habituated to the living standard of a tiny fraction of what existed in Organization for Economic Cooperation and Development (OECD) countries. This of course put downward pressure on wages in the rich countries, aided by the technological revolution that was taking place and the development of global supply chains, which made capital transfer to where costs are lowest.

And so, as I have further put forward (Standing, 2020b), we have had a situation where the proportion of the share of national income all over the world, in the US, in China, in Britain and in Germany, has gone down and down as part of the crisis. This means stagnant wages and an attempt by millions of people to try to maintain a standard of living that their wages cannot support, which has created the basis of a growth of private debt. This situation is coupled with the fact that neo-liberals were not worried about monopolies, resulting in what economists called Schumpeterian monopolies, because they expected that competition would lead to a gradual loss of the monopoly power to put up prices and gain rent (Schumpeter, 1942).

What has happened is a growing concentration of capital in a smaller and smaller number of corporations which have been taking more and more of the rental income within their sectors and become completely dominant in the world (Standing, 2021). A few global corporations are therefore now taking a leadership role, expanding by both acquisition and competition – so that the Big Five tech companies, for example, have bought up 519 medium to large corporations in ten years. This has enabled them to continue with monopolistic prices while at the same time the leadership of corporations has moved to remove any notion of a free market system.

They did it in part through the World Trade Organization, with the passage of the Agreement on Trade-Related Aspects of International Property Rights (TRIPS). TRIPS introduced a global system based on the American intellectual property rights model, centered on patents and copyrights and industrial brands. This enabled a single corporation to have monopolistic profits for 20 years, or in the case of pharmaceuticals 40 years. This is very critical for understanding the response to COVID-19 with the vaccine. More broadly, it has led to a situation where over 14 million patents are in force at the moment, enabling more and more of the income to go to rent.

Thus, we have a system of rentier capitalism (Standing, 2021) that has seriously impacted the COVID-19 situation. If you look historically at the Spanish flu, something like 550 million people worldwide may have died in 1918 and 1919 (Abdo, 2020). This was not followed by a global economic slump thanks to quite a quick recovery led by the US. This will not happen this time, because rentier capitalism has generated eight giants that are blocking our road forward.

The eight giants blocking the way forward

As I have argued previously (Standing, 2020b), we have to confront eight giants, drawing on the analogy of the five giants from William Beveridge, whose classic

1942 report in Britain set the ceiling for the post 1945 era – a welfare state capitalism representing the embedded phase of the great transformation. His five giants were disease, ignorance, idleness, squalor, and want. We have not yet beaten those five giants, but rentier capitalism has created eight modern giants which will shortly be outlined in an economic slump that is a crash waiting to happen. In this, the pandemic will be a trigger for a slump that we are going to see – just as the shooting of the Archduke Ferdinand in August 1914 was the trigger to the First World War but was not the actual cause. And the excess deaths and the excess morbidity that will flow thereafter are going to be far worse than the deaths so far directly from COVID-19 itself.

The first of the eight giants is inequality (Standing, 2020b). Inequality is greater today than at any time in modern history by far, and it reflects a growth of wealth inequality greater than income acquired wealth, which is an island vastly greater than income. In some countries, wealth has risen to three, four or five times national income, and wealth inequality as measured by the Gini Coefficient, a measure of statistical dispersion intended to represent the income inequality or the wealth inequality within a nation or social group (Dorfman, 1979), is much greater than income inequality. Therefore, more and more of income is flowing to the wealth holders and thereby to the property owner's actual property – physical property and intellectual property.

Inequality creates conditions for the growth of the other giants – the second of which is insecurity. And here, millions and millions of people before the pandemic were facing insecurity, even in the richest part of the world. They are insecure and facing something that is relatively new and which is uninsurable through social or national insurance, as in the post-war era, which creates uncertainty and the unknown. People feel they could be hit by a shock wave at any moment, but they do not know where it is coming from. They do not know how to prepare for it. They do not have resilience because this is something out of their control.

Insecurity goes with the third giant. The third giant is one of the immediate causes of this endemic slump we are going to face and that is the growth of private debt. Private debt has risen to record levels in the US, paralleling that at the worst time of the Depression in the 1930s. Here, at the very worst point, private debt reached 140 percent of GDP before the pandemic hit, but after this US private debt was over 150 percent of GDP – and now it is well above that level, as in Britain. It is the same all over the world, with private debt at a level such that if there is even a modest shock millions more people are going to face destitution, death, despair, suicidal tendencies, rising hypertension, cardiac disease and many other symptoms that go with that. And here we are in a situation where – as a result of austerity and other privatization measures – many countries have weakened health services.

Aside from being unable to respond to COVID cases, the health services are not even able to look after traditional cases of ill health (World Health Organization, 2020). This leaves many more people exposed to lack of diagnosis, lack of prognosis, lack of treatment and early death and is the result of a situation that was waiting to happen. This of course relates to the fourth giant – that of stress. We have a global pandemic of stress – in an age where stress has become a central part of our vocabulary (Jackson, 2013). And stress can induce many of those other things previously mentioned, including morbidity and mortality.

The fifth giant is the growth of the precariat, which I have written most about. We now have a situation where not only is the marginal army of people expanding with low wages, temporary contracts, insecure employment and a lack of a workplace identity (Standing, 2011), but this group is also facing an ever-increasing loss of rights. The United Nations talks about the importance of leadership and rights, but if you are in the precariat, every single day you realize you are losing rights – such as economic rights, cultural rights and civil rights. That is the real problem for the precariat, as I have recently highlighted in Britain in the broader context of the increasing plundering of the Commons (Standing, 2019). Elsewhere, I have outlined a detailed Precariat Charter which underlines the importance of redefining our social contract around notions of associational freedom, agency and the Commons (Standing, 2014).

The sixth giant, of course, is robots, artificial intelligence and automation. Here, the images are misleading, in the sense that such changes are extremely disruptive – even if they appear to be progressive. However, despite the views of some commentators (see, for instance, Susskind, 2020), they are not going to destroy employment, as there will certainly be plenty of work for us to do for the rest of our lives, and for many, many generations to come. However, automation is enabling the growth of inequality to increase and by itself has become a perceived threat.

The next giant is the giant of our age, extinction. And it has been both a causal factor in this pandemic and the one that is actually the most threatening of all, which is naturally the threat of extinction. We need bold new responsible leadership at every level of society to confront this threat, recognizing the moral dilemmas involved (Gottlieb, 2019). I support the extinction rebellion 100 percent because it provides an ecological base for this transformation (Farrell et al., 2019). It goes with being part of the precariat, this growing mass class, who identify with the ecological threat and want to lead the transformation.

This leads to the eighth giant, where we, every single one of us, have to show some degree of leadership against the threat of populism and, in particular, neo-fascist populism. Today, millions of people globally are turning to authoritarian leaders, to populists who promise to bring back yesterday (Moffitt, 2016). They prey on insecurities. They play on stresses – including the fears and traumas of people. And in terms of showing leadership, what we have is a very odd phenomenon which needs to be carefully analyzed by all those wanting to provide political and intellectual leadership.

This is because the new class structure in the world is providing a strange set of alliances which have to be understood in order for us to have astute strategic leadership to overcome the worst of them. The new class structure has at its top a plutocracy. This plutocracy is made up almost entirely of rent-seeking multi-billionaires.

The growth of the plutocracy and in the number of billionaires has been incredible by any standards. In this area, I had the peculiar honor of being invited to talk about this subject, alongside the growth of the precariat, to the Bilderberg Group. This Group consists of billionaires and elite far-right politicians, whose names are all familiar. I thought I would not receive a positive reception because I was saying that you leaders are the problem as you are taking the rent, exploiting the situation to increase your power, and using this to manipulate politics and corrupt the system.

Instead, I was further invited by one multi-billionaire present to speak about these phenomena in Los Angeles to the tech barons in California. At this event, he publicly agreed with me – along with a number of people in the audience – that it was immoral, unsustainable and could lead to social violence. Unfortunately, the billionaires are not in a position to provide the necessary leadership out of the crisis.

Thus responsible leadership must come from younger people in the precariat. Those outside the precariat do not know what it is like to live a life of insecurity. The precariat does not want to go back to the old social democratic model and longstanding full-time boring jobs. They are looking for a politics of paradise. And at the moment, the leaders out there are not providing it. As a result, we have Brexit and other regressive developments floundering around with lack of vision (Burton, 2022; Hopkins, 2020). That leads to the last related point – namely, the irretrievable breakdown of the twentieth century income distribution system.

Conclusion: Responsible leadership and the contemporary income distribution

We shall probably not see a rise in real wages, but we have to find alternative ways of recycling rental income by enabling everybody to have basic income security as a protection against poverty. I believe that the case for a basic income for all is fundamentally an ethical one. It is the only way to have common justice, sharing in public wealth and to really enhance freedom (Standing, 2017). We must therefore trust in people as the only way to give everybody basic security. I believe this crisis has turned basic income from being a desirable policy to being an absolute essential one, economically as well as ethically. I think that even some of the timidest politicians are coming to realize this essential truth, which is that if some groups in society are left economically insecure and vulnerable then all of us will remain economically and socially vulnerable. If we leave millions behind in the rescue, if you leave millions without resilience, none of us will have resilience.

This leads me to two historically astute comments made by President Roosevelt in the US (Dallek, 2018). At the height of the Depression in 1932, he classically said we have "nothing to fear, but fear itself". However, I think he was slightly wrong. We do have things to fear besides fear. But he was right in that we need to make sure our new leaders do not have spaghetti backups. Many politicians have told me over the years when I have explained basic income that they agree with the principle but do not know how to give it and come out in support of it. Well, now is the time to show responsible leadership.

The other statement from Roosevelt maybe is apocryphal, but I like to believe it. A delegation reputedly went to visit him in the White House with a particular policy, and he listened to what they had to say for about 40 minutes then asked questions. By the end, they had convinced him to go out on the streets to force him to do it. That is the kind of leadership he felt we have to be brave enough to encourage. And that is the sort of leadership people of the older generation should be motivating the young to participate in. In this context, positive change will require a collective vanguard effort by the precariat. But I believe this energy and leadership will come from below. And that is the best form of leadership in the world.

References

Abdo, K. (2020) *Spanish Flu*, Oxford: Blackwell.
Beveridge, W. (1942) *Social Insurance and Allied Services*, London: HMSO (Cmd. 6404).
Burton, M. (2022) *From Broke to Brexit: Britain's Lost Decade*, Cham: Palgrave Macmillan.
Dallek, R. (2018) *Franklin D. Roosevelt: A Political Life*, London: Penguin Books.
Dorfman, R. (1979) 'A formula for the Gini Coefficient', *Review of Economics and Statistics* 61(1): 146–49.
Farrell, C., Green, A., Knights, S. and Skeaping, W. (eds) (2019) *This Is Not a Drill: An Extinction Rebellion Handbook*, London: Penguin Books.
Gottlieb, R. S. (2019) *Morality and the Environment Crisis*, Cambridge: Cambridge University Press.
Hopkins, M. (2020) *Brrrexit! Why England Will Be Left Out in the Cold: The UK Decides upon Perpetual Winter*, Amazon, UK. Available at: https://www.amazon.com/Brrrexit-England-will-left-cold-ebook/dp/B0849ZLN7G
Jackson, M. (2013) *The Age of Stress: Science and the Search for Stability*, Oxford: Oxford University Press.
Moffitt, B. (2016) *The Global Rise of Populism: Performance, Political Style and Representation*, Stanford, CA: Stanford University Press.
Polanyi, K. (1957) *The Great Transformation: The Political and Economic Origins of Our Time*, Boston, MA: Beacon Press.
Schmidt, M. S. (2020) *Donald Trump vs. the United States: Inside the Struggle to Stop a President*, New York: Random House.
Schumpeter, J. A. (1942) *Capitalism, Socialism and Democracy*, New York: Oxford University Press.
Standing, G. (2011) *The Precariat: The New Dangerous Class*, London: Bloomsbury Publishing.
Standing, G. (2014) *The Precariat Charter: From Denizens to Citizens*, London: Bloomsbury Publishing.
Standing, G. (2017) *Basic Income: And How To Make It Happen*, London: Penguin Books.
Standing, G. (2019) *Plunder of the Commons: A Manifesto for Sharing Public Wealth*, London: Penguin Books.

Standing, G. (2020a) *Battling the Eight Giants: Basic Income Now*, London: Bloomsbury Publishing.
Standing, G. (2020b) 'Trust and responsible leadership in the COVID-19 pandemic', United Nations Institute for Training and Research/Institute for Responsible Leadership Webinar, June, Geneva.
Standing, G. (2021) *The Corruption of Capitalism: Why Rentiers Thrive and Work Does Not Pay*, 3rd edition, London: Biteback Publishing.
Susskind, D. (2020) *A World Without Work: Technology, Automation and How We Should Respond*, London: Allen Lane.
Wapshott, N. (2008) *Ronald Reagan and Margaret Thatcher: A Political Marriage*, New York: Sentinel.
World Health Organization (2020) *Maintaining Essential Health Services: Operational Guidance for the COVID-19 Context*, Geneva: WHO.

Chapter 8

Corporate Social Responsibility, Sustainability and Leadership

Michael Hopkins

Introduction

Sezekely and Knirsch (2005) note in their research that they have found that it always takes a leader to transform a company into a sustainable, socially responsible enterprise. Companies and public institutions should of course behave responsibly, especially in their leadership. However, there are many instances of leaders who say they will act responsibly where their actions fall way short of that goal. Still worse, some leaders lead but are not responsible on whatever definition is invoked. Here Marques and Gomes (2019: 1) see responsible leadership as exploring "concepts such as responsibility, ethics, sustainability, and stakeholders' interests". They claim that the study of responsible leadership throws light on how the various parties involved in an organization develop a more holistic, inclusive and responsible management approach. This chapter, which is heavily based on the arguments in my most recent book (Hopkins, 2022), advances some reflections on responsible leadership and its link to responsible management as found in both the Corporate Social Responsibility (CSR) and sustainability literature.

DOI: 10.4324/9781003129189-11

What Corporate Social Responsibility is about

The definition of CSR is based on the original definitions that arose in the 1960s but has steadily been improved and changed as time and experience has moved on. Thus, it is argued in Hopkins (1998; 2006) that:

- CSR is a process concerned with treating the stakeholders of a company or institution ethically or in a responsible manner. 'Ethically' or 'responsibly' means treating key stakeholders in a manner acceptable according to international norms.
- Social responsibility includes economic, financial and environmental responsibility. Stakeholders exist both within a firm or institution and outside. It includes at a minimum the organization's leaders, staff, shareholders and suppliers as well as the consumers and users of their public goods and services. It may also include media, government and the wider society.
- The broader aim of social responsibility is to create higher and higher standards of sustainable living while preserving the profitability of the corporation or the integrity of the institution involved, for those within and outside their boundaries. The key is how profits are made, not the pursuit of profits at any cost.
- CSR is a process aimed at achieving the goal of sustainable development in societies. Both the notions of CSR and sustainability address multi-stakeholders and their materiality. Thus CSR and sustainability are interchangeable concepts, with the former more process and the latter more goal oriented.
- Corporate means any private, public or non-governmental organization (NGO). Thus the definition applies outside the traditional private corporate sphere and covers all institutions, public or private.
- There must be a business case for working with stakeholders. These include the wider society, and, as such, being a responsible company or institution means working in partnership with society and part of its long-term development. Longer-term 'big' issues are key to prevent collapse and are the responsibility of institutions.

This definition is very wide ranging, but the major part is that CSR is about treating key stakeholders responsibly. A good definition is essentially based on a model from which all the other elements can readily be derived. I discussed the above definition in more detail in my recent book on *From the Margins to the Mainstream* (Hopkins, 2016), but confidence can be placed in this definition because it developed from the great United States (US) thinkers of the twentieth century and the European Union (EU), and other international standards employ it. Moreover, it covers just about every element of what we want to say. Perhaps the key element, and the link to sustainability, lies in adding in the definition of sustainable development, which is development that meets the needs of the present without compromising the ability of future generations to meet their own needs. This follows the definition of the United Nations (UN) (1987) in its sponsored report on *Our Common Future* chaired by Brundtland. Consequently, CSR centrally aims to seek sustainable development as its goal.

In my work, I use the definition to develop a model designed to help companies and organizations with CSR and sustainability. In fact, CSR is simply a business strategy with a view to the long-term and not purely the quarterly financial report or the daily stock market ratings. Thus CSR and sustainability emphasize profit making with reference to 'how' a company makes profits, not profits at any cost. It is also a strategic systems approach that examines and influences the behavior of a company while preserving its competitive advantage. In this way, we can say:

- CSR means treating the primary stakeholders of a company in a responsible manner
- Corporate means any group of people working together in a for-profit or not-for-profit company or organization
- Social means the social system and includes finance, economy, environment and social issues
- Responsibility is about taking issues affecting the corporate body seriously and acting within – and sometimes even beyond – societal norms
- Strategic means having a strategy that is taken into a working model
- A systems approach means including all aspects of the system in decision-making
- Competitive advantage is the implementation of a value-creating strategy not simultaneously being implemented by any current or potential competitors.

The longstanding issue of CSR and sustainability has raised questions of responsible management and responsible leadership. Here we should be mindful of the distinction that Kotter (1990) makes between leadership and management – where managing is about coping with complexity, and leading is about the rather different process of coping with change. In this sense, managers plan and prepare budgets, whereas leaders set directions. Managers too are focused on organizing and staffing, as well as controlling and problem solving, whereas leaders are concerned with aligning and motivating people. In addition, managers endeavor to do things right, whereas leaders strive to do the right thing. These facets of the managerial and leadership roles are not mutually exclusive but actually complementary. Moreover, both are needed in organizations as integral parts of exercising Corporate Social Responsibility.

In this vein, Monbiot (2019) has argued that political hucksters using aggression, lies and outrage to drown out reasoned argument are becoming increasingly successful. He lists a range of leaders from Donald Trump in the US and Boris Johnson in the United Kingdom (UK) to Narendra Modi in India and Jair Bolsonaro in Brazil, who have discovered that the digital age offers rich pickings. From this viewpoint, CSR and sustainability can only take place where there is an active leader and/or manager who champions transforming an organization into a sustainable, socially responsible enterprise (Szekely and Knirsch, 2005). This requires the person concerned to be both a good leader and a good manager. Their sustainability work begins with the examination of the various internal and external factors related to the sustainability performance of their company and its suppliers.

We should now set out the three critical success factors in achieving sustainable performance in organizations. These are as follows:

- *Leadership and vision*: This requires the full and honest commitment of management, backed by incentives and training to reinforce the right messages and drive performance from the top – including product and process innovations.
- *Flexibility to change*: Key managerial staff must be committed to CSR and sustainability if sustainability values and vision are to be integrated into business strategy, policies and culture and communicated effectively to all employees – with appropriate goal and target setting and a coordinated approach to monitoring and evaluating progress.
- *Openness*: It is vital to engage with key stakeholders openly and transparently to develop a shared understanding of approaches and expectations beyond simply short-term profits, including the provision of benchmarks – only in this way will there be an associated increase in credibility, commitment and innovation in the learning process.

The relationship between Corporate Social Responsibility and responsible leadership

The influential US group the Business Roundtable, comprised of Chief Executive Officers (CEOs) representing top corporations, recently rephrased the company rule book from maximizing shareholder value to maximizing stakeholder value (Kaplan, 2019). This is a highly significant move because for more than forty years, following Milton Friedman (1970), corporate boardrooms had focused primarily on increasing profits at the expense of a worsening distribution of income to workers in capitalist economies (see, for instance, Standing, 2019). Moreover, this turnaround was accompanied by a pledge by the Business Roundtable to ensure that issues of sustainability, ethics and the public interest are addressed in the private and public sectors to the benefit of more than just shareholders – in line with CSR goals.

This broadening of the constituencies to take into account groups ranging from clients, directors, owners, to employees, suppliers, environmental lobbyists, the community, citizens and future generations clearly is a major watershed. However, I would go further and argue that each key stakeholder group should have a responsible leader to ensure their responsible treatment. Three further issues stem from this. First, a golden rule is that, where appropriate, leaders should imagine themselves in subservient roles and then agree with the leadership taken.

A second issue concerns what is meant by a 'key' stakeholder. Kenny (2014) poses five questions and gives some examples that a responsible leader must address:

- Key importance is central in terms of whether the stakeholder has a fundamental impact on the organization's performance and it is wise for the organization in question to respect this – not least to avoid expensive legal battles.
- What you really want a key stakeholder to do – which is a crucial consideration if constituencies like the community are to be heard.
- Whether the relationship with key stakeholders is dynamic and you want it to grow – a significant dimension of which is whether this is needed.
- Whether you can exist without, or easily replace, the key stakeholder from another source without undue detriment.
- If the key stakeholder has already been identified through another relationship – as organizations would wish to avoid double counting.

Kenny (2014) also points out that responsible leadership was important for employees as shown by Krister Ungerboeck, CEO of Courageous Growth. When Ungerboeck first became a business leader, he thought that the CEO should be the smartest person in the organization, which led him to doubt the capabilities of his team – resulting in an unproductive work environment. However, after receiving feedback in an employee survey, he realized that this leadership style did not work in terms of motivation and made a 360-degree transformation. He acknowledged that criticism from above is lazy leadership that makes employees feel inferior. Since then, he has tried to lead through encouragement and endorsement of the deeds of his employees.

A further issue arises when stakeholders unite to influence a company or institution, which can have knock-on consequences. This was the case when Greenpeace criticized Shell in 1995 for its plan to dump the Brent Spar Oil Rig into the North Sea (Reuters, 2010). The combination of Greenpeace and the media – two key stakeholders that Shell had previously ignored – led to mass press coverage and a decision by Shell to locate the rig elsewhere. This classic case eventually resulted in NGOs being more involved in the operations of Shell and other oil companies. To further muddy the water, if all stakeholders are key and equally important then there may be too many concerns – meaning that no one is important. So the selection by the organizations involved of the most significant stakeholders is pivotal.

Enhanced performance and responsible leadership

Kung and Rupp (2018) claim most academic research has found companies engaged in CSR have larger stock returns as a result of establishing greater trust among employees, customers and shareholders. Here a good example of a responsible leader was Anita Roddick, who was one of the first to introduce CSR into a company, such that she became known as the Queen of Green in expanding her Body Shop chain, paralleled by strong concerns for her staff and their fair trade suppliers. The original shop in Brighton became a global retailing phenomenon – with almost two thousand stores in fifty countries and revenue of $986 million being generated by the time of her death in 2005. This is practical testimony by a responsible leader that CSR can bring great rewards to organizations prepared to embrace it (Saks and Search-Whittaker, 2018).

But not all leaders are benevolent in the business sphere. For instance, the Koch brothers, who supported Americans for Prosperity (AFP) with its focus on anti-union legislation, were arguably rather too driven by a libertarian approach to free markets and limited government. AFP recognized that to make lasting change in US politics, the Koch network would need to permanently weaken the organizations that support liberal candidates and causes – and, above all, the labor movement. This it has done through the enormous wealth generated by Koch Industries, one of the largest privately held conglomerates in the US, which – through investment in support of conservative idea generation, leadership training, election campaigning and policy advocacy – has helped to reduce public union membership rates, as well as erode the political clout of the labor unions. This had a consequent negative impact on the Democratic Party, especially in states like Wisconsin, where Donald Trump gained a surprise success in the 2016 elections. Robinson (2019) therefore suggests that the anti-democratic thrust of the political campaigning through the Koch brothers puts them at the other end of the responsible leadership spectrum.

The primary thrust of CSR has been to promote a form of responsible capitalism. However, in some quarters, there is an increasing concern that capitalism itself is to blame for all the ills in society. Capitalism has many definitions and forms, and so I would like to be clear on what we mean by it. We have certainly moved on from Karl Marx, who described capitalism, with the private ownership of the means of production, critically and argued for its replacement by socialism (Marx, 2004). The latter led to the Russian Revolution and the destruction of the Tsar and his family. But eventually in this context socialism turned sour (Service, 1997). It is not surprising that in Eastern Europe there was a *volte-face* as the populations of previous Soviet states wanted the benefits of freedom and democracy that came from a mixed economy. Marx understated the rise of trade unions that led to increases in the standard of living of workers and gave them a voice. Today trade unions are seen as much as a constraint to prosperity as an enabling mechanism to promote prosperity for all, which underlines the need for CSR and sustainability in the stakeholder equation.

Leaders matter but Africa needs more responsible leaders

So far, I have concentrated my commentary on capitalist societies in the Global North, but it is important to consider other parts of the world too. Here I make some observations on Africa in the Global South as a particular case with which I am very familiar. Here Nelson Mandela, the figurehead of the Institute for Responsible

Leadership, was inconvertibly a remarkable leader, and it was clearly highly regrettable that 27 years of his life were spent in jail on Robben Island. Nonetheless, after coming out of prison without remorse, he showed the sympathetic, peaceful and understanding attitude that I have found myself among most Africans – especially in Kenya, where I have spent a large part of the last few years.

There have been other brilliant leaders, some of whom are relatively unsung as compared to Mandela. One of my heroes, Habib Bourguiba, was instrumental in the huge success of Tunisia over some fifty years; while fighting the French, he managed to take Tunisia to where it is today – a reasonably well-educated and developed country (Bessis and Belhassen, 2012). This remains one of the best hopes of resisting the darker forces of Islam as well as other elements of the world that have turned against democracy.

Even in Kenya, highly troubled by corruption and great inequality at present, Jomo Kenyatta was a largely responsible leader post-independence (Angelo, 2020). He, like subsequent leaders, believed in the value of education and laid the foundations for its subsequent impressive multi-faceted development. The uplifting result can be seen today with roads packed in the mornings and evenings with every form of transport taking Kenyan children to school. Yet Kenya still needs leadership to stop corruption at the grassroots and elsewhere. Encouragingly, though, while leadership skills have been mixed, there are green shoots in other parts of Africa, including in countries like Botswana, Liberia and Rwanda. These are to be set against the example of countries like Zimbabwe, where Mlambo (2014) underlines the serious economic decline and human rights violations under Mugabe – making his country a pariah state.

There are rumors that ex-President Barack Obama is investing in land in Kenya so as to start a Foundation. That gives me great hope, since Obama, of Kenyan origin, can be the visionary leader and superb role model with a warm, sympathetic manner that Africa needs – a new Mandela. Not with the power of a President but with the power of example. Socially responsible leaders matter, and they do not have to be ex-Presidents – as philanthropic entrepreneurs like Bill Gates, the co-founder of Microsoft, have shown – but there is no doubt that it is an advantage. Obama demonstrated this in two terms in the White House in his various engagements over healthcare, the US gun lobby, climate change, fiscal responsibility, growing the economy, negotiations with Iran and his attempt to close Guantanamo Bay. All this took place in face of one of the most hostile Congresses with which any US President has had to deal. However, now free of the constraints of Presidential office, Obama (2020) can use the power of his words from his new base in Africa and elsewhere to drive human rights, democracy, education and, most importantly, socially responsible leadership.

Responsible leadership in the era of COVID-19

The focus finally should switch to responsible leadership and CSR in dealing with the COVID pandemic, which has so shaken our conceptions of what is normal. Here most small, medium and large-scale enterprises in the private sector have suffered deeply in the wake of the pandemic in which, amongst other things, many flights have been cancelled, social distancing has led to places of entertainment closing and large numbers of activities have been prohibited. There has consequently been even more need, with the virus spreading and accumulating numbers being hospitalized and dying, for strong socially responsible leadership from both the private and the public sector to meet the needs of stakeholders.

As I note elsewhere (Hopkins, 2022), the stakeholders that need to be treated responsibly in the modern COVID-19 era and beyond include the following:

- *Board members*: In the case of CSR, it is often the independent directors who take the longer-term view and understand that a short-term focus simply on profit-making can ruin an organization's reputation and sustainability.
- *CEOs*: They often appoint task forces to advise them on the main issues for the companies they command. These are usually based on factors such as profits, reputation centered on service to the local/national community, and how the pandemic is being addressed.
- *All leaders*: A key question is how far leaders can treat a subordinate responsibly in the hierarchies in which they are embedded. It is commendable if leaders can put themselves in the subordinate's position and think whether they would consider their actions to be responsible in this light.
- *Shareholders*: They need to keep investing if the company is helping to reduce COVID cases and is increasing its reputation in a way that will lead to eventual increased profitability.
- *Managers*: Managers must respect the need for employees to observe social distancing, remain at home if not required to physically be at work, and have regular teleconferencing meetings.
- *Employees*: Management should keep employees informed of issues and problems both at the workplace and at home, especially if there is extensive homeworking.
- *Suppliers*: They should ensure that sufficient personnel are available and explain any difficulties in delivery of products and services that have been requested.
- *Community*: Donations should be accepted gratefully, and the organization should keep the community informed of its problems and achievements – while generating community leadership.
- *Government*: It should ensure that companies and other bodies work together to avoid duplication and fragmentation of tasks, and to ensure key issues are being addressed without unnecessary waste.
- *Media and social media*: Evidence-based journalism is vital in times of crisis, as in the case of COVID-19. False accusations are not needed. Messaging should also promote responsible behavior and social cohesion – as well as positive aspects of organizational work.
- *The environment*: It is essential that urban areas greatly decrease the pollution from carbon dioxide and allow species to recover numbers in their natural environment.

An example of how private companies could respond responsibly to stakeholders was through messaging its customers to make sure, during the peak of the COVID-19 era, that:

- Masks were worn whenever possible, as the virus spreads through the air in droplets
- Social distancing of one or two meters was observed between individuals
- Hands were washed frequently with soap and water if disposable surgical gloves are not worn
- Flat surfaces were regularly cleaned where the virus can thrive.

Interestingly, when the results of our CSR Rating App (https://www.csrfi.com/rate-your-company) were analyzed, we found that most large private companies, if not all, have a higher CSR rating score than public institutions. This highlights that more and more large companies are realizing that multi-stakeholder capitalism is more praiseworthy and profitable if it does not merely focus on shareholder value. Given the current suspicion and lack of confidence in some of our public sector leaders, this bodes well for the future.

The COVID-19 worldwide pandemic has thrown into relief the arguments put forward in this chapter. Pleasingly many, but not all, companies and large corporations now see the need to extend their responsibilities to the big issues of the day. They have already been involved in a range of initiatives from trying to prevent global warming and reducing car exhaust emissions to substituting biodegradable plastics and creating alternative energy devices. To underscore this, in response to a recent question from the head of CSR at a company in Kosovo about what might be done in progressing their country, I gave a reply that generalizes to other nations at a similar stage of development, namely:

- Work with other companies to prevent needless overlapping activity
- Engage with the government and help them with management and priorities
- Ensure there is a business case for what your company does
- Communicate through Internet conferencing such as Zoom and Skype, with less travel to improve the environment
- Given that less movement has led to many business failures, not least amongst small companies, ensuring a basic income needs to be seriously considered by governments.

While CSR is normally applied to the private sector, there is no reason why it cannot be applied to other corporate entities in the public sector. A CSR strategy is based on defining the key stakeholders of an institution and treating them with responsibility. At the peak time of COVID-19, the key stakeholders included, amongst others, the public at large, civil servants, important players in the private sector such as in health, and the vulnerable population. Discussions between the government and each of the stakeholder groups, especially labor, are ongoing, and there are often cases of irresponsible, as well as responsible, behavior on both sides. From all perspectives, there is clearly now an imperative to preserve employment and wages, as well as to care for the newly unemployed.

In the private sector, many are cynical about large private corporations and their social responsibility, but there are many examples of exemplary behavior as well as many of poor behavior. On the exemplary side, as Parsons (2022) notes, the Bill and Melinda Gates Foundation has recently committed $150 million to the Coalition for Epidemic Preparedness and Innovation (CEPI) to fight COVID-19 and prepare for future pandemics. The CEPI is also in part responsible for the initiative to distribute vaccines across the developing world, and it also helped bankroll the development of the AstraZeneca and Moderna vaccines. Nevertheless, there is no doubt that almost all organizations could have done much more to meet the social responsibilities of their own stakeholders, as well as the wider community. I write in the hope that organizations can think seriously about these responsibilities, work together and protect their customers as well as communities across the globe.

Governments themselves could also do more in terms of CSR and sustainability. In Britain, there is the much cited case of Brexit, where the UK is more often than not seen as lurching to disaster as it dissociates itself from scientific and other fruitful links with the EU (Hopkins, 2020). Some public leaders, moreover, have willfully destroyed treaties, like the UN (2015) Paris Agreement on Climate Change, for their own personal glorification rather than acting in accord with their social responsibility. As previously noted, it is important too that responsible governments committed to CSR look more systemically at the case for basic income in light of the plight of the poor (Standing, 2017) – although this should not necessarily extend to richer constituencies as this may skew further an already imbalanced income distribution.

Conclusion

In conclusion, therefore, while private companies are heavily involved in helping to reduce the effects of COVID-19, they could extend their engagement – not least in more extensively supporting the public sector. The extent of this depends on the country concerned. The rich countries have not come out as well as might be expected in the pandemic, where responses to COVID-19 have been highly varied. Meanwhile, most developing countries have tended to lag even further behind. Private sector companies with responsible leadership could help more, but whatever their contribution, it is difficult when host countries have a negative reaction to the agenda of the World Health Organization. There is no doubt that strong responsible leadership is of benefit with increased rates of vaccination and other controls, as seen in New Zealand (Corlett, 2021). Kenya, from where I write, has also seen impressive leadership in response to COVID with its political leader symbolically wearing a mask in public – which has not always been the case elsewhere. However, lack of resources, especially in virus testing, has severely hampered efforts to contain the pandemic – while hospitals have struggled through lack of such critical items as proper protective clothing, masks and ventilators.

Taking a more general view of CSR, sustainability and leadership, the suffering in many countries of the poor who have lost employment and their livelihoods in the welter of curfews and social distancing and for other reasons is of major concern. This situation is exacerbated by the fact that there is still no basic income for the most financially distressed in any country of the globe – aside from in relatively small-scale pilots. To advance the introduction of this safety net, more resources and careful management are needed on a large scale. Here the private sector could greatly assist by backing such an initiative and lending its skills to the implementation process. As I point out elsewhere (Hopkins, 2022), the key to the CSR and sustainability theme of this chapter is respect for stakeholders. Here Friedman (2020) has said, in the context of his critique of ex-US President Donald Trump as a responsible leader, that "if you show some people respect, if you affirm their dignity, it is amazing what they will let you say to them or ask of them. Sometimes it just takes listening to them, but deep listening – not just waiting for them to stop talking. Because listening is the ultimate sign of respect".

References

Angelo, A. (2020) *Power and the Presidency in Kenya: The Jomo Kenyatta Years*, Cambridge: Cambridge University Press.

Bessis, S. and Belhassen, S. (2012) *Bourguiba*, Tunis: Elyzad.

Corlett, E. (2021) 'New Zealand ends 2021 with one of the world's best Covid outcomes', *Wellington*, 23 December.

Friedman, M. (1970) 'The social responsibility of business is to increase its profits', *New York Times*, 13 September. Available at: https://www.nytimes.com/1970/09/13/archives/a-friedman-doctrine-the-social-responsibility-of-business-is-to.html

Friedman, T. (2020) 'Who can win America's politics of humiliation?' *New York Times*, 8 September. Available at: https://www.nytimes.com/2020/09/08/opinion/biden-trump-humiliation.htm

Hopkins, M. (1998) *A Planetary Bargain: Corporate Social Responsibility Comes of Age*, Basingstoke: Macmillan.

Hopkins, M. (2006) 'What is corporate social responsibility all about?', *Journal of Public Affairs* 6(3–4): 298–306.

Hopkins, M. (2016) *CSR and Sustainability – From the Margins to the Mainstream: A Text Book*, London: Greenleaf.

Hopkins, M. (2020) *Brrrexit! Why England Will Be Left Out in the Cold: The UK Decides upon Perpetual Winter*, Amazon, UK. Available at: https://www.amazon.com/Brrrexit-England-will-left-cold-ebook/dp/B0849ZLN7G

Hopkins, M. (2022) *CSR and Sustainability: The Big Issues of the Day*, London: Anthem Press.

Kaplan, S. (2019) 'Are companies right to abandon the shareholder-first mantra?', *Financial Times*, 27 August. Available at: https://www.ft.com/content/f99b0098-c4d1-11e9-ae6e-a26d1d0455f4

Kenny, G. (2014) 'Five questions to identify key stakeholders', *Harvard Business Review*, 6 March.
Kotter, J. P. (1990) *A Force for Change: How Leadership Differs from Management*, New York: Free Press.
Kung, F. and Rupp, N. (2018) 'Corporate Social Responsibility and firm value: Recent developments', IntechOpen Book Series. Available at: https://www.intechopen.com/chapters/60650
Marques, T. and Gomes, J. (2019) 'Responsible leadership and/versus responsible management', in Laasch, O., Suddaby, R., Gustavson, P. B., Freeman, R. E., Olsson, S. and Jamali, D. (eds) *Research Handbook of Responsible Management*, Cheltenham: Edward Elgar.
Marx, K. (2004) *Capital*, New edition, London: Penguin Books.
Mlambo, A. S. (2014) *A History of Zimbabwe*, Cambridge: Cambridge University Press.
Monbiot, G. (2019) 'Demagogues thrive by whipping up our fury: Here's how to thwart them', *The Guardian*, 3 October. Available at: https://www.theguardian.com/commentisfree/2019/oct/03/demagogues-fury-violence-outrage-discourse
Obama, B. (2020) *A Promised Land*, New York: Penguin Books.
Parsons, J. (2022) 'Bill Gates warns that future pandemics could be even worse than Covid', *The Metro*, 20 January.
Reuters (2010) 'Brent Spar: Battle that launched modern activism', 5 May. Available at: https://www.reutersevents.com/sustainability/business-strategy/brent-spar-battle-launched-modern-activism
Robinson, N. (2019) 'The Koch brothers tried to build a plutocracy in the name of freedom', *The Guardian*, 28 August.
Saks, M. and Search-Whittaker, J. (2018) 'Responsible leadership in challenging times', *Brite Innovation Review*, December.
Service, R. (1997) *The Penguin History of Modern Russia: From Tsarism to the Twenty-first Century*, 3rd edition, London: Penguin Books.
Standing, G. (2017) *Basic Income. And How to Make It Happen*, London: Penguin Books.
Standing, G. (2019) *Plunder of the Commons: A Manifesto for Sharing Public Wealth*, London: Penguin Books.
Szekely, F. and Knirsch, M. (2005) 'Responsible leadership and Corporate Social Responsibility: Metrics for sustainable performance', *European Management Journal* 23(6): 628–47.
United Nations (1987) *Our Common Future: The World Commission on Environment and Development*, Geneva: UN.
United Nations (2015) *The Paris Agreement*, New York: UN.

Part IV

Communication and Responsible Leadership

Chapter 9

Emotional Intelligence, Social Cohesion and Responsible Leadership

Mike Eldon

Introduction

This chapter suggests that responsible leadership brings people together and creates social cohesion, and that to do so successfully requires strong interpersonal skills. This implies possessing high emotional intelligence and being able to communicate effectively. These two attributes are elaborated on, along with several supporting models, in the Transactional Analysis of Berne (1961), Theory X and Theory Y of McGregor (1960), the Managerial Grid of Blake and Mouton (1964), the Appreciative Inquiry of Cooperrider and Srivastva (1987) and the Humble Inquiry of Schein (2013). The chapter also draws on personal experience, which includes my time in Africa, where I have been living in Kenya since 1977, and the United Kingdom (UK), where I grew up and started my career, as well as the United States (US).

Many of the skills involved revolve around resolving conflict and aligning the energy of individuals and groups, and this implies a talent for mediation, with its desired win-win outcomes. Responsible leaders find the strength, the boldness and the courage to hold on to and effectively communicate positive visions and values, and to bring people together in cohesive sustainable organizations and societies,

DOI: 10.4324/9781003129189-13

from the smallest to the largest scale. The Institute for Responsible Leadership theme of 'being fair to all key stakeholders' is implied throughout, and attention is also drawn to the United Nations (UN) Sustainable Development Goal (SDG) to "promote peaceful and inclusive societies for sustainable development, provide access to justice for all and build effective, accountable and inclusive institutions at all levels" (United Nations, 2015). This means building social cohesion, which requires tackling inequality and finding ways of helping those who have been, or are likely to be, left behind.

By contrast to intellectual intelligence – commonly referred to as IQ (Intelligence Quotient) – Emotional Intelligence (EI) relates to the soft skills that enable positive interpersonal relations. Those with a high Emotional Quotient (EQ) are self-aware, in touch with their feelings and emotions and manage them well (see Goleman, 1998; Goleman, 2006; Goleman and Boyatzis, 2008). They also keenly observe the feelings and emotions of those with whom they interact. They listen openly and show empathy – thus enabling them to build win-win relationships of high trust. As for social cohesion, this exists in organizations and societies where there is good cooperation and trust between members, where they agree on how to move forward together without wasting undue energy on conflict and gridlock. Such entities share common aspirations, and there is equitable allocation of resources and a respect for diversity.

Responsible leadership and the possibility of social cohesion cannot be effective without the presence of EI. Responsible leaders possess and apply this vital attribute to bring people together around common visions and values, enabling them to develop a sustainable existence together. It is through EI that leaders are able to communicate with influence. To put it simply, EI is about helping people to negotiate adequately win-win outcomes – the very objective of responsible and cohesive groups and their leaders. Given that the Institute for Responsible Leadership defines responsible leadership as treating all key stakeholders fairly, this implies the need for give and take among these stakeholders, mediated by the entity's leadership. And it is an assumption of fairness in how consensus about the sharing of costs and benefits is arrived at that allows for social cohesion. This expectation of give and take, leading to a feeling that there is an overall spirit of fairness, applies at all levels of organizations, from the family and the community to the country and ultimately globally; from the smallest informal micro-business to the largest multinational organization, be it a government body, a for-profit corporate or a not-for-profit entity.

Win-win outcomes to issues typically involve the participants making compromises in order to build consensus around agreed solutions, as described by Stephen Covey (1989), whose fourth habit of highly effective people is 'Think Win/Win'. Some such outcomes result from 'a third way' emerging. But as often as not some of those involved end up being better off (the 'winners') than others (the 'losers'). In a fair society – one that enjoys social cohesion – those who emerge less well-off will have been prepared to make sacrifices in the short term because of a reasonable expectation that those who emerge better off will in turn be prepared to be generous to them at some point in the future. Responsible leaders know how to nurture such a culture in their sphere of influence. To motivate those they lead to indulge in equitable and sustainable give-and-take flexibility over time requires both parties to behave with EI. This is what it takes to build consensus, where leaders play the role of mediators between different interests.

On the topic of responsible leaders helping their people to deal with loss, on 7 January 2021 I heard an interview on CNN with Dan Kildee, the Democratic Congressman for Michigan. It was on the morning after the Congress met to confirm Joe Biden as President, during which a mob of angry Trump supporters invaded the Capitol. In the interview, Kildee recalled this definition of leadership offered by his favorite professor at the Harvard Kennedy School: "Leadership is disappointing your people in ways they can absorb." I assume this Professor was Ronald Heifetz, with whose Adaptive Leadership approach I am very familiar (Heifetz and Linsky, 2002; Heifetz, Linsky and Grashow, 2009).

Emotional Intelligence, Social Intelligence and Transactional Analysis

Like many others, I was introduced to the concept of EI by Daniel Goleman (2006), who offered new insights into the brain architecture underlying emotion and rationality in the twenty-fifth anniversary edition of his book. The book by Goleman (1998), *Working with Emotional Intelligence*, made me an even more enthusiastic promoter of the development of EI. But throughout my life as a leader, consultant and coach, going back to the 1970s, I have always been conscious of the vital importance of interpersonal skills, the non-technical ones that complement the technical ones. The concepts and language of EI as laid out by Goleman significantly enhanced my thinking in this area (Eldon, 2007), helping me to develop myself and others. Goleman and Boyatzis (2008) also introduced the related concept of Social Intelligence, and indeed brought this together with EI; if a person behaves with social intelligence, they are at ease in interacting with others, knowing how to read moods and to react appropriately.

At this stage, I wish to introduce my interpretation of the allied concept of Transactional Analysis (TA), set out by Eric Berne (1964) in his book *Games People Play*. In it he discerned the "Parent", the "Adult" and the "Child" within us – our three 'ego states'. Thomas Harris (1968) was also heavily influenced by Berne in his book *I'm OK – You're OK*. My own enthusiasm for TA stems from my long experience in introducing people to its concepts, which I have found to be by far the most effective way of developing their EI, which unlike intellectual intelligence is much more amenable to development.

For me, there are two basic components to the TA framework which help us examine how we 'transact' with one another – the child and the parent. Some of us never really grow up, remaining either childlike (spontaneous, curious, open . . .) or childish (irresponsible, immature . . .) or some combination of the two. Others seem to copy the behavior of parents or parent figures and live their lives as stern and controlling, assuming all around are naughty children, or they play out the indulgent parent and adopt a nurturing, supportive, trusting approach. Berne (1964) can be seen to insert a third component into our personalities – one he calls the 'adult', who slots in between the parent and the child. The adult within us learns from history in order to build a better future. The adult is mature and solution-oriented, an open listener and respectful of others. The adult prefers horizontal relationships with other adults over vertical ones with parents or children. We are all familiar with what is meant when we describe someone as 'the adult in the room'.

In addition, Berne (1964) divided people into four categories, again relating to 'ego states'. It is about how, generally, we feel about ourselves and about others. The first of the four categories is "I'm not OK, You're OK". This is how we are born, utterly dependent on our mothers. And, says Berne, it is in this "I'm not OK, You're OK" mindset where a vast majority of the world's population exist until they die. The second state is "I'm OK, You're not OK", and the other two are "I'm not OK, You're not OK", and finally "I'm OK, You're OK". The last three are states people may evolve into largely depending on their early life experiences. While so many remain stuck in the first state, which is full of the insecurities that fuel inferiority complexes (however deserved or undeserved), many others move to the next two unfortunate ones. Pity the miserable souls who feel that neither they nor others around them are OK. And worry about those who while feeling 'OK' about themselves imagine (or at least give the impression that they imagine) they are surrounded by lesser mortals. Finally, rejoice in that positive subset of humanity which feels the good in both themselves and others.

I hasten to add that ego state is about 'being' rather than about 'doing'. It is not about how competent we think we are in one area or another but simply about whether we feel at peace with ourselves and with others. While our ego state may vary during our life and depend on who we are interacting with in the moment, we are likely to occupy one dominant or normal position. This leads us on to a complementary framework associated with TA, albeit not one articulated explicitly by Berne or Harris, which further helps us to place ourselves in the universe. If we relate an 'OK' state to the 'win' option and the 'not OK' state to the 'lose' option, we see how an "I'm not OK, You're OK" character is likely to assume they will end up in lose-win situations. The other three fits are immediately apparent, with only the "I'm OK, You're OK" group assuming that win-win outcomes are not only desirable but also possible.

Bringing the frameworks together, the 'adult' is an "I'm OK, You're OK" type, who aims at win-win outcomes. Stern parents assume that they are the only OK ones around, and as often as not they will expect to win at the expense of some unfortunate 'child'. (What they forget is that win-lose is not sustainable and tends to degenerate to lose-lose, as the child will most likely either withdraw or rebel, to the disadvantage of the parent.) It is our past that determines where we fit into these frameworks. We are who we are thanks to our early childhood influences: OK or not OK with ourselves and with others; some combination of parent and adult and child; assuming personal or mutual victories or defeats. What about our future? It does not have to be a mere extension of our history, provided we find the strength to treat the dysfunctional elements of who we are as unwanted baggage.

We are capable of growing into more of the world of "I'm OK, You're OK", 'win-win' and 'adults'. Indeed, just reflecting on these frameworks has led many in my workshops and coaching groups (including my children and grandchildren) to life-transforming thoughts. We must and do make many behavioral decisions, like when to be the 'adult' and when turning on a touch of 'stern parent' is what is called for if faced with a consistently naughty child, following up with the nurturing parent to promote healing. However, EI is about building positive relationships, and for me sharing the concepts of TA have provided the means to do so.

Parental influence and its consequences for responsible leadership: Obama vs. Trump

My first case to illustrate TA is that of former President Barack Obama (2020), whose autobiography *The Promised Land* reaffirms the nurturing parent he has shown himself to be. He also seems to have been at ease playing with his children as child-to-child. Between them all a sense of "I'm OK, You're OK" prevails, leading to win-win all round – he and his wife Michelle are true role models for a happy family life. While Obama's father was not with him growing up, his mother and her parents provided the uplifting influence that formed him and led him to develop into the adult he became.

By contrast to Obama's predominantly adult persona (Eldon, 2021b), I turn to the case of former President Donald Trump. To the casual observer, Trump normally displays an extreme "I'm OK, You're not OK" ego state, always expecting to win, no matter how, while enjoying seeing others lose at his expense. And he is the stern, controlling 'parent'. Yet however much he behaves as "I'm OK, You're not OK", it may merely be a cover for how he really feels and who he really is. So how does he feel, and who is he?

Mr Trump seems to be a desperately insecure person, as was so vividly suggested by his niece Mary Trump (2020) in her book about him, *Too Much and Never Enough*. Behind the bluster and the boasting, he may be an "I'm not OK, You're OK" character, acting the spoilt child, the villain complaining he is the victim (Eldon, 2021a). Trump's niece, a psychologist by profession, explains her uncle's development by telling us about his controlling father Fred – who, she wrote, had no real human feeling and treated his children with contempt – while Trump's mother was largely absent from his life. Mary Trump claims that his deep-seated insecurities created in him "a black hole of need that constantly requires the light of compliments that disappears as soon as he's soaked it in".

It could be suggested that Trump does possess EI – in the sense that he, like other populists, knows how to build trusting relationships with his base (Friedman, 2020). What he appeared to lack as President, however, were the pure motives that are associated with responsible leadership. His style of win-lose, divisive politics worked only in so far as getting him the presidency in 2016; despite the fact that he came very close to being re-elected in 2020, it was ultimately not sustainable. Like many who are most in need of help in such areas, the likelihood of him wanting it or benefiting from it appeared very slim.

Other helpful behavioral frameworks

There are several other behavioral frameworks that are helpful in supporting responsible leadership. These include the Theory X and Theory Y of social psychologist Douglas McGregor (1960), who developed these contrasting theories to explain how managers' beliefs about what motivates people can affect their management style. Drawn from *The Human Side of Enterprise*, these are outlined in Figure 9.1 below.

Theory X

- Humans are lazy, untrustworthy and hate work
- So they must be controlled and pushed around.

Theory Y

- Work is as natural as play
- If the environment is right, humans will get on with it, be committed, do good things, seek responsibility
- Most people are under-utilized.

Figure 9.1 McGregor's Theory X and Theory Y

Theory X refers to an authoritarian style of management, and Theory Y refers to a participative style. Theory X managers assume that workers are disengaged and do not inherently possess a good work ethic, which leads them to wield the big stick and to micromanage. On the other hand, Theory Y managers assume that people take pride in their work and are basically trustworthy, which allows for the adoption of a participative style of leadership. Organizational pyramids are then flatter, with fewer and lesser power gaps between levels. It can readily be seen how the emotionally intelligent – the 'adult-adult', "I'm OK, You're OK", 'win-win' type of people – are more likely to be adherents of Theory Y and hence responsible leaders that act fairly to all key stakeholders. The challenge for responsible leaders is to develop high trust cultures, which allow for participative styles of management.

Another helpful framework was devised by Robert Blake and Jane Mouton (1964). Known as the Blake–Mouton Management Grid, it consists of nine-point horizontal and vertical axes. As set out in Figure 9.2, the horizontal axis represents concern for tasks, where 9 shows high concern and 1 low concern – and the vertical axis represents concern for people, similarly calibrated.

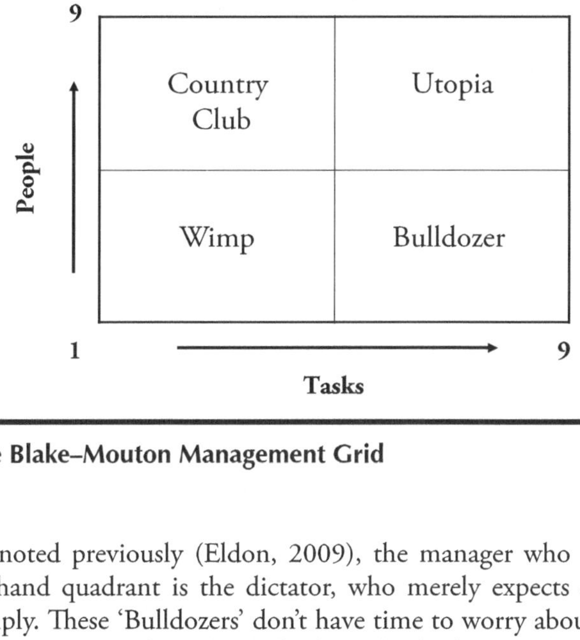

Figure 9.2 The Blake–Mouton Management Grid

As I have noted previously (Eldon, 2009), the manager who falls within the bottom right hand quadrant is the dictator, who merely expects subordinates to listen and comply. These 'Bulldozers' don't have time to worry about people issues, so focused are they on results. They talk about leadership not being a popularity contest, and do not 'waste' time consulting, for they and only they have the answers. All very efficient? Well, yes, except for the frustration and resentment this will cause, and the dreadful consequences thereof, such as suppressed creativity and ownership, demotivation, and possibly even a desire to see the whole thing foul up. It should be added, however, that in times of crisis, in life-and-death situations, there may well be a strong case for swift decisiveness without consultation. How about the person in the top left quadrant, who so wants to be liked that production suffers? Warm, friendly souls, these 'Country Club' managers try hard to keep the workers happy, are embarrassed by conflict and fail to stretch their people.

In the bottom left hand quadrant, there are 'impoverished' or 'indifferent' managers, who lie low, blow with the wind, agree with everyone and keep out of trouble. In the middle at 5.5, we find managers who push – but not too hard. They follow the rules, conform with the culture, avoid big risks or changes and compromise all too easily. They will talk candidly about the small, easy issues but hold back on the hard things. Next there is the top right quadrant manager, who understands how to work the synergy between the people and the production. Here is the person who seeks facts and views from all around, assuming that there is much value to be obtained from doing so. Dogma and personalities play no role in decision-making; disagreements are raised and resolved without them degenerating into fruitless conflict; and if emotional barriers exist, the root causes of frustrations and misunderstandings are identified and handled.

Other models can also be discerned, like the 9.5 benevolent autocrat with a strong production focus, who seeks the welfare of the staff while insisting on taking all the decisions. Or the paternalist, who combines the 9.1 of controlling activity with the 1.9 of caring and warmth. They both breed dependency and resentment. I concluded an article on this topic by quoting the late Pakistani banker Agha Hasan Abedi, who suggested that: "The conventional definition of management is getting work done through people, but real management is developing people through work" (Eldon, 2009). Now that is 9.9, which is the place occupied by responsible leaders with EI.

Emotionally intelligent communications

It goes without saying that responsible leaders with EI can only be influential if they are good communicators. Indeed, it is often the most intellectually brilliant among us who have neglected to develop their communications and other interpersonal skills. As I mentioned at the outset, responsible leadership brings people together around common visions and values, helping them to negotiate win-win outcomes. This is achieved through, first, humble and open listening, seeking to understand before seeking to be understood. *Humble Inquiry* by Schein (2013) reminds us of the many leaders – not least board members – who do too much telling and not enough asking or open listening. Such 'stern parent', "I'm OK, You're not OK" directors do not know what they do not know about what management may actually be working on and accomplishing quietly. They tell management what they should be doing that they are not doing, wagging their fingers at them disapprovingly, and it is only once they have finished pontificating that the respectful reaction is that what is being proposed is exactly what they have been quietly spending their time on all along.

This is why the technique known as Appreciative Inquiry, evolved by David Cooperrider and Suresh Srivastva (1987), is so helpful. This kind of inquiry acknowledges and appreciates the good in people and in organizations, affirming what is working well and the strengths that explain the achievements. It contrasts with the far more common approach of identifying what is not working and the weaknesses that prevent success. It takes us from over-focusing on the negatives, as in 'exception reporting' with an emphasis largely on overcoming weaknesses, to building further on strengths. Management simply by exception reporting on performance gaps saps self-esteem and self-confidence, motivation and energy, and makes people timid and lethargic. Here we can learn much about what motivates and what demotivates from the research carried out by Frederick Herzberg (1966) in his Motivation-Hygiene Theory. In this vein, Appreciative Inquiry aligns people with their strengths, stimulates boldness and creativity, and allows for risk-taking, enjoyment and self-actualization. It implies the possession by leaders of effective communication skills, which they deploy to inspire their people into buying into an uplifting common vision and to help them accept that living healthy values is a good idea.

A few years ago, as an associate faculty member of the Aga Khan University Graduate School of Media and Communications, I facilitated workshop sessions on themes such as 'The Voice of Leadership' and 'Communicating for Influence', where I shared these concepts with leaders from around Africa. I and my fellow facilitators led conversations on communicating vision and strategy; communication in crisis and conflict; and communicating to encourage creativity, innovation and change. So much of what we discussed in these sessions – which I do in many of my other workshops with clients from both the public and private sector – revolved around the challenge of energy alignment, of reducing the amount of energy that is wasted on poor or no communication, on misunderstandings and conflicts. Often the problem arises from the unhelpful individualistic ways in which Key Performance Indicators and incentives are defined – ways that stimulate selfish and unhealthy competition. We must also worry about people's egos and about clashes of personalities and attitudes.

The aim is to align individuals and teams, both horizontally and vertically. There must be a softening of the walls between departmental and project silos like back office and front office; head office and field offices; boards and senior management; and senior and middle management. To become more productive by generating synergy, I suggest the players exchange offers and requests with a view to negotiating win-wins. As I have mentioned before, the responsible leader acts as the mediator between the parties – or may bring in an external consultant to facilitate the process. Conducting such mediation myself, I have noted that the offers by one side almost perfectly pre-empt the requests made by the other. Each one knows what disturbs the other, as the challenges are not shrouded in mystery. What is frequently lacking is making the time and finding the mind space to discuss the issues openly and with a solution-oriented, win-win mindset.

Before moving on to the government context, it is helpful to set out in Table 9.1 below a summary of the theories introduced above, identifying how each relates to EI.

Table 9.1 Theoretical constructs and how they relate to Emotional Intelligence

Theoretical constructs	*Link to Emotional Intelligence*
Transactional Analysis	Behaving as an "I'm OK, You're OK" adult-adult
Theory X and Theory Y	An optimistic view of human nature
Humble Inquiry	Asking and listening more than telling
Appreciative Inquiry	Building on the positive
Blake–Mouton Grid	Being focused on the tasks *and* the people

Responsible leadership in government: Democracy, dictatorship and social cohesion

There is perhaps no greater challenge to leadership in government – not least to political leadership – than that of promoting social cohesion. The very fact that politicians compete in elections where winners and losers inevitably emerge – except where coalitions are formed – defines a relentlessly adversarial way of life. This may at least partially explain why lawyers are so naturally attracted to politics. Much time and energy are consumed in campaigning when promises of imminent inclusive Utopias are made. And once elected, it is not just impossible to please all the people all the time, but it may even seem hard to ever please anyone, as identified by Obama (2020).

The need for EI is nowhere greater than in the political sphere. This is much less so in dictatorships, where leaders are feared and can drive their agenda without opposition. No wonder some countries yearn for autocratic leadership, where there is greater scope for utilizing resources efficiently. It is possible to plan for the longer term, uninterrupted by the disruptive nuisance of opposition and by fiercely contested elections that may well result in a new team with a different agenda. Some African countries like Rwanda and Ethiopia, as well as China, have adopted such a model, but while they have benefited from strong economic growth, there are worries because as levels of prosperity, education and urbanization rise, it becomes far harder to rule with an iron fist. The Rwanda genocide in 1994, signaling social collapse, led to a perhaps justifiably more authoritarian style of leadership and indeed a more responsible one. It has at least led to a peaceful and highly disciplined environment, if not one where there is full freedom of expression or where underlying healing has been achieved. But the question remains as to whether the peace is sustainable in the long term, not least once President Kagame hands over to a successor. There are parallels in Ethiopia (Matfess, 2015), where seriously destabilizing tensions have been witnessed as different ethnic groups have pursued win-lose zero-sum political options, harming both economic development and the case for strong centralized direction.

Messy and undisciplined as real democracies are, they do ensure the protection of human rights, including freedom of expression and the airing of diverse views.

Yet here too social cohesion is not guaranteed. Where irresponsible leadership is in power, social cohesion can too easily also be ruptured in democracies. This is illustrated by the accusations of police brutality against African Americans in the US, and the partisan divisiveness that has in recent years resulted in legislative gridlock in Congress – not to mention the denial by President Trump that he lost the November 2020 election, which ultimately led to the Capitol attack by a pro-Trump mob in Washington DC in January 2021 (Dan, McIntire and Rosenberg, 2021).

The weakening of social cohesion was also supported by certain US media outlets and some Republican members of the two chambers of the US Congress, who – despite what many regard as President Trump's irresponsible behavior – for self-interested reasons supported him to the end of his term. What joy this brought to the world's autocrats, able to point to the divisiveness and negative emotions that populist democracy can so easily generate, stoked by an arguably irresponsible President and exacerbated by social media. Populist politics also led to the Brexit saga and to the disruption of social cohesion in the UK (Hopkins, 2020). Here some media moguls supported Brexit – perhaps not because they felt it was necessarily a good idea in itself, but because they saw it would benefit their audience rating, while some politicians knew they had to support leaving the European Union or face losing their seats. David Goodhart (2017) argues that in Britain we can separate two constituencies: those coming from 'somewhere', who are rooted in small towns or communities in the countryside, socially conservative, and often less educated and left behind; and those from 'anywhere', who are typically urban and geographically mobile, socially liberal and university educated. There can only be limited social cohesion in such divided and unequal societies, where the challenge to leadership is to take responsibility for closing the gap.

In Kenya, we have also experienced challenges to social cohesion, thanks again to irresponsible leadership, which in this case has largely exploited ethnic conflict based on competing (win-lose and zero-sum) tribal interests. That is why after the post-electoral violence in 2008 a number of initiatives concerning the strategic need for healing and social cohesion were introduced to develop long-term solutions to the underlying societal issues that had created the unrest. As a result, a number of independent commissions were formed, one of which was the Truth Justice and Reconciliation Commission and another the National Cohesion and Integration Commission (NCIC). The violence of 2008 was thus followed by less disruption around elections (Hornsby, 2013). I have worked closely with the NCIC, which for the most part works quietly behind the scenes to resolve conflicts and build peace between different communities. In Kenya, as elsewhere, in First World democracies as much as in the Third World, the challenge is to see leadership elected that possesses sufficient EI to bring people together in a socially cohesive society. This requires civic education that takes citizens beyond having their awareness raised about who is a responsible leader to actually voting for them at the ballot. However, in Kenya, as in many other places, politicians too often indulge in irresponsible populist 'hate speeches' that fire up their supporters. Indeed, one of NCIC's core functions is to pursue those who give such speeches and hand them over for prosecution.

During the Donald Trump era, the very essence of his 'America First' policy was win-lose. In his time, the US lost influence and soft power due to the relative absence of his EI, even if he knew how to appeal to his base. And in his final days, the more enraged and weak Trump became, the more he drove himself down a lose-lose path, deluding himself and his supporters that the election had been stolen from him thanks to a plot by the Democrats, the mainstream media and the elite (Wolff, 2022). His irresponsible media and social media backers amplified the alternative reality he proclaimed to those who were his loyal supporters. And this made it very hard for his successor, however responsible a healer he may be, to bring the country together and to reduce the terrible waste of energy and lack of direction that comes from a polarized society.

How are those who are left behind, who feel like losers, to be helped to find positions of dignity in their societies? How is inequality and marginalization to be reduced? How do political, corporate and other leaders assist stakeholders in making short-term sacrifices that require immediate discomfort but enable longer-term sustainability? How do education systems nurture children to recognize responsible leaders who aspire to bring people together rather than populists reliant on social divisiveness? And what will it take for children to later become responsible leaders themselves? Heifetz, Linsky and Grashow (2009) explain how leaders can aid those who are losing out through the Adaptive Leadership framework, but 'experts', on the other hand, can lack the empathy to help those left behind. Joe Earle, Cahal Moran and Zach Ward-Perkins (2016) have underlined the perils of leaving economics to experts, showing how the UK and other countries have become 'econocracies' – that is, societies in which improving the economy has become the main purpose of politics. They demonstrate how this undermines democracy, in turn increasing the power and authority of economic technocrats, who lack the EI to show the necessary empathy to support the vulnerable in increasingly unequal societies and to express themselves in terms to which non-experts can relate.

Conclusion

I would finally like to return to the UN SDG that seeks to "promote peaceful and inclusive societies for sustainable development, provide access to justice for all and build effective, accountable and inclusive institutions at all levels" (United Nations, 2015). This surely requires responsible leadership to bring about social cohesion. And for such leadership to be effective, it must display EI, thereby demonstrating understanding of how to listen openly and empathetically, communicate with influence, and focus people's minds on attaining consensual win-wins. This is so needed yet so hard to achieve – not least in the political sphere. Even the most responsible leaders, possessed of the finest skills and values, face relentless resistance from irresponsible and selfish leaders, who appeal to our lesser selves. It is the readers of this book, from whichever sector and at whatever level, who are the ones most likely to aspire to offer responsible leadership. You are urged to find the strength, the boldness and the courage to hold on to positive visions and to develop the skills to bring people together in cohesive, sustainable organizations and societies.

References

Berne, E. (1961) *Transactional Analysis in Psychotherapy*, London: Souvenir Books.

Berne, E. (1964) *Games People Play*, London: Penguin Books.

Blake, R. and Mouton, J. (1964) *The Managerial Grid: The Key to Leadership Excellence*, Houston, TX: Gulf Publishing Co.

Cooperrider, D. L. and Srivastva, S. (1987) 'Appreciative inquiry in organizational life', in Woodman, R. W. and Pasmore, W. A. (eds) *Research in Organizational Change and Development*, Volume 1, Stamford, CT: JAI Press.

Covey, S. R. (1989) *The 7 Habits of Highly Effective People*, London: Simon & Schuster.

Dan, B., McIntire, M. and Rosenberg, M. (2021) '"Our President wants us here": The mob that stormed the Capitol', *New York Times*, 9 January. Available at: https://www.nytimes.com/2021/01/09/us/capitol-rioters.html?partner=IFTTT

Earle, J., Moran, C. and Ward-Perkins, Z. (2016) *The Econocracy*, London: Penguin Books.

Eldon, M. (2007) 'Emotional intelligence takes centre stage at the workplace', *Business Daily*, 27 July.

Eldon, M. (2009) 'Keeping production and people in fine balance', *Business Daily*, 15 October.

Eldon, M. (2021a) 'Analysing impact of spoilt child in Trump', *Business Daily*, 7 January.

Eldon, M. (2021b) 'Dissecting behaviour of Obama the "adult"', *Business Daily*, 4 February.

Friedman, T. (2020) 'Who can win America's politics of humiliation?' *New York Times*, 8 September. Available at: https://www.nytimes.com/2020/09/08/opinion/biden-trump-humiliation.htm

Goleman, D. (1998) *Working with Emotional Intelligence*, New York: Bantam Books.

Goleman, D. (2006) *Emotional Intelligence*, New York: Bantam Books.

Goleman, D. and Boyatzis, R. (2008) 'Social intelligence and the biology of leadership', *Harvard Business Review*, September.

Goodhart, D. (2017) *The Road to Somewhere: The Populist Revolt and the Future of Politics*, London: Penguin Books.

Harris, T. A. (1968) *I'm OK – You're OK*, London: Avon Books.

Heifetz, R. A. and Linsky, M. (2002) *Leadership on the Line: Staying Alive Through the Dangers of Leading*, Cambridge, MA: Harvard Business School Press.

Heifetz, R. A., Linsky, M. and Grashow, A. (2009) *The Practice of Adaptive Leadership: Tools and Tactics for Changing Your Organization and the World*, Cambridge, MA: Harvard Business School Press.

Herzberg, F. (1966) *Work and the Nature of Man*, Cleveland, OH: World Publishing.

Hopkins, M. (2020) *Brrrexit! Why England Will Be Left Out in the Cold: The UK Decides Upon Perpetual Winter*, Amazon UK. Available at: https://www.amazon.com/Brrrexit-England-will-left-cold-ebook/dp/B0849ZLN7G

Hornsby, C. (2013) *Kenya: A History Since Independence*, London: I. B. Tauris.

Matfess, H. (2015) 'Rwanda and Ethiopia: Developmental authoritarianism and the new politics of African strong men', *African Studies Review* 58(2): 181–204. Available at: https://doi.org/10.1017/asr.2015.43

McGregor, D. (1960) *The Human Side of Enterprise*, New York: Penguin Business Library.

Obama, B. (2020) *A Promised Land*, New York: Penguin Books.
Schein, E. H. (2013) *Humble Inquiry – The Gentle Art of Asking Instead of Telling*, San Francisco, CA: Berrett Koehler.
Trump, M. (2020) *Too Much and Never Enough*, London: Simon & Schuster.
United Nations (2015) *Transforming Our World: The 2030 Agenda for Sustainable Development*, Geneva: UN.
Wolff, M. (2022) *Landslide: The Final Days of the Trump Presidency*, London: The Bridge Street Press.

Chapter 10

Intercultural Communication Competence for Responsible Leadership

Lixian Jin and Martin Cortazzi

Introduction

The responsible leadership required to meet the United Nations (UN) Sustainable Development Goals (SDGs) centrally involves intercultural communication (IC). Developing IC is sometimes thought of as a means to overcome the cultural distances between people from different nations. Since all nations are collectively charged to achieve the SDGs, this communication is important. However, IC is much more than this. In IC, language skills are used for exchanging meaningful messages between different cultural groups and diverse communities. The range of community diversity includes combinations of differences in communication styles across languages, ethnicities, generations, genders, professions, institutions and organizations. Moreover, there are significant variations of language use among members of social, cultural, political and economic communities.

Within this diversity, organizational leaders endeavor to ensure communication is efficient and effective. Characteristically, IC also needs to be appropriate. It is adapted to the diverse people and dynamic cultural contexts at hand. Speakers striving for IC

DOI: 10.4324/9781003129189-14

aim at achieving mutual understanding, improving relationships and solving problems or resolving conflicts in a wide range of situations. Since positive relationships are often at the heart of effective human action, IC also needs to be meaningful and satisfying for everyone. Hence, part of the IC process is to develop humane characteristics and positive feelings, such as empathy (Jin and Cortazzi, 2017). Further, the diverse identities and values of those who participate may sometimes seem threatened, so IC deeply involves respect, rapport, rights and responsibilities.

Thus, developing IC competencies is a moral imperative. Current textbooks introducing IC are based on ethical, humane and social justice perspectives for global citizenship (Jackson, 2020; Sorrels, 2020; Ting-Toomey and Chung, 2021). Conversely, leadership textbooks stress cultural understanding for socially responsible leadership within global diversity (Daft, 2018; Gupta and Van Wart, 2016; Northouse, 2019). To enhance their communication skills, leaders need to develop a sound knowledge of relevant cultures, to show an empathetic understanding of relevant community values and ways of living. They also need to practice skills of mindfulness in interpreting and expressing the cultural ways of speaking in different development contexts. Leaders can be seen as models of communication and can mediate IC competences within their organizations in achieving the SDGs.

In this chapter, we elaborate these ideas with examples related to China and Chinese ideas of leadership. We look at leadership in relation to eliminating poverty in China, one of the SDGs recognized by the UN, before outlining some theoretical approaches to IC relevant to leadership and elaborating on the notion of IC competences. Using further Chinese cases, we report on two metaphor-based studies of leaders in their fields: university teachers and senior managers in international companies.

Intercultural communication in poverty alleviation in China

In the big picture, each SDG goal involves leaders from many cultures in diverse fields. The goals are interdependent, so leaders need to collaborate for co-development across goals. For many SDG-related activities, senior leaders must communicate appropriately with others, and this means leading within four tiers. There is a primary tier of global, regional and national leaders. Generally, these require support from a second tier of experienced professionals and technical experts in organizations and institutions. From an IC perspective, these second-tier leaders may need a third tier of support through specialist advisors and knowledge exchange experts, mediators, language interpreters and translators. These in turn work with fourth-tier local leaders and communities. Across all these tiers, diverse leaders need to practice IC mindfully to achieve the SDGs.

The project to eliminate extreme poverty in China shows how the tiers of leadership are interlinked. Poverty reduction is listed first by the UN as 'an indispensable requirement' (United Nations, 2015). In older people's living memory in China, poverty was widespread. Living conditions in many rural areas were severely under-developed. From the 1950s, there was slow but gradually accelerating progress. Then, between 2013 and 2021, one hundred million rural people were systematically lifted out of poverty through a nationally-directed, long-term scheme. This poverty reduction plan involved huge investment to innovate in agricultural production, to provide rural medical clinics, improve rural schooling and develop infrastructure for water and energy supplies and road and rail transport. In this way, progress towards meeting the SDG of alleviating poverty was interwoven with other SDGs. It became a national goal in 1979, reiterated by successive leaders, and was re-focused specifically in 2012 for achievement in 2021. This immensely challenging goal has now successfully been met as a result of long-term leadership strategies and collective effort – officially resulting in 'a moderately prosperous society' (State Council Information Office, 2021a).

Responsible leadership was key to realizing this long-term strategy (State Council Information Office, 2021b). After surveys to identify each poor household, local issues were identified through consultation between officials and rural residents. Local targets were agreed, typically to boost incomes, improve housing, provide skills training and create jobs. Local leaders conducted spot checks to monitor progress and sought feedback on problems and progress. Officials were appointed from outside to live with villagers for 2–3 years and were themselves accountable at district, county and provincial levels. Any leaders who did not perform responsibly were demoted or transferred. Figures from the State Council Information Office (2021b) show residents in 832 counties and 128,000 villages were lifted out of poverty. Program consolidation will continue until 2026, with further steps in 'rural revitalization'.

In this context, IC refers to exchanging ideas, strategies and plans and implementing them into work tasks between tiers of leaders who liaise with different cultural groups in different communities. Communication has a crucial role between and among diverse communities, especially given the huge social linguistic and cultural diversity of the 1.41 billion population in China. IC is implicated in leadership networks crossing urban-rural or coastal-inland divides and in uses of ethnic minority languages and numerous dialects. Communication issues are inherent in the technical training related to the SDG on innovation in agriculture to improve food production. Infrastructure development includes expanding Internet connections so that villagers can develop online marketing skills to communicate in new ways with distant customers and distribute food produce. Significant face-to-face communication also occurs with incoming tourists who visit scenic spots, stay in new hotels, sample local food in new restaurants and purchase handmade art and craft products.

The case of achieving the SDG to alleviate poverty in China thus reveals intricate communication networks. Leaders need to communicate effectively and appropriately with experts. Experts need to communicate with professionals, researchers and technical innovators. In turn, these groups need to communicate with practitioners and local residents. As the attainment of the SDGs progresses worldwide, engaged participants and beneficiaries encompass a vast global diversity of cultures. Some communication is expert-to-expert and needs to be translated across disciplines. Still more communication is between experts and novices or the general public, which again needs to be translated into accessible non-specialist language. These multiple networks underline the imperative for IC skills and competences among leaders, albeit with reciprocal rather than one-way communication. Responsible leaders listen in culturally-responsive dialogue, and IC competencies are vital too for *followership*. This latter concept refers to the capacity to respond to leadership in the processes of accepting, being influenced by and accomplishing shared goals, which is constructed through communication and active participation (Daft, 2018; Northouse, 2019). The Chinese success with the SDG on poverty confirms the significance of followership. Here huge numbers of communities accepted the influence of leaders' guidance to accomplish common goals, which were understood through communication and negotiated for agreed action. Followers assumed common responsibility towards recognized common purposes which are held to benefit everyone.

Globally, leadership communication with cultural communities is becoming more complex. There are significant cultural variations in ideas about leadership and followership which raise questions about the universal applicability of Western ideas, for example amongst Asian, Middle Eastern and indigenous populations (Cotter-Lockard, 2018; Intezari, Spiller and Yang, 2021). The majority of populations that are included in SDGs are multi-ethnic, multi-cultural and multi-lingual. Even among those who use a common language like English this is far from simple. English is a first language in some countries. Yet the majority of the world's English speakers currently use the language as a second or foreign language. They use English not only with mother-tongue speakers but more frequently as a *lingua franca*, with others who also use English as an additional language. In doing so, many communicators show surprising linguistic and cultural diversity in how language is used. Social and cultural habits of expression reflect the different location and origins of participants, their styles of learning, their cultural heritages, personal histories and identities. Diversity within English has increased in its multiple worldwide uses so that many linguists now describe the language as Englishes (plural) or global English, or English as a *lingua franca*.

Interpreting communication patterns in cultural communities

Examples of trends in using different languages across cultures show contrasts and possible difficulties for IC (Carbaugh, 2017). These relate to intercultural uses of English as a *lingua franca* in face-to-face communication. Speakers of different languages can use apparently 'normal' features quite differently (Saville-Troike, 2002). Such features can be transferred into English so that, as a *lingua franca*, communication is characterized by considerable multi-lingual diversity (Jenkins, 2020). Most obvious are different uses of pronunciation, vocabulary or grammar. These are not necessarily mistakes, which can be identified and may be forgiven. Frequently, they are unconscious transfers of speech patterns into English from another language. Less obvious may be different ways in which particular words or phrases are emphasized by patterns of pitch, loudness, tone of voice, and the rise and fall of intonation. If these uses are unfamiliar to outsiders, they can distract attention from meaning. They can be misinterpreted as showing emotions such as annoyance, aggression or anger. Even less obvious are diverse ways of interpreting slow rates of speech, pauses and silence. Silences can be mistakenly seen by hearers to indicate disengagement, disagreement or lack of understanding rather than showing respect or thoughtfulness, or a need for extra thinking time to express something in another language. In contrast, more rapid speech and swift responses in interaction which overlap with the talk of a previous speaker may seem like impatient or domineering interruptions rather than signaling social solidarity through rapid understanding. Hence what are diverse uses of language can be erroneously considered attributes of the speaker or of the speaker's community. Such judgments can accumulate difficulties, reinforcing possible prejudice and exacerbating conflicts.

Uses of discourse patterns can also lead to different interpretations, not only of the message but of the speaker as a person. If a speaker, with the customary indirect politeness of many languages, avoids giving a direct negative answer by using circuitous phrases, this may be understood as vagueness or even agreement by those who – according to their own language habits – expect short, immediate and direct responses. Again, a person may answer a question by leading listeners gently up to the main point by first presenting a context of background information. This establishes the common ground needed to understand the upcoming answer. However, this can seem frustrating to a hearer who expects a main point to be expressed immediately if it is important. The listener may conclude that the speaker is avoiding the question and may mentally switch off, so missing the answer when it comes. A general awareness of how IC varies in such examples is helpful, combined with knowledge of specific cultural uses related to a target community. We outline below some skills and mindsets to use in such situations.

In working towards the SDGs, the leaders and participants involved will use many other languages besides English, but similar variations are evident in the major world languages and in minority languages. Even within a single identifiable 'culture' there are differences of views, values and ways of expression so that our definitions of culture have to include notions of diversity in its dynamic, flexible, adaptive characteristics. Cultures influence each other – many appear to overlap or blend, even while members hold onto the distinctiveness of their local identity.

Approaches to intercultural communication and leadership

Contemporary theoretical approaches to leadership include cultural theories. In leadership textbooks, this is often discussed in a separate chapter, with relatively little attention given to IC (see, for example, Daft, 2018; Northouse, 2019). However, the imperative to develop leaders within the social, cultural and linguistic diversity of humanity means that IC should be a major strand throughout leadership learning. Well-known examples of cross-cultural theories for management communication refer to national groups, based on large-scale surveys in many countries. Extensive data are analyzed to give profiles to nations using multiple dimensions or scales (Hofstede, Hofstede and Minkov, 2010) – particularly to leadership style in the massive Global Leadership and Organizational Behavior (GLOBE) studies (House et al., 2004). Such profiles identify tendencies and predict some behavior so that comparisons between countries and regions can be made. However, leaders drawing on these theories need to remember the strong caveat that national tendencies never apply to all individuals or groups and that the profiles may conceal communicative diversities within nations.

For instance, for Hofstede, Hofstede and Minkov (2010), the United Kingdom (UK) is recognized as being high on 'individualism', with more loosely-knit groups compared to China, which is generally high on 'collectivism', where most people harmonize within groups. China is also considered much higher than the UK on 'power distance', with greater acceptance of vertical hierarchies in which everyone has their place, rather than more equal distributions of power. Combining these orientations might help to understand the Chinese success in combatting poverty, together with a third dimension on which China is characteristically high. This is a pragmatic approach towards 'long-term', as opposed to 'short-term', goal orientations. The overall profile suggests that when participants understand a situation they are likely to follow responsible leaders' guidance and act in a cohesive way for long-term benefits. In terms of the SDG relating to the alleviation of poverty, and with regard to efficient and effective action in the COVID-19 situation, Chinese leaders seem to have successfully drawn upon positive features of the combined dimensions to work for the common good. While leaders elsewhere can gain deep insights from the Chinese approach, it is likely that culturally adaptations would need to be made for more individualistic, low hierarchically-oriented and short-term oriented societies. Importantly, these tendencies are themselves constantly changing and developing. Indeed, with increasing globalization, leaders are becoming more aware of cultural preferences and intercultural adaptation needs.

The GLOBE studies (House et al., 2004), using results from different surveys, likewise cluster countries with similar cultural characteristics to consider leadership profiles. For instance, there is an 'Anglo' cluster (the UK, Ireland, United States, Canada, Australia and New Zealand) contrasted with a 'Confucian' cluster (China, Japan, South Korea and Singapore). Within the Confucian cluster, China appears low for 'participative decision-making' compared with the UK, where leaders are more likely to involve others. However, China is higher for a 'self-protective leadership' style than the UK, where leaders seem less concerned with face-saving and are more willing to take risks. Nonetheless, China and the UK both appear more 'team-oriented' than countries in the Middle East, although not as high as Latin America. Nevertheless, all such tendencies, like identified trends in IC, may be modified in specific contexts, not least because leaders need to have flexibility in face of different circumstances. In relation to the Chinese response to poverty and the COVID-19 situation, the leadership appears authoritarian with high power distance and low involvement with other levels in decision-making. However, the Chinese poverty-reduction project was carefully planned long-term, with local consultation for maximum participation (State Council Information Office, 2021a; 2021b). This minimized risks, so that face-saving is less relevant, while teamwork for the project seems noticeably high.

Intercultural communication competences

Other IC approaches focus on competencies. The concept of IC competencies brings together four major strands (Deardorff, 2009; United Nations Educational Scientific and Cultural Organization, 2006; 2013). First, the cognitive abilities and skills related to communication include raising awareness and knowledge of language uses and associated variations in cultural values and practices. This suggests a process of conscious inquiry so that an increasingly competent communicator comes to know, understand and appreciate less familiar cultural uses of language in interaction. Second, there are the behavioral elements associated with customs and taken-for-granted ways of doing things. IC competences imply the ability to recognize and reflect on these mindfully, in relation to one's own culture and other cultures, and to be flexible in adapting and developing different skills. Third, awareness of feelings, which often influence reactions and assessments and communication, means establishing respect and rapport, and showing empathy and perhaps compassion towards others to establish confidence and trust. The fourth strand is that there are personal qualities related to successful intercultural interaction and collaboration within and between cultural communities. Such qualities include open-mindedness and curiosity; adaptability and flexibility; patience and tolerance; persistence and resilience; creativity and criticality; and ethical responsibility and cultural humility (Jin and Cortazzi, 2017).

Such qualities are necessary for IC competence but are also developed in the effort to attain it. This means that engaging in the process mindfully is already incorporated. Hence, leaders need to consider how to develop such qualities both in themselves and collectively among followers, and how to focus self-reflective thinking towards mindful ways of applying IC competencies (Ting-Toomey and Chung, 2021). Significantly, these qualities are not confined to IC but are key leadership-followership characteristics. This aspect of the humane and personal aspects of developing IC competencies indicates that leadership is not simply a matter of getting the job done, however efficient, effective or beneficial. Rather, for long-term participation, responsible leadership is equally important – for example, through establishing truth and trust through consultative collaboration, and developing cultures of reciprocal learning, compassion and cultural humility (Jin and Cortazzi, 2022). To further illuminate this theme, we now report on two studies of metaphors relating to IC in China.

Intercultural communication for leadership in China

University teacher-leaders

The first is our study of Chinese university teachers' conceptualizations of IC. These teachers were themselves leaders in their field and among their students are the next generation of leaders for continuing sustainability. Some teachers in this group are city consultants or provincial advisors in education related to languages and business and technology, so potentially this study scales up well beyond university classrooms. At a national conference, within ethical parameters, we collected 332 metaphors for IC from 134 university teachers in over 80 different Chinese universities. They were highly experienced teachers of English, with strong awareness of language use in international contexts. Most of them already teach some IC and all were aware that to develop IC for many professions is a significant trend in China and internationally.

The method used to analyze these metaphors extends recognized research approaches in cognitive linguistics, albeit with socio-cultural applications (see Cortazzi and Jin, 2020a; 2020b; Jin and Cortazzi, 2020). A metaphor, as an analogy, typically compares something abstract, complicated or less familiar with something accessible, more immediate and familiar. For instance, in the metaphor expression "*Intercultural communication is a bridge*", the abstract concept of IC is compared to the familiar idea of a bridge. This metaphor has implications about how the communication makes connections between two sides or opposite riverbanks, or between two cultures or communities. This research method of eliciting metaphor data is comparable to questionnaire or interview data but often with more creative, imaginative and emotional involvement from participants when they make their own metaphors.

Briefly, we asked teachers to complete proforma sentences, like "*Intercultural communication is . . .*", using their own metaphors to express their own ideas; for instance, "*Intercultural communication is . . . a journey*". Metaphors are compact comparisons, so they can have various elaborations or interpretations, giving different levels of meaning. We therefore asked the teachers to explain their metaphors by giving reasons. For example, "*it's a journey . . . because you go to many unknown places, you can enjoy the confusion and enlightenment of cultural shock on the way; because it starts with diversities but broadens horizons and deepens insights*". In principle, participants have a completely open choice. They can add practically any metaphor with a wide choice of appropriate reasons. Their metaphors may be commonplace, conventional, or more creative and deliberative. However, the metaphors are not arbitrary. All metaphors arguably relate intimately to cognition (Lakoff and Johnson, 2003) and to culture (Kövecses, 2005) because they employ fundamental analogical processing of thought. Our analysis attends closely to patterns of both the metaphors and the explanations in the entailments. We quote the teachers' own words (in italics) to portray their ideas in their own voices.

The teachers' metaphors emphasize their understanding of how IC *bridges differences* and *establishes interpersonal connections* in order *to overcome barriers*. It *helps to solve misunderstanding and conflict*. As *a tool*, IC *promotes cooperation*; as *a key*, it *opens gates to mutual understanding and more harmonious relationships*; as *a window*, it *offers views of others' perspectives and new ways of thinking*, as *a door*, it *opens to a splendid world outside your own culture* so that *you can walk towards a new cultural environment*. Some teachers saw IC as *a ball game*, typically *ping pong*, in which players *must know the rules*, and while it can be a *fast and furious* competition *to win*, one can also *cooperate* in *interacting with others* to *play peacefully*. Teachers recognized difficulties: IC can be *a war* or *a battle of minds with winners and losers* and *people can be hurt in confrontations, conflicts and clashes*. *Intercultural weapons*, like *double-edged swords*, can *attack and defend*. People in intercultural situations may *be confused* in *the maze* of IC, and *like mice running in it get lost in it if they are too passive*. Nevertheless, with effort IC can be a source of learning, like *an encyclopedia, full of help for living; it helps you to understand the world like a wise friend*.

The teachers, as leaders and expert communicators, were well aware that IC is not simply about exchanging information and knowledge, but as *a light* it *enlightens the way to a bright future* and *both minds and hearts*, and as *a book* it *spreads both ideas and values* among people. IC deeply involves emotions: *the journey of* IC *involves bitterness and happiness*; like *coffee* it *may taste bitter at first* but *sweetness comes later*. Like *marriage*, IC means those involved *tolerate*, *negotiate*, and *compromise in conflicts* before *full contentment*; *each side has to learn from the other*, but the process can be *full of sweetness and bitterness* as those involved *make progress together*. The intercultural journey means *to go from the heart of one person to the heart of another person*. Leaders developing much-needed IC might, like these teachers, see this as *a tree* or *a plant* which *needs care and patience* and *takes time to cultivate*. Leaders might follow the '*tai ji*' metaphor, which sees the slow movements of the *Taiji* Chinese martial-arts activity as exercise for physical, mental and emotional well-being: *it involves interactions, balance, practice, competition and patience*. As *a dance*, IC *means sometimes you go forward, but sometimes you need to move backwards*.

Significantly, the teacher-leaders see IC as reflexive: *it can reflect what you are and make you think about who you are; it can reflect your value orientations*. Like *looking in a mirror*, it enables people such as leaders *to see their own self* and re-assess their *identity*, *reflected in diversified ingredients* of *a mixing bowl, blended for something new* as *they come to know their own culture better* while they *understand other languages and cultures.* They see situations and problems *through a prism in diversified lights to achieve some targets* and *relate to the wider terrain, in a multi-dimensional view of the world.* Admittedly, this might be seen as trendy, like wearing *a fashion garment* in which *everyone wants to be seen in because they want to be thought of as at the international leading edge.* Yet IC requires hard work, like *building a scaffold* to *learn knowledge and* a willingness *to learn more to connect the East and the West* and make *a building to house different beliefs and ideas.* Perhaps surprisingly, teachers see these intercultural learning processes in aesthetic terms – *it is artistic* in *the beauties and varieties of this process.* It is like *poetry* and *music,* which through interaction with counterparts *makes us closer and shows us beauty* as people *join others to make a beautiful song* and *build friendships* across geographies of *cultures, societies and nations* towards *new horizons, towards beauty and charm, towards dreams.* Like *a drama on the stage, its performance needs constant updating with knowledge and understanding of the cultures of the East and West.* It is *beautiful but powerful.*

This reflexive quality shows how these teachers as leaders believe they must continue to develop IC further as they reflect upon themselves. This kind of self-reflection for self-correction represents a strong strand of Chinese leadership. While learning avidly from the best of the West, Chinese leaders tend to model themselves on key Chinese leadership values, which are noticeably supported in Chinese followership (Bell, 2015; Bell and Li, 2020). Leaders must show high capability and have solid recognized professional experience. These qualities should be combined with the moral character of showing responsible values and virtues. These are exemplified in the dedication, self-sacrifice and service to communities of leaders at all levels in how China advances the SDG in alleviating poverty.

Over decades, such leadership has been nurtured in a consolidating meritocracy in which those who are more capable and demonstrate the requisite responsibility rise to senior positions and are recognized and supported by their peers (Bell, 2015; Bell and Li, 2020). In significant ways, this continues a 1,300-year tradition in China of assessing well-educated officials through intensive examinations to select the most able, knowledgeable, morally suitable and loyal candidates for all administrative levels. Senior leaders have decades of competent performance at lower levels. They have likely accumulated extensive relationships through peer networks so that their decisions receive supportive agreement. Those selected seem less likely to make mistakes and take risks without proper assessment of relevant evidence. As seen in the SDG poverty achievement, this conception of leadership is a long-term, stable but still-evolving project. Leaders in China, as elsewhere, face unexpected challenges, but their step-by-step planning is normally designed with specific goals for 5, 10 or 30 years ahead.

A key characteristic is learning from experience – that is, developing consciously and cautiously, with careful evaluation of pilot projects before more rapid general applications. Characteristically in China, once such policies are considered, agreed and formulated, they tend to be promoted, implemented and enforced energetically with large-scale participation. The handling of the COVID-19 situation is an example of this. In broad outline, other SDG goals are approached with similar responsible leadership strategies. For example, the SDG to control climate change and its impacts is formulated in China to minimize disruption over time but to maximize uses of new technologies and piloted innovations – as in world-leading solar and wind power generation, in re-forestation, or in digital technologies and electric vehicles (Holzmann and Grünberg, 2021). Case studies of Chinese companies show similar increasingly responsible 'green leadership' (Lee, Ramasamy and Rhee, 2016), and companies and local officials are now pressured by the state to formulate long-term strategies to ensure they take responsibility for climate change, which is part of their performance evaluation (Holzmann, Meinhardt and Sebastian, 2021).

Senior leaders in international companies

A second study investigated metaphors for IC in a project related to communication among senior leaders in international companies in China and the UK (Jin, 2014). Data were gathered ethically during project meetings. The study shows basic differences in views over IC and the positive effect of an IC training program. The metaphors show far less richness than those of the university teachers, which probably reflects greater unfamiliarity and uncertainty about IC and that English teachers professionally give ongoing attention to communication issues. The analysis included considering data on 47 metaphors from 105 questionnaires to Chinese participants and 47 questionnaires completed by non-Chinese in the UK, plus other metaphors mentioned in interviews with 44 Chinese leaders and 19 British leaders in international companies.

Among the Chinese leaders, 74 percent believed it was important to have both a good command of the working language and cultural-business understanding of the context in China or elsewhere, whereas 70 percent of the British leaders thought that, while cultural understanding was important, knowledge of the language was unnecessary – presumably because using English as a *lingua franca* was considered sufficient internationally. This stance towards language by the British leaders seemed to ignore possible communication mismatches of the kind outlined above and indicated a need for IC training. Other clear differences in perceptions of IC emerged through an analysis of the participants' metaphors. Over 50 percent of Chinese leaders in the study felt that working with people from different cultures is like *overcoming barriers* or *trying to adapt to others*. In contrast, over 50 percent of the British leaders perceived that working interculturally made them *feel uncertain* or, more positively, *curious* or *adventurous*.

Thus, the managers in China thought that working interculturally was like *figuring out a math problem*, but lacking certainty they realized that *any answers depend on the methods employed to find solutions*. Some considered that working across cultures is like *going through a wall, difficult and painful*, but *very satisfying once achieved*. These managers readily used food metaphors to express uncertainty or early difficulty: IC is *tasting a variety of dishes – some might be amazing but there might be a mixture of tastes;* IC is *eating Japanese sashimi – we are not used to it from the beginning but later we really appreciate it*; or IC is *eating durian fruit – we appreciate its amazing glamour, though it cannot easily be swallowed the first time.* IC is also like *a blind date – a couple cannot understand each other; only through a long-term relationship can they get along with each other.* These leaders' metaphors therefore appear to emphasize the initial uncertainty and negative anticipation but solid achievement in the end. This fits well with a Chinese belief that life is bitterness first and sweetness last.

The British managers used food metaphors about IC too, often with similar ideas about variety plus a sense of surprise or excitement: IC is *eating a buffet meal, you see all different types of dishes; it's choosing a chocolate from a variety box – you never know what you will get.* These metaphors stress the positive variation felt by British leaders rather than a linear bitterness-to-sweetness development. The British managers also referred to classic well-known images: IC is *seeing an iceberg – initially you only see a very small amount, most is hidden waiting to be uncovered*; it's *opening Pandora's box – the results are unexpected, sometimes challenging*; or in the Indian fable, *it is touching an elephant – seven blind men feel it, and everyone has a different interpretation of the same object.*

Later, a group of senior marketing, technology and finance leaders from a well-known Chinese state international company were sent to their subsidiary UK company for two months working alongside their counterparts in the UK. Their goals included enhancing their awareness of IC, which was helped by including brief training sessions at the beginning and end of their program. Questionnaires were completed initially and at the conclusion of the program. Analysis showed a considerable shift of mindset towards a more open understanding and globalized view after their work experience abroad and IC training. In the final data, they were more likely to see *working with people from different cultures* as *exciting* (+11 percent) and find *mutual understanding of benefit* (+22 percent) and *not frustrating* (+27 percent), although it was more frequently felt that *hardship* could lead to *achievement.* They also showed a shift towards *something desired, to explore*, and towards *making an effort to understand* (+80 percent), despite being more *aware of difficulties* and *the need to be careful* in communication. IC after training was viewed as *watching flowers in the fog*, although *understanding cultural background* could *clear the fog.* IC was *traveling to a completely unfamiliar place: you know a little bit and you need to explore by yourself gradually.* IC was *making friends between boys and girls: we need to understand each other well and communicate efficiently for further development.*

For the Chinese leaders, therefore, the IC program was limited; it was fitted into a busy professional schedule with other priorities. Nevertheless, even brief training seemed effective in raising awareness. In an ideal world, the university teachers in China would help train Chinese leaders regarding IC in such globalized state companies, as well as more broadly, to help achieve further SDGs. Some university teachers – while strongly aware of, and to some degree competent in, some aspects of IC – asked for further training, which our studies show would be beneficial. The teachers' metaphors, as quoted here, certainly show broad understanding of IC; such insight could be shared with leaders. Encouragingly, they show sensitive feelings towards IC and teaching students, at least some of whom will become future leaders.

Conclusion

Striving to attain the UN SDGs needs a willingness, engagement and effort linked to IC because so many participants come from linguistically and culturally diverse communities. Interactionally, developing IC competences on a desirable scale implies a vison beyond globalization towards 'planetization' – a concept which seems prescient in relation to the SDGs. It was advocated by the French philosopher Pierre Teilhard de Chardin (1959), who included the vision of all life in the planet's ecology to emphasize how people need to change to protect the planet. Distinctively, writing in Beijing, he proposed the evolution of human consciousness towards maximum unification by concentrating profound reflection on the planet and on the socialization of humanity. Developing IC competences has a key role in planetization: it not only relates to the external environment but also an internal reflexive environment which involves humanity as a whole in thinking, feeling and acting in a social and spiritual evolution. Planetization means responsibility for all life on the planet, in leadership and followership.

For leaders, IC competences as part of responsible leadership imply developing humane qualities in focused contexts. This involves positive learning about community preferences, priorities and practices of communication. Studies of Chinese conceptions and actions in relation to the SDGs show a significant mindset comprised of the following:

- Clear agreed goals and long-term planning
- Consideration of contexts and identities
- Leading through competence combined with moral responsibility
- Learning continually and self-correcting through experience
- Communicating in multiple networks across levels
- Engendering firm forms of collective and cohesive action.

Both traditional and contemporary Chinese ideas of leadership (Fu, Wu and Yang, 2012) emphasize how knowledge and technical competence need to be combined with moral and social responsibility: leaders are responsible *to* and *for* those within their organizations, as well as in the broader society.

Developing IC for the achievement of the SDGs involves learning about, and developing skills in, communication aligned to multi-cultural and multi-lingual communities. This means learning from others. IC develops a leadership responsibility not only to learn to see how others see us but also to communicate flexibly without sacrificing identity or purpose, to adjust to an other-oriented vision while conveying our own vision – and reciprocally to help others do this too. Chinese conceptions of IC portray highly collective, interactive communication within diverse communities to achieve a mutual understanding of perspectives and negotiated, harmonious relationships. This is understood to be effortful striving, which is not easy and can be bitter-sweet. It involves values and virtues. It is mind-to-mind and heart-to-heart. It is beautiful but powerful artistry. To lead *with* these qualities and communicate *through* them is responsible leadership.

References

Bell, D. A. (2015) *The China Model: Political Meritocracy and the Limits to Democracy*, Princeton, NJ: Princeton University Press.

Bell, D. A. and Li, C. (eds) (2020) *The East Asian Challenge for Democracy; Political Meritocracy in Comparative Perspective*, New York: Cambridge University Press.

Carbaugh, D. (ed) (2017) *The Handbook of Communication in Cross-cultural Perspective*, New York: Routledge.

Cortazzi, M. and Jin, L. (2020a) 'Elicited metaphor analysis: Approaching teaching and learning', in Delamont, S. and Ward, M. (eds) *Handbook of Qualitative Research in Education*, 2nd edition, Chichester: Edward Elgar.

Cortazzi, M. and Jin, L. (2020b) 'Good teachers: Visions of values and virtues in university student metaphors', *KEMANUSIAAN Asian Journal of Humanities* 27(2): 145–64.

Cotter-Lockard, D. (ed) (2018) *Authentic Leadership and Followership in Intercultural Perspective*, Basingstoke: Palgrave Macmillan.

Daft, R. (2018) *The Leadership Experience*, 7th edition, Boston, MA: Cengage Learning.

Deardorff, D. K. (ed) (2009) *The Sage Handbook of Intercultural Competence*, Thousand Oaks, CA: Sage.

Fu, P. P, Wu, R. and Yang, Y. K. (2012) 'Chinese culture and leadership', in Chhokar, J. S. Brodbeck, F. C. and House, R. J. (eds) *Culture and Leadership across the World: The GLOBE Book of In-depth Studies of 25 Countries*, New York: Routledge.

Gupta, V. and Van Wart, M. (2016) *Leadership across the Globe*, New York: Routledge.

Hofstede, G., Hofstede, G. J. and Minkov, M. (2010) *Culture's Consequences: Comparing Values, Behaviors, Institutions and Organizations across Nations*, 3rd edition, New York: McGraw-Hill.

Holzmann, A. and Grünberg, N. (2021) *'Greening China': An Analysis of Beijing's Sustainable Development Strategies*, Berlin: Mercator Institute for China Studies.

Holzmann, A., Meinhardt, C. and Sebastian, G. (2021) *China Industries Briefing*, Berlin: Mercator Institute for China Studies.

House, R. J., Hanges, P. J., Javidan, M., Dorfman, P. W. and Gupta, V. (eds) (2004) *Culture, Leadership, and Organizations: The GLOBE Study of 62 Societies*, Thousand Oaks, CA: Sage.

Intezari, A., Spiller, C. and Yang, S. Y. (eds) (2021) *Practical Wisdom, Leadership and Culture: Indigenous, Asian and Middle Eastern Perspectives*, London: Routledge.

Jackson, J. (2020) *Introducing Language and Intercultural Communication*, 3rd edition, London: Routledge.

Jenkins, J. (ed) (2020) *The Routledge Handbook of English as a Lingua Franca*, London: Routledge.

Jin, L. (2014) 'Intercultural communication competence for leaders with a global vision', *China Leadership Science Review* 1: 118–34.

Jin, L. and Cortazzi, M. (2017) 'Intercultural communication', in Hinkel, E. (ed) *Handbook of Research in Second Language Teaching and Learning*, Volume III, London: Routledge.

Jin, L. and Cortazzi, M. (2020) 'Reaching for the gold standard: Metaphors and good university teachers', *Chinese Journal of Applied Linguistics* 4(2): 131–49.

Jin, L. and Cortazzi, M. (2022) 'Teaching intercultural communication: Principles and practices', in Hinkle, E. (ed) *Handbook of Second Language Teaching and Learning*, London: Routledge.

Kövecses, Z. (2005) *Metaphor in Culture, Universality and Variation*, Cambridge: Cambridge University Press.

Lakoff, G. and Johnson, M. (2003) *Metaphors We Live By*, 2nd edition, Chicago, IL: University of Chicago Press.

Lee, S. Y., Ramasamy, A. and Rhee, J. H. (2016) *Green Leadership in China: Management Strategies Form China's Most Responsible Companies*, London: Routledge.

Northouse, P. G. (2019) *Leadership, Theory and Practice*, 8th edition, Los Angeles, CA: Sage.

Saville-Troike, M. (2002) *The Ethnography of Communication: An Introduction*, 3rd edition, Oxford: Wiley Blackwell.

Sorrels, K. (2020) *Intercultural Communication; Globalization and Social Justice*, 3rd edition, Los Angeles, CA: Sage.

State Council Information Office of the People's Republic of China (2021a) *Full Text: Moderate Prosperity in All Respects: Another Milestone Achieved in China's Human Rights*, Beijing: Foreign Language Press.

State Council Information Office of the People's Republic of China (2021b) *Poverty Alleviation: China's Experience and Contribution*, Beijing: Foreign Language Press.

Teilhard de Chardin, P. (1959) *The Future of Mankind*, New York: Harper & Row.

Ting-Toomey, S. and Chung, L. (2021) *Understanding Intercultural Communication*, 3rd edition, New York: Oxford University Press.

United Nations (2015) *Transforming Our World: The 2030 Goals for Sustainable Development*, Geneva: UN.

United Nations Educational Scientific and Cultural Organization (2006) *Guidelines on Intercultural Education*, Paris: UNESCO.

United Nations Educational Scientific and Cultural Organization (2013) *Intercultural Competencies: Conceptual and Operational Framework*, Paris: UNESCO.

Chapter 11

Co-Responsible Leadership and Partnership

Rhiannon Lloyd and Brigid Carroll

Introduction

For many keen to see global commitment to climate change mitigation, the pace of change and the scale of national obligations to lowering greenhouse gas (GHG) emissions has been disappointing, if not frightening. The scene was particularly bleak after a disheartening Copenhagen Summit in 2009, which failed to bind nations to new targets. As a result, notwithstanding their centrality to the United Nations (UN) Sustainable Development Goals (SDGs) (2015b), the processes of the UN relating to climate diplomacy and environmental multilateralism were increasingly being met with skepticism, doubt and distrust by environmental commentators and the wider climate change community (Dimitrov, 2016; Obergassel et al., 2016). Given this context, when the Paris Agreement (PA) was developed at the 2015 Paris Summit it was hailed as constituting a "new era for climate policy" (Rogelj et al., 2016: 637), representing "the first truly collective effort by the world community to tackle climate change" (Obergassel et al., 2015: 245).

It is from this truly collective effort that we wish to explore co-responsible leadership and partnership. We build our exploration on a number of related theories, concepts and models: responsible leadership, co-responsibility, partnership, global

DOI: 10.4324/9781003129189-15

leadership and, most significantly, the social connection model of responsibility. We use these in a retrospective case study on the Paris Climate Agreement (United Nations, 2015a) and its push to overcome historical failures in collaborating on such a scale across multiple partners. Our aim in this chapter is to challenge the assumptions of liability, blame, punishment and penalties that can creep into discussions of responsibility, and we highlight the importance of co-responsibility and partnership as a means of forging a different conversation about engagement, collaboration, encouragement and reciprocity.

Responsible leadership

Pless and Maak (2011: 4) argue that responsible leadership is "a multilevel response to deficiencies in existing leadership frameworks and theories", by which they mean "high-profile scandals on individual, organizational, and systemic levels" developing situations such as "new and emerging social, ethical, and environmental challenges" and a fundamental change in the context within which leadership happens "in an increasingly connected world". This would suggest that responsible leadership provides a correction and reset to a terrain which still privileges leadership in mostly linear manager/managed relationships within boundaries and contexts that focus on performance above all else. Responsible leadership is therefore a perspective for which we have a great deal of sympathy, given that it firmly reframes leadership around assumptions of complexity, ambiguity and uncertainty, with which much leadership theory has traditionally struggled.

The above would suggest that we do not approach responsible leadership as a singular leadership theory but as an "umbrella concept to rethink the concept of leadership" (Gond et al., 2011: 116), particularly in terms of leading within contexts with multiple stakeholders, where much leadership happens outside of defined organizational and team relationships and at the intersection of multiple interests and agendas. That means responsible leadership overlaps with other leadership(s) such as global, ethical and relational leadership. If it is such an umbrella concept, one would expect an "inherent diversity of its paradigmatic and conceptual orientations" (Miska and Mendenhall, 2018: 117) and a rich set of debates about what it means to be responsible, what we are individually and collectively responsible for, and how responsible leadership can be enacted. This chapter argues in relation to responsible leadership that:

- It incorporates co-responsibility as part of a more expansive repertoire of responsibility- related concepts
- Co-responsibility is particularly orientated to partnership and new governance configurations
- Both co-responsibility and partnership lie at the intersection of responsible and global leadership
- Co-responsibility and partnership are centered on social connection theory and social interaction.

From responsible to co-responsible

Pless, Maak and De Jongh (2011: 1) claim that "from the 'me' to the 'we' to the 'us'" requires a shift to global citizenship and collaboration but also applies to leadership studies in general and responsible leadership specifically. Put starkly, there is no form of leadership that is accomplished by a single individual and does not require the contribution of others. While we respect the right and expertise of scholars to investigate the individual leader within broader collective leadership, at the same time the tendency to speak of leadership as something individuals do has created a leader-focused industry, a media frenzy on 'leadership superheroes' and the exclusion of multiple leadership actors and activity. Responsible leadership is distinctive in that it largely responds to these issues through the advocacy of a multi-level approach designed to incorporate a focus on leadership at individual, organizational and societal levels (Laasch et al., 2020). Working with such an approach in practice is nevertheless challenging, with the majority of studies selecting the level with which they want to work, as opposed to examining levels that cross and placing individuals within their organization and the wider society. For the latter to happen, we need to resist talking simply about responsibility and instead talk more about co-responsibility.

Co-responsibility as a concept arose in reaction to the 'denial of collective' in the literature on responsibilities (Isaacs, 2011) and its failure to grapple with "the macro-dimension of humankind's fragile existence on the finite earth" (Strydom, 1999: 66). Co-responsibility is defined by Strydom (1999: 69) as where "all those whose concern is being raised and whose support is being sought equally bear co-responsibility for the observed consequences and side-effects of collective activity". Co-responsibility is therefore predicated on a form of responsibility that can be mobilized through collective activity to address challenges that are universal and felt by humanity in its broadest sense, globally and intractably across time (Strydom, 1999). Climate change would of course appear the quintessential challenge of this type. Importantly, co-responsibility is not simply an aggregate of the responsibilities that different individuals hold but a relocation of responsibility within relational, communal and discursive processes. Given its relationality, it is centered on "the participation of individuals, groups, collective agents and the public" and is therefore geared towards "accommodating a variety of distinct social actors who maintain different yet changing cultural and institutional relations" (Strydom, 1999: 80).

The context of partnership

This chapter extends the more recent research by Carroll (2016: 56) on co-responsibility and its positioning within an ethos of community and "new discourses, mindsets, and practices" by locating it within the context of partnership. Maak and Pless (2009: 546) are amongst the few to discuss responsible leadership with respect to partnership, reminding us that "leadership in a global stakeholder society is a partnership effort to contribute to a sustainable future". While they talk of shared leadership but not co-responsibility, they characterize the partnership effort as one requiring leadership actors to "*engage* themselves among equals" through a "*participative* stakeholder dialogue" orientated to achieve "an *inclusive* approach" (Maak and Pless, 2009: 546, emphasis added), which would appear to be exactly the conditions that mobilize co-responsibility.

The language of engagement, participation and inclusivity is central to our definition of partnership in this chapter. Here we do not refer to the legal form of partnership or to business structures but instead to the notion of partnership in the sense of "complex interdependence adopted by the UN itself, which states any actor's action has reciprocal, consequential effects in the international system" (Barbanti Jr., 2004). Thus, we see partnership as driven by an imperative of co-operation, relationships that are voluntary and flexible, and expansive engagement (Sondermann and Ulbert, 2020). These characteristics are increasingly evident in partnerships which represent innovative forms of governance, including those associated with the UN, but also cross-sector configurations encompassing government, community, indigenous entities and social movements such as Black Lives Matter and Me Too. We argue that a co-responsibility approach fuels new and much needed processes for such partnerships.

In drawing on the PA, this chapter focuses on a particular form of global partnership best described as one of a series of "self-regulatory initiatives that address governance gaps on the global level" (Voegtlin and Pless, 2014: 180). The UN SDGs and the UN Global Compact (UNGC) are the other prime and well researched examples. Sondermann and Ulbert (2021) characterize such global governance as governance/partnership hybrids which encompass seemingly conflictual roles of guardian and watchdog and rely on what they call 'meaningful participation' and 'meaningful accountability' between participants. Not surprisingly, perhaps given their hybrid nature, there is debate over the efficacy of these partnerships as they do not directly monitor individual participants, sanction non-compliance or exclude those who might be exhibiting minimal standards. On the other hand, they do encourage dialogue, shared learning, a consensus on ethical standards, peer influence, resource sharing, and collaborating networks (Voegtlin and Pless, 2014). In this sense, they are a prime area for co-responsible leadership and for future responsible leadership research into how they operate, how leadership actors navigate them, and how they move from principle to action.

Going global

In setting out to investigate co-responsible leadership and partnership through the PA, we are undergoing the journey that other recent scholars have made to the intersection of responsible and global leadership (Maak and Pless, 2009; Miska, Stahl and Mendenhall, 2013; Voegtlin, Patzer and Scherer, 2012). This seems a natural journey given the stark need and growing call for leadership to address intractable and significant challenges that extend beyond the terrain and prerogative of any one part of the world. Miska and Mendenhall (2018) warn, however, that going global requires definition and theorization and cannot be assumed to be simply a scaling up of context. We argue that the concept of global leadership reflects more than leadership activity for cross-globe issues. Instead, it is a purpose, set of principles and repertoire of practices for engaging with genuinely global challenges, with an active realization of 'being of the planet' and part of a 'world community' (Adler, 1997). We therefore present global leadership as transcending cross-cultural and international multi-stakeholder management (Bird and Mendenhall, 2016) and apply theories that help us understand global leadership as a complex and collective process.

For example, Miska and Mendenhall (2018: 128) theorize global leadership along three dimensions, the first of which is complexity that they understand as a "continuous, non-linear, mutual interaction of core processes of multiplicity, interdependence, ambiguity, and flux". The second is flow, which is presented in relational terms as channels of information and communication spanning all manner of boundaries and positions including those leading as 'a cultivator and facilitator of relationships' (Maak and Pless, 2006). The third dimension is the spatial-temporal dimension of presence, which speaks to the need for 'tangible interactions among multiple stakeholders' (Miska and Mendenhall, 2018). Taken together, complexity, flow and presence highlight that global leadership is a distinctive milieu where traditional models and conventions of leadership are unlikely to apply. This chapter argues that a co-responsible framing of leadership aligns and works with global leadership, participative partnerships and the need for increasingly responsible 'global work' and governance structures (Mendenhall et al., 2012).

The social connection model of responsibility

The social connection model of responsibility of Young (2006) is particularly attuned to the challenges of global responsible leadership and partnership, as it theorizes responsibility in the context of structural injustice and transnational challenges. The model is therefore actively searching for an alternative understanding of responsibility different from that traditionally applied to an individual leadership actor. In this model, responsibility is always a shared social practice that

> derives from belonging together with others in a system of interdependent processes of cooperation and competition through which we seek benefits and aim to realize projects. Even though we cannot trace the outcome we may regret to our own particular actions in a direct causal chain, we bear responsibility because we are part of the process.
>
> (Young, 2006: 119)

Furthermore, the social connection model of responsibility states that "all agents who contribute by their actions to the structural processes that produce injustice have responsibilities to work to remedy these injustices" (Young, 2006: 122). We are then able to draw a direct line, not just between multiple leadership actors but between institutional participation on the one hand and global injustice on the other.

Although Young (2006) does not use the exact term, there are five core features of the model that speak to what we term as co-responsibility. The first is that it does not isolate responsibility to one or even a few leadership actors and absolve the rest. If we participate in social structures that play some part in injustice, then we are to a degree responsible. Secondly, it does not assume a normative judgment of a 'wrong' for which someone needs to take the blame but rather understands that structural injustice comes about through accepted and often sanctioned adherence of rules and conventions that are taken for granted and need ongoing critical scrutiny. Thirdly, it understands responsibility in forward-looking terms, where responsibility is "an ongoing set of processes that we understand is likely to continue producing harms unless there are interventions" (Young, 2006: 122). Fourthly, responsibility is shared between those who participate or contribute to the structural processes that underpin injustice, where all are "personally responsible for outcomes in a partial way, since he or she alone does not produce the outcomes" – which means that "the specific part that each person plays in producing the outcome cannot be isolated and identified . . . and thus the responsibility is essentially shared" (Young, 2006: 122). Finally, responsibility must be actioned as a collective where change is only possible "if many actors in diverse social positions work together to intervene in these processes to produce different outcomes" (Young, 2006: 123).

Ultimately, these five core features locate responsibility in those who have a social connection to an injustice. The action required to meet such a responsibility is likely to be political and require 'public communicative engagement' (Young, 2006). Voegtlin (2016: 604) has done much to champion this social connection model within the responsible leadership literature, noting that such leadership "shifts the focus toward communication, shared responsibility, and collective problem solving" with the participation of stakeholders. At the same time, it is recognized that we know little about the leadership required for such complex dialogue and problem-solving work, particularly with regard to social and environmental challenges. It is this closer examination of leadership that is offered by the illustrative case of the PA – which was a key stepping stone to the subsequent and much heralded COP26 held in Glasgow in November 2021, which made further progress in stemming climate change (United Nations, 2021).

The Paris Agreement

Co-responsible leadership is therefore scrutinized here through the PA, together with a selection of the processes that led to the Paris Summit from which it was born. This Summit challenges us to see leadership at multiple levels and discourages attempts to locate the 'leading' of complex global issues with discrete and isolated people.

Instead, co-responsible leadership is seen in the complex global partnership of the then 191 UN Parties voluntarily accepting their connections to climate change mitigation, climate justice and responsibilities to injustice at a supra-national level. As a truly global, legally binding international treaty, the PA has been celebrated as a successful feat of facilitated diplomacy and an effective collective accomplishment which created a base for progressively ambitious climate action from all countries associated with the UN Framework on Climate Change (UNFCCC).

The Paris Summit, also known as Conference of the Parties (COP) 21, was the culmination of a drawn-out diplomatic process characterized by a 'cooperative spirit' (Savaresi, 2016) and a "genuine collective effort to reach mutual compromise" (Dimitrov, 2016: 2). This spirit is evident in its technical components and principles, which makes it a particularly helpful case for examining the collective forms of responsible leadership present in climate governance and moving it away from the ineffectual, "rancorous and largely circular and sterile rhetoric that has long characterized international climate negotiations" (Savaresi, 2016: 26). As such, the PA is an important outcome of new forms of climate diplomacy, and its exploration through a leadership lens can help us determine better ways of leading collaborative responses to the climate emergency.

On 12 December 2015, COP21 formally adopted the PA as a treaty of the UNFCCC. The PA specified obligations related to climate mitigation and climate-resilient development and committed all members to limit global warming to below 2 degrees Celsius, and to pursue actions which will keep global warming to under 1.5 degrees Celsius. The mix of binding and non-binding obligations in the PA guided all member nations to reach net-zero GHG emissions in the second half of the century. It also recognized the need for members to ensure that all countries have the capacity, technology and financial resources to adjust to changing environmental circumstances. Whilst some provisions are unequivocal obligations, others are expressed in less categorical terms, and others have an enabling character, in that there is considerable leeway on how to undertake actions which align with the Agreement's aims.

The journey to finalizing the PA was tumultuous. Since the 1997 Kyoto Protocol, global climate governance has required renewal and increased international commitment, which has been far from global, with only 36 countries fully committing. Difficult negotiations in the early 2000s set the scene for the 2009 Copenhagen Summit and resultant Copenhagen Accord, which is often considered a "low point in the history of the climate regime" (Savaresi, 2016: 18). Whilst disappointing, the Summit in Denmark triggered a succession of working groups and negotiations which set up the PA to exemplify a 'new geometry' of commitments which would be applicable to all UNFCCC Parties, replace or supplement the Kyoto Protocol, and provide legally binding targets and provisions for the period post-2012. To rejuvenate climate governance, the Paris Summit needed to produce an outcome that would have real global impact and be binding on all Parties to the UNFCCC.

The 2015 Paris Summit was a microcosm of activity within a broad global and complex climate governance process and a specific place and space in time where representatives participated in shaping the final version of the Agreement. It was hosted and facilitated by the French Presidency and has been hailed as being a successful display of strategic facilitation and climate leadership. Whilst there are few academic commentaries which analyze the detailed goings-on within the Summit negotiations, Dimitrov (2016) has shown that the choreographing of open collaborative processes and more secretive and private negotiations, alongside smart timing, provided a political dynamic and diplomatic process which was a major contributor to the success of the Summit in finalizing the PA. When difficult and contentious issues were in the spotlight, such as those regarding financing support for developing countries, ongoing informal negotiations and a facilitated method of negotiation were used to enable concessions and open up conversation and agreement (Obergassel et al., 2015).

Significantly, the Paris Summit approached the global participatory process differently from previous COPs. Rather than a traditional top-down architecture which sets targets and timetables at the highest level and thereafter pushes them downwards onto Parties, the PA adopted a pledge and review bottom-up model, which required Parties to unilaterally declare the contributions they were willing to undertake to meet the goals set out by the Agreement (Savaresi, 2016). Parties autonomously submitted Nationally Determined Contributions (NDCs) which outlined a voluntary contribution of their own design to climate change mitigation. These were required to be "successive, increasingly ambitious . . . [and] subject to strong transparency guidelines" (Rogelj et al., 2016: 637). It was also agreed that these would be reviewed as part of the global stocktake process to occur every five years from 2023 onwards. Parties were expected to both meet NDCs and support the ability of others to do the same. Importantly, a non-backsliding clause was built in, which means that each global stocktake process pushed members to ramp up the level of ambition of their own commitments over time. The NDCs therefore were required to escalate in terms of objectives, actions and intentions.

The process of escalating NDCs is tied to a core communication and transparency principle which is woven throughout the Agreement and embedded in its ongoing processes. Such a principle is designed to enable ongoing collective action and can be seen most clearly in the global stocktake process. Parties are required to report on the extent to which they are meeting their commitments and to ramp up their commitments each time. The standardization of measures and metrics to be used in these stocktakes further improves information transparency and comparative analysis. These measures are designed to sustain and grow the partnership and facilitate community dialogue. Central to this Agreement is the wider network of actors, particularly non-Party stakeholders. As Rogelj and colleagues (2016: 637) note, "the recent unprecedented engagement of non-state actors such as businesses, citizens and religious organizations illustrates a more profuse awareness and an increased momentum for climate action . . . [where] supporting and enabling national and non-state action will be critical."

Previous UNFCCC agreements had applied classification systems which subdivided countries across Annex-I, Annex-II and Least Developed Countries categories based on the Organization for Economic Co-operation and Development (OECD) (2013) Intercultural Competencies framework. OECD proxies were used initially in 1992 for such purposes, but this outdated and over-simplified approach to the differentiation of Parties has been displaced by the NDC process, which requires commitments from all countries to meet the Agreement objectives, regardless of OECD classification. In line with the spirit of collaboration and partnership, developed countries were encouraged to take the lead in reducing emissions and to provide support to other countries as required. Driving the PA through autonomously determined NDCs illustrates a complex interdependence between the Parties as well as the connections between the individual Parties and the supra-national partnership. The Parties therefore must participate by determining their own responsibilities towards the goals of the collective whilst also understanding the dependencies and connections between all those involved in taking responsibility for meeting PA objectives.

Whilst the PA was hailed as a success, there nevertheless continue to be challenges in determining both responsibility and distributive justice measures. The UNFCCC has always had within it a differentiated responsibility principle whereby Annex I countries were expected to bear more responsibility to redress the burdens of climate change as their historical contributions to emissions were higher than other countries (Venn, 2019). NDCs meant that Parties could not be forced to offer support. This was therefore controversial as the Least Developed Countries wanted their industrialized counterparts to have stricter obligations and commitments without conditions attached. Industrialized countries, on the other hand, supported unconditional mitigation commitments from all Parties (Obergassel et al., 2015). The use of language in the Agreement is important here as 'loss and damage' relating to damage done by climate change that cannot be fixed or mitigated is a particularly contested issue. This is because it brings up issues of historical liability and expectations of financial compensation. Although many developing countries wanted loss and damage to be a part of the Agreement, other groups like the Umbrella Group – a coalition of Parties formed after the adoption of the Kyoto Protocol – feared that compensation language would result in liability issues for developed countries (Obergassel et al., 2015). Thus the final outcome provides a compromise whereby loss and damage were featured in the Agreement but cannot be used for liability claims against Parties.

Whilst flexibility and compromises have been pivotal in getting the PA off the ground amidst the complexity of numerous national and institutional conditions, contexts, politics and policies, there were no specific obligatory commitments for implementation by any members. Procedural obligations were expected, as opposed to obligations to implement or achieve that set out in NDCs. NDCs do not lead to outcome-orientated obligations on Parties, as this would give them the same legal status as in the Kyoto Protocol, which was rejected by many of them (Bodansky,

2016). With its collection of NDCs at the time, the Agreement would not work because the intended NDCs submitted were not enough to limit global warming to 2 degrees Celsius. As Obergassel and colleagues (2015: 251) point out, "the effectiveness of the Paris Agreement in limiting global warming therefore depends on the quick strengthening of the national determined contributions". In other words, the PA was a ground-breaking collective achievement, but it could only be helpful in the long term if there was the will and collective co-relational leadership to rapidly and ambitiously intensify commitments.

Identifying co-responsible leadership

The global climate change challenge is unquestionably an important context for those looking to offer impactful responsible leadership theory and practice which confronts structural injustice and transnational challenges. In exploring the Paris Summit and Agreement within a broader international climate struggle, the case provides a glimpse into the nature of large and complex participatory governance structures and co-responsibility and the need to engage in multiple levels of analysis. We now revisit and apply the social connection model of responsibility (Young, 2006) to this case and conceptualize co-responsible leadership as a shared social practice which cannot be isolated in one individual (Voegtlin, 2016). Rather, all Parties both individually and collectively bore responsibility and aimed to realize the Agreement's goals through "interdependent processes of cooperation and competition" (Young, 2006: 119). The following analysis shifts the focus of leadership onto "communication, shared responsibility, and collective problem solving" (Voegtlin, 2016: 604).

What we can firstly learn from the PA about co-responsibility and partnership are the practices which seek to separate responsibility from liability, blame, punishment, shame and penalties. A raft of these practices was referred to in the case study, such as sensitivity, compensation and liability alongside restrictions on their application, self-differentiation of partners in terms of their context and resources, and the use of both binding and non-binding obligations. It is worth revisiting the social connection model of Young (2006) at this point, as it complicates the traditional relationship between an identifiable party (individual or group) and a harm or injustice. If too causal a relationship is assumed then it is difficult to evade connotations of guilt, harm and blame. It is not that such a relationship should never be drawn but that it is not 'sufficient' to limit responsibility to this relationship. This is because all "agents who participate in structural social processes with unjust outcomes" (Young, 2006: 118) need to have co-responsibility to sustain an ongoing partnership to solve challenges that are universal and irreversible. Liability thus constrains the potential, scale and time required to sustain such a partnership. The PA sought to create an enduring approach with multiple entry points, a plethora of choice and decision points and a self-regulatory ethos. In this, it maximized progressive and future-orientated structural social processes and minimized the significance of causal and direct entity/harm relationships in determining members' actions.

A liability orientation also focuses on critical, adverse and contestable points as opposed to an unfolding, day-by-day process. Again, it is worth quoting Young (2006: 120), who notes that unlike a liability approach to responsibility a social connection approach "evaluate[s] harm that deviates from the normal and acceptable" and brings into question the "background conditions that ascriptions of blame or fault assume as normal". The PA worked strongly with what we could call background conditions: mutual compromise, a co-operative spirit and an enabling orientation. Young (2006: 120) makes the point that we participate in "the production and reproduction of structural injustice precisely because we follow the accepted and expected rules and conventions of the communities and institutions in which we act". Background conditions like compromise, co-operation and enablement act as principles to embed alternative norms, legitimate alternative routines and shape a proactive culture with different conventions. In other words, they disrupt accepted ideas to forge a different spirit and way of working. For the Paris Summit, this meant reworking established patterns of global governance that had proved ineffectual and inviting new modes of negotiation and facilitation.

In addition, the PA case signals the importance of "the temporality of assigning and taking responsibility" (Young, 2006: 122). Liability models by their very nature look back retrospectively at something that has already occurred (or not occurred), often wanting to seek redress, sanctions, penalties or even compensation. Connection models of responsibility need to be forward looking to keep building, refining and extending progress towards the collective vision and goals. The PA looked forward through mechanisms such as global stocktakes, non-backsliding clauses and the standardization of measures and metrics. Such mechanisms essentially created a flow of evidential data, knowledge resources and methodologies with a focus on forward movement and momentum. In addition, barriers to recommitting (such as we have seen with the United States) are deliberately minimized to avoid any associations of blame and shame. As Young (2006: 122) confirms, "the point is not to blame, punish, or seek redress . . . but rather to enjoin those who participate by their actions in the process of collective action to change".

Finally, the PA points to communicative practices designed to build and sustain positive relationships, share and distribute learning amongst partners and encourage supportive relationships between partners from diverse contexts. In the case study, we see the juxtaposition of open, collaborative processes alongside private and sometimes secret negotiations, cross-sector stakeholder dialogue with not-for-profit, corporate and community groups, and capacity-building forums for the transfer and translation of learning. Young (2006) calls this attention to the politics of responsibility, given it is about managing relationships, co-ordinating responses and moving into collective action. Overall, this reframes co-responsibility as a process within a partnership and, like all processes, one requiring sophisticated relational, facilitative and negotiation practices. As co-responsible leadership unfolds in partnerships, leadership may consistently or temporarily rest on individuals with power and political might at particular junctures. Indeed, the hosts and facilitators of the Paris Summit itself should not be overlooked, given their contributions to progressing and mobilizing conversation. Moreover, by recognizing the multi-level configurations of individuals and groups engaged in co-responsible leadership, we see how action-orientated practices shift form from the individual to collective at various times, as those engaged in the process represent themselves and their nations and participate as a broader part of the UN. Ultimately, then, co-responsibility must be actioned collectively where change is only possible "if many actors in diverse social positions work together to intervene in these processes to produce different outcomes" (Young, 2006: 123). This speaks to the earlier discussion of the three dimensions of global leadership, whereby co-responsible practice unfolds as an interdependent and multi-level process of individual and collective interactions which relate and connect across boundaries in a bid to seek and mobilize responsibility through partnership.

Conclusion

Through an application of the social connection model of responsibility of Young (2006), this chapter has illustrated how co-responsible leadership is particularly orientated to partnership and new governance configurations which aim to deal with "the observed consequences and side-effects of collective activity" (Strydom, 1999: 69) such as climate change and other global challenges invoking issues of international social injustice and environmental degradation. In responding to such issues, we have shown how a co-responsible leadership approach "shifts the focus toward communication, shared responsibility, and collective problem solving" (Voegtlin, 2016: 604) to mobilize new forms of partnership which are required to drive urgent global action. Central to co-responsible leadership are the principles and practices of engagement, collaboration, encouragement and reciprocity, which align with the assertion by Young (2006: 119) that "our responsibility derives from belonging together with others in a system of interdependent processes of cooperation and competition". Whilst a co-responsibility approach encourages new and much needed partnership processes for increasingly complex global contexts, in concluding we wish to briefly draw attention to some of the challenges the PA continues to face, and how framing this in terms of co-responsible leadership addresses these.

Whilst we are appreciative of the Paris Summit's successes and recognize it as a celebrated example of the kinds of co-responsible leadership we champion, we are also acutely aware of the Agreement's ongoing failures. These include the liability-orientated contentions surrounding loss and damage, as well as social and distributive injustices, which have continued to be major inhibitors to the effectiveness of the PA. Co-responsible leadership calls for an engagement with forward-focused responsibility and activities which are "morally appropriate . . . and aiming for certain outcomes" (Young, 2006: 119). However, we argue that all actors in the UNFCCC bear responsibility for the structural injustices that underpin the climate emergency. The liability model of distributive justice, which has traditionally been core to the approach of the UNFCCC, is nevertheless continuing to underpin a "false dichotomy between development and environmental protection [, which] has been particularly pervasive in the field of climate change, where, reinforced by a binary approach to common but differentiated responsibility, it has served to entrench the pre-Paris impasse on mitigation action between developed and high-emitting developing states" (Venn, 2019: 118). Continuing to hold responsibility as dependent on linear, causal and direct relationships between emitting states and liability sits uncomfortably with shared responsibility and will continue to limit collective progress.

We mentioned earlier that whilst partnerships do not directly monitor individual participants, sanction non-compliance or exclude those who might be exhibiting minimal standards, they do encourage dialogue, a consensus on ethical standards, peer influence, resource sharing, and collaborating networks (Voegtlin and Pless, 2014). We note that although the PA is a success story in these terms, it is also a victim of non-compliance. Without obligatory commitments regarding implementation for members, the Agreement's NDCs do not lead to outcome-orientated obligations on Parties (Bodansky, 2016). As such, the collection of voluntary targets is not sufficient to limit global warming to 2 degrees Celsius and hence "the effectiveness of the Paris Agreement in limiting global warming . . . depends on the quick strengthening of the national determined contributions" (Obergassel et al., 2015: 251). In other words, the PA was a ground-breaking achievement, but its principles will only succeed in the long term if commitments are escalated quickly and ambitiously. With many Parties including France not meeting its NDC commitments in 2020, there is legitimate concern that progress in climate change mitigation and adaptation will fall short – to catastrophic effect.

A co-responsibility leadership frame encourages climate governance configurations to continue their transformation into increasingly participative and partnership-orientated spaces wherein contributing actors are encouraged to maintain communicative practices over time. Summits and dialogues such as the Paris Summit in 2015 – and indeed the more recent COP26 meeting in Glasgow in 2021 – are short-term one-offs, whilst global partnerships solidify collective action by making it ongoing. As Voetglin (2016: 599) notes, "collaboration and dialogue do not mean having all parties meet just once to discuss an issue". Co-responsibility and partnership speak to the intersection of responsible and global leadership by highlighting how ongoing social connection, interaction and conversation are needed for effective partnerships to continue crossing boundaries, engaging multiple levels and fostering future-forward approaches which transcend traditional models and conventions of leadership.

References

Adler, N. J. (1997) *International Dimensions of Organizational Behavior*, 3rd edition, Boston, MA: PWS-Kent Publishing.

Barbanti Jr., O. (2004) 'Global partnerships and development', *Beyond Intractability*. Available at: https://www.beyondintractability.org/essay/partnership-and-conflict

Bird, A. and Mendenhall, M. E. (2016) 'From cross-cultural management to global leadership: Evolution and adaptation', *Journal of World Business* 51(1): 115–26.

Bodansky, D. (2016) 'The legal character of the Paris Agreement', *Review of European, Comparative and International Environmental Law* 25(2). Available at: https://doi: 10.1111/reel.12154

Carroll, B. (2016) 'From responsibility to responsibilities: Towards a theory of co-responsibility leadership', in Kempster, S. and Carroll, B. (eds) *Responsible Leadership: Realism and Romanticism*, New York: Routledge.

Dimitrov, R. S. (2016) 'The Paris Agreement on Climate Change: Behind closed doors', *Global Environmental Politics* 16(3): 1–11.

Gond, J-P., Igalens, J., Swaen, V. and El Akremi, A. (2011) 'The human resources contribution to responsible leadership: An exploration of the CSR – HR interface', *Journal of Business Ethics* 98(S1). Available at: https://doi: 10.1007/s10551-011-1028-1

Isaacs, T. (2011) *Moral Responsibility in Collective Contexts*, Oxford Scholarship Online. Available at: https://doi: 10.1093/acprof:oso/9780199782963.001.0001

Laasch, O., Suddaby, R., Freeman, R. E. and Jamali, D. (2020) 'Mapping the emerging field of responsible management: Domains, spheres, themes, and future research', in Laasch, O., Suddaby, R., Gustavson, P. B., Freeman, R. E., Olsson, S. and Jamali, D. (eds) *Research Handbook of Responsible Management*, Cheltenham: Edward Elgar.

Maak, T. and Pless, N. M. (2006) 'Responsible leadership in a stakeholder society: A relational perspective', *Journal of Business Ethics* 66(1) 99–115.

Maak, T. and Pless, N. M. (2009) 'Business leaders as citizens of the world: Advancing humanism on a global scale', *Journal of Business Ethics* 88(3): 537–50.

Mendenhall, M. E. et al. (2012) 'Defining the "global" in global leadership', *Journal of World Business* 47(4): 493–503.

Miska, C. and Mendenhall, M. E. (2018) 'Responsible leadership: A mapping of extant research and future directions', *Journal of Business Ethics* 148(1). Available at: https://doi: 10.1007/s10551-015-2999-0

Miska, C., Stahl, G. K. and Mendenhall, M. E. (2013) 'Intercultural competencies as antecedents of responsible global leadership', *European Journal of International Management* 7(5): 550–69.

Obergassel, W., Arens, C., Hermwille, L., Kreibich, N., Mersmann, F., Ott, H. E. and Wang-Helmreich, H. (2015) 'Phoenix from the ashes: An analysis of the Paris Agreement to the United Nations Framework Convention on Climate Change – Part I', *Environmental Law and Management* 27(6): 243–62.

Obergassel, W., Arens, C., Hermwille, L., Kreibich, N., Mersmann, F., Ott, H. E. and Wang-Helmreich, H. (2016) 'Phoenix from the ashes: An analysis of the Paris Agreement to the United Nations Framework Convention on Climate Change – Part II', *Environmental Law and Management* 28(1): 3–12.

Organization for Economic Co-operation and Development (2013) *Intercultural Competencies: Conceptual and Operational Framework*, Paris: OECD.

Pless, N. M. and Maak, T. (2011) 'Responsible leadership: Pathways to the future', *Journal of Business Ethics* 98(S1). Available at: https://link.springer.com/article/10.1007/s10551-011-1114-4

Pless, N. M., Maak, T. and de Jongh, D. (2011) 'Foreword to Special Issue on Responsible Leadership', *Journal of Business Ethics* 98(S1). Available at: https://link.springer.com/article/10.1007/s10551-011-1117-1

Rogelj, J. et al. (2016) 'Paris Agreement climate proposals need a boost to keep warming well below 2 °C', *Nature* 534: 631–39.

Savaresi, A. (2016) 'The Paris Agreement: A new beginning?', *Journal of Energy and Natural Resources Law* 34(1): 16–66.

Sondermann, E. and Ulbert, C. (2020) 'The threat of thinking in threats: Reframing global health during and after COVID-19', *Zeitschrift für Friedens-und Konfliktforschung* 9(2): 309–20.

Sondermann, E. and Ulbert, C. (2021) 'Transformation through "meaningful" partnership? SDG 17 as metagovernance norm and its global health implementation', *Politics and Governance* 9(1). Available at: https://doi: 10.17645/pag.v9i1.3656

Strydom, P. (1999) 'The challenge of responsibility for sociology', *Current Sociology* 47(3): 65–82.

United Nations (2015a) *The Paris Agreement*, New York: UN.

United Nations (2015b) *Transforming Our World: The 2030 Agenda for Sustainable Development*, Geneva: UN.

United Nations (2021) 'Climate change conference outcomes', World Leaders Summit COP26, Glasgow, November. Available at: https://ukcop26.org/the-conference/cop26-outcomes/

Venn, A. (2019) 'Social justice and climate change', in Letcher, T. M. (ed) *Managing Global Warming: An Interface of Technology and Human Issues*, London: Elsevier.

Voegtlin, C. (2016) 'What does it mean to be responsible? Addressing the missing responsibility dimension in ethical leadership research', *Leadership* 12(5). Available at: https://doi: 10.1177/1742715015578936

Voegtlin, C., Patzer, M. and Scherer, A. G. (2012) 'Responsible leadership in global business: A new approach to leadership and its multi-level outcomes', *Journal of Business Ethics* 105(1). Available at: https://doi: 10.1007/s10551-011-0952-4

Voegtlin, C. and Pless, N. M. (2014) 'Global governance: CSR and the role of the UN Global Compact', *Journal of Business Ethics* 122(2). Available at: https://doi: 10.1007/s10551-014-2214-8

Young, I. M. (2006) 'Responsibility and global justice: A social connection model', *Social Philosophy and Policy* 23(1): 102–30.

Part V

Education, Professions and Responsible Leadership

Chapter 12

School and College Education and Responsible Leadership

Julie Search-Whittaker and Adrian Sladdin

Introduction

Audrey Azoulay, Director General of the United Nations Educational, Scientific and Cultural Organization (UNESCO) has described education as a human right, a public good and a public responsibility. As such, education is an essential tool that imparts knowledge to improve the lives of individuals and plays a significant role in molding the ethics and culture of the society. It is therefore of paramount importance that those who influence the education agenda and have the power to make changes that will impact significantly on those who access education in its broadest sense lead responsibly. Decisions must consider the interests of all key stakeholders – including those who access the various pathways to education – as well as the wider community. The role of the educational leader, therefore, is to focus on teaching and learning, putting the interests and needs of learners at the heart of the agenda. It is also to collaborate with educators and to effectively implement a rich educational offer that is diverse and inclusive. Fads and fashions may come and go in relation to educational delivery, but the core emphasis must always be to educate, improve, enrich and equip learners with the tools they need for now and the future.

DOI: 10.4324/9781003129189-17

In this chapter, we shall refer to leaders in educational settings internationally – first focusing on primary education and then on secondary schools and colleges. Having said this, education is a lifelong process, and making sense of the world is our main business in life. Babies universally explore their surroundings using all their senses, identifying faces and communicating their needs via cries, expressions and noises. Spoken recognizable words are not at the start of language and communication. As Whitehead (1996: 2) comments: "A child's first word has behind it a personal history of listening, observing and experimenting with sounds and highly selective imitations of people." The learning process continues throughout our lives, but the formative years are vital for providing the foundations and pathways for learning to develop and flourish. Educational methods of learning during this time include, amongst others, teacher-led and pupil-led teaching, training, storytelling, discussion and directed research. As Whitehead (1996: vii) summarized: "At most times in history and in most parts of the world, the first eight years of life have been seen as the first phase of living. Ideally, during this period, children learn who they are; about those who are significant to them; and how their world is."

The value of education and responsible leadership

Those of us involved in education know that it is not only powerful but also essential to help level the playing field and reduces inequalities. It can break the cycle of poverty, empower people to live healthy and sustainable lives, help to foster tolerance between people, and contribute to more peaceful societies. These are at the heart of the Sustainable Development Goals (SDGs) of the United Nations (UN) (2015). Here education is a force for the good, not least because it gives people across the world the skills needed to realize their potential. However, education can also be seen as dangerous and threatening because it is so powerful. A UNESCO (2010) report on *Protecting Education from Attack* discusses the many thousands of teachers and pupils, in various parts of the world, living in war zones and under dictatorships who are physically attacked and have their lives threatened. Aloni and Weintrob (2017: 7) further observe that: "Attacks on education occur in many countries that face armed conflict and insecurity . . . Such attacks are directed against learners, educators, education aid workers, education trade unionists and educational institutions at all levels."

Nonetheless, education can be valued, important and worth defending. It can be a ticket out of one section of society to another or, more broadly, a route from one situation to another. Nelson Mandela once said: "education is the most powerful weapon which you can use to change the world". The acquisition of knowledge is part of education but not the whole story. Having a holistic, rich, wide, varied and inclusive curriculum providing new experiences as well as giving knowledge is what is most valuable and important for all. A focus on overall wellbeing is necessary to help maintain positive mental and physical health. As Irina Bokova observed: "Young people and learners need the cognitive and socio-emotional skills (such as creativity, empathy, compassion, sense of solidarity and responsibility)" (Aloni and Weintrob, 2017: ix).

Some have been victims of what the American writer Fredrik de Boer (2020) calls 'the cult of smart', the pervasive modern idea that intelligence is the defining human quality and academic performance is necessary to have real human value. We need to value a range of different types of intelligence and appreciate other admirable human qualities. In fact, some of the admiration for academic achievement itself could be on shaky ground. This is illustrated in schools in England with the Standard Assessment Tests (SATS), but the pressures of a target-led agenda can lead to corruption. A BBC TV Panorama program recently showed how a boss in an Academy, an independent state school funded directly by government, ordered staff to cheat on SATS (Thompson, 2020). The pressure to obtain high published test results that influence parental choice of school, and affect the amount of money available to them, is a strong driving force. Responsible leaders must rise above these pressures and focus on the moral purpose of their role: educating children in the best possible way. There needs to be a government re-think on SATS, which were cancelled in 2021 due to COVID.

Some writers, however, do not see education as a valued commodity, particularly in a school setting. Illich (1973), for example, once called for schools to be disestablished, as he saw their formal organization as an impediment to, rather than a facilitator of, learning. Instead, he favored informal, individually self-directed education through learning webs. Contributors such as Bowles and Gintis (1976) also had a negative take on schools because they viewed them as a major mechanism of social class reproduction in capitalist societies – creating docile workers ripe for exploitation by the dominant class through the hidden curriculum of schooling. This chapter goes beyond those critiques by focusing on the virtues of education and its potential when managed by responsible leaders. A. S. Neill was one of these in the United Kingdom (UK); he cared more about psychology than about education. He believed that all crimes, hatred and wars could be reduced to unhappiness and, to counteract this, held that children should be provided with a 'free' education where they had real choices unlike the existing state system (Neil, 1960). He set up a pioneering school called Summerhill; while providing a traditional academic education and being proud of the academic achievements of its pupils, it had educational benefits which were far more profound, as observed by Lamb (1992).

Leadership in education is pivotal. Put simply, responsible leadership in an educational setting means providing the best possible teaching and learning opportunities and making sustainable business decisions which consider the interests of all stakeholders: teachers, pupils, parents, governors and the wider community. The role of the educational leader is to focus on teaching and learning, drawing on research and putting the interests of the children at the center. It is also to collaborate with educators and provide curriculum direction and guidance, supporting staff to effectively implement the cycle of planning to enhance learning and lead the development and implementation of an effective and appropriate educational offer. Responsible leadership in an educational context therefore requires adherence to ethical principles. Some argue that there are no common ethical principles as they are culturally generated. However, the argument here is not that such principles are universal but rather that in relationships with others a leadership position cannot be maintained unless it is seen to be fair, listening to all sides, coming to just decisions and keeping to promises (Donlevy and Walker, 2011).

Being a leader such as a headteacher in schools and a principal in colleges is a demanding task which requires relevant skills. Meeting the educational needs of children, young people and adults is underpinned by ethical expectations and may include functions such as protecting, providing resources, understanding, catering for individual differences, and ensuring all have equal access to educational opportunities and resources. Aloni and Weintrob (2017) suggest that educators need to generate trust and lead mutually uplifting exchanges, be an advocate for their students, believe in them and seek to empower them to flourish. Educational leaders have diverse and challenging roles. Targets are to be met, but, above all, the children need to learn effectively. In England, the Office for Standards in Education, Children's Services and Skills (Ofsted) is an inspection service that checks and monitors educational standards – even if these may not fully represent the learning that is taking place and in what context. For example, in England, as Gorard (2018: 111) notes, "schools deemed to be failing are more likely to be in urban centers, and so-called good schools are more often in leafy suburban settings". However, he goes on to observe that "there is little evidence-based research for educational leaders to draw on to support improvement [,] and leadership itself must be among the weakest education research in the world".

Primary education

This notwithstanding, teachers strive to enable children in primary education to reach their full potential by removing barriers and providing effective support for learning. The allocation of resources to redress the imbalance is a daily task for educators. As such, responsible leadership in a primary school context entails clarity of vision and engagement and a belief in the essential work in which children are engaged. The thoughts, opinions and expertise of all the stakeholders need to be valued. Responsible and effective leaders understand the importance and value of diverse perspectives and maximize the opportunities for inclusivity. The responsible leader will enable the education process to happen by removing barriers and embracing opportunities for learning, including outside the classrooms, and by utilizing all available resources to help learners achieve, which involves motivating and engaging them. Within the primary school system, a responsible leader will also need to lead by following a moral path. Much has been written in recent years highlighting the scandals in schools, which are often the result of external pressures on leaders in the education system. For example, Thompson (2020) recently noted that parental pressure on admissions officers could affect access to first-choice primary schools.

One approach in England is not to start with the National Curriculum requirements but first consult with children, parents and the wider community to find out about what they consider to be the most important things to learn about (Reed et al., 2012). Once the core content has been established, National Curriculum edicts can be included in line with reports such as that by Rose (2006) on early reading. However, there are different philosophies in educating primary age children. Some schools operate completely outside the National Curriculum with an alternative curriculum for children. For instance, Steiner schools in England give priority to providing a creative and unhurried learning environment where children can find joy in the learning experience and the richness of childhood; early academic specialism is not encouraged (Rawson, 2021). Montessori schools meanwhile emphasize learning through all five senses, where children learn at their own pace and make individual choices of activities (Davies, 2019). Dewey believed that the aim of education was to allow children to gain the capacity to grow knowledge and experience it as the foundation of learning (Simpson, Jackson and Aycock, 2005).

We have much to learn from such educational pioneers and need to consider how their work is incorporated in schools at primary and other levels. We must not forget that intelligence is only one admirable human quality among many. Since the examination system has been disrupted due to COVID-19, it may be time for a re-think and finding ways to value education by preparing our children for an uncertain future. This by no means undermines those who want to specialize or follow a particular academic pathway, but other types of attributes need to be valued – such as technical and creative skills – whilst enabling the basics to be covered. One of the co-authors has been involved in storytelling projects that involve young children recounting their favorite personal stories to elders and vice-versa. Such projects value creative thinking and enable schools to be linked more closely with their local communities. Valuing technical and creative skills is vital in order to attract able individuals into pathways which will lead to respected and vital jobs for economic growth. These pathways should not be simply for those who are less academic. Indeed, all work needs to be valued because all jobs interrelate holistically and provide for economic growth and sustainability.

We also need to be aware of how other societies educate their young children and consider what can be learned from other approaches. One example is illustrated by the first-hand experience of one of the co-authors of working in Sweden, visiting nurseries and schools, and lecturing to a group of teacher training students who asked about a day in the life of a 4/5 year old in an English school. They all found the formality, timetable and expectations we had for our young children alarming. The experience of education for children of the same age in Sweden was in stark contrast.

Swedes would have perceived that leadership from government was not responsible because of the demands on teachers in England to make primary children take tests, have breaks in the flow of learning, and sit for relatively long periods of time in large assembly gatherings. The view from educators in Sweden was that more attention should be given to research on how children learn and what their basic needs are in early school life because a day in a typical English primary school did not sound like it reflects this.

Preliminary findings of the Russian team from the International Consortium on Families and Community in the Time of COVID-19 (I-CoFACT) project were that it had similarities with England and Sweden in relation to learning during the pandemic (Yurchenko, 2021). Their research was based on a survey of over 2,000 parents across Russia involving in-depth online interviews and ethnographic observations, including in the primary sector. The study revealed that there were no strong relationships between the schools and families and that the lack of clarity and transparency experienced by parents inhibited learning. Parents in routine work also found it more difficult to support children with learning. The study discovered that such children lacked self-regulated learning skills and found it hard to understand and analyze information in textbooks without help from the teacher. Headteachers in England have reported more effective communication with parents but also noted that some children lacked the self-motivation to learn, as in the Russian study.

Another similarity between Russia and the UK during the pandemic was that the digital divide widened in primary education because some children did not have access to computers or the means to use the online materials effectively. This was also evident in Sweden. The Swedish Schools' Inspectorate (SSI) (2020) published a report which underlined that the public education system was not able to deliver online digital education on equal terms. Some schools were seen to be better prepared than others. The lack of mandatory standards for online education resulted in a large variation in how different schools were digitized. This showed deep inequalities not just in who has Internet devices and sufficient bandwidth but also who has the skills to self-direct their learning, and parents who have the time to help them. The report from the SSI highlighted the critical importance of school as a place of learning, socialization, care, coaching and shared community space – as well as the necessity for cultivating vital new skills for future generations. Responsible leadership should be based on principles and ethics of equality of educational opportunity and should ensure that all relevant stakeholders are considered when decisions are made.

In England, Wales and Northern Ireland (but not Scotland), state primary schools must provide a National Curriculum. Subjects include Art and design, Technology, Geography, History, Computing, Language, Music and Physical education, with a focus on the core subjects of English, Mathematics, and Science. Although this does not apply to private schools, leaders of state primary schools are required to fulfill the duty of providing a curriculum that both covers these areas and enriches and engages other interests. Young children are tested on a regular basis to ensure they reach expected targets, and if they do not achieve, they will have additional help provided. Leaders need to incentivize staff to maintain momentum and achieve these targets. It is therefore especially important that responsible leaders fully engage with their staff so that they can work together in this task, especially during the challenging COVID-19 pandemic. Some teachers may be more vulnerable to the implications of coronavirus than others in terms of shielding, and classes have more generally had to be adapted to online delivery, with children needing to be motivated as far as possible. Primary headteachers have also had to create rotas and hire extra help to ensure cleaning regimes are in place and that children are taught in safe 'bubbles' in the classroom. Despite these actions, tens of millions of children missed school due to COVID-19 globally, when some 150 countries fully closed them for a year or more (United Nations Children's Fund, 2021).

Changes will inevitably follow from lessons learned from the pandemic which will affect primary and other forms of education in England and throughout the world. Questions are being asked about how much more can be done online and whether other kinds of curricula can be offered in schools on a different pattern. One of the reasons cited by the UK government as to why the economy was at risk was because some parents of young children were unable to leave them and easily access job roles. Perhaps there is too much emphasis being put on educational establishments as childminding establishments? Maybe there are better alternative ways of caring for children outside the school timetable? Either way, it is important for primary school and other educators to understand the powerful and vital role they have in society to demonstrate their responsible leadership.

Schools in the primary and secondary sector are generally the hub of a community. Often, the headteacher or a teacher hears about incidents that happen in the lives of children and their families. They have had the training and have a sound understanding of the needs of children from an educational point of view, and their voice should be heard when policies and curriculum changes are made. We now have an opportunity to re-think our educational curriculum, structure and pattern and can learn lessons from the pandemic, including in relation to reducing inequalities with the digital divide and teaching children the skills of resilience in learning how to learn. Once the foundations of learning have been achieved in primary education with effective leadership, secondary education must build on this so that everyone can strive to fulfill their potential. We need to ensure that we enable children to be the best they can be. As Nelson Mandela once said: "There is no passion to be found in settling for a life less than one you are capable of living."

Secondary education

Despite the comparative absence of research on leadership in schools and colleges (Foster, 2006), in modern secondary schools, leadership must embrace a range of different areas – from knowledge and skills to responsibilities and autonomies. The deconstruction of schools and other learning centers should therefore be paramount, including their architecture, classroom environment, technology, timetables, staff and student relationships, curriculum, and pedagogy to deliver on academic outcomes and address concerns like wellbeing, positive mental health and preparation for life. As Khaideen (2015: 43) comments, "today's education landscape is being re-shaped by rapidly developing technologies, innovative teaching and learning practices, demanding accountability and a growing realization that education reform is necessary within a globalized world."

This requires innovative thinking and radical rewriting, as well as inspirational leadership allied to ethical and sustainable goals. Education should not be detached from the realities of life and work; it should have a greater range of diverse voices to ensure education is fit for purpose and future proofed in a fast-changing world. It is the responsibility of those charged with leading secondary establishments to ensure that this is not just top-down but inclusive of the whole educational community. It is also important that strong leadership ensures schools and colleges are a beacon for societal good and not simply inward-looking. Therefore, it is crucial that they have a global view of how they best serve our students now and in the future, as there are no short cuts to implementing and managing educational change (Holmes, Clement and Albright, 2013). Here we should always look forward rather than back in our educational views, given that much of what we have inherited in the modern world has changed little over time. Khaideen (2015) in fact observes that our education system has been organized on an industrial model, with pre-determined curricula and textbooks, learning through standardized assessment, and the goal of maintaining the *status quo*.

Kress (2000) echoes this, noting that the current educational curriculum is largely inherited from the nineteenth century and still assumes it is educating young people into older dispositions; this is despite the coming era demanding an education for instability, which could enable a refreshing change from the stranglehold of exams and a reversal of a learning journey that is often simply based on the grinding accumulation of knowledge and is thus a joyless experience for many young people. In his seminal work *The Cult of Smart* (2020), the Marxist academic Fredrik de Boer deals with some of the long-held beliefs about equality in the classroom. Responsible leadership in this context means that we should scrutinize all we do in schools because they will otherwise be little more than a state-sponsored form of childcare.

Several hundred years of education have therefore looked very similar, with the same pedagogy, architecture and classrooms and just another version of a teacher with chalk and a board getting young people to commit facts to memory. The prescient view of Kress (2000) is that new circumstances demand a new response with new goals and curricula. He also notes that it is now becoming possible to see the dissolution of the former framings and the tentative emergence of new configurations. That then leaves the task of attempting to establish the shape of a secondary school curriculum. What remains constant is the fundamental aim of all education – namely, to provide those skills, knowledges, aptitudes and dispositions that allow young people to lead rich and productive lives in society as adults. However, as the experience of COVID-19 has indicated, with more online learning and the temporary removal of exams in the UK and elsewhere, now is the time for change. So what is it that we value in terms of learning, and how should responsible school leaders in the secondary sector implement this?

To help answer this, we shall now look at some interesting new ways of learning within secondary education from around the world, as witnessed by one of the co-authors. The Island School in Hong Kong addresses the issue of education as leisure. On a staff training day, teachers were asked to abandon their professional development and instead think about their own passions, interests and enthusiasms with the aim of establishing 'clubs'. In many cases, these were to be scheduled off-site, in line with Kress (2000) on the ideological potency of the shift from sites of education to sites of leisure – going out to the community rather than remaining in the educational establishment. Two days per week were to be given to these 'alternative' activities in lieu of lessons. A range of fascinating clubs emerged, from photography and sport to fashion, as well as physical activities that were new to the secondary students, such as scuba-diving, which was not only exciting but had an immediate value in the context of Hong Kong harbor. With this activity, students were free to explore the ecology and the sea-life, and environmental concerns around fishing were addressed. Aside from skill development, this experiential learning contributed to confidence-building, physical wellbeing and mental health.

There was also a positive effect on how students at the Island School related to the other three main curriculum days of the week. Every teacher had their own story to tell, but it was certainly a lesson in leadership in the staff room and school. Headteachers, who allowed their teachers freedom, trust and opportunity, reaped rich rewards from their responsible leadership. The numbers of school achievers were high, with a 97 percent pass rate for GCSEs A*–C and 100 percent IB and BTEC passes, which is impressive for a non-selective comprehensive school. Global comparisons were positive too, suggesting that the positive school ethos is working. As noted by Davis (2016: 242): "Change leadership and visionary leadership are related but different", and driving change, for her, is a captain's problem: once a new route has been established, the captain must ensure it arrives safely at a destination. As she says, though, what is "even harder is convincing the ship's owners and shareholders to agree the new course in the first place" (Davis, 2016: 242–43) and Island School had that new course in place.

Looking at further examples of responsible leadership, it is interesting to reflect on best practice. In relation to the Islington summer program in the UK, Kress (2000: 137) observes that secondary and primary students were offered the chance to attend off-site, free of charge activities including: "Rap & Scratch courses; Dance; Maths GCSE revision; Women's football; Fabric painting; Canoeing; African dance & drumming; Making music through computers; Drama; Art; Vocals/singing classes; Sailing; Discussion Groups; Music Technology & Recording Skills". This was again predicated on the notion that "learning is fun, that the knowledge which it offers is fun, that 'doing a course' at university is like leisure time activity more than like work time activity" (Kress, 2000: 135).

A scheme titled 'Hearts, Hands and Heads' at Roedean School, just outside Brighton in the UK, which began around five years ago, has some comparable elements, with a unique take on the curriculum. The new Headteacher showed how leadership can take a school in a different direction without entirely losing its long-established ethos and values. Aside from attempting to modify the ancient perception of the school being 'the Eton for girls', there was clearly a need to modernize, from the curriculum, accommodation and buildings to the culture of the school. The main thrust of these changes in secondary education gave less focus to academic outcomes for the students and introduced a more rounded, holistic education program to let the students develop at their own pace and feel confident and unpressurized. Languages were incorporated such as Russian, Mandarin and Sign. And other new subjects were introduced like Photography, Dance, Drama, Philosophy, Psychology, Cookery and the School Farm. All this was approached in the spirit of curiosity, enquiry and innovation within the school's new holistic education commitment. Examinations were still important but not a be all and end all. Students were able to pursue their passions and develop a range of new skills while learning to value qualities such as participation, creativity and confidence away from the stresses of academia.

It may be argued that this vision is resonant with the ideas of Kress (2000: 140), who noted that the new philosophy

> suggests a very different curriculum, a very different pedagogy and a fundamentally different notion of learning. It sees the learner as fully agentive, as becoming fully aware of the potentials, capacities and affordances of the materials to be used in the designs. It sees design as the making of signs (whatever the materiality in which they appear: material/three-dimensional, spoken/temporal, written/two-dimensional) whether in the science classroom, in English or in art. Of course, this is a fundamental realignment of the curriculum: a realignment from a curriculum focused on knowledge as a stable, even if complex, 'entity', to a curriculum focused on uses of knowledge-as-information in relation to specific domains of application.

China is the final stop on this educational leadership journey. In this example, again drawn from one of the co-author's experiences, leadership in secondary education came not from a single individual but from a collection of school leaders daring to try something different. The schools in question were home to some of the brightest 'A' Level students, with guaranteed top grades across the board and a seemingly glittering future. However, there was little to differentiate one student from another in terms of 'quality', and so it became apparent that skills and autonomies could be the most useful way of measuring students' overall capabilities. What the headteachers came upon here was a UK Level 3 Qualification in Personal Effectiveness, based upon the successful wider key skills qualifications but with added emphasis on communication and research. This in turn had been adapted to become a 'Mini Business MBA' with international travel, commercial visits and language skills all built into the overall package. Visits to both the UK and mainland Europe ensured a broad organizational and cultural reach for the program. The Chinese schools had believed quite rigidly in the benefits of academia and learning by rote, so success in exams was seen as the way forward, with students working impossible amounts of time to be the best. What was suggested was untried and unknown – pushing them into brand new pedagogy and thinking.

Initially, the program yielded varying numbers of students, some more keen to see the Eiffel Tower and shop at Galerie Lafayette than to interview managers at the BMW factory or analyze the work of the Frankfurt Stock Exchange. Results were patchy, but gradually each school increased its numbers, and more teachers and senior leaders joined the trips to see the program in real terms. The students compiled portfolios of the work they were completing, including films they had made and detailed plans of action and execution. The results grew ever more impressive, and the actual number of schools participating increased as more school leaders found out about the program. Clearly, the attraction of allying academic rigor to lifelong transferable skills was not just a brave educational choice but also an attractive one. To note Kress (2000: 134): "What remains constant is the fundamental aim of all serious education: to provide those skills, knowledges, aptitudes and dispositions which would allow the young who are experiencing that curriculum to lead productive lives in the societies of their adult periods." Nurturing productive lives means embracing the need to equip the next generation with the knowledge and skills needed for employment and to contribute to an effective economy. The way in which knowledge is transmitted, the kind of subjects taught and the creativity that is encouraged is part of the process to achieve this goal.

A number of examples of strong and responsible leadership at secondary school level from around the world have now been offered. No example is accompanied by hard data, and none come with a research methodology to indicate that they definitely work, but all come from educational leaders who have a future vision of what schools could and should look like – these are the innovators who believe there are certain rules we can abandon. In the wake of a pandemic, the time to stop and think will perhaps filter down to more school leaders so that they too can show strong leadership for a better educational world. Clearly, in the examples here, there is the long-term need to conduct more research to judge whether responsible leadership results in not just winning educational battles but – more significantly – the educational war. We need to ensure that school education opens doors for students and does not reinforce an unfair *status quo* in 'the legitimization of inequality' as Bowles and Gintis (1976) described.

Many secondary schools and colleges may return to the way they were, with the same classrooms, subjects and the like. However, one strand that may well develop is the outdoor learning agenda. In the UK and more widely there is now increasingly a green curriculum and a commitment to the UN SDGs, and organizations for young environmental leaders are springing up in the firm belief that this is part of the way ahead. Strong educational leadership may well take us further in this direction and lead the way through post-pandemic educational confusion, offering access to a more inclusive, holistic education for all and taking us beyond the specter of schools driven by academic tests as the sole arbiter of success.

Conclusion

Education is an essential tool that imparts knowledge to improve life. It is a key process that plays a significant role in molding the ethics and culture of a society. It empowers and helps to equip us to face the challenges of life more efficiently and prepare for future employment. Additionally, education, in its fullest sense, improves skills, abilities and knowledge and can broaden attitudes, influence views, and help enable everyone to live a fuller and richer life by opening doors for discovery and exploration. UNESCO (2010), as the sole UN agency with an exclusive mandate in this area for the associated SDG, believes that education is a human right for all throughout life and that access must be matched by quality and not be dependent on socio-economic influences in certain parts of a single country or internationally. Inclusion should also more broadly be recognized as best practice, and more opportunities should be provided for this going forward. Greater inclusion would allow more acceptance of educating learners across the spectrum of age, ability, culture, economic background, ethnicity, gender and more.

In the UK, the universal right to access education has formally been achieved, but not all experiences are satisfactory from the viewpoint of equality for all children. What we are expecting of children with regular testing, routines and other demands may not echo what many educationalists have said about what young children need and what is required to prepare the next generation with the skills to live a full and rewarding life. The latter includes obtaining the skills and knowledge to gain, sustain and achieve in different pathways for employment. As such, the economy is central to the educational opportunities provided.

Changes will inevitably follow in schools throughout the world from lessons learned from the COVID-19 pandemic. A key change is an increase in the use of technology for online learning. One essential and responsible action required from leaders is to ensure appropriate access and support to narrow digital divides where they exist. More generally, we can now re-think and plan for various pathways to success, which includes valuing different types of achievements and human qualities. It is important to capitalize on growing educational research internationally and draw on lessons from the pandemic in relation to online learning, access to digital learning and the pressures of the examination system, and to teach children skills of resourcefulness, agency and resilience. This will require widening our children's educational experiences inside and outside the classroom. Changes to the pattern of the day and to the delivery of learning may be needed, and the requirements of childcare may need to be revised.

As noted in the specific UN (2015) educational SDG, there is no place for complacency until all children universally have access to appropriate quality education in its broadest sense as a human right. We cannot return to the world as it was before COVID but instead must revise and create an education system that is fit for purpose for all. Learning must prepare students of all ages creatively to find solutions for the challenges of today and the future. Education should be transformative and allow us to make informed decisions and take individual and collective action to change our societies and care for the planet.

References

Aloni, N. and Weintrob, L. (eds) (2017) *Beyond Bystanders*, Rotterdam: Sense Publishers.

Bowles, S. and Gintis, H. (1976) *Schooling in Capitalist America: Education Reform and the Contradictions of Economic Life*, Chicago IL: Haymarket Books.

Davies, S. (2019) *The Montessori Toddler: A Parent's Guide to Raising a Curious and Responsible Human Being*, New York: Workman Publishing.

Davis, J. (ed) (2016) *The Greats on Leadership*, London: Nicholas Brearley Publishing.

De Boer, F. (2020) *The Cult of Smart: How Our Broken Education System Perpetuates Injustices*, London: Macmillan.

Donlevy, J. and Walker, K. (2011) *Working Through Ethics in Education and Leadership*, Rotterdam: Sense Publishers.

Foster, R. (2006) 'Leadership and secondary school improvement: Case studies of tensions and possibilities', *International Journal of Leadership in Education*. Available at: https://doi: 10.1080/1360312042000299233

Gorard, S. (2018) *Education Policy: Evidence of Equity and Effectiveness*, Bristol: Policy Press.

Holmes, K., Clement, J. and Albright, J. (2013) 'The complex task of leading educational change in schools', *School Leadership and Management* 33(3). Available at: https://doi: 10.1080/13632434.2013.800477

Illich, I. (1973) *Deschooling Society*, London: Marion Boyars.

Khaideen, R. (2015) 'Leading in the twenty-first century learning environment: Challenging the deanship', in Elliott-Johns, S. E. (ed) *Leadership for Change in Teacher Education: Voices of Canadian Deans of Education*, Rotterdam: Sense Publishers.

Kress, G. (2000) 'A curriculum for the future', *Cambridge Journal of Education* 30: 133–45.

Lamb, A. (ed) (1992) *The New Summerhill*, London: Penguin Books.

Neill, A. S. (1960) *Summerhill: A Radical Approach to Child Rearing*, New York: Hart Publishing Company.

Rawson, M. (2021) *Steiner Waldorf Pedagogy in Schools: A Critical Introduction*, London: Routledge.

Reed, J., Maskell, K., Allinson, D., Bailey, R., Bates, F., Davies, S. and Gallimore, C. (2012) *The Adventurous School: Vision, Community and Curriculum for Primary Education in the Twenty-First Century*, London: IOE Publishers.

Rose, J. (2006) *Independent Review of the Teaching of Early Reading*, London: Department for Education and Science.

Simpson, D. J., Jackson, M. J. B. and Aycock, J. C. (2005) *John Dewey and the Art of Teaching: Toward Reflective and Imaginative Practice*, Thousand Oaks, CA: Sage.

Swedish Schools Inspectorate (2020) *Education under the Influence of the Corona Pandemic*, Stockholm: SSI.

Thomas, C. (ed) (2012) *A Call for Engaged Leadership*, Rotterdam: Sense Publishers.

Thompson, P. (2020) *School Scandals: Blowing the Whistle on the Corruption of Our Education System*, Bristol: Policy Press.

United Nations (2015) *Transforming Our World: The 2030 Agenda for Sustainable Development*, Geneva: UN.

United Nations Children's Fund (2021) *Covid-19 and School Closures: One Year of Education Disruption*, New York: UNICEF.

United Nations Educational Scientific and Cultural Organization (2010) *Protecting Education from Attack*, Paris: UNESCO.

Whitehead, M. (1996) T*he Development of Language and Literacy*, London: Hodder & Stoughton.

Yurchenko, O. (2021) 'Responsible leadership in schools and colleges', United Nations Institute for Training and Research/Institute for Responsible Leadership Webinar, Geneva, June.

Chapter 13

Responsible Leadership and Higher Education

Enver Yücel

Introduction

There is not one consistent definition of responsible leadership. Early on, the Globally Responsible Leadership Initiative (GRLI) highlighted ethically correct and values-based behavior and action in the context of understanding the interconnectedness of the world in its call for globally responsible leadership. In the GRLI report (2005: 2), responsible leadership is defined as "the global exercise of ethical, values-based leadership in the pursuit of economic and societal progress and sustainable development". A common understanding among researchers is that responsible leadership centers attention firmly on matters of responsibility, including accountability, appropriate moral decision-making and trust. In other words, responsible leadership seeks to define what 'responsible' means in the context of leadership. Moreover, being accountable for actions, answerable for decisions and reliable and trusted are not just semantic variations on the term 'responsibility' but rather constitute inherently relational concepts. By definition, then, responsible leadership is geared toward the concerns of others and asks for what and to whom leaders are responsible.

Responsible leadership necessitates leaders addressing the challenges of globalization effectively, building trusting relationships and facilitating stakeholder engagement for the sake of both business success and the common good (Maak and Pless, 2006). Responsible leaders think about the consequences of their decisions for all affected constituencies and engage in an active stakeholder dialogue, balancing

DOI: 10.4324/9781003129189-18

different interests (Voegtlin, Patzer and Scherer, 2012). The 2015 annual meeting of the European Organizational Studies Group was devoted to responsible leadership (Pless, Stahl and Voegtlin, 2015). The aim was to encourage more research on the concept and to advance the discussion on responsible leadership, particularly on its relationship with individual ethics, decision-making, stakeholder participation and corporate social responsibility. Today, the concept of responsible leadership has expanded the traditional understanding of leadership by shifting the focus from the leader-subordinate(s) relationship to the multifaceted relationships between leaders and corporate stakeholders in an increasingly complex and uncertain global business world (Stahl, Sully de Luque and Waldman, 2017; Waldman, 2011).

This chapter discusses the concept of responsible leadership as so defined in the context of higher education. This is held to involve the United Nations (UN) Sustainable Development Goals (SDGs), since cross-reference to them can be seen to be at the root of responsible leadership. As McCowan (2019) notes, such goals have increasingly been adopted by a range of universities globally – in rich and low-to-middle income countries. However, this chapter focuses on the exemplary application of the SDGs in terms of responsible leadership in Bahçeşehir University (BAU), one of the newest, larger universities worldwide. First, though, the chapter turns to discuss the SDGs more generally in relation to higher education.

The Sustainable Development Goals and responsible leadership in higher education

The beginning of the twenty-first century brought important advances at the international level to increase the viability of a more sustainable form of development. In the year 2000, the UN launched the Global Compact, which was a serious attempt to engage the international business community in sustainable development via the implementation and dissemination of policies and practices with an inclusive and multi-participatory orientation (Buono, 2014; Kell, 2012; Parkes, Buono, and Howaidy, 2017). In 2015, the UN (2015) launched the 2030 Agenda for Sustainable Development to guide societies on issues that should be a priority to improve people's quality of life and the world's environmental conditions. The Agenda covers a series of 17 goals and 169 targets that focus on solving a wide range of challenges, such as the eradication of extreme poverty and hunger, the promotion of health and wellness across the globe, gender equality and quality education for all, as well as urgent concerns regarding water, energy, economic, infrastructure, consumption, climate, ecosystems, institutions for peace and sustainable development (Parkes, 2017). The introduction of the SDGs brought the issue of policy decisions to be co-designed and co-produced with the pertinent stakeholders to the fore. As such, the depth and breadth of the SDGs has necessitated concerted and coordinated efforts across all sectors and actors – in which training and education have been regarded as crucial elements to achieving sustainable development and a sustainable planetary future.

In this sense, there is an emphasis that sustainable development occurs in environments where there is effective education.

The UN Agenda was built collaboratively by several societal actors. Within this framework, universities are seen as well placed to lead the cross-sectoral implementation of the SDGs and advance the 2030 goals. Higher education institutions play a significant role in achieving the SDGs because, in association with schools and colleges, they can equip the next generation with the skills, knowledge and understanding to address sustainability challenges and perform research that advances the sustainable development agenda. They can also provide valuable sources of expertise in research and education in all sectors of the SDGs. Thus, fostering partnerships with governments and communities has gained increased prominence as the mission of universities gradually moves beyond the tradition of education and research towards a 'third mission' related to their ability to address social needs and to achieve societal impact (McCowan, 2019).

As Saks (2019) notes, universities and other higher education institutions can contribute to the SDGs by, amongst other things:

- Defining appropriate learning objectives and contents (such as providing sustainable kitemarks for programs)
- Offering courses supporting sustainability (for instance, on environmental studies and climate change)
- Introducing relevant pedagogies and initiatives that empower learners (as illustrated by *pro bono* legal work for the poor)
- Conducting research promoting sustainability (for example, on crop growth, economic development and tropical medicine)
- Including sustainability principles in their own management structures (like carbon reduction and widening participation).

These points are generalized further in the recent report by Quacquarelli Symonds (QS) (2020) on *The Rise of Social Responsibility in Higher Education*. This report stresses the role of higher education institutions in sustainable development as follows:

- Universities have an obligation to act in society's interests
- Universities can be a major fulcrum for change through research and other mechanisms
- Cultural shifts can be born in universities with responsible curricula and philanthropic projects
- University impacts can be at a local or wider national or international level – which are both complementary and essential.

Although there can be important variations between universities in how far and in what ways they deliver on sustainable development, this is an area in which the report by QS (2020) shows many universities are keen to progress. Indeed, there is a QS star system which highlights their very different and stratified strengths in such areas as partnering, meeting skills shortages and student volunteering – as well as their contribution to more substantive issues from reducing carbon footprints and addressing changing weather conditions to encouraging bike riding to work as a means of transport and building hydropower dams. Here it is not always those universities that are based in the richest countries or are placed highest in the world rankings on purely academic criteria that do the best. Indonesia and Mexico currently host most of the fifty or so universities with five stars for social responsibility – with eight and four institutions represented respectively. Moreover, examples of the higher education institutions that received the top five QS stars range from UniRitter in Brazil and the Universidad Privada del Norte in Peru to Massey University in New Zealand and the University of Northumbria in the United Kingdom (UK).

Interestingly, drawing on the critical role that universities play at the vanguard of innovation, there are also national sustainability university tables. For instance, as Saks (2019) points out, there is a sustainability league table that runs parallel to the QS system that is compiled by the student network in the UK. It covers areas from carbon reduction and ethical investment to human rights and sustainable education. In terms of impact, the existence of this table – the stratified nature of which is influential in areas such as student recruitment – seems to have variously encouraged UK universities to disinvest from fossil fuel companies; respond positively to organized climate change demonstrations; and lobby government to cancel substantial amounts of debt owed by developing countries. This underlines the value of the UN SDGs in moving universities forward.

As the aforementioned indicates, responsible leadership is rooted in an ethic of care driven by a desire to serve others (Pless, 2007) in the form of attentiveness, responsibility and competence, and to care for their needs (Tronto, 1993). According to some scholars, responsible leadership is beyond relationship and emotion; it is conceptualized spiritually in terms of virtuousness and service to the wider society, not to say the whole world (Cameron, 2011). Within this framework, a university assuming the role of responsible leadership is obliged to serve the community as a whole, including future generations, and consistently seek desirable ends that meet the needs of a wide range of stakeholders by focusing on virtuous outcomes (Crilly, Schneider and Zollo, 2008; Waldman, 2011). This further reinforces their relationship with the SDGs.

In this chapter, we will present the responsible leadership of BAU both in preparing young people to participate as active citizens of the global community and in establishing collaboration among stakeholders for active engagement for equal and inclusive education – and the SDGs in general. As previously implied, universities have three functions: teaching, research and community outreach and extension. Our main focus in this chapter will be BAU's leadership regarding the third function. Initiatives taken by BAU will be shared to highlight by example BAU's leadership in advancing the SDGs for the good of the whole community.

Bahçeşehir University: The higher education context

BAU is a competitive foundation university in Istanbul, Turkey, established in 1998. Today, there are nine Faculties, one School of Applied Sciences, one Conservatory, one School of Foreign Languages, one Vocational School and the Graduate School – with some 20,000 undergraduate students, 1,500 associate degree students, 5,500 masters students and 500 doctoral students at the time of writing. Of these students, over 5,500 are foreign students from different countries. The University has had over 37,000 graduates so far. BAU also has ten campuses internationally and is a member of the BAU Global Education Network, which offers worldwide education opportunities in cities such as Berlin, Toronto, Washington DC, Batumi, Cyprus, Hanoi, Kyiv, Pueblo and Brockville. According to the *Times Higher Education* 2022 World University Rankings, in a short time BAU had risen to the rank of between 801–1000 and was rated ninth among all universities in Turkey.

Since its founding, BAU has defined innovation, sustainability, ethics and leadership as its guiding concepts both in internal management policies and educational practices. BAU underlines the principle that education is the key catalyst for sustainable development and the material and cultural wealth allowing societies to flourish. In BAU, courses integrating new methods in the pursuit of knowledge and innovation are promoted. In most of its Faculties, students are offered courses in which real world solutions are sought by confronting practical problems and pragmatically applying the derived solutions. Both at the undergraduate and graduate levels in BAU, projects leading to transformative action linked to the UN SDGs have replaced traditional forms of education based on knowledge transmission.

What makes Bahçeşehir University a responsible leader in education?

The CIFAL Center and BAU Global Citizen Program

One of the most noticeable examples of responsible leadership initiatives at BAU is the establishment of the Istanbul Centre International de Formation des Autorités et Leaders (CIFAL). The CIFAL was established in 2019 in collaboration with the UN Institute for Training and Research (UNITAR) and BAU. The Center is a part of the UNITAR-affiliated CIFAL Global Network, which consists of 22 international training centers in 19 countries. BAU is the only university in Turkey where such collaboration exists. The aim is to enhance sustainable development and provide quality, accessible and inclusive education, particularly for under-represented and disadvantaged people in Turkey and around the world. Since its foundation, CIFAL Istanbul has provided guidance to all institutions and individuals within the network and worked with the network to internalize the necessity of the SDGs. The Center has provided online and offline education and training for students from kindergarten to doctorate level, including professionals, teachers and academics.

This has made quality education accessible and inclusive for all, reducing waste production and unnecessary consumption, increasing recycling, supporting sustainable agriculture, decreasing practices harmful to the environment, remedying inequalities of gender, belief, ethnicity, socio-economic status and cultural background, and empowering immigrants through skills development to gain global employability. All the content and programs initiated by CIFAL Istanbul are prepared and conducted in both English and the local language of the partner institutions to maximize the dissemination of quality education on sustainable development across the globe. As a global organization, CIFAL Istanbul works in partnership with educational institutions located in Turkey, the United States, the UK, Germany, Italy, Canada, Cyprus and Georgia, and provides education, training and consultancy services to all students, professionals and partners of those institutions. A key mission of CIFAL Istanbul is to empower students, Turkish and international, to experience studying and working in settings in different parts of the world with people from multicultural backgrounds. To that end, CIFAL Istanbul has initiated training programs with UNITAR to enable students to see international organizations and global policymaking on site and receive training from professionals and experts from disparate fields.

As a sign of responsible leadership, each work area of BAU Global – including school construction, classroom design, energy consumption, waste disposal, water usage, student and staff inclusion and the accessibility of classes – was re-envisioned and updated based on building a sustainable, inclusive and accessible framework of operations and a safe and healthy educational environment. To that end, the Global Citizenship Program was initiated in more than 125 schools in Turkey with the partnership of Harvard University. The program educates kindergarten, elementary and high school students on the basics of sustainable development by solving real-life issues on sustainability. Each year, the program reaches 70,000 students with the aim of educating global citizens who are aware of, and sensitive to, global problems. A wide range of undergraduate and graduate courses were initiated at BAU and the universities within the BAU Global network, such as the Introduction to Agenda 2030, Sustainable Curriculum Design, Sustainable Management and Sustainable Maritime Operations. This enables BAU to inform and educate future managers, engineers, teachers, doctors and social scientists on the globally vital issues of equality, prosperity, peace and justice, as represented in the SDGs, and to empower them to find innovative solutions to make the world a better, healthier and safer place.

BAU, gender equality and the COVID pandemic

Another example indicating the responsible leadership of BAU is the Equality and Inclusion Committee (BAU EQUAL). BAU made a declaration in December 2019 of its intention to pursue institutional studies on gender equality and anti-harassment, especially in terms of sexual harassment and workplace violence, and the prevention of all kinds of discrimination. Following this declaration, as of October 2020, a group of expert BAU faculty members started to work together with the aim of bringing an equality and inclusion-based approach to all university-run operations. BAU is pleased to announce that BAU EQUAL has now started working on a program to develop policies and procedures to prevent and support incidents of sexual harassment and gender-based violence, as well as workplace and discrimination-based violence. So far BAU EQUAL has examined national and international models to determine the steps necessary to create a non-violent campus and an inclusive learning and working environment and started research to better understand the internal situation at the university. BAU EQUAL not only works on training programs and activities such as preventive measures to create positive learning/working environments but is also designing procedures as a response to incidents. In this context, BAU EQUAL aims to constitute a point of contact, so that BAU members can be in touch if they are subjected to sexual harassment, gender-based violence, or other forms of discrimination in line with the relevant SDGs.

The responsible leadership steps of the university can particularly be witnessed in times of crisis, such as natural disasters and pandemics. This has been especially important in face of COVID-19, which has been highly disruptive to higher education, involving everything from the decline of face-to-face contact to increases in remote learning and assessment – with all of its implications for inequalities in terms of access to computer technologies (Saks, 2020). The Department of Psychological Counselling and Guidance (PCGD) in the Faculty of Educational Sciences always takes the lead in addressing the urgent needs of students and the wider public regarding anxiety, fear and loss of resilience by providing psychosocial support services, and it frequently shares information through television programs and online seminars with stakeholders in the university and with the general public. These programs, together with individual and group sessions, are aimed at helping to overcome trauma in society. To give a more specific example, after the destruction caused by the 6.8 magnitude earthquake in Elazığ in January 2020, Bahçeşehir Global Education Network was among the first body to implement psychosocial support activities to assist families. Teams of graduate volunteer students and instructors at the PCGD reached around 1,670 children to heal their trauma.

The COVID-19 crisis and its socio-economic effects have disproportionately affected women, especially with reference to such economic sectors as catering, hospitality and services. The pandemic has exacerbated existing inequalities between women and men in almost all areas of life, both in Europe and beyond, rolling back the hard-won achievements of past years. In developing countries, conditions appear to have been more serious due to scarce social protection mechanisms and effective protection rights in relation to women. Women in Turkey also suffered from a disproportionate impact of the pandemic. Studies on the effects of COVID-19 revealed that the pandemic has further sharpened gender inequalities in Turkey, which already had the second widest gender gap in unpaid work time in the Organization for Economic Co-operation and Development (OECD), with women on average performing 4.5 times more unpaid work than men. As an extension of this, it has the lowest female employment rate at 32.2 percent, as against an OECD average of 61.3 percent of the population of working age women. Research conducted during the pandemic investigated the possible impacts of the pandemic on the private sector from a gender perspective. The two most frequent challenges reported by employees were related to work-life balance and domestic violence. A large difference between women and men was observed, in which women reported challenges including longer working hours due to remote working, anxiety, psychological stress and exhaustion, as well as limited access to communication and Information Technology at home (TÜSİAD, TÜRKONFED and United Nations Women Turkey, 2020).

Research conducted by UN Women Turkey (2020) on the gender assessment of the social and economic impact of COVID-19 in Turkey demonstrated that while both women and men have been significantly negatively impacted by the crisis they have not been affected in the same way or equally. Instead, it has resulted in a deepening of pre-existing gender inequalities. The survey revealed that women experienced a higher rate of job loss and reduced working hours, a larger uptake of unpaid leave from work, and a higher workload within the household for domestic and care responsibilities. These findings prompted BAU to set up a panel to make proper emergency and other responses to address this issue. The panel strove to encourage diverse inputs from women leaders in sectors ranging from business to diplomacy and media, to develop a coordinated response to the global challenge of promoting female roles in society and women's empowerment in light of the effects of the COVID-19 pandemic. Forward strategies were discussed on this panel, with a particular focus on three outstanding themes: labor and economic empowerment and work-life balance; socio-economic inclusion; and the inclusion of women in leadership positions. The panel aimed to contribute to a transformative agenda with a high degree of multilateral coordination promoted at national level through an integrated and shared strategy including all sections of civil society, institutions, the world of culture and work. It was attended interactively by students, academicians and civilians.

Moreover, the foundation established in my name and my wife's name, Semra Yücel, in 2019, aimed to take various steps to empower women and promote equality in education. Members of the foundation provided education to children and families in disadvantaged areas, in accordance with the socio-economic conditions of their regions. Together with seminars for parents, a number of activities were organized for children. For example, the 'Young Entrepreneurs Competition' strove to share the concept of entrepreneurship with high school children and encouraged them to consider how to start their own business. In addition, the foundation organized talks and panels to raise awareness of gender equality. One of the panels about violence against women received nationwide appeal, with many of the well-known women panelists having been exposed to violence themselves.

In September 2021, with the leadership of BAU, a workshop on the role of youth and women in agriculture and cooperatives was held in collaboration with The United Nations Agriculture and Food Organization (FAO) in Giresun in Turkey. It focused on introducing local agricultural products in the development of the country to contribute to sustainable development and address the central role of women and youth in agricultural cooperatives, smart agriculture practices, digital agriculture and sustainable food systems. With BAU's instructors and FAO's technical experts, a series of activities were organized to empower women and make cooperatives more effective. For two days, training focused on revealing the role of women in agriculture, supporting women's entrepreneurship and ensuring the access of local products to the market under the leadership of women.

BAU, migration and refugees

Finally, in terms of the contribution of BAU to responsible leadership, the influx of migrants, particularly those from Syria, has created serious social and economic problems in Turkey. Moreover, the changing situation in Africa and the Middle East in recent years has forced millions to migrate to Europe, crossing from the Turkish coast. These migration movements, which have accelerated throughout the world in recent years, require more detailed investigation. For this purpose, BAU Migration and Urban Studies Center (BAUMUS) was established in 2014 to deal with migration and urban studies with an interdisciplinary perspective. The main purpose of BAUMUS is to create realistic and applicable solutions for the management of these issues by blending theory and data obtained in the field. It has an active working tempo with its growing academic staff and students from various faculties such as social sciences and architecture.

BAUMUS has created a wide academic network and also collaborates with both government institutions and non-governmental organizations. The work of BAUMUS includes national and international projects, field studies, various publications, symposia and conferences. BAUMUS, which is also active on social media, has expanded its working area day by day with webinars, campaigns, documentaries and awareness studies. This underlines the importance of migration and its proper management – as well as other issues like refugee crisis and climate change. In August 2019, BAUMUS was one of the few institutions invited to the 'Activities of the Centers for Migration Studies and Research' session at the Temporary Protection Workshop organized by the UN Refugee Agency and the Turkish Republic Ministry of Interior General Directorate of Migration Management. Together with BAUMUS, BAU Documentary and the Social Project Research Center prepared a film titled *Lives Matter*, which deals with the asylum process of refugees and their transition to Europe. The film, which was dedicated to refugees who lost their lives, greatly expanded awareness of the subject.

Conclusion

A key aim of this chapter is to highlight the initiatives taken by BAU to fulfil its role as a responsible leader in the context of a wider rise in the sensitivities of higher education institutions globally to the need to advance the UN SDGs. Universities such as BAU are expected to contribute not only to their local communities but also to the global community. In this respect, they are expected to instill their graduates with a well-rounded education and global awareness. BAU has followed the UN SDG framework for examining local and global challenges while encouraging students to progress the SDGs both as student groups and in collaboration with other stakeholders. For universities to truly adopt the SDGs, the administration must make sustainability a priority in their operations and hold themselves accountable. In BAU, the establishment of several offices of sustainability was a great start, but sustainability had to enter the conscience of faculty members and students to make the most difference.

As an academic institution committed to every single SDG, BAU has helped students understand the roots of social issues and natural problems and motivated them to seek out sustainable practices. It has also focused on the causes of injustice, together with the employment of models of justice and humaneness. Such education has provided an opportunity to promote critical awareness, exchange ideas and develop projects and research to increase the value of education for sustainability by including the SDGs in the academic curriculum. Higher education plays a vital role in educating the current and next generation of leaders, driving the research agenda for both the public and private sectors and playing a critical role in shaping the direction of national economies.

BAU has used its capacity to generate, translate and disseminate knowledge relevant to achieving the SDGs to its full extent, working with policymakers and other stakeholders to identify and evaluate policy priorities and problems, assess policy options and implement solutions. Many of the SDGs were translated into measurable and country-specific targets by actively matching academic capital with public policy priorities and making knowledge and resources readily available to the government and community. With most of the initiatives, BAU engaged in collaborative knowledge generation alongside other stakeholders, leading to knowledge co-production or co-creation, to increase the societal impact of research through dynamic, locally adaptive partnerships, power sharing and ongoing conflict resolution. With the creation of many centers and interdisciplinary and collaborative initiatives, BAU has played a very important, responsible leadership role in seeking to achieve the SDGs by 2030. In these terms, it is an exemplar that other universities may helpfully follow in acting as responsible leaders moving forward.

References

Buono, A. F. (2014) 'Setting the stage: Facilitating global partnerships for a better world', *SAM Advanced Management Journal* 79(4): 4–7.

Cameron, K. (2011) 'Responsible leadership as virtuous leadership', *Journal of Business Ethics* 98: 25–35.
Crilly, D., Schneider, S. C. and Zollo, M. (2008) 'Psychological antecedents to socially responsible behavior', *European Management Review* 5: 175–90.
Globally Responsible Leadership Initiative (2005) *Globally Responsible Leadership: A Call for Engagement*, Brussels: GRLI. Available at: http://www.grli.org/images/stories/grli/documents/globally_ responsible_leadership_report.pdf
Kell, G. (2013) '12 years later: Reflections on the growth of the UN Global Compact', *Business and Society* 52(1): 31–52.
Maak, T. and Pless, N. M. (2006) *Responsible Leadership*, London: Routledge.
McCowan, T. (2019) *Higher Education for and beyond the Sustainable Development Goals*, London: Palgrave Macmillan.
Parkes, C. (2017) 'How social science is driving a sustainable future', *Elsevier Connect*. Available at: https://www.elsevier.com/connect/how-social-science-is-driving-a-sustainable-future-with-special-issue
Parkes, C., Buono, A. F. and Howaidy, G. (2017) 'The Principles of Responsible Management Education (PRME): The first decade – What has been achieved? The next decade – Responsible management education's challenge for the Sustainable Development Goals (SDGs)', *International Journal of Management Education* 15(2b): 61–65. Available at: https://doi.org/10.1016/j.ijme.2017.05.003
Pless, N. M. (2007) 'Understanding responsible leadership: Roles identity and motivational drivers', *Journal of Business Ethics* 74(4): 437–56.
Pless, N. M., Stahl, G. K. and Voegtlin, C. (2015) 'Responsible leadership: Addressing the social, environmental and business implications of leadership', presentation at the Colloquium of the European Group for Organizational Studies, Athens, July.
Quacquarelli Symonds (2020) *The Rise of Social Responsibility in Higher Education*, London: QS.
Saks, M. (2019) 'Universities and sustainable development', presentation at United Nations Institute for Training and Research Workshop on The Role of Educational Systems in Sustainable Development, Geneva, Switzerland.
Saks, M. (2020) 'Higher education and coronavirus in the UK', presentation at United Nations Institute for Training and Research Webinar on Coronavirus and Its Impact on the Higher Education Sector, Geneva, Switzerland.
Stahl, G. K., Sully de Luque, M. F. and Waldman, D. A. (2017) 'Responsible leadership in global organizations: Antecedents, consequences, interventions', *Academy of Management Proceedings*. Available at: https://doi.org/10.5465/ambpp.2014.11089symposium
Tronto, J. (1993) *Moral Boundaries: A Political Argument for an Ethic of Care*, New York: Routledge.
TÜSİAD, TÜRKONFED and United Nations Women (2020) 'The effects of the Covid-19 outbreak on women employees'. Available at: https://tusiad.org/tr/tum/item/10661-covid-19-salgininin-kadin-calisanlar-acisindan-etkileri-arastirmasi.
United Nations (2015) *Transforming Our World: The 2030 Agenda for Sustainable Development*, Geneva: UN.
United Nations Women (2020) 'The economic and social impact of Covid-19 on women and men: Rapid gender assessment of Covid-19 implications in Turkey', UN Women Ankara. Available at: https://www2.unwomen.org/-/media/field%20office%20eca/attachments/publications/2020/06/rapid%20gender%20assessment%20report%20turkey.pdf?la=en&vs=438

Voegtlin, C., Patzer, M. and Scherer, A. G. (2012) 'Responsible leadership in global business: A new approach to leadership and its multi-level outcomes', *Journal of Business Ethics* 105: 1–16.

Waldman, D. (2011) 'Moving forward with the concept of responsible leadership: Three caveats to guide theory and research', *Journal of Business Ethics* 98: 75–83.

Acknowledgments

Many thanks go to Professor Derin Atay, Dean of Faculty of Educational Sciences at BAU, for her assistance with the content, and to Professor Başak Akdemir, CEO of MLA College, London, for translating this chapter from the Turkish original.

Chapter 14

Professions and Responsible Leadership

Mike Saks

Introduction

This chapter deals with professions at a group level rather than an individual level, although both are interconnected if not synonymous. It also focuses particularly on their role in neo-liberal societies such as the United States (US) and the United Kingdom (UK). As such, their associations cover a wide range of groups from accountancy and architecture to law and medicine where they are most fully developed. Brint (1994) in fact classifies professions into five categories – business services, applied sciences, culture and communications, civic regulation and human services – which highlights their pervasive influence on society. This said, there are many debates about how to define professions – with definitions ranging from those based on lay definitions of those engaged in paid skilled work as opposed to unwaged amateurs, to more sophisticated theoretical conceptions of such groups (Saks, 2021).

However, although there is some variation across neo-liberal societies, professions are viewed primarily here in neo-Weberian terms as groups which have gained legally underpinned exclusionary social closure in the marketplace – in which privileged groups of insiders have obtained various kinds of monopolies related to their claimed expertise. Their monopolistic jurisdiction is typically based on registers of practitioners with codes of ethics that are legitimated through their higher education credentials. In this light, the chapter discusses the extent to which professions can and do exercise responsible leadership, while recognizing that professions have powers ranging from control over title to that of knowledge. Despite their common

DOI: 10.4324/9781003129189-19

title of 'profession', they are also hierarchically organized – in which medicine, for instance, sits above allied professions like physiotherapists and podiatrists in the pecking order (Nancarrow and Borthwick, 2021).

Notwithstanding the ongoing existence of state and provincial regulation in countries like Australia and Canada (Adams, 2017), their national and now increasingly international professional self-regulated nature has its origin historically in the US and UK in more localized medieval guilds. These were based on the production of goods and services by occupations from bakers and milliners to apothecaries and surgeons – initially through apprenticeships but increasingly with links to the developing university system (Krause, 1996). Thereafter there was a transition from 'status professionalism', where groups such as lawyers, physicians and the clergy gained the highest standing from a wealthy, leisured lifestyle, to 'occupational professionalism', where professions justified their position primarily with reference to an ideology of public responsibility (Elliott, 1972). In all this, the growth of federalized, country-specific professions was by no means unilinear. Contradictory images of them have also arisen in the modern context, as will now be outlined.

Debates about modern professions

The very different theoretical views on professions here give counterposed interpretations of the extent to which they engage in responsible leadership. Early writing by trait and functionalist writers up to the 1960s held that professions possessed unique bodies of expertise of great benefit to society. Historically, trait writers, who attempted to categorize the key features of professions, classically saw them as bulwarks of democracy – bastions of freedom, dignity and responsibility forming a stable element of society (Carr-Saunders and Wilson, 1933). Other elements of the varied lists of trait writers included features of a profession, like an altruistic orientation, in which professional self-interests were subordinated to those of clients and/or the public, esoteric knowledge and education and training (Millerson, 1964).

Functionalist contributors took a no less positive view but endeavored to link such selected features of a profession together to meet the needs of the social system. Here it was felt that there was a functional trade off in which professional groups were accorded high socio-economic rewards in exchange for employing knowledge of great significance to society in a non-exploitative manner (Barber, 1963). However, too frequently functionalists – like trait theorists – simply presumed, rather than empirically substantiated, that professional groups were virtuous and exercised responsible leadership. This benevolent view of professions was to be increasingly challenged from the 1960s onwards, following the early literary attack on doctors in the first half of the century by George Bernard Shaw (1946), who famously suggested that all professions were conspiracies against the laity.

In a rather different vein, free market economists like Milton Friedman (1962) questioned the integrity of professions in terms of responsible leadership based on their monopolistic obstruction of the play of market forces. Groups such as physicians in the US were thereby charged by Friedman to be engaged in, amongst other things, stifling innovation, limiting access opportunities to the profession by suitably qualified entrants, and expanding their own income in a self-interested drive to increase their market value against the public interest. Although interactionist contributors have stressed on a micro-level that the concept of a profession was simply a symbol used to legitimate the privileges of a profession and not a substantive indicator of how they actually operated (Roth, 1974), more macro-oriented criticisms followed.

These critics included Marxist writers, who from the 1970s onwards typically viewed professions negatively as agents of capitalist class control in neo-liberal countries. Thus Poulantzas (1975) saw groups such as social workers and teachers as engaging in the ideological inculcation and political repression of the working class alongside engineers, who were held to be actively involved in their management and supervision. Moreover, Esland (1980) viewed even apparently people-serving welfare professions like careers advisers and counsellors as helping to preserve capitalism by individualizing, rather than collectivizing, issues that actually have their roots in the dynamics of the capitalist system. Similar comments too have been made by Navarro (1986) on the role of medicine in preserving the *status quo* in capitalist societies by policing the boundaries of sickness.

Foucauldian contributors, on the other hand, have viewed the normalizing, legitimating and regulating activities of professions at a macro-level as part of the incorporation of populations into increasing state control through a process of governmentality. This is expressed in the work of Foucault (2001) through his challenge to the notions of scientific progress in the development of psychiatry, which is seen as suppressing spontaneity and freedom through a value-laden bourgeois frame of reference. It is also apparent in the Foucauldian criticisms of the assumed benefits of the professional gaze in areas from social work (Donzelot, 1979) to dentistry (Nettleton, 1992) because of the implicit subjection of populations to state control. Like the Marxist analysis, though, the approach is weakened by being somewhat self-fulfilling from an empirical, evidence-based viewpoint.

Neo-Weberians themselves have also not been averse to criticizing professions. In their case, it has primarily been because of claims about the application of self-interests by professional bodies to gain, maintain and extend the privileges restricted to a small group of insiders, to the exclusion of outsiders. In this vein, for example, Johnson (2016) argues that the emergence of auxiliary professions in medicine in the UK was based on doctors' own definition of their roles and led to an 'irrational' utilization of resources. He also claims that lawyers and other professions do not act in the public interest because of the irrelevance of their services to black and feminist groups. Unfortunately, as has sometimes been the case in neo-Weberian work – but is not intrinsic to the approach – he offers no evidence for either of these denigratory comments.

Most importantly, when rigorously applied, this model of self-regulatory professions fits the Anglo-American context well and potentially enables us to transcend the embedded positive and negative assumptions of the previously discussed perspectives. While there is some variation in the form of professionalism in neo-liberal societies as in some parts of continental Europe such groups are creatures of the state bureaucracy (Sciulli, 2005), it has value in depicting professions on a spectrum of types. And, although some neo-Weberians have overstepped the mark in making unsubstantiated adverse claims about the professions, the model itself does not prejudge by *fiat* whether they act responsibly in practice. Halliday (1987) illustrates this in his detailed analysis of the Chicago Bar Association in the US, in which he argues that its quest for monopoly was more oriented towards the public through responsible leadership than self-interested in nature.

The contemporary attack on professions

The relevance of this quick headline overview of the history of theories of professions over the past few decades is that it is reflected in contemporary real-world debates. More specifically, in tandem with the recent more critical theoretical approach to professions, there has been a heavy attack on professional groups over the past half century in the wake of the 1960s/70s counterculture that swept the modern world at this time. The counterculture challenged materialistic values and the all too easy technocratic solutions to problems advanced by professional groups – with an emphasis on greater public empowerment and self-help. Illich (1973) was one of the most vociferous critics of professional monopolies, seeing their implementation in practice as a form of imperialism, which has alienated the public – casting further doubt over the degree to which they are able to engage in responsible leadership.

This attack on professions has been fueled by a series of public scandals that have surrounded them – in which the relevant professional bodies are not seen to have acted swiftly enough to correct disastrous failings. These range from the widely-publicized deficiencies in the role of accountants in the 2008 financial crash to shocking child sex abuse by priests and the mass serial killing of patients by a doctor in general practice in the UK (Saks, 2021). Two further trends have exacerbated this critique of the professions – first, the subsequent emergence of a nihilistic 'war on expertise' such that everyone's opinion is of equal value, which has fueled the spread of fake news, and second, growing political support for the previously mentioned free-market approach favoring market determinations rather than professional intercession and judgment (Leicht, 2018).

The ensuing attack on professions in recent times has come from three main quarters, which can be set out as follows:

- The increasing backlash by clients against professional groups
- Growing encroachment by the state on the turf of professions
- Increasing influence of corporations over their operation.

In terms of clients, after ever-rising public pressure, users in neo-liberal societies have become more empowered through the 'extension of voice and choice'. This is manifested in more public participation in health and other areas through professional and interlinked committees, greater availability of information about professionals to enable more consumer choice in the market, and enhanced steps to increase the extent to which people can take responsibility for their own situation through self-help (Tonkens, 2016).

A second aspect of the endangerment to professions has been through the state, which while underwriting their exclusionary closure has also had a role in protecting the welfare of its citizens. Since the time of Margaret Thatcher as Prime Minister in the UK, this engagement has had the most dramatic effect of reducing the medical profession to a position of 'regulated self-regulation' – particularly through a raft of reforms, from the requirement for regular peer-reviewed re-accreditation to independent disciplinary oversight of fitness-to-practice regulation (Roche, 2018). As in other neo-liberal countries, this has been seen metaphorically as a shift from zoos, in which professions create their own self-regulatory cages, to a circus, in which a state ringmaster assumes greater control of the creatures therein (Saks, 2014).

As regards growing corporatization, the greatest effect has been in the US, where in one of the most privatized nations on earth the plethora of commercial health insurance companies have limited the income, status and power of the medical profession through much reduced standardized fee setting (Saks, 2015). In parallel with this, a growing number of large law firms in the US have been driven to place a greater proportion of legal work with staff other than lawyers to limit costs in the marketplace (Krause, 1996). However, for all these changes related to rising pressure from users as well as the growing role of the state and increasing corporatization – which have spread to many other neo-liberal countries beyond the UK and US – professions have not been completely emaciated.

Instead, professions have still been able to retain a good deal of autonomy – although they have often been disempowered in ever-more bureaucratized settings, in some countries more than others. Despite efforts by users of their services in the private and public sector, as well as governments and corporations, to rein back their powers, professional associations of groups like doctors, nurses, the police and teachers have been able to defend their independence and material privileges. Mechanisms like hybridization – based on skillful management of the conflict between organizational and professional logics (Noordegraaf, 2018) – have been important here in protecting the turf of professions. We are therefore far from the deprofessionalization of the workforce once vaunted by some writers, although in some cases there have been changes in the internal management and rewards associated with professional work (Saks, 2021).

The biggest challenge to the backlash against the professions has arguably been from ever-expanding large-scale international professional service firms like Ernst & Young, which go beyond the boundaries of professions within the nation state

(Saks and Muzio, 2018). As such, their increasingly commodified services – most heavily focused on accountancy and law – exist outside the professional regulatory framework of any one country, with the main bounding parameter to their operation being international law. In these terms, functioning more as enterprising business corporations than traditional professional bodies, such firms pose major regulatory dilemmas as they are not legally recognized or certified in any single country (Boussard, 2018). Wherein, though, lies the future of professions – should they survive and, if so, in what form?

The future of professions

There is much debate about the future of professions – not least in terms of the type of leadership that they can provide. Some critics argue that, in light of the foregoing theoretical discussion of recent critiques of professional groups, they should be disestablished as they have little to contribute to responsible leadership. One of the virtues of the neo-Weberian approach, though, is that while its proponents can use the bounding framework of exclusionary closure to make sustainable or otherwise claims that are critical of the role which professional self-interests have played in decision-making, it is also a platform that can highlight the real benefits of professions to society, of which there are many – especially if it is appreciated that professional self-interests and the public interest are often not in conflict but can coalesce (Saks, 1995).

The benefit of professions to society is underlined by considering what the world would look like without their protection. On the one hand, there may be some advantages in turning to the 'law of the jungle' as far as the market is concerned, from cheapening the costs of services to giving more direct consumer control of the professions involved. Against this, though, deregulation may lead to a dystopian world in which, amongst other things, clients must be extremely cautious in the absence of certified and tightly regulated expertise where *caveat emptor* ('let the buyer beware') would necessarily prevail. There would also be a lack of an intermediary buffer between users and the state potentially acting in the public good – in a system that may well have to be centered on more costly increased bureaucracy in a sea of unregulated competitors (Saks, 2015).

Still others claim that the role of professional groups in society should simply be shifted. Some of this discussion revolves around specific professions. For example, as I have noted elsewhere (Saks, 2021), it has been argued that the antiquated division between solicitors and barristers in a divided legal profession in the UK should be abolished to avoid needless duplication, with a one stop shop for clients. In parallel, it has been claimed that trading off the quality of legal services for lower prices has not been worthwhile in the US – as it has led to insecure working conditions for poorer paid attorneys to the prejudice of the marginalized groups who primarily use them. By the same token, accountants may need to be more public facing on both sides of the Atlantic, deploying more independent critical thinking in dealing with high-profile clients, if we are to avoid world economic crises like that precipitated by the collapse of Enron in the early 2000s (Brooks, 2018).

As regards more generic future changes in the role of professions, Noordegraaf (2020) observes that professions should no longer work protectively within well-defined jurisdictional silos given the increasing heterogeneity, fragmentation and interweaving of professional fields and other dependencies in the external world. Susskind and Susskind (2015) meanwhile argue that professional groups should give greater emphasis to using new technologies, whether through increasing use of CAD systems in architecture or video consultations by doctors in the wake of the experience of COVID-19. They claim artificial intelligence could both improve the work of professions and further empower clients. Leicht (2018) indeed believes that with increasing public access to information through the Internet professions should become risk managers or trusted interpreters of information instead of simply purveyors of expert knowledge.

Professions and responsible leadership

Leicht (2018) also rightly sees future professions as playing a further key role in the new age in bringing values to clients, policymakers and the public. While these values are not well defined, his position highlights the crucial part that professions could play in responsible leadership in future. The role of professions in responsible leadership can be seen as vital for their future for two reasons. The first is as a key part of the professional repertoire in the years ahead. The second is as a mainstream feature of professions in transitioning to a better future world, in which profession are central in working with clients, citizens, governments and corporate bodies in the private and public sector. In making this statement, though, it is initially necessary to consider in more detail what is meant by the much-contested notion of responsible leadership.

Defining responsible leadership

Our academic guides here are Kempster and Carroll (2016), who rightly comment that although there are many books on leadership the concept of responsible leadership has been rarely studied in depth. To date, it has largely been discussed in the context of corporate social responsibility (Hopkins, 2016), although there is a growing range of publications on subjects such as rules for global justice (Scholte, Fioramonti and Nhema, 2016) and ethical decision-making (Savur and Sandhu, 2017). According to Kempster, Maak and Parry (2020), though, what is at the heart of responsible leadership is not just the qualities, abilities and effectiveness of individual leaders but also the purpose, responsibilities and activities of leadership in realizing value for a broad span of stakeholders.

Even in these terms, as Kempster and Carroll (2016) note, the nature of responsible leadership in practice is not self-evident, as its provenance lies between romanticism and realism. As such, it raises further questions as to exactly who is responsible and why. They argue that there are ten key inter-related aspects of responsible leadership, which can be concisely outlined as follows:

- The attention and commitment given to social responsibility.
- Its applicability at all levels, from the individual to the team, organization and society.
- Its stakeholder perspective transcending a focus purely on shareholders.
- The reliance on our ethical duty to do no harm and do good.
- Its sensitivity to global intercultural issues, citizens and cosmopolitanism.
- The broad outcome orientation, going beyond humanitarianism alone.
- Its engagement with sense-making and sense-giving, pivoted on questions of purpose.
- Its focus on shared opinions, connecting stakeholders together.
- The central focus on the use of resources, including where and when disruption should occur.
- Its long-term stakeholder view, as opposed to a short-term shareholder perspective.

This helpful list for considering the future role of responsible leadership in the professions has been further developed by Kempster, Maak and Parry (2020), who argue that – even in corporate business – responsible leaders should look beyond seeking simply financial dividends and aim to produce a wider range of sustainable 'good dividends' for society. These ambitions may of course sometimes converge as indicated by the recent detailed longitudinal statistical study by Grant Thornton (2019) on the performance of FTSE 350 companies, which showed that companies with stronger corporate governance generate greater financial value for shareholders and lenders in terms of indicators like dividends and liquidity. In this sense, corporate citizenship both builds reputation and delivers to the bottom line.

It can therefore be said that it makes sense for private companies to incorporate societal purpose into their business model, which importantly brings into play more than just the financial kind. However, in applying the concept of responsible leadership to the professions in the private and public sectors, the definition outlined by Kempster and Carroll (2016) needs to be extended further in a global context in line with the focus of this book – as it is in the work of Kempster, Maak and Parry (2020). In the latter, it encompasses in a highly resonant way the United Nations (UN) (2015) Sustainable Development Goals (SDGs), which range from combatting poverty and inequality to enhancing the environment and reversing climate change.

Here it should be stressed that the significance of achieving such UN goals, which is a central theme of this book, has been accentuated by the COVID-19 pandemic. Whilst devastatingly disruptive on a global scale, this has sharpened the need to address through the professions not only health issues directly related to coronavirus but also faltering economies and financial markets, given the indirect implications of unemployment and declining income for public health. This harmonizes with the views of Greenwood, Hinings and Prakash (2017), who argue that the social purpose of professions has previously been neglected – and should be taken more fully into account, not least in the business environment. But how might the concept of responsible leadership be applied to the professions in this context?

The concept of responsible leadership applied to the professions

Fortunately, a wider collectivity ethos of professions has for long existed in modern neo-liberal societies such as the UK and the US. In this respect, a broader commitment to the public interest has typically been built into their modern codes of ethics (Saks, 1995). This, indeed, was a major component of the earlier trait and functionalist conceptions of the professions explored towards the beginning of this chapter (Millerson, 1964). Although this rather sugar-coated view of professional groups, reflecting the ideologies of professions themselves, was felt to be the dupe of those seeking to depict the actual practice of professions (Roth, 1974), it certainly highlights that the notion of responsible leadership is by no means alien to professions at the ideological level.

Marxist contributors considered in our earlier commentary on theories of professions would doubtless query whether professional groups by definition can be responsible leaders in class-divided capitalist societies, as would Foucauldians, given the perceived negative links of professions to the process of governmentality in modern states. However, for all their criticisms of the self-interests of professional associations in neo-liberal regimes from a neo-Weberian perspective, this approach sidesteps the frequent self-confirming ethos of the previous two critical perspectives – and entertains the possibility of an enlightened role for professions in which they put the public interest before their own interests whenever the two are in conflict (Saks, 2016b).

As such, the altruistic ideologies of professions at least have the potential to deliver more responsible leadership in future, however self-seekingly they may have operated in the past. One of the difficulties, though, of a number of the writers urging change in the positioning of professions going forward is that their analysis, like that of Susskind and Susskind (2015), centers on overly technical aspects of developing their role and does not always sufficiently address the importance of the type of value orientation possessed by such groups. Yet the desire for professions to lead responsibly should now be the driving force shaping their direction in the years ahead – the how, and not just the what, of their future behavior (Saks, 2021).

In emphasizing the significance of the professional altruism ideal, which – at an ideological level – lies at the core of the concept of responsible leadership, it should be recognized that its particular form can vary in different socio-political contexts. Thus, in the UK codes of ethics have tended to be more oriented towards the wider public as opposed to clients specifically, whereas the reverse is true in the US (Saks, 1995). It is this orientation to a broader range of stakeholders that should be particularly encouraged in the most responsible professional leadership. At the most generic level, this can be seen as being represented by advancing the UN SDGs (2015), against which so many organizations now benchmark themselves. In so doing, as a central part of the global agenda, professional bodies will also need to work in a more interdisciplinary and collaborative manner in future (Noordegraaf, 2020).

This underlines that professional groups are not simply islands. For some neo-Weberians, they are seen through a neo-institutionalist lens by extension as one institution vying with others in a wider economic, political and social landscape (Saks, 2016a). This helpfully enables us to view responsible leadership in the professions as involving an interface with other players in a broader politicized ecology – as exemplified by Cockerham (2018) in discussing the obstacles and opportunities available in the global governance of public health. Moreover, if professions are to act in a more responsible manner as leaders in future, not least in a COVID-19 world, it is essential that they are encouraged to do so not just through methods of recruitment and socialization over which they still have some independent control but also with support from the state, public and private corporations, and clients and citizens.

This is very important in neo-liberal societies, even though autonomous professions are largely absent in countries like China and Russia, where they are heavily subject to state control linked to their socialist pasts (Saks, 2015). While occupational groups like doctors have considerable university education and expertise in such societies, their income, status and power are much less as compared with the Anglo-American context. Similarly, as I have noted elsewhere (Saks, 2021), in the developing world – including in Brazil and India – where independent professions do exist, the discriminatory legacy of colonialism may still taint their operation and provide limits on the extent to which they can provide responsible leadership. This underlines that the continuance of professions is not inevitable and that the ongoing protection from their ethical codes cannot be assumed – even if it is very likely in Western countries.

Conclusion

Quite clearly, therefore, for all their contemporary critics, professions have a strong potential role as independent intermediary groups with high levels of expertise offering responsible leadership in the neo-liberal world going forward. Here, given my belief in the importance of metaphor in enhancing our understanding of the professions and other occupational groups (Liljegren and Saks, 2016), I would like to conclude this chapter by briefly recounting the tale of Aladdin from the Arabian Nights, as outlined in my last book on this subject (Saks, 2021). In this story, as is well known, the evil sorcerer tricks Aladdin's wife while he is away into giving him the lamp with the powerful genie on the pretext of swapping 'new lamps for old'. However, Aladdin is able to retrieve the original lamp and hence the genie that grants the owner's wishes.

The key message of the tale of Aladdin is that when we talk of exchanging the old lamps of the professions for glittering new ones going forward, it is vital that we do not surrender the most important lamp of all – the one that contains the magic genie. In this case, the lamp with the genie is metaphorically the one that houses the altruistic ideologies of professions so strongly embedded in the past. If we are to reshape the professions in the future from a technological and positional viewpoint, it is critical that such ideologies are retained and put more fully into practice to enable the world to successfully meet the challenges ahead through responsible leadership – in step with the public interest as now heavily embodied in the UN SDGs (Schuyler, Baugher and Jironet, 2016).

References

Adams, T. (2017) 'Self-regulating professions: Past, present, future', *Journal of Professions and Organization* 4(1): 70–87.

Barber, B. (1963) 'Some problems in the sociology of professions', *Daedalus* 92: 669–88.

Boussard, V. (2018) 'Professional closure regimes in the global age: The boundary work of professional services specializing in mergers and acquisitions', *Journal of Professions and Organization* 5(3): 279–96.

Brint, S. (1994) *In an Age of Experts: The Changing Role of Professionals in Politics and Public Life*, Princeton, NJ: Princeton University Press.

Brooks, R. (2018) *The Bean Counters: The Triumph of the Accountants and How They Broke Capitalism*, London: Atlantic Books.

Carr-Saunders, A. M. and Wilson, P. A. (1933) *The Professions*, Oxford: Clarendon Press.

Cockerham, G. B. (2018) *Global Governance and Public Health: Obstacles and Opportunities*, London: Rowman & Littlefield.

Donzelot, J. (1979) *The Policing of Families*, New York: Pantheon.

Elliott, P. (1972) *The Sociology of the Professions*, London: Macmillan.

Esland, G. (1980) 'Diagnosis and therapy', in Esland, G. and Salaman, G. (eds) *The Politics of Work and Occupations*, Milton Keynes: Open University Press.

Foucault, M. (2001) *Madness and Civilization: A History of Madness in the Age of Reason*, London: Routledge Classics.

Friedman, M. (1962) *Capitalism and Freedom*, Chicago, IL: University of Chicago Press.

Grant Thornton (2019) *Corporate Governance and Company Performance*, London: GT.

Greenwood, R., Hinings, C. R. and Prakash, R. (2017) '25 years of the Professional Partnership (P2) form: Time to foreground its social purpose and herald the P3?', *Journal of Professions and Organization* 4(2): 112–22.

Halliday, T. C. (1987) *Beyond Monopoly: Lawyers, State Crises, and Professional Empowerment*, Chicago, IL: University of Chicago Press.

Hopkins, M. (ed) (2016) *CSR and Sustainability: From the Margins to the Mainstream*, Sheffield: Greenleaf Publishing.

Illich, I. (1973) *Tools for Conviviality*, New York: Harper & Row.
Johnson, T. (2016) *Professions and Power*, London: Routledge Revivals.
Kempster, S. and Carroll, B. (2016) *Responsible Leadership: Realism and Romanticism*, London: Routledge.
Kempster, S., Maak, T. and Parry, K. (eds) (2020) *Good Dividends: Responsible Leadership of Business Purpose*, London: Routledge.
Krause, E. (1996) *The Death of the Guilds: Professions, States and the Advance of Capitalism, 1930 to the Present*, New Haven, CT: Yale University Press.
Leicht, K. T. (2018) 'Professions and entrepreneurship in international perspective', in Saks, M. and Muzio, D. (eds) *Professions and Professional Service Firms: Private and Public Sector Enterprises in the Global Economy*, London: Routledge.
Liljegren, A. and Saks, M. (2016) 'Introducing professions and metaphors', in Liljegren, A. and Saks, M. (eds) *Professions and Metaphors: Understanding Professions in Society*, London: Routledge.
Millerson, G. (1964) *The Qualifying Associations*, London: Routledge & Kegan Paul.
Nancarrow, S. and Borthwick, A. (2021) *The Allied Health Professions: A Sociological Perspective*, Bristol: Policy Press.
Navarro, V. (1986) *Crisis, Health and Medicine: A Social Critique*, London: Tavistock.
Nettleton, S. (1992) *Power, Pain and Dentistry*, Buckingham: Open University Press.
Noordegraaf, M. (2018) 'Enterprise, hybrid professionalism and the public sector', in Saks, M. and Muzio, D. (eds) *Professions and Professional Service Firms: Private and Public Sector Enterprises in the Global Economy*, London: Routledge.
Noordegraaf, M. (2020) 'Protective or connective professionalism? How connected professionals can (still) act as autonomous and authoritative experts', *Journal of Professions and Organization* 7(2): 205–23.
Poulantzas, N. (1975) *Political Power and Social Classes*, London: New Left Books.
Roche, W. (2018) 'Medical regulation for the public interest in the United Kingdom', in Chamberlain, J. M., Dent, M., Saks, M. (eds) *Professional Health Regulation in the Public Interest*, Bristol: Policy Press.
Roth, J. (1974) 'Professionalism: The sociologists' decoy', *Work and Occupations* 1: 6–23.
Saks, M. (1995) *Professions and the Public Interest*, London: Routledge.
Saks, M. (2014) 'The regulation of the English health professions: Zoos, circuses or safari parks?', *Journal of Professions and Organization* 1(1): 84–98.
Saks, M. (2015) *The Professions, State and the Market: Medicine in Britain, the United States and Russia*, London: Routledge.
Saks, M. (2016a) 'Professions and power: A review of theories of professions and power', in Dent, M., Bourgeault, I., Denis, J.-L. and Kuhlmann, E. (eds) *The Routledge Companion to the Professions and Professionalism*, London: Routledge.
Saks, M. (2016b) 'Review of theories of professions, organizations and society: Neo-Weberianism, neo-institutionalism and eclecticism', *Journal of Professions and Organization* 3(2): 170–87.
Saks, M. (2021) *Professions: A Key Idea for Business and Society*, London: Routledge.
Saks, M. and Muzio, D. (2018) 'Introduction: Professions and professional service firms', in Saks, M. and Muzio, D. (eds) *Professions and Professional Service Firms: Private and Public Sector Enterprises in the Global Economy*, London: Routledge.
Savur, S. and Sandhu, S. (eds) (2017) *Responsible Leadership and Ethical Decision-making*, Bingley: Emerald Publishing.
Scholte, J. A., Fioramonti, L. and Nhema, A. G. (eds) (2016) *New Rules for Global Justice: Structural Distribution in the Global Economy*, London: Rowan & Littlefield.

Schuyler, K. G., Baugher, J. E. and Jironet, K. (eds) (2016) *Creative Social Change: Leadership for a Healthy World*, Bingley: Emerald Publishing.
Sciulli, D. (2005) 'Continental sociology of professions today: Conceptual contributions', *Current Sociology* 53(6): 915–42.
Shaw, G. B. (1946) *The Doctor's Dilemma*, Harmondsworth: Penguin Books.
Susskind, R. and Susskind, D. (2015) *The Future of the Professions: How Technology Will Transform the Work of Human Experts*, Oxford: Oxford University Press.
Tonkens, E. (2016) 'Professions, service users and citizenship: Deliberation, choice and responsibility', in Dent, M., Bourgeault, I., Denis, J.-L. and Kuhlmann, E. (eds) *The Routledge Companion to the Professions and Professionalism*, London: Routledge.
United Nations (2015) *Transforming Our World: The 2030 Agenda for Sustainable Development*, Geneva: UN.

Part VI

Responsible Leadership, the Environment and Global Health

Chapter 15

COVID-19 and Global Human Health

Miwako Hosoda

Introduction: Global health as a global issue

We are now living in a global society in which in the last few decades national borders have been transcended and people and goods have moved more fluidly. With the spread of the Internet, knowledge and information are circulating around the world. The same is true for infectious diseases. The more globalization progresses, the more the risk of spreading infection increases, so health issues need to be resolved on a global scale. This has been reaffirmed by COVID-19, a pandemic that began at the end of 2019 and engulfed the world. Almost all countries have taken measures to prevent infection, and many have taken measures at their borders – often labelled as 'waterfront operations'. However, since we are all globally connected, no amount of border sealing will spare the entire world from the danger of infection unless strong healthcare systems are established everywhere on the planet. Dr Tedros, the Director-General of the World Health Organization (WHO), recognized that COVID-19 had reached pandemic status on 11 March 2020, the first time the WHO has declared a pandemic since the 2009 H1N1 influenza pandemic. As of June 2021, the COVID pandemic had infected 200 million people worldwide and claimed four million lives (Center for Systems Science and Engineering, 2021).

Once the vaccine was developed at the end of 2020, vaccination proceeded swiftly, and the cumulative number of vaccinations worldwide exceeded 2.9 billion by 28 June 2021. By country/region, the number of vaccinations in China, the United States (US) and India was particularly outstanding, with the three

DOI: 10.4324/9781003129189-21

countries accounting for about 60 percent of the total. The number of vaccinations is also rapidly increasing in European and Asian countries, even if less so in more impoverished African societies. In addition, an international framework called COVAX (COVID-19 Vaccine Global Access), which was launched in 2020 under the leadership of the WHO, has been established to jointly purchase and distribute COVID-19 vaccines to developing and other countries. Such a coordinated global response in healthcare is becoming necessary not only in the fight against infectious diseases but also in areas such as chronic diseases and mental disorders. It is also known that the protection of people's health is not limited to medical care but also involves the combined influence of factors such as poverty, gender, ecological balance and the environment. We need to leave a peaceful and livable environment for future generations. To achieve this, we need international solidarity, cooperation and exchange across multiple fields. This is the basic idea behind the United Nations (UN) (2015) Sustainable Development Goals (SDGs).

Problems in a COVID-19 situation

Since the spring of 2020, when the pandemic was declared, many countries have taken various measures to prevent the spread of COVID-19 infection, including urban lockdowns; orders to shut down stores, bars and restaurants; mask mandates that are supposed to inhibit the spread of the virus; school closures; and large-scale Polymerase Chain Reaction (PCR) testing. Chillingly, in spite of these measures, the outbreak has continued to spread, and many people have died. It is perhaps not surprising therefore that another feature of COVID-19 is the use of the metaphor of war. Here politicians around the world have said they are 'at war' with coronavirus, and the media has described intensive care units and emergency rooms as 'war zones' where doctors, nurses and other 'foot soldiers' are fighting a desperate battle. While it is not uncommon for responses to illness to be cloaked in metaphors of 'war' and 'struggle' (Liljegren and Saks, 2016; Niland, 2020), there are many problems with this. It underestimates the actual meaning of war and risks turning medical preventive measures into a means of social control by referring to it as 'wartime'. It is therefore important to stop embellishing illnesses with metaphors and see them only as illnesses anyone can get (Hosoda, 2020).

The COVID-19 outbreak revealed a variety of other issues including those related to such areas as medical resources, bioethics, health disparities and school closures, as well as urban lockdowns and reduced economic activity. In particular, people who are vulnerable on a daily basis, such as those with disabilities and illnesses, low-income groups, racial and ethnic minorities, immigrants and foreign workers, women and girls, sexual minorities, and essential workers became more difficult to reach due to the spread of COVID-19 and the response to it. Moreover, the initial spread of COVID in China made the situation more difficult. Discrimination against Asians, who were the first to be infected, were reported in many places in North and South America and Europe. It is now becoming a common understanding that pandemics are global in nature but also global in resolution. In this chapter, the problems that have arisen in health resources, education, socio-economic status, and discrimination and stigma are summarized in more detail. Following this, by overviewing the efforts that are needed by the international community, governments, academia and civil society, the qualities of a responsible leader are discussed.

Health resources

COVID-19 causes severe respiratory distress, so ventilators and extracorporeal membrane oxygenation (ECMO) are used as symptomatic treatment. However, the number of such medical devices was not able to keep up with the number of patients who needed these devices. This is why triage, a concept associated with disaster medicine, was adopted. The triage determines who can use a ventilator and who can use ECMO according to the severity of the physical and other conditions presented. It can be said that in a COVID world healthcare professionals were forced to shift from medical care in peacetime, when they do their best for each patient, to emergency medical care that saves as many lives as possible.

In this context, some places created guidelines for the placement of such ventilators in advance. For example, by May 2020 in the US, 26 states had developed guidelines for ventilator placement (Piscitello et al., 2020). In the *Guidelines for the Use of Ventilators in the Event of a Global Epidemic of Infectious Diseases* published by the New York State Department of Health (2015), criteria such as the color code index are said to be determined by 'current severity' alone, and "if the patient does not recover after 48 hours of treatment, the ventilator may be removed". Even so, medical practitioners were not able to provide the necessary care in severe cases of COVID-19 without feeling guilt and embarrassment.

In many countries, medical personnel have been forced to make decisions about the allocation of ventilators in the event of an infection explosion, which has caused great psychological damage. In addition, ventilator users and related victims of COVID-19 also became very anxious about triage because they found the atmosphere of selecting 'lives worth living' eugenic in nature. This raises matters of bioethics in the selection process. It is necessary for health personnel to prepare for emergencies in normal times and to consistently be aware of what criteria to employ in case of a shortage of medical care, both at the management and field level respectively. This limitation of health resources is one of a number of issues created by the pandemic.

Education

As COVID-19 spread worldwide, social distancing was shown to be an important preventive measure. Therefore, many countries closed their schools to prevent the spread of the infection, which presented a further problem. According to the United Nations Educational, Scientific and Cultural Organization (UNESCO) (2022), there are more than 180 countries and regions that closed schools throughout the country. Over one and a half billion people, or more than 91.3 percent of the world's pupils and students, were unable to attend school due to COVID closures. In places like refugee camps, international educational non-governmental organizations were forced to retreat. Only food and health safety were considered as top priorities. UNESCO Director-General Audre Azoulay (2020) said, "The previously unthinkable has become a reality: a world without schools."

In order to cope with the school closure, a number of schools started to offer online classes, while many others moved to self-study mode. This was due to the difference between schools where the teachers were actively involved in online classes and those where they were not. At the same time, there was a difference in whether or not the students had access to online classes at home. There was also a concern here that the education gap would widen further. 'Educational disparity' does not mean that there are children who can do well and children who cannot. It refers to the problem that the results of education, such as future occupation and income, are strongly correlated with the initial conditions that are beyond the control of the individual, such as socio-economic class and region of origin, and gender (Cole, 2018). This is another aspect of the problems to be solved.

Even in countries that appear to be equal on the surface, the level of education may differ depending on where people live and factors such as cultural background. In some areas, primary and secondary education is based on the premise that students will go on to university, while in other areas it is not. For example, it has been pointed out in Japan that teachers in urban and rural areas have different expectations and pressures from parents and that there is a difference in the enthusiasm of teachers for education (Hosoda, 2021). In addition to these educational disparities, some schools have had difficulty conducting online classes because not all children could participate as they did not have their own computers or private rooms, so educational disparities widened in the period of school closure related to COVID-19. The digitization of education will be one major future trend, but the most important issue will be to 'leave no one behind'. It is therefore necessary in terms of a wider definition of health to continue to search for ways to make learning more accessible to children around the world.

Socio-economic status

Many public health studies have shown that populations with lower socio-economic status are less healthy. In the US, for example, it has been shown that, in general, the higher the income, the longer the life expectancy when comparing high-income and low-income populations (World Economic Forum, 2015). In addition, notwithstanding Medicaid, a lower percentage of low-income people have health insurance. And even if they do have insurance, the plans have low premiums, so the co-payments for medical visits are high, and for this reason many people do not seek medical attention even when they are not feeling well – at a great potential cost to their relative health status (Saks, 2015).

COVID-19 highlights these health disparities, since the risk of contracting the virus varies by race and ethnicity, occupation, and access to healthcare. Thus, in the US, Hispanics are about twice as likely to be infected with COVID-19 as Whites. The death rate from COVID-19 among Black people and Hispanics is twice that of Whites. When it comes to native Americans, the mortality rate is 2.4 times higher (Centers for Disease Control and Prevention, 2021). In fact, low-income people who work in low-wage service and manual labor jobs, such as essential workers and infrastructure workers, are often most affected. This is because they have difficulty with social distancing, have more contact with other people, find teleworking problematic, and travel by public transportation. They also tend to live in multigenerational households, which means that if one person is infected it can readily spread within the family. Although anyone can be infected, the spread of COVID and the circumstances of those infected are extremely unequal (Owen, Carmona and Pomeroy, 2020).

Outside of the US, disparities in access to healthcare, as well as disparities in social conditions such as working environment and income, have led to significant health differences in COVID-19 settings. As long as these health disparities exist, it will remain difficult to control infectious diseases – not least because societies are connected. Some countries tried to combat COVID by sending a lump sum to all citizens, regardless of whether they are infected or not. This is a measure reminiscent of putting in place a basic income scheme for all citizens (Standing, 2017), and it is worth seriously considering this as a way of providing some form of financial security to facilitate control of a pandemic. In terms of the problems associated with COVID-19, it is also important to focus on socio-psychological considerations such as stigma and mental health issues such as loneliness and suicide – and it is to this we now turn.

Discrimination and stigma

Erving Goffman (1963) referred to stigma as a social mechanism that divides people into two groups: the normal and the downtrodden. Stigma is deeply rooted in people's attitudes and values throughout society, culture and history, and it affects behavior in various aspects of daily life. Stigma in the context of health is the socially demeaning labelling of people with certain diseases, treating them differently from normal people and discriminating against them by forcing them to undergo experiences that undermine their social status. This stigma extends not only to people with the disease but also to healthcare providers, caregivers, family, friends and the community, affecting them in similar ways. Therefore, people around them may try to cut off relations with those who have the disease. Thus, the infected person and their family is at risk of becoming isolated and lonely.

In general, discriminatory acts that occur during pandemics tend to target 'outsiders', such as foreigners and ethnic and other minorities. However, during COVID-19, the target of discrimination was Asians and people of Asian descent, as the infection was initially reported from Wuhan in China. Discrimination included verbal attacks in public places and harassment on social media, as well as instances of violence. It is said that the prejudice against Asians that existed in the past was heightened by COVID-19. There have been responses to this by civil society groups and researchers, and some countries have strengthened their laws to prevent hate crimes. Italian physicist Paolo Giordano (2020: 13) thus wrote during the COVID pandemic: "Infectious diseases are diseases that invade our various relationships", reflecting on an episode where a Japanese mother and her daughter were yelled at by a couple of men in a supermarket in Rome with the ringing condemnation that everything is your fault, now go back to your country.

There is also discrimination against infected people. In Japan, infected people, those in close contact with infected people, health personnel, people in accommodation facilities where the patients stayed, and their families, were sometimes subjected to stigma. In some cases, the infected people had to leave their jobs or move out of the community because of the accusations or unkind words, while the children of healthcare workers were bullied at school or refused care at day care centers. The government took the situation very seriously and set up a working group on prejudice, discrimination and privacy in the Subcommittee on Countermeasures against COVID-19, and prefectural governments and human rights organizations conducted educational activities to prevent prejudice, discrimination and bullying.

Mental health problems such as loneliness caused by COVID-19 and resulting depression and suicide have also been pointed out to be occurring worldwide (Centers for Disease Control and Prevention, 2020, Shrestha et al., 2021). In order to solve the problems of fear of others, anxiety and loneliness that are behind the stigma and mental health problems, we need to deal with uncertainty, social capital and social solidarity. Art can be one of the mechanisms. It is said that art therapists see how creativity can help relieve people's stress and process the heaviness of thought that they are carrying. Under COVID-19 situations, where people might have felt unusually lonely and isolated, it was thought they could develop their inner artist and find peace by creating some kind of art (Cleveland Clinic, 2020).

The WHO (2020a; 2020b; 2020c) has also repeatedly pointed out that stigma weakens social cohesion and promotes greater social isolation for those who are targeted. Throughout the history of infectious diseases and stigma, people have repeatedly been forced to hide their diseases for fear of discrimination, leading to further spread of the disease. Reducing stigma not only protects the sick from discrimination and isolation but also contributes greatly to stopping the spread of infectious diseases. According to the UN Secretary-General António Guterres, stigma and discrimination arise from the instability and fear caused by pandemics, and certain groups are targeted, exacerbating human rights issues (United Nations COVID-19 Response, 2020). Discriminatory incidents have been reported by international organizations, mass media and social media, confirming that it is a global phenomenon. In this respect, large-scale data analysis has revealed that social networking sites such as Twitter, Instagram, YouTube, Reddit and Gab had a significant impact on the spread of misinformation about COVID-19. Some of these have been called 'infodemics', which promote discrimination (Clinelli et al., 2020).

We therefore need to take action against media that promote stigma, threaten health and divide people (World Health Organization, 2020b). We also need to pay close attention to the language used in the media about COVID-19 itself and COVID patients. It is recommended by the WHO (2020b) to say 'people recovering from COVID-19' or 'people who have died from COVID-19' rather than using pejorative phrases. It was also suggested that mutant strains be given alphabetical names, such as Alpha to Omega, instead of being referred to by country or region – as in the cases of the so-called 'Indian variant' and 'South African variant'.

International collaboration: A key to solving the COVID-19 problems

As described above, COVID-19 not only causes physical damage but is also a social disease that divides our society and promotes inequality and prejudice. In response, we can improve the situation through our own perceptions and actions. It is important for people to have a sense of solidarity and not a sense of division that separates communities. With the vaccine developed at the end of 2020, more cooperation was needed. The previously mentioned COVAX organization promoted by the WHO and the Gavi Vaccine Alliance and Coalition for Epidemic Preparedness and Innovation (CEPI), in which more than 180 countries participated, can be said to be one good example of positive international collaboration.

As of June 2021, a total of 2.3 billion doses of vaccine had been secured, and at the G7 Summit an agreement was reached to provide one billion doses of vaccine to developing countries. As we saw at the beginning of this chapter, unless COVID-19 is controlled in all countries, the spread of the disease cannot be prevented. As Dr Seth Berkley, Chief Executive of the Gavi Vaccine Alliance said: "If everyone doesn't win, no one wins" (World Health Organization, 2021a). He went on to note: "This is an important moment of global solidarity and a critical milestone in ensuring that those most at risk everywhere are protected . . . We look forward to working with countries to ensure that the pledged doses are administered rapidly toward the goal of ending the acute phase of the pandemic." Dr Richard Hatchett, Chief Executive of CEPI, added: "This is a historic moment, bringing together the leaders of the wealthiest countries to ensure that all regions of the world have access to life-saving vaccines" (United Nations Children's Fund, 2021).

The WHO Director-General, Dr Tedros, noted early in the pandemic that we need to realize that health is an investment in the future. Countries invest heavily in protecting their people from terrorist attacks but not against the attack of a virus, which could be far more deadly, and far more economically and socially damaging. A pandemic can bring economies and nations to their knees. This is why health security cannot be a matter for ministries of health alone. These words have been underlined through the international coordination that COVAX has promoted (World Health Organization, 2021b). Equitable global access to vaccines, especially to protect vulnerable populations and healthcare workers and others most at risk, is the only way to reduce the public health and economic impact of a pandemic.

COVID-19 and the Sustainable Development Goals

The UN (2015) SDGs, with their integrated approach, can be a countermeasure to COVID-19. The SDGs, adopted by all member states, set out common goals of what it should look like for people and the planet to be peaceful and prosperous in the present and into the future. At the center of this agenda, the 17 SDGs cover a range of areas from the eradication of poverty and hunger and the improvement of health and education to gender equality and environmental protection. The UN also indicates that in order to achieve one goal, all other goals must be achieved. For example, to eliminate poverty and other deprivations, we need to improve health and education, reduce inequality and promote economic growth while at the same time addressing climate change and conserving oceans and forests. And the SDGs can be achieved by all countries, developed and developing alike, acting in global partnership.

The UN Department of Economic and Social Affairs (2020) has shown that countries can recover from the human and economic devastation caused by COVID-19 by accelerating their efforts to achieve a wider range of SDGs. The SDGs as a whole encourage people to take action to make this world a better place. This is certainly true for COVID-19. Since it is a response to an infectious disease, the SDG for healthcare and wellbeing for all is central, but it is not enough. Other SDGs also need to come into play. For example, we need to fulfill the SDG giving access to clean water to wash our hands and keep them clean. In addition, to reduce exposure to the virus, it is important to avoid congestion and to maintain sufficient social distance from the city and living environment in line with the SDG to establish sustainable cities and communities. Moreover, while many lives are still being lost and livelihoods are threatened by the spread of COVID, the world's Gross Domestic Product is declining (Office for National Statistics, 2021). We are suffering from the largest contraction of economic activity since the Great Depression, which is much more severe than the 2008 global financial crisis. As a result, many people may lose their livelihoods, fall into poverty and be unable to receive societal protection. Therefore, it is necessary to achieve the SDG of achieving decent work and economic growth as well in combatting the ills of COVID-19.

In addition to the aforementioned interlinked SDGs, the World Food Program (2020) reported that COVID-19 was expected to increase the number of children in the world who face acute malnutrition, with the numbers facing food insecurity expected to almost double to 265 million compared to 2019. This links to the SDG on achieving zero hunger. In a situation where schools are closed and people are forced to work from home, ensuring access to the Internet means that the SDGs on providing quality education for all and building a foundation for industry and technology are extremely relevant. Such achievements will enable a more sustainable and equitable world where no one is left behind and where the multi-faceted threats posed by a pandemic are diminished. By engaging in cross-sectoral dialogue, people from different areas like government, research, the healthcare industry, civil society and the international community can find integrated and sustainable ways to solve current and future health crises. Engaging in this work now is our responsibility to the future.

Conclusion: Responsible leadership in relation to COVID-19

In this chapter, I have written about how COVID-19 is not only a contagious respiratory disease but also poses various complex problems to the community at large. I have also discussed the need for global collaboration to resolve these. With responsible leadership, the resolution will take more than the efforts of healthcare and medical professionals; it will require diverse actors to seek political, economic and infrastructural change. Responsible global health leaders will therefore be required to take an integrated perspective in their search for solutions. This integrated approach importantly overlaps with the framework of the UN SDGs.

The WHO constitution defines health as a state of complete physical, mental and social wellbeing and not merely the absence of disease or infirmity. A well-balanced diet, good sleep and moderate exercise are all important for good health, but at the same time, not being poor, not being unemployed, having a place to live, and having good relationships with others are also very important for good health. People can be healthy if their body and mind are in a healthy state and if they lead a stable social life with good human relationships. The fact that all social activities are connected to people's health, or public health, is captured in the term 'the social determinants of health' (Kawachi and Kennedy, 2001) on which responsible leadership needs to focus.

This point about responsible leadership is reinforced by the fact that it has become clear that there are differences in health – like enhanced life expectancy and the absence of chronic diseases – which depend on socio-economic status, including factors such as income, education, race/ethnicity, place of residence and type of work. Reducing such health disparities is the goal of public health – everyone will be healthier if the natural environment is protected, peace is maintained, economic activities are stable, employment and educational opportunities are available, medical care is improved, and good human relations are maintained throughout the world. National and global leaders therefore have this responsibility to increase the health of all people living on this planet.

In the context of COVID-19, we have seen that the poor, women and racial minorities are more affected, the vulnerable are increasingly challenged, and there is a great need here too for joined-up solutions based on the SDGs. In response to COVID, multilateral dialogue and coordination are important, and international cooperation such as COVAX, which involves countries from all over the world, has pleasingly been put into practice. It may be that through the response to COVID-19 the world is now able to take a more responsible and integrated approach to achieving the SDGs. However, in the event of a pandemic, donor countries' public support for assistance in development may weaken due to concerns about personal health and the national economy, which may translate into an associated decline in trust in government (Schneider et al., 2021). Attention should therefore be paid to making the need for international collaboration in donor countries understood by the public, parallel to domestic issues, including the most vulnerable stakeholders and care for others.

COVID-19 is not the only health issue in the world. Other important health issues include infectious diseases such as Ebola and West Nile fever, chronic diseases, and dementia. As UN Secretary-General António Guterres (2021) recently said: "COVID-19 cannot be seen in isolation from the fundamental problems with our health systems: inequality, underfunding; complacency, neglect. With the right primary health care systems in place, we will recover more quickly from this pandemic, and prevent the next before it takes hold." In order to grasp that COVID-19 is a complex problem, to think of solutions, and to implement them, it is necessary for responsible leaders to have a dialogue with all stakeholders, including users of services, patient groups, peer supporters, family members, medical professionals, caregivers, media, researchers, companies, policymakers, and governments in local, national and global communities.

References

Azoulay, A. (2020) 'Global Education Coalition: Message from Audrey Azoulay'. Available at: https://bangkok.unesco.org/content/global-education-coalition-message-audrey-azoulay-unesco-director-general

Center for Systems Science and Engineering (2021) *COVID-19 Dashboard*, Johns Hopkins University MD. Available at: https://coronavirus.jhu.edu/map.html

Centers for Disease Control and Prevention (2020) 'Mental Health, Substance Use, and Suicidal Ideation During the COVID-19 Pandemic – United States, June 24–30'. Available at: https://www.cdc.gov/mmwr/volumes/69/wr/mm6932a1.htm

Centers for Disease Control and Prevention (2021) 'Risk for COVID-19 Infection, Hospitalization, and Death by Race/Ethnicity'. Available at: https://www.cdc.gov/coronavirus/2019-ncov/covid-data/investigations-discovery/hospitalization-death-by-race-ethnicity.html

Cleveland Clinic (2020) 'How art can help you cope with the pandemic', *Health Essentials*. Available at: https://health.clevelandclinic.org/how-art-can-help-you-cope-with-the-pandemic/

Clinelli, M. et al. (2020) 'The COVID-19 social media infodemic', *Scientific Reports* 10. Available at: https://doi.org/10.1038/s41598-020-73510-5

Cole, M. (ed) (2018) *Education, Equality and Human Rights*, London: Routledge.

Giordano, P. (2020) *Nel Contagio*, Tulin: Einaudi.

Goffman, E. (1963) *Stigma: Notes on the Management of Spoiled Identity*, Englewood Cliffs, NJ: Prentice-Hall.

Guterres, A. (2021) 'Step up global plan for COVID-19 vaccines, UN chief says in message to World Health Assembly'. Available at: https://news.un.org/en/story/2021/05/1092592

Hosoda, M. (2020) 'COVID-19 and the metaphors of war', *Budhi* 24(2): 131–40.

Hosoda, M. (2021) 'Pandemic and schooling: Emerging educational inequality in Japan', in Ahmed, I. (ed) *COVID-19: The Otherside of Living through the Pandemic*, Dhaka: Pathak Shamabesh Book.

Kawachi, I. and Kennedy, B. (2001) *The Health of Nations: Why Inequality is Harmful to Your Health*, New York: New Press.

Ledford, H. (2019) 'Millions of black people affected by racial bias in health-care algorithms', *Nature* 574: 608–9.

Liljegren, A. and Saks, M. (eds) (2016) *Professions and Metaphors: Understanding Professions in Society*, London: Routledge.

New York State Department of Health (2015) *Guidelines for the Use of Ventilators in the Event of a Global Epidemic of Infectious Diseases*, New York State Task Force on Life and the Law, November. Available at: https://www.health.ny.gov/regulations/task_force/reports_publications/docs/ventilator_guideline.pdf

Niland, N. (2020) 'An unhealthy combination: War, Covid-19 and the politics of metaphor', *Focus*, 14 July.

Office for National Statistics (2021) 'International comparisons of GDP during the coronavirus (Covid-19) pandemic', London: ONS.

Owen, W. F. Jr., Carmona, R. and Pomeroy, C. (2020) 'Failing another national stress test on health disparities', *Journal of the American Medical Association* 323(19): 1905–6.

Piscitello, G., Esha, M., Kapania, E. and Miller, W. D. (2020) 'Variation in ventilator allocation guidelines by US state during the coronavirus disease 2019 pandemic: A systematic review', *Journal of the American Medical Association, Network Open* 3(6): e2012606.

Saks, M. (2015) *The Professions, State and the Market: Medicine in Britain, the United States and Russia*, London: Routledge.

Schneider, S., Eger, J., Bruder, M., Fausta, J. and Wieler, L. H. (2021) 'Does the COVID-19 pandemic threaten global solidarity? Evidence from Germany', *World Development* 140, April. Available at: https://www.sciencedirect.com/science/article/pii/S0305750X20304848

Shrestha, R., Siwakoti, S., Singh, S. and Shrestha, A. P. (2021) 'Impact of the COVID-19 pandemic on suicide and self-harm among patients presenting to the emergency department of a teaching hospital in Nepal', *PLOS ONE*, 30 April.

Standing, G. (2017) *Basic Income and How We Can Make it Happen*, London: Penguin Books.

Tedros, G. (2020) 'Urgent health challenges for the next decade'. Available at: https://www.who.int/news-room/photo-story/photo-story-detail/urgent-health-challenges-for-the-next-decade

United Nations (2015) *Transforming Our World: The 2030 Agenda for Sustainable Development*, Geneva: UN.

United Nations Children's Fund (2021) 'COVAX Joint Statement: Call to action to equip COVAX to deliver 2 billion doses in 2021'. Available at: https://www.unicef.org/press-releases/covax-joint-statement-call-action-equip-covax-deliver-2-billion-doses-2021–0

United Nations COVID-19 Response (2020) 'COVID-19: UN counters pandemic-related hate and xenophobia'. Available at: https://www.un.org/en/coronavirus/covid-19-un-counters-pandemic-related-hate-and-xenophobia

United Nations Department of Economic and Social Affairs (2020) 'SDGs still offer best option to reduce worst impacts of COVID-19 and to recover better'. Available at: https://www.un.org/en/desa/sdgs-still-offer-best-option-reduce-worst-impacts-covid-19-and-recover-better

United Nations Educational, Scientific and Cultural Organization (2022) 'COVID-19 school health and safety protocols: Good practices and lessons learnt to respond to Omicron', Paris: UNESCO.

World Economic Forum (2015) 'How income affects life expectancy', Geneva: WEF.

World Food Program (2020) 'Coronavirus threatens global surge in malnutrition, jeopardizing future of an extra 10 million children'. Available at: https://www.wfp.org/news/coronavirus-threatens-global-surge-malnutrition-jeopardizing-future-extra-10-mil lion-children

World Health Organization (2020a) 'A guide to preventing and addressing social stigma'. Available at: https://www.who.int/docs/default-source/coronaviruse/covid19-stigma-guide.pdf

World Health Organization (2020b) 'Infodemic management: Promoting healthy behaviors in the time of COVID-19 and mitigating harm from misinformation and disinformation'. Available at: https://www.who.int/news-room/events/detail/2020/09/23/default-calendar/infodemic-management-promoting-healthy-behaviors-in-the-time-of-covid-19-and-mitigating-harm-from-misinformation-and-disinformation

World Health Organization (2020c) 'Social stigma associated with COVID-19'. Available at: https://www.who.int/docs/default-source/coronaviruse/covid19-stigma-guide.pdf

World Health Organization (2021a) 'COVAX: Working for global equitable access to COVID-19 vaccines'. Available at: https://www.who.int/initiatives/act-accelerator/covax

World Health Organization (2021b) 'G7 announces pledges of 870 million COVID-19 vaccine doses, of which at least half to be delivered by the end of 2021'. Available at: https://www.who.int/news/item/13-06-2021-g7-announces-pledges-of-870-million-covid-19-vaccine-doses-of-which-at-least-half-to-be-delivered-by-the-end-of-2021

Chapter 16

Responsible Leadership, the Climate Crisis and Preserving Planetary Health

David Zakus

Introduction

Despite many good intentions and commitments from across most sectors of society, Earth will continue to experience increasing global atmospheric warming, leading to more and more serious global climatic and weather events with increasing human suffering. Given our science, technology and knowledge, we have the tools to deal with this, but there are doubts as to whether we have the will and leadership. Are we content to keep assaulting nature and aggravating an already very serious situation?

Since the beginning of recorded human history more than six thousand years ago, we have been living off the largesse of a planet that is home to a great spectacle of life within a narrow range of physical parameters, mainly of temperature and weather events (Xu et al., 2020). This range is now being challenged, as are our lives and future. Our existence is being greatly and negatively impacted by an ever-increasing population and the scientific, technological and industrial revolutions that have so greatly benefited us. In the twenty-first century, we are products of technologies associated with communications, health, work, agriculture, manufacturing,

DOI: 10.4324/9781003129189-22

transportation and daily healthy living. The impacts are both caused and augmented by our profligate use of mined and processed carbon-based fuels on a global scale.

Initially, up to two million years ago, wood was used to make fire as a first acquired external energy source. This was added to very many years later by the discovery of natural materials containing much higher concentrations of energy. Oil from olives and seeds was first employed some three thousand years ago and then obtained from animals like whales, before coal came on the scene in early China and the Roman Empire. Subsequently, around one hundred and fifty years ago, we began to use refined oil/petroleum-based products like gasoline, kerosine and diesel. When they are burned, they release water vapor, carbon dioxide, methane, nitrous oxide and fluorinated gases, which collectively (along with ozone) are called greenhouse gases (GHGs). These can absorb radiation and emit heat. Any substantial increase of them in the atmosphere causes a heat imbalance directly affecting Earth's life-sustaining features. A century ago, this imbalance started happening in profound and measurable ways.

Industrialized countries – especially the United States (US), China, India and Europe – are responsible for most of the increase in carbon dioxide and other GHG emissions. As the atmosphere is flooded with large amounts of GHGs – now about 50 billion tons annually – temperatures and other related weather phenomena increase, altering the blanket that has for long protected all life on Earth. We are now heating the world to a degree not seen since millions of years ago (Harvey, 2020). The damage began in earnest fifty years ago and has been accentuated in the last twenty years. According to the National Aeronautics and Space Administration (NASA) (2021), the planet's average surface temperature has risen by about 1.18 degrees Celsius since the late nineteenth century, and according to the Intergovernmental Panel on Climate Change (2021), it is projected to increase to 2 degrees Celsius by the mid- twenty-first century and 3 degrees Celsius by the end.

Earth, home to over 7.5 billion humans, is now experiencing uncharacteristic and dangerous heating, winds, floods, droughts, wildfires, ice melt, ocean rising, warming and acidification, forest anomalies and air pollution. As this chapter makes clear, to address all these risks, responsible leaders in all spheres of life must step up and tackle the many challenges to our very existence.

The pressing need for change

Significant societal changes and progressive thinking are now needed to avoid greater climate, environmental and health tragedies in future in all regions of the world. GHGs in excess cause climate change – big shifts in global weather patterns over a long period of time. Building on decades of experience and scientific knowledge, we have now reached the stage of climate crisis. All humankind and ecosystems on Earth are potentially affected – hence the recent record-breaking temperatures and catastrophic wildfires in Western Canada, the US, Greece, Turkey, Algeria, the

Middle East, Russia and Australia. Against this, amongst other signs, there has been unheard of flooding in Western European countries, China, West Africa, South Sudan and the US.

Moreover, the International Union for Conservation of Nature (2021) notes that our oceans are heating up and, along with polar and glacial ice-melt, expanding their mass. This leads to rising sea levels and extraordinary wave surges affecting many countries like Bangladesh and small island states such as Barbados and the Maldives, as well as coastal cities from Miami and Manila to Singapore and Venice, the latter of which has for long been sinking (Bhateja, 2021). Ocean warming is also causing widespread coral destruction in the Caribbean, Australia, Southeast Asia and Oceana. Glaciers in Greenland, Iceland, Switzerland, North America and Antarctica are melting away, and sea ice cover is rapidly disappearing in the Arctic. Add to this the warming and clear cutting of Amazonian rainforests and Canada's giant boreal forest, resulting in big parts of them now moving from being carbon sinks to becoming net contributors of carbon dioxide to the atmosphere. In short, we already have a climate catastrophe related to the excessive use of carbon-based fossil fuels.

The scientific consensus of this human-induced change is almost absolute as it is amongst most senior political and institutional leaders worldwide. This includes not just governments at national and sub-state levels but also multilateral agencies like the United Nations (UN) and its associated agencies, the World Bank and the International Monetary Fund, as well as national and transnational governmental and non-governmental organizations, centers and institutes for environmental policy, universities, financial, industrial and transnational corporations, and religious organizations (Winfield, 2021). Individual citizens too are also becoming directly involved and providing leadership – as groups like Farmers for Climate Solutions will testify. Although there remains limited resistance from recalcitrant scientists and conspiracy theorists, the vast majority are now in agreement. Even the giant global oil companies understand and acknowledge what is happening. Most, though, together with banks, pension funds and investment companies, do not engage in meaningful action or responsible leadership and spread misinformation – arguably because of the threat to profits (Hanbury, 2021).

While, as we shall see, this crisis was predicted decades ago, by scientists all over the world, it is now coming to fruition faster than imagined because appropriate actions have not been taken. Most of the warming has occurred in the past forty years, with the seven most recent years being the warmest and the years 2016 and 2020 tied for the warmest years on record. We are now barely short of the elusive upper target set under the Paris Agreement (United Nations, 2015a) of keeping Earth's warming to below 2 degrees Celsius and, ideally, no more than 1.5 degrees Celsius. At the Paris meeting, all the attending 180 countries agreed to reduce their GHG emissions. The United Nations Framework Convention on Climate Change (UNFCCC) (2021), the world's guiding framework for climate change, originated at the Conference on Environment and Development in Rio de Janeiro, where it was signed by 197 nations pledging to prevent "dangerous anthropogenic interference with the climate system" (United Nations, 1992: 9). Since 1995, regular Conference of Parties (COP) policy meetings of the world's political, civil and scientific leadership have occurred under the auspices of the UN and the UNFCCC, at which consensus is sought for avoiding global meltdown. The Paris meeting (COP21) in 2015 was part of this.

The UNFCCC and COP meetings remain the main guiding forces today to provide regular global solidarity and leadership, building on the 1988 formation of the UN Intergovernmental Panel on Climate Change, mandated to provide scientific assessments of human-induced climate change, its natural, political and economic impacts and risks, and possible response options. It quickly became fundamental to support the UNFCCC and COP process and has continually produced state-of-the-art documents, including its most recent unanimously approved report (Intergovernmental Panel on Climate Change, 2021). By December 2020, 194 UNFCCC members had signed the legally binding Paris Agreement. Unfortunately, current country commitments on reducing GHGs are insufficient to stabilize the global ecosystem and prevent more serious consequences, despite the promise of COP26 in Glasgow in November 2021. It is no surprise that some of the world's richest people have started programs to colonize space.

This focused environmental effort was also accompanied by several decades of developing and implementing a broad set of global development goals, starting in 2000 with the Millennium Development Goals (MDGs). The current UN Sustainable Development Goals (SDGs) (United Nations, 2015b), with a global development framework lasting until 2030, then took over from the MDGs. The SDGs express the collective aspiration for achieving a better and more sustainable world while affirming everyone's human rights (Yimbesalu and Zakus, 2019). One of the 17 SDGs specifically directs decision-makers to take urgent action to combat climate change and its impacts, while another promotes clean energy. The alleviation of what is now the crisis of global warming, environmental destruction and ensuring environmental justice is related to all the SDGs, especially that of conserving and sustainably using the oceans, seas and marine resources, and protecting, restoring and promoting sustainable use of terrestrial ecosystems, sustainably managing forests, combatting desertification, halting and reversing land degradation, and halting biodiversity loss. It is also linked to eradicating poverty, ending hunger, achieving food security and improved nutrition, promoting sustainable agriculture, and making cities and human settlements inclusive, safe, resilient and sustainable. Moreover, given the major effects of population growth, some scientists are now calling for a new SDG in this area (McGavin, 2021).

The synergistic SDGs around climate change, though, are now in jeopardy because of decades of unrelenting global warming affecting the complex interplay of physical and social factors on planet Earth. We now know unequivocally that this is caused by increasing concentrations of atmospheric GHGs, which directly results from human activity (Intergovernmental Panel on Climate Change, 2021). Now is the time for action. Leaders must come forward from all sectors of society. We are all on spaceship Earth and have a duty to help ensure safe traveling.

The solid pieces of research that assure us that climate warming is happening and is caused by human activity fall into nine independently studied, but physically related, lines of evidence (Ocko, 2021):

- Simple chemistry of carbon dioxide and methane being emitted on burning carbon-based materials.
- Basic accounting of what we burn, including how much carbon dioxide we emit.
- Measuring increasing carbon dioxide and other GHGs in the atmosphere and trapped in ice, with levels higher than for nearly a million years.
- Chemical analysis of the atmospheric carbon dioxide that reveals the increase is coming from burning fossil fuels.
- Basic physics that shows us that all GHGs absorb heat.
- Monitoring climate conditions to find that the air, sea and land is warming, as expected with rising greenhouse gas emissions, causing ice to melt and sea levels to rise.
- Ruling out natural factors that can influence climate like the sun and ocean cycles.
- Employing computer models to run experiments of natural versus human-influenced simulations of Earth.
- Consensus among scientists who consider previous evidence and form conclusions.

The role of responsible leadership in the climate crisis

These pieces of evidence highlight the pressing need for change, but why, then, are we in this predicament now? How is it that we have a climate crisis? And, aside from the physically damaging impacts of climate warming, why are we so concerned at this point? The reasons are plentiful. First, GHG emissions from our activities are rising year after year into uncharted territory for life on Earth. Various other actions are compounding this like deforestation, population growth and the consumer society. Second, some reject the scientific consensus by either refusing to acknowledge there is a problem or not believing that human activities are the cause, and by obfuscating this reality they protect vested interests. And third, and just as important, there is a serious problem with leadership.

Many leaders only operate on a short-term horizon within election, planning or annual profit cycles, believing there is no problem in delay. Many are not willing to make the necessary hard or unpopular decisions. Many make promises and then fail to deliver on them, despite good intentions. Many also try to subvert the science and mislead to maintain power, profitability and financial advantage. Many too see it as an inconvenience affecting their privileged lifestyles and wealth and reject any notion of change and obligation to society. All this is heading us in the wrong direction and without the needed pace and scale of change. This, though, must change quickly. Ultimately, combatting climate change comes down to an issue of responsible leadership (Attenborough, 2020).

Ensuring achievement of the SDGs, human rights and a physically stable world demands we cannot accept the distortions, misconstructions and rejection of climate science. If we do, and all forms of leadership do not get on board, we will surely suffer the consequences. Lives are already being hugely disrupted, businesses are collapsing, and societies are being pushed to the edge.

The impact of climate change

Each of the occurring and impending climate change-related events have two widely recognized impacts – on the health of humans and other living things, and that of the ocean. This can be summarized as set out below.

Health of humans and other living things

The climate crisis is affecting human as well as animal and plant health. More severe and prolonged heat waves, temperature variability, increased length and severity of the pollen season, air pollution, forest fires, droughts, soil salinization, heavy precipitation events and floods present various risks and outcomes. As variously documented (see, amongst others, Alderman, Turner and Tong, 2012; Anders, 2021; D'Amato et al., 2014; The Energy Mix, 2021; Welsh, 2015) these include:

- An increase of infectious, food and water borne diseases
- Heat effects which can be severe, especially in the elderly, the young and those with chronic conditions and pregnancy
- Putting respiratory health at risk
- A direct assault on agriculture, with drought, floods and soil salinization causing a decrease in the amount and nutritional quality of food
- Growth in mental health problems including associated sickness, hunger, loss of life, home and income, and imposing added stress on healthcare providers during catastrophes
- Increased suffering of those with limited access to medical care and less well-developed medical services, including disadvantaged groups, migrants and areas of population growth
- Serious societal effects including social conflict, war and tens of millions fleeing crop failures, droughts, floods and rising sea levels.

Ocean health and stability

The health of Earth's life-giving ocean is also being seriously affected by climate change. As atmospheric temperatures rise, so too do the upper layers of the ocean.

As the ocean warms, it naturally expands and rises, just as it does from glacier melt. The biggest present danger, though, is from accentuated storm surges, which cause flooding around the globe. Many Pacific Island states have lost land and fresh water to ocean storms, and many inhabitants have fled to other countries, as was vocalized at COP26 in 2021 in Glasgow.

Warming sea waters are also anathema to coral reefs, which provide sustenance and livelihood to 1.2 billion people and huge numbers of fish and other sea creatures. Corals live in a symbiotic relationship with microplankton/microalgae that live within them, providing not only 90 percent of the corals' nutrients but all their amazing colors. In response to excessive sea warming, the coral polyps expel the microalgae, leaving them white or blanched. If the algae loss is prolonged and the stress continues, the coral will die. Already at least half of the world's coral reefs have experienced bleaching episodes since the mid-1970s. In 2020, Australia's Great Barrier Reef experienced its most extensive and second most destructive bleaching event on record. If current climate and societal trends continue, by 2050 90 percent of all Earth's coral reefs will be dead (Becatoros, 2017).

The warming ocean also affects the lives of its many other inhabitants, including fish, either by impacting their health directly or by causing them to migrate to new homes in cooler waters. Like the giant forests, the ocean is a carbon sink, absorbing about 25 percent of yearly human emissions. Annual excessive carbon emissions are now saturating the ocean, impairing another of Earth's protective systems. This increase in dissolved carbon dioxide leads to acidification, affecting the health of molluscs and other creatures. Billions of mussels, clams, oysters, barnacles, sea stars and other intertidal species died during the heat wave in June 2021 in the Pacific Northwest (Leahy, 2021). Coastal ecosystems have also been found to be highly degraded by warming water and acidification. In addition, the ocean must contend with melting glaciers, melting sea ice, disrupted ocean currents, and declining species numbers – such as shorebird populations in North America, which have decreased by 70 percent over the last fifty years (Munro, 2017) – as well as severely damaged biodiversity (Merrington, 2021).

Warnings of catastrophe

With all this happening, it is surprising that our political, governmental, business and other leaders do not say and do more. It is not because there is a shortage of knowledge or an absence of clear warnings throughout history. For example, even over a century ago the *Rodney and Otamatea Times* (1912: 7) stated:

> The furnaces of the world are now burning about 2,000,000,000 tons of coal a year. When this is burned, uniting with oxygen, it adds about 7,000,000,000 tons of carbon dioxide to the atmosphere yearly. This tends to make the air a more effective blanket for the earth and to raise its temperature. The effect may be considerable in a few centuries.

Several decades later, Meadows and colleagues (1972) published a landmark report, *Limits to Growth*, on behalf of the Club of Rome, a group of global intellectual and business elites. It forewarned of impending societal collapse due to the overexploitation of planetary resources in the next fifty to seventy-five years. But this warning was largely ignored, although its path was prepared by a popular book by Paul and Anne Ehrlich (1971), titled *The Population Bomb*. This also predicted societal collapse, albeit from large, sustained population growth.

Although the predictions did not all pan out on given timelines, subsequent reworking of the data concluded that most of the predictions are in line for becoming real in the next twenty years (Herrington, 2021). These prophetic documents, though, did not stand alone. In 1992, the first 'Warning to Humanity' was issued – a call to action signed by over 1,700 scientists, including 104 Nobel laureates, from 71 countries. A 'Second Warning' was produced in 2017, signed by 15,364 scientists from 184 countries, and was swiftly followed by a 'Third Warning' in 2019 signed by 11,258 scientists representing 153 countries. Thereafter, the World Economic Forum (2020) published a report by a group of scientists from the US, China and the European Union warning of the catastrophic consequences of climate change – highlighted by COP26 in Glasgow in 2021.

The climate crisis, thrust upon us by ever increasing GHGs in our atmosphere from activities on Earth, is now on full display. It does not take a climate scientist to see that something is drastically wrong. For instance, in Canada at the beginning of summer in 2021, a small town in British Columbia set an all-time Canadian record for temperature in a 'heat dome' at 49.6 degrees Celsius, hotter than the Sahara Desert, and then two days later lost 90 percent of its infrastructure from a wildfire. And about four months later, many areas of southern British Columbia were hit by an 'atmospheric river', a prolonged deluge, destroying neighborhoods, roads and farms, and killing hundreds of thousands of animals. The town of Merritt had to completely evacuate, as the high flood waters rendered their wastewater treatment plant inoperable. Two months later, this same and many other western Canada locations had record-breaking cold temperatures, touching the -50 degrees Celsius range, the coldest on Earth.

The Arctic, Siberia and Canada's north are the most rapidly changing areas of the world, warming by more than 2.2 degrees Celsius since the 1960s, with many other areas not far behind (Rosen, 2021). Above freezing temperatures are now being recorded in the winter and way above average temperatures in the summer. Even Lake Superior, the world's largest body of fresh water, is now among the world's fastest warming lakes (Lester, 2021). Life in all these areas is rapidly changing – affecting food, water sources, employment, infrastructure and transportation. Many are now talking of a new normal of extremes. A comprehensive global assessment measuring heat waves from 1950 to 2000 found that their frequency, duration and intensity had risen significantly (Perkins-Kirkpatrick and Lewis, 2020). In the Middle East and much of Africa, such indicators had increased by

50 percent every decade. In other parts of the world, the increase ranged from 10 to 30 percent each decade. While the impacts of drought have received much attention, heat waves are now considered a 'major global threat' to plants, animals and ecosystems (Breshears et al., 2021).

Despite continued, widely broadcast and reliable warnings over many years, leadership in government, business and other sectors has failed to act and take the necessary measures to reduce atmospheric warming. Many have given into pressure from fossil fuel and allied companies and their lobbyists. It is well known that they relentlessly continue to get political, financial and other support to protect and subsidize their industries and promote intensive carbon use in agriculture, transportation, manufacturing and other industrial operations. While some countries are now adopting policies to encourage green energy sources, it is not enough. Despite the COP26 rhetoric of phasing out the use of coal, its use is currently increasing. If existing energy infrastructure – power plants, industrial plants, buildings, vehicles and more – continue to operate as they have in the past, with similar lifespans, according to the International Energy Agency (2020), this alone will push global temperatures to 1.65 degrees Celsius above pre-industrial levels.

Many political and business leaders continue to support and foster the extraction and use of fossil fuels as an economic imperative, out of their perceived fiduciary, financial and employment responsibilities. While no one is calling for the immediate demise of fossil fuels, there must be a globally coordinated plan to phase them out. But even during the COVID-19 pandemic when many societal activities including air travel were curtailed, CO2 concentrations increased over the previous year, albeit at a lesser rate.

What has been done and what to do next?

It is crucially important that we believe the easily understandable science and learn from today's experiences. This issue is so immense that we must mobilize our knowledge and move from understanding to action. We must encourage and directly reduce our emissions of GHGs and proactively adapt to the consequences to protect lives and livelihoods today and into the future. Our choices for survival are clear, and we can act and change current patterns. Leadership must quickly wise up and act.

Governments should make and implement appropriate policy, including incentives to encourage behavior in the right direction, like subsidizing and encouraging electric cars, solar generating parks, rooftop solar panels, wind energy generation, energy and ecosystem conservation, waste reduction, and enhancing food security and educational programs encompassing retraining. They must lead the way and work side by side with the public and private sectors. Thankfully much of the private sector is now getting on board with huge investments in such areas as solar and wind electrical generation, personal and business-related electric vehicle technologies, as well as manufacturing, agriculture, communications, medicine, finance, mining and water supplies.

The necessary wholesale change from the internal combustion engine vehicle to battery-powered vehicles is now taking place within both major and new manufacturing brands. Many countries have targeted the end of internal combustion vehicles in the next decade. New and more sustainable methods of agriculture are being developed and implemented – together with the enforcement of laws to ensure forests are not being destroyed without replacement. Working together with indigenous peoples is imperative so that we learn from their wisdom and knowledge of nature and the environmental rights and responsibilities that lie at the cornerstone of their legal systems.

What has been done about rights

Fifty years ago, the concept of a human right to a healthy environment, reflecting "the need of humans to be able to live and enjoy a beneficial ecosystem, that doesn't endanger health, doesn't disrupt the quality of life and ultimately that permits human activity to continue in the far future" (Contralbrigo, 2020) was viewed as a novel, even radical, idea. Today, after its first formal articulation fifty years ago in the Stockholm Declaration, it is widely accepted in international law and endorsed by an overwhelming proportion of countries in recognition of the consequences of an unhealthy environment, which threaten human freedoms at the core of fundamental rights. Despite their recent emergence, environmental rights now enjoy legal protection in over one hundred countries – with most UN member nations recognizing these, even if simply through such means as the ratification of an international agreement. This recent upturn is having a remarkable impact, including stronger environmental laws, greater enforcement of those laws, the clean-up of pollution hotspots, and the provision of safer drinking water.

In parallel with this, the first global earth summit gave birth to the United Nations Environment Program (UNEP) based in Nairobi in 1972. Then in 1976 the legally-binding International Covenant on Economic, Social and Cultural Rights, to which almost all countries signed up, came into force. Amongst other things, the Covenant stated that the parties concerned recognize the right of all to the enjoyment of the highest attainable standard of physical and mental health, as well as the improvement of all aspects of environmental and industrial hygiene (Contralbrigo, 2020). Moreover, in the 1970s, Portugal and Spain became the first countries to establish this right to a healthy environment in its Constitution, while in 2008 Ecuador amended its Constitution to recognize the rights of nature – giving species and ecosystems rights similar to fundamental human rights (Foundation for Democracy and Sustainable Development, 2015). Since then, court decisions in some countries have legally recognized the rights of nature, mainly relating to rivers – most notably in Australia, Bangladesh, Columbia, India, New Zealand and the US.

What should we do next?

In terms of next moves, government, business, multilateral and civil society leaders have several options available to them. Effective governance of climate change requires the establishment and fostering of institutions responsible for coordinating multiple sectors from education, the media, agriculture and the environment to welfare, the economy, health, entertainment and the military. This needs to take place at local, regional, national and global levels, with key actors being governments, civil society, the private sector and international bodies. Positive outcomes will be engendered by participation, learning, flexibility, cooperation and following through on commitments. Delivering effective outcomes promoting mitigation of, and adaptation to, climate change can most productively involve policies suitably designed and aligned across many departments. Here we should learn from the multilayered experience of fighting against COVID-19 as we aim for a more sustainable world.

Civil society has lately been active in targeting the financing and insuring of the investments of fossil fuel companies, particularly those constructing pipelines and coal plants, to get them to stop. Large institutions and pension funds are also being targeted to continue disinvesting from fossil fuel. Pension funds alone manage $50 trillion of investments. Adam Scott, Director of Shift Action (2021), an organization advocating pension wealth for planetary health, recently said: "Decisions over whether this capital is invested in causes of the climate crisis, or in the solutions, are critical to achieving safety for our savings and the planet." Its work has attracted international news coverage, which led to commitments from five of the top six banks involved in the trade of oil from the Amazon to end their financing. Even business lobby groups are now calling for the development of national climate strategies and for corporations to show how they are integrating climate change risks into their long-term strategies, despite still not having good metrics to help determine this (Meyer, 2019).

Speaking in July 2021 at the Venice International Conference on Climate, a side event of the G20 meeting of finance ministers and central bank governors, the Chief Executive of Blackrock, Inc., a major investor in fossil fuels and the largest asset manager in the world with some $9 trillion of assets, called on governments to develop stronger long-term climate finance plans to unlock the private capital needed to fund the transition to a low-carbon economy (Jessop and Jones, 2021). He also called on the International Monetary Fund and the World Bank to reform their practices in emerging markets, provide capital to protect the returns of private investors, and make themselves more capable of tackling the climate crisis, which he said represented a $50 trillion opportunity for investors. His credibility, though, was put to the test a month later, when he led a $15.5 billion investment in new Saudi natural gas pipelines (Martin, 2021).

In another positive sign of private sector responsible leadership, the former governor of the Bank of Canada and Bank of England, Mark Carney, is now the UN Special Envoy on Climate Action and Finance and Chair of the new Glasgow

Financial Alliance for Net Zero (GFANZ). GFANZ comprises over 450 firms from 45 countries with $130 trillion in assets, bringing together leading net-zero initiatives across the financial system to accelerate the transition to net-zero emissions by 2050 and deliver on the Paris Agreement. It is to set science-aligned interim and long-term goals in line with the UN Climate Change Champion's Race to Zero campaign, which rallies leadership and support from businesses, cities, regions and investors around the world. Existing and new net zero finance initiatives are also to be part of the Alliance, including the Net Zero Asset Managers Initiative, the UN-convened Net-Zero Asset Owner Alliance and the newly launched Net Zero Banking Alliance, which links 43 of the world's leading banks, is hosted by UNEP's Finance Initiative, and was co-launched by the Financial Services Taskforce of the Prince of Wales' Sustainable Markets Initiative.

As the United Kingdom (UK) Prime Minister Boris Johnson observed just before COP26: "Uniting the world's banks and financial institutions behind the global transition to net zero is crucial to unlocking the finance we need to get there – from backing pioneering firms and new technologies to building resilient economies around the world" (United Nations, 2021). US Special Presidential Envoy for Climate, John Kerry, has echoed this:

> The largest financial players in the world recognize energy transition represents a vast commercial opportunity as well as a planetary imperative. As countries around the world move to decarbonize, the large sums these institutions are dedicating to climate finance also reflect a growing understanding of how critical a low-carbon global economy is to their business models. Ultimately, their commitment of capital and assets, as well as adherence to high standards and reporting, will accelerate the transition to this new economy, create a massive number of new jobs, and increase our collective ability to tackle the climate crisis.
>
> (United Nations, 2021)

Some of the largest manufacturing companies in the world are also getting on board. Firms like General Motors, Ford, Volkswagen, Nissan, Volvo, Chrysler and Daimler AG are continually adding electric conveyances to their production lines and making pledges to build more, to the detriment of internal combustion engine vehicles. Airlines and the shipping industry are working on the development of electric- (or hydrogen-) powered engines too. Thus United Airlines flew its first commercial flight in December 2021 with one of two engines totally powered by biofuel, while a small airline in Vancouver in Canada and its partners have launched a commercial electric plane (Harbour Air Seaplanes, 2021).

Companies are also working hard to develop new technologies, either to directly remove CO2 from the air or to decarbonize production and products. Google achieved net zero status in 2007 and then in 2020, through the purchase of high-quality carbon offsets, reduced its lifetime net carbon footprint to zero. Others are investing in battery storage technologies to accompany the explosion in the production and deployment of electric vehicles and solar panel and wind technologies, which together now comprise some 10 percent of global electricity generation. There is still plenty of room to expand renewables, though, especially as they are increasingly favored financially over fossil fuels. The world's best solar power schemes now offer cheaper energy as compared to coal and gas in most major countries, according to the International Energy Agency (Evans, 2020), and wind energy too is one of the lowest cost new electricity options without subsidies (Canadian Wind Energy Association, 2021).

However, globally coal is still widely used, producing about 38 percent of electricity, mainly in Asia, and is the single largest source of energy-related CO2 emissions. It is still widely supported and funded in China, which consumes about 65 percent of the world's total – although it is now beginning to pull back from this energy source (Alloway and Weisenthal, 2022). All coal mining and use must cease soon, and in the interim emissions capture technologies should be deployed. Both China and the US have encouragingly pledged to stop financing coal plants internationally, and many countries are eliminating its use. The UK plans to phase out coal generation by 2024, while the US is committed to carbon free electricity by 2035. At COP26, all Parties agreed to reduce unabated coal power and end inefficient fossil fuel subsidies. This was the first time fossil fuels were mentioned in a COP declaration. Nonetheless, there is a long way to go, with a great need for responsible leadership.

Enabling conditions to achieve net zero include multi-level governance and multi-sector institutions and multiple policy pathways, and, in this regard, cities have a major role to play. The SAFE Cities movement of municipalities blocking fossil fuel expansion and accelerating a just transition is progressing (Stand.earth, 2021). Dozens of SAFE ordinances were passed in 2021, showing that they can be very involved, including in banning new gas stations, electrifying public transport, encouraging bicycle use, promoting community solar power generation, planting trees, and providing cool decarbonized buildings. Cities can also minimize risk by updating building codes, preventing development in certain areas, funding community-led buyout programs, and addressing inequality. Moreover, the capacities of local emergency-management agencies can be strengthened. Leaders too need to prevent disasters from happening and ensure we have equitable systems in place – which, as the case of New York illustrates, they have frequently failed to do (McKibben, 2021)

The role of individual citizens

Reducing emissions, engaging in mitigation, and funding those hardest hit are not only the responsibility of government and business but of everyone. There is so much that each individual citizen can do including through the ballot box, pressing politicians for net zero policies and joining organizations to make a difference. Everyone can also exert agency and control over their energy use, whether for heating, transportation or diet. Moreover, youth are becoming much more vocal, including the 'Fridays for Future' campaign started by Greta Thunberg (Giannella, 2019).

It has been suggested by Lober (2019) that we should, amongst other things, do the following:

- Fly sparingly, carpool and take public transport
- Keep cars as long as possible and buy a hybrid or electric replacement
- Recycle as much as possible and use recycled items
- Compost organic waste instead of putting it in the trash
- Eliminate single use plastics in purchases
- Buy fresh foods with little packaging
- Keep reusable grocery bags on hand and avoid plastic bags
- Reduce red meat intake
- Shop and eat locally, walking if possible
- Turn off lights and unplug devices when not in use
- Insulate all dwellings and switch to more efficient appliances
- Assist poor and vulnerable populations
- Lobby politicians.

The enormity and challenge of the climate crisis can feel overwhelming. Disasters are often considered rare events and not of great general concern. But now, given the increasing frequency and severity of climate-related incidents, many populations fear that they will be next, their homes are not safe from flood or wildfire, their land might dry up, and they might be struck down while out of their homes. Together, though, we can protect forests, move the world away from fossil fuels, and build a better future. What is more, the greatest antidote to despair is action. But to ensure this, equitable transitions and public acceptability are needed with respect to jobs and changing industrial and financial directions. If leadership in all sectors does not step up, it signals that the issue is unimportant or undeserving of concern.

Conclusion

This world is getting hotter. Temperatures are increasing. Ocean and lakes are warming. Huge areas of the world are becoming drier as others are getting wetter. The climate crisis is not something that is lingering, waiting to swing past by the end of the century. It is happening now and disrupting and ruining lives, crushing industries, displacing communities, and forcing societies to the edge. For anyone who was waiting for the crisis to become so big that it was undeniable, we passed that milestone long ago. This is an emergency, and it deserves to be treated like one. The idea that any piece of legislation is 'too green' no longer makes any sense (Sumner, 2021) – especially in light of the imperative of the UN SDGs.

Great leaders know how to inspire trust – in them and their decisions. But what type of trust and decisions? Is responsible leadership defined only in terms of the bottom line for businesses? Or does it relate to building a united society, with a secure future for all. Indigenous communities in North America are known to make decisions based on what will be the effect several generations down the line. This seems a responsible formula for providing leadership and ultimately stewardship of Earth's atmosphere, lands, waters and other resources. Increasing current wealth at the expense of an impoverished and highly threatened future does not make sense.

Our leaders and citizens must look honestly at where we are going and how we are going to get there. We have to think about the life support systems that are needed to ensure we arrive, and also our children, and their children. We must understand our current predicament as a preview of what is yet to come and do whatever we can to adapt and help lessen the ills of the future. All of us, no matter what our position in society, have a vital role to play in addressing the climate crisis, by raising our voices, communicating about it, and doing all we can to be part of the solution. We must reverse and eliminate our 'addiction' to fossil fuels and question our consumer society and its reliance on continued economic growth.

We have the science, and we have been warned. Exemplary leadership is present in the scientific, education and health communities alongside many excellent government, business, union, and other leaders. The general public too must be key players. All leaders, whomsoever they are, wherever they are, must be educated and pressured to be responsible and be held accountable. Our future climate depends on decisions made today and tomorrow. We have the time of about one generation to set things right. We must focus on taking responsible decisions to halt the emissions working their way through the ecosystem. This is the challenge we have today, to ensure that coming generations will prosper. We must do all we can to overcome the propensity of people to resist change, despite supporting evidence. The health of the planet and all of its life depend on it. We are *homo sapiens*, supposedly wise people. Let us use our wisdom by tackling our climate crisis with all the resolve, resources and compassion we can muster.

References

Alderman, K., Turner, L. R. and Tong, S. (2012) 'Floods and human health: A systematic review', *Environment International* 47: 37–47.

Alloway, T. and Weisenthal, J. (2022) 'China is changing its coal use, and it affects the whole world', *BloombergQuint*, 31 January. Available at: https://www.bloombergquint.com/business/china-is-changing-its-coal-use-and-it-affects-the-whole-world

Anders, C. (2021) 'Canada's farmers brace for new heat wave as scorching summer leaves cherries roasting on trees', *Washington Post*, 17 July. Available at: https://www.washingtonpost.com/climate-environment/2021/07/17/heat-wave-canada-agriculture/

Attenborough, D. (2020) *A Life on Our Planet: My Witness Statement and a Vision for the Future*, London: Witness Books.

Becatoros, E. (2017) 'More than 90 percent of world's coral reefs will die by 2050', *The Independent*, 13 March. Available at: https://www.independent.co.uk/climate-change/news/environment-90-percent-coral-reefs-die-2050-climate-change-bleaching-pollution-a7626911.html

Bhateja, A. (2021) 'These 11 cities are sinking: They could be gone by 2100', *Fodor's Travel*. Available at: https://www.fodors.com/news/photos/these-11-cities-are-sinking-they-could-be-gone-by-2100

Breshears, D. D. et al. (2021) 'Underappreciated plant vulnerabilities to heat waves', *New Phytologist*, 17 March. Available at: https://doi.org/10.1111/nph.17348

Canadian Wind Energy Association (2021) 'A wind energy vision for Canada', Ottawa: CWEA. Available at: https://canwea.ca/vision/

Contralbrigo, S. (2020) 'The "right to a healthy environment" protection', *Sustainable Development Watch*, 19 July. Available at: https://sdwatch.eu/2020/07/the-right-to-a-healthy-environment-protection/

D'Amato, G., Cecchi, L., D'Amato, M., Annesi-Maesano, I. (2014) 'Climate change and respiratory diseases', *European Respiratory Review* 23: 161–69.

Ehrlich, P. and Ehrlich, A. (1971) *The Population Bomb*, Revised edition, London: Macmillan.

Evans, S. (2020) 'Solar is now "cheapest electricity in history", confirms IEA', *Carbon Brief*, 27 October. Available at: https://www.carbonbrief.org/solar-is-now-cheapest-electricity-in-history-confirms-iea

Foundation for Democracy and Sustainable Development (2015) 'The Ecuadorian Constitution was the first national constitution to give rights to nature', London: FDSD. Available at: https://www.fdsd.org/ideas/ecuadorian-constitution-rights-to-nature/

Giannella, V. (2019) *We Are All Greta: Be Inspired to Save the World*, London: Laurence King Publishing.

Hanbury, S. (2021) 'Oil executives deny misinformation on climate change, despite evidence', *Mongabay*, 2 November. Available at: https://news.mongabay.com/2021/11/oil-executives-deny-spreading-lies-on-climate-change-despite-evidence/

Harbour Air Seaplanes (2021) 'Harbour Air, magniX and H55 partner for the world's first certified all electric commercial airplane', Harbour Air Seaplanes, 20 April. Available at: https://www.harbourair.com/harbour-air-magnix-and-h55-partner-for-the-worlds-first-certified-all-electric-commercial-airplane/

Harvey, C. (2020) 'Earth hasn't warmed this fast in tens of millions of years', *Scientific American*, 13 September. Available at: https://www.scientificamerican.com/article/earth-hasnt-warmed-this-fast-in-tens-of-millions-of-years/

Herrington, G. (2021) 'Data check on the world model that forecast global collapse', Club of Rome. Available at: https://www.clubofrome.org/blog-post/herrington-world-model/

Intergovernmental Panel on Climate Change (2021) *Assessment Report 6 – The Physical Science Basis*, Geneva: IPCC. Available at: https://www.ipcc.ch/report/ar6/wg1/

International Energy Agency (2020) *World Energy Outlook*, Paris: IEA. Available at: https://www.iea.org/reports/world-energy-outlook-2020

International Union for Conservation of Nature (2021) 'Ocean warming', Gland: IUCN. Available at: https://www.iucn.org/resources/issues-briefs/ocean-warming

Jessop, S. and Jones, G. (2021) 'BlackRock CEO calls for stronger climate finance plan at G20 meet', *Reuters*, 11 July. Available at: https://www.reuters.com/business/sustainable-business/blackrock-ceo-calls-stronger-climate-finance-plan-g20-meet-2021-07–11/

Leahy, S. (2021) 'If the hardiest species are boiled alive, what happens to humans?' *The Atlantic*, July. Available at: https://www.theatlantic.com/ideas/archive/2021/07/billions-victims-heat-dome/619604/

Lester, G. (2021) 'Lake Superior is warming faster than many of the world's big lakes', Michigan Environment Watch. Available at: https://www.bridgemi.com/michigan-environment-watch/lake-superior-warming-faster-many-worlds-big-lakes

Lober, D. (2019) 'List of 10 human causes of global warming for 2020', *Ramblings of an Occupy Liberal*, 18 April. Available at: https://www.reusethisbag.com/articles/10-human-causes-of-global-warming

Martin, M. (2021) 'BlackRock co-leads $15.5 billion Aramco gas pipelines deal', *Bloomberg*, 7 December. Available at: https://www.bloomberg.com/news/articles/2021-12-06/aramco-agrees-15-5-billion-gas-pipeline-deal-with-blackrock?sref=gPAG2MJ8

McGavin, B. (2021) 'Top scientists call for new UN sustainable development goal on population', The Overpopulation Project, Gothenburg: University of Gothenburg.

McKibben, B. (2021) 'Can a border tax help slow a borderless crisis?' *The New Yorker*, 21 July. Available at: https://www.newyorker.com/news/annals-of-a-warming-planet/can-a-border-tax-help-slow-a-borderless-crisis

Meadows, D. H., Meadows, D. L., Randers, J. and Behrens III, W. W. (1972) *Limits to Growth*. New York: Universe Books.

Merrington, A. (2021) 'Coastal ecosystems being "burned" by double whammy of rising temperatures and ocean acidification', Plymouth: University of Plymouth. Available at: www.plymouth.ac.uk/news/coastal-ecosystems-being-burned-by-double-whammy-of-rising-temperatures-and-ocean-acidification

Meyer, C. (2019) 'Canada's chief executives call for companies to disclose climate risks', *National Observer*, 31 October. Available at: www.nationalobserver.com/2019/10/31/news/canadas-chief-executives-call-companies-disclose-climate-risks

Munro, M. (2017) 'What's killing the world's shorebirds?', *Nature* 541: 16–20.

National Aeronautics and Space Administration (2021) 'Climate change: How do we know?' Washington, DC: NASA. Available at: https://climate.nasa.gov/evidence/

Ocko, I. (2021) '9 ways we know humans triggered climate change', Environmental Defense Fund. Available at: www.edf.org/climate/9-ways-we-know-humans-triggered-climate-change

Perkins-Kirkpatrick, S. E. and Lewis, S. C. (2020) 'Increasing trends in regional heatwaves', *Nature Communications* 11. Available at: www.nature.com/articles/s41467-020-16970-7#Sec2

Rodney and Otamatea Times (1912) 'Coal Consumption Affecting Climate', *Rodney and Otamatea Times, Waitemata and Kaipara Gazette*, 14 August. Available at: https://paperspast.natlib.govt.nz/newspapers/ROTWKG19120814.2.56.5

Rosen, J. (2021) 'The science of climate change explained: Facts, evidence and proof', *New York Times*, 6 November. Available at: www.nytimes.com/article/climate-change-global-warming-faq.html?

Shift Action (2021) 'Shift Action for pension wealth and planet health'. Available at: www.shiftaction.ca/Shift

Stand.earth (2021) 'What are SAFE cities?' Available at: www.stand.earth/page/fossil-fuel-free/what-are-safe-cities

Sumner, M. (2021) 'The climate crisis is here, steadily getting worse, and should be treated like an emergency', *Daily Kos*, 27 July. Available at: www.dailykos.com/stories/2021/7/27/2042290/-Floods-fires-sandstorms-droughts-what-kind-of-sign-were-you-waiting-for?detail=emaildkre

The Energy Mix (2021) 'Prairie drought could threaten global food supplies', 5 August. Available at: www.theenergymix.com/2021/08/05/prairie-drought-could-threaten-global-food-supplies/

United Nations (1992) *United Nations Framework Convention on Climate Change*, Geneva: UN. Available at: https://unfccc.int/files/essential_background/background_publications_htmlpdf/application/pdf/conveng.pdf

United Nations (2015a) *The Paris Agreement*, New York: UN.

United Nations (2015b) *Transforming Our World: The 2030 Agenda for Sustainable Development*, Geneva: UN.

United Nations (2021) 'Biggest financial players back net zero', Geneva: UN. Available at: www.un.org/en/climatechange/biggest-financial-players-back-net-zero

United Nations Framework Convention on Climate Change (2021) 'What is the United Nations Framework Convention on Climate Change?', Bonn: UNFCCC. Available at: https://unfccc.int/process-and-meetings/the-convention/what-is-the-united-nations-framework-convention-on-climate-change

Welsh, C. (2015) 'Climate change helped spark Syrian war, study says', *National Geographic*, 2 March. Available at: www.nationalgeographic.com/science/article/150302-syria-war-climate-change-drought?loggedin=true

Winfield, N. (2021) 'Pope, faith leaders sign joint climate appeal before summit', *CTV News*, 4 October. Available at: www.ctvnews.ca/climate-and-environment/pope-faith-leaders-sign-joint-climate-appeal-before-summit-1.5609974

World Economic Forum (2020) *A Decade Left: Confronting Runaway Climate Threat*, Geneva: WEF.

Xu, C., Kohler, T. A., Lenton, T. M., Syenning, J-C. and Scheffer, M. (2020) 'Future of the human climate niche', *Proceedings of the National Academy of Sciences of the United States of America* 117(21): 11350–55.

Yimbesalu, J. and Zakus, D. (2019) 'The Sustainable Development Goals as human rights', in Izarali, R. (ed) *Expanding Perspectives on Human Rights in Africa*, London: Routledge.

Chapter 17

Biodiversity and Responsible Leadership

Edward Milner

Introduction

Victor Hugo once prophetically said that "it is a sad thing to think that nature speaks, and that humankind does not listen". In this vein, Sir David Attenborough (2020) recently recorded a witness statement based on his book *A Life on Our Planet* – reflecting on his 70-year career as a broadcaster and celebrating the astonishing beauty and diversity of nature. He began not in a rainforest or on an incredible coral reef but walking among the ruins of Chernobyl – polluted and abandoned to the wild, a place rendered uninhabitable by human misadventure, a combination of hubris, misjudgment and incompetence. He saw this deserted city as "a monument to the capacity of humankind to lose everything it needs, and everything that it treasures" (Attenborough, 2020: 5). After observing the deterioration of every habitat and ecosystem across the globe, he is not the first to believe it is time to rethink our entire relationship with the natural world.

Much of the debate around climate science has focused on global heating and the urgency of cutting carbon emissions. This will not be enough. Monitoring studies have revealed habitat loss and fragmentation resulting from "an explosion in global trade, consumption, human population growth and urbanisation" (World Wildlife Fund, 2020: 6). We are effectively degrading the biosphere at a rate that far exceeds sustainability (Dasgupta, 2021). Dangerous declines in populations of mammals, fish, reptiles, birds and amphibians have been recorded. Insect numbers

DOI: 10.4324/9781003129189-23

too are diminishing at a perilous rate, trending towards a global insect apocalypse; thousands will disappear before we even know of them. The impact of modern society has to change before the entire planet becomes uninhabitable.

What is biodiversity?

This planet provides unique and sustainable conditions for life – seasonal solar energy, rain and wind, natural circulation of atmospheric and ground water, circulating oceans, and regular tides. While some of these features have varied over time – in which sea level has been particularly changeable – the planet benefits from the combination of 'ecosystem services' that recycle water and vital elements such as carbon, nitrogen, phosphorus and potassium, resulting in our prolific and diverse biosphere. Biodiversity is understood to mean not only all the millions of individual life forms but even more importantly their myriad interdependencies – plant and herbivore, predator and prey, decomposer and waste – that make up the complex and sustainable network of the Earth's biosphere.

Ecologists have found that once the carrying capacity of a particular environment is reached, total growth is replaced by increasing complexity and specialization, within the constraints of the geographical location and climate. This provides stability and resilience, often with extraordinary productivity, which for millennia humanity has harvested sustainably. Where this has been disrupted – for example, by deforestation, pollution, overexploitation or industrial transformation – the outcome is often unpredictable and can lead to collapse of harvests, desertification and catastrophic loss of biodiversity.

The planetary biodiversity crisis

The Stockholm Resilience Centre has calculated that of nine key planetary boundaries, three – biodiversity loss, interference with the nitrogen cycle and atmospheric carbon dioxide – have already breached safe levels (Rockstrom et al., 2009). To these should perhaps be added total chemical and plastics pollution. Recent assessments of living nature by a forum of international scientists "show worsening trends and a rapidly narrowing window for (restorative) action" (Diaz et al., 2020: 411), while international scientists at both the United Nations Environment Programme and the Intergovernmental Science-Policy Platform on Biodiversity and Ecosystem Services (IPBES) have warned that biodiversity losses are now critical, with 75 percent of the land and 66 percent of the seas significantly 'altered' – that is, degraded by human activities. Satellite images show vast areas of natural habitat being destroyed year by year, especially in some of the most sensitive areas like the Amazon. In the oceans, overfishing, eutrophication and pollution combine to produce a deteriorating biome, with plastic waste ubiquitous and oxygen-starved 'dead zones' proliferating.

Biodiversity is still not specifically prioritized and cuts across several of the United Nations (UN) (2015) Sustainable Development Goals (SDGs). IPBES estimates that current negative environmental trends will undermine progress towards 80 percent of the assessed targets of the eight SDGs related to poverty, hunger, health, water, cities, climate, oceans, and life on land (Intergovernmental Science-Policy Platform on Biodiversity and Ecosystem Services, 2019). All current trends are alarmingly negative, as has been pointed out by hundreds of the world's environmental scientists (Ripple, 2017). Hamstrung by commercial and sectional interests, political leadership has failed; we have truly reached a critical moment for the future of life on Earth. The way forward urgently calls for more responsible leadership managing significant innovation on a global scale, but perhaps even more important is curtailing harmful current trends.

Historical damage to biodiversity

Historically, it was the sheer abundance of nature rather than its diversity that has been seductive. Flocks of the passenger pigeon darkened the North American sky a century ago, but hunting reduced billions to total extinction in half a century (Hung et al., 2014). The vast herds of grazing animals in Africa and North America must have seemed infinite to the first Western hunters, encouraging a wildly irresponsible attitude. A popular sport in the 1860s was shooting buffalo from the windows of the newly completed Kansas Pacific Railroad – where carcasses lined the tracks by the thousand. The vast shoals of Atlantic cod off the Newfoundland Banks fed millions until 1962, when overfishing caused the collapse of the entire commercial fishery. Such wanton destruction and lack of foresight can only be explained by ignorance, greed and stupidity – and, ultimately, irresponsible leadership.

Widespread degradation of ecosystems still goes on, although today's hunters, forest destroyers and land converters can hardly claim ignorance anymore. Contemporary agrobusiness is perhaps the worst offender along with the illegal wildlife trade, worth £15 billion per year (World Wildlife Fund, 2020) and targeting individual species that play a vital role in their own ecosystems. In Borneo, deforestation has reduced the orangutang populations by over 90 percent, mostly to make way for vast oil palm plantations. Orangutangs depend on over two hundred different plants, but when this biodiverse forest community is replaced by a single alien species, large areas can become dangerously vulnerable to disruption by violent weather events, disease or pest invasions. The entire ecosystem is damaged, displacing forest people, affecting soil stability and the water cycle, causing heat stress and droughts, and encouraging dangerous effects of climate change like flash flooding (University of Helsinki, 2021).

Where did this contempt for nature come from?

For responsible leaders to make sense of this situation, it is worth considering the origins of today's destructive attitudes. Many of the problems addressed by the UN SDGs have built up over many years from actions which originated in past centuries. The 'civilizing mission' of the colonial enterprise through conquest or settlement was fueled by superior firepower and what Lynn White (1967), the historian, provocatively termed its 'orthodox Christian arrogance' belittling 'primitive' alien beliefs and customs. Imperialism was highly profitable to the colonizers, maximization of profits being an imperative. Celebrated by its supporters as the expression of free enterprise, what developed was the single-minded and often barbaric pursuit of riches at the expense of supposedly inferior lands and peoples. The brutal reality of Belgian imperialism in the Congo horrified the author Joseph Conrad, not least because of the distorted worldview of the colonizers; what he had seen was indeed a 'heart of darkness'. His words still resonate, as the continued destruction of both forests and forest communities has been witnessed in horror by more recent observers such as Caufield (1985). In 2020 alone it is estimated that the Earth's tropics lost 12.2 million hectares of tree cover, around a third of it virgin tropical forest on land converted for agriculture (World Resources Institute, 2021).

Capitalist economists, from Adam Smith to Milton Friedman, hardly considered any limits to resources as the capitalist system must be 'unhampered' (Von Mises, 1944). The abundance of nature was a given, the absolute right to exploit it unquestioned, dictated by market forces. As a result, the transformation of all environments – physical and human – became not only legitimate but a moral imperative. The effects on biodiversity were, in many places, catastrophic; the past five hundred years have been truly an age of extinctions, as illustrated by the casual introduction of alien species like rats and cane toads into pristine environments. In the twentieth century, giant corporations have vigorously pursued profit maximization based on a model of export-led development in the Global South, backed by Western aid and international agencies. While this has been largely profitable for banks, donors and local elites, collateral damage to the environment has been devastating, ignored or written off as the inevitable cost of modern 'progress'.

Warnings disregarded

When Fairfield Osborn (1948: 196) decried humanity's failure to attend to "the most basic purpose of all, namely that of conserving the living resources of the Earth", his views were considered alarmist, and his concerns were ignored. In the 1960s, scientists at Massachusetts Institute of Technology (MIT) projected human activities and environmental trends to show inescapable and disastrous limits to growth on a finite planet that could lead to total societal collapse (Meadows et al., 1972), while Schumacher (1973) warned against the misuse of the Earth's 'natural capital' putting at risk the welfare of future generations. The Brundtland Report (United Nations, 1987) confirmed the adverse planetary trends but was criticized by theoretical economists for urging preferential resource allocation to future generations at the expense of present-day need, while the fossil fuel industry has constantly sought to question the scientific basis of any global limits. Even now, leading economists regard themselves as no more than 'growth agnostic' (Raworth, 2017), although others have pointed out the 'illusion' of infinite economic growth (Dhara and Singh, 2021). Even the concept of 'green growth', popular among some politicians, must now be regarded with the utmost skepticism (Hickel, 2018).

In the current way of thinking, problems are broken down into component parts and simplified for convenience of focus and profitability. The drawback of this reductionist approach is its incompatibility with the complexities and linkages of biodiversity. The predominant food supply is now largely a simplified input intensive system based on a few varieties of just seven major crops, providing a highly processed diet for an increasingly urban population prioritizing speed and convenience. Corporate decision-making in the agro-food industry is overwhelmingly wedded to the demands of short-term profitability and maximum shareholder benefit.

Not only is modern industry careless about collateral damage, it also actively supports harmful action by encouraging irresponsible regimes bent on promoting prestige projects for political gain. Amazon Watch and Global Witness report major finance houses such as JPMorgan, Bank of America, Blackstone Investments and Chinese banks are still financing coal-fired power stations, fossil fuel exploration, tropical deforestation, dam building and inappropriate tourist projects in fragile ecosystems. At the same time, like other multinationals that plunder and pollute nature, they claim to support campaigns to 'preserve wildlife' or 'raise awareness of environmental problems', attaching their logos to universities or Museums of Natural History, while ensuring these institutions are comprehensively gagged by their sponsorship agreements (Webster, 2021). That this level of hypocrisy and hubris survives is a serious indictment of leadership at every level, with compliant media, irresponsible law firms, biddable 'experts' and self-serving politicians all playing their part. To break out of this cycle, responsible leaders need the vision to see a bigger picture, find ways to resist the influence of ruthless business models that currently still enjoy overwhelming political support, and instead choose new directions based on new priorities.

Another way

Some years ago, I spent a week with the Yucuna people living in a circular communal *maloca* on sovereign indigenous land on the Miritiparana river in the Amazon region of Colombia. They have maintained a stable population in their remote forest for millennia, as have other indigenous peoples (Piperno et al., 2021). They hunt and gather in the forest and clear and burn small areas to grow manioc and sweet potatoes for two seasons, using no synthetic pesticides or artificial fertilizers, before planting selected trees for fruit and timber, herbs and healing. After two seasons they move on, leaving an area already enriched by a diversity of saplings.

The Yucuna people are aware of an optimum size for individual settlements if the health of the forest is to be maintained. Through their oral records, they know the plots their ancestors planted and can therefore harvest timber or collect fruit grown from seedlings their forbears nurtured. They regard the forest as sacred; maintaining its health is their responsibility. Whether fishing, farming or foraging, they work together, observing complex rules about where, when and how much to harvest (leaving enough fruit for other mammals in the forest, for example), and how to encourage forest regrowth. Seasonally, they sell renewable forest products like fruits, rubber and honey, but otherwise their entire existence is lived deep in the forest and in harmony with it. One of the elders told me: *the forest is like a mother to us; it provides all our needs*. He was at one with his forest world, deeply aware of his place in it between ancestors and the wellbeing of generations to come. He expected to pass on a similarly rich, sacred forest that his generation had inherited; he tended to talk about the group collectively – not I but *us*: *this is the life we believe in*.

What I experienced has been confirmed by researchers for Latin America as a whole: land governed and curated by indigenous communities suffers less deforestation and biodiversity loss than other similar lands (Food and Agriculture Organization, 2021). Even timber extraction is managed sustainably. Sensitive scientists have managed to bridge the two worlds, pointing out the proven value of much traditional ecological knowledge (Kimmerer, 2020), while the appointment in 2021 of Deb Haaland of Native American heritage to lead the US Interior Department builds on this understanding. In this context, the 2007 UN Declaration of the Rights of Indigenous Peoples has been a step in the right direction, although indigenous communities are still under violent pressure in many countries – even in some that supported the UN Declaration. Attitudes that date back to the colonial era are still mainstream in the modern world, as a result of which we are all the poorer. Hopeful signs include the acceptance of indigenous peoples as full members of the International Union for the Conservation of Nature with direct input into future policy (Rubiano, 2021) and the allocation at COP26 of over $1.7 billion to indigenous organizations for forest protection.

There are ways to manage ecosystems to be both productive and sustainable without artificial inputs, as the Yucuna people have shown. Their system is more complex and labor intensive than an equivalent area on a modern industrial farm. Indigenous peoples across the globe make use of myriad species of plants and animals – a hint at the wealth of neglected food plants and medicines which the rest of humanity could be using. Scientists are also aware that the genes of wild crop relatives are essential if plant breeders are to adapt our crops to changing conditions like higher temperatures, increased soil salinity and new diseases (Smith et al., 1992). In 2020, Nemonte Nenquino, leader of the Waorani people of the Ecuadorian Amazon, said: "the whole planet is in trouble because you don't respect it". What the dominant society can learn from indigenous peoples is not a whole way of life perhaps, but a better approach to the natural world, summed up in the phrase 'respect the planet and emphasize wellbeing'. This view is echoed by the leaders of several UN agencies (Azoulay et al., 2021). Reafforestation projects like the Great Green Wall across the Sahel are already building on this philosophy and showing the multiple benefits of promoting biodiversity.

New directions: Some principles for responsible leadership

What are the implications for responsible leadership? I want to suggest some principles that are familiar but often neglected – that can be relevant. A key principle, borrowed from natural ecosystems, is that diversity should be understood as a positive value in itself: from the opening up of commercial decision-making, involving a wider group by heritage, age, background and training, to concerted research-based and community-led restoration of damaged ecosystems. Reductions in diversity can destabilize whole ecosystems and increase their vulnerability just as decision-making by limited groups of elderly Caucasian males has contributed to today's planetary insensitivities. Natural systems almost always turn out to be more complex than they first appear, and responses need to be sophisticated. New linkages need to be developed, such as through partnerships with other businesses or civil society groups, as envisaged in the SDG on partnerships, and by widening access to decision-making, as urged by young people across the world through the 'Fridays for Future' campaign in over 150 countries (Thunberg, 2019).

The 'polluter pays principle' can guide the understanding of the effects of industrial processes which cascade down several levels. At every stage in manufacture, use, and disposal of goods, there are both profits made and planetary costs incurred. Many industrial processes, from rearing livestock to mineral extraction, cause major pollution problems, but powerful lobbying by the companies concerned is often successful in avoiding associated costs, whether upstream or downstream. Plastic waste is suffocating the biodiversity of our oceans – the chain of responsibility must be traced, starting with the inadequacy of plastic end-use recycling, upwards to the retailer, the soft-drink manufacturer, the maker of the plastic bottle and ultimately to the chemical company where the polymer originated. At present, most plastic will never be recycled; according to some observers the manufacturers could not care less, because it cuts into profits (Mahdawi, 2020). In fact, from polymer manufacturer to end-user, each level bears some responsibility; when the associated costs are ignored, they become effective subsidies that distort the economy and alienate opinion.

Pollution caused by the fossil fuel industry and resultant damage to ecosystems and public health has been estimated to have cost society $62 billion, but such sums do not typically appear on balance sheets (Kotchen, 2021). Similarly, the increasing environmental damage caused by the global food industry goes unaccounted for. Commentators have suggested that this trend is dangerously unsustainable and will need the wholesale transformation to a more environmentally sensitive model (Rockefeller Foundation, 2021). In the oceans, while some moves are being made to curtail illegal, unreported and unregulated fishing (Lundquist, 2021), the sources of marine pollution and destruction may be more difficult to identify along with associated costs. The need for a comprehensive ocean charter to protect biodiversity becomes more urgent every year (Bullett, 2021); indeed, learning to account fully for the impact of all our interaction with nature as a principle is urgently needed (Dasgupta, 2021).

A third consideration is the 'precautionary principle', which is routinely neglected for new products and processes under commercial pressures. New industrial techniques can cause untold damage to biodiversity before this is recognized – the devastation caused by bottom trawling only came to light after years of unrestricted misuse. The lethal effects of synthetic chemicals were first exposed, in face of furious commercial hostility, by Rachel Carson (1962) in her classic *Silent Spring*. Yet, as the European Food Standards Agency (2018) reports, dangerous chemicals like glyphosate and neonicotinoids are still aggressively marketed by companies profiting from them, ignoring the damage caused in the wider environment. Effects include the rise of herbicide-resistant super-weeds, declines in bird numbers and losses of pollinating insects, whose value alone has been estimated at around £500 billion a year. Repeated efforts by the international scientific community to urge better compliance with even the existing limited regulations have failed due to an all too familiar lack of political will, often associated with corruption (Diaz, 2020).

The role of governments

While national governments are responsible for the welfare of all their citizens, their environmental performance, including enforcement of environmental regulations, varies enormously. The reinsurance giant Swiss Re Institute (2020) suggests ten criteria including aspects of biodiversity, such as habitat intactness, numbers of pollinators and the extent of standing forest, together with strategic aims and capacity trends. Superficially, this looks like a reductionist approach, but in fact it is more sophisticated; their criteria include not just the numbers of pollinators but their diversity and the extent as well as the quality of forests. Using these criteria, they produce overall performance scores and rank countries, identifying areas in most urgent need of improvement, with likely influence on the costs of insurance. This is valuable, although the scores so far have proved to be distressingly low. Some of the more disputed, but relevant, factors not yet included are the level of civil society activity, free trade unions, degree of press freedom, protection for whistle-blowers and activists, and independence of the judiciary.

While Swiss Re's work is impressive, there is clearly an urgent need for a generally accepted assessment system to measure net biodiversity losses or gains. Several independent bodies have made limited progress in this direction. The thinktank Global Footprint Network is developing an assessment of what it terms positive or negative biocapacity. An international Task Force on Nature-related Financial Disclosures has also been launched by the independent Financial Stability Board, while the World Benchmarking Alliance is working to establish internationally accepted criteria applicable for rating both countries and companies.

Ambitious goals are frequently set, even if rarely achieved. Of those for the decade ahead set by the 2010 meeting of the Convention on Biological Diversity, it was recently admitted that none of the targets have been reached, and only six partially achieved. One target partially achieved was nothing better than an increase in the number of countries announcing new protected areas. Perhaps target-setting is the wrong approach, and specific legislation and enforceable regulation are more useful. In China, political moves are being made towards prioritizing biodiversity conservation in connection with the much-delayed Convention on Biological Diversity in Kunming in 2022, but whether this process will make any real difference is questionable. Even the proposed 30 percent of land and oceans fully protected by 2030 has only partial support – with little from countries such as Brazil, Indonesia and Papua New Guinea with the richest biodiversity.

The corporate response

In the corporate world, even nominal support for the UN SDGs is inconsistent. The word 'sustainability' is currently ubiquitous, although it is often treated as a relative term, its meaning debased by being linked with permanent growth. Although the main concern of business managers remains profitability with an eye to corporate stock price, environmental issues are generally a secondary consideration. Vogtlin (2017) claims that business managers are now feeling pressure to contribute to a sustainable future for people and planet, but how they might do this is often vague and generalized. Economists tend to see seven key stakeholders, starting with shareholders and ending with the natural environment and the communities within which the business operates (Hopkins, 2003). Neither approach is adequate to protect biodiversity. Without a sustainable planet, humanity has no future, yet current trends are inescapably compromising the welfare of future generations, who are not included as relevant stakeholders. Changes are now urgent, however inconvenient this is for business executives facing shareholders, and politicians facing their electorate.

A major factor preventing change is timescale; business cycles are annual or even quarterly, while politicians are similarly constrained by electoral cycles or, in some countries, five-year plans. As a result, pledges are frequently made that make little sense. For example, the Chinese government recently announced a commitment to targets including net zero emissions by 2060, at the same time claiming that their Gross Domestic Product will double in 15 years. Targets for 2050 and even 2030 are easy to declare but are rarely followed up, as today's politicians know they are unlikely to be held to account. Short-termism is baked into these systems. At COP26 in Glasgow in 2021, Vanessa Nakate, a young activist from Uganda admitted: "we are drowning in pledges", while Greta Thunberg asked: "Future plans are all very well but what are the actions for the here and now?" This is important, as, according to a recent report, widespread deforestation continues on a vast scale, financed by many international finance houses (Global Canopy, 2022).

The corporate world is increasingly involved with the system of performance disclosures known as Environmental, Social and Governance (ESG) risk, with various commercial agencies offering ratings assessments, although they admit that the process is hardly unbiased – aimed as it is at improving a company's financial standing rather than influencing actual business practice. Discussion of ESG matters at board level is even deprioritized according to Farnham (2021). More cynical commentators ridicule the approach, suggesting it is no more than a temporary fad (De Rugy, 2021) which fraudulently silences difficult investors and impresses the media. Others are scathing about the likelihood of corporate good faith (Reich, 2021). Even Greta Thunberg is unconvinced, referring to the whole ESG process as 'greenwash' and a displacement activity, a view evidenced by the internal communications between Exxon executives, leaked by Greenpeace. Meanwhile, bodies such as the Global Reporting Initiative (2016) try to encourage corporate transparency, but to many observers this is still far short of what is required. While international standards are an important aspiration, any system of voluntary disclosure is inferior to a robust framework of regulation properly enforced.

While there is considerable cynicism about ESG in some circles, in others it is winning acceptance and stimulating important innovation. A UN (2017) financed initiative known as National Benchmarking may have started changing business practice in Brazil by improving business standards and producing reputational gain for participating companies – leading to improved recruitment and staff retention. While no official progress reports are yet available, and joining the scheme is voluntary, positive developments have been observed. Lacking the appropriate in-house expertise, some companies have developed partnerships with civil society groups and green digital start-ups to improve their environmental footprint and interrogate their supply chain. One of Brazil's major meat packing firms JBS, for example, recently cancelled a supplier who was raising stock on deforested land, in partial response to consumer pressure and the benchmarking scheme (Global Witness, 2020).

Civil society

There is a planetary cost to every commodity, raw material and industrial product, which all affect biodiversity directly or indirectly. Basic standards for most consumer items are established by law in many countries, while civil society groups have begun to devise and monitor these independent of the industries – or governments – concerned. An early example was Consumer Action Penang, established more than fifty years ago. Sustainably harvested, sustainably farmed or bycatch-free fish is now guaranteed by the Marine Stewardship Council, while the Forest Stewardship Council certifies timber products according to source, although critics are alarmed that this certification is now so compromised by lobbying as to be actually misleading. Responsible leadership is needed to ensure that these efforts are made more independent of debilitating commercial influence. The Better Cotton Initiative limits itself to monitoring aspects of cotton growing, although not yet actual cotton garment production, as it claims the supply chain for cotton clothing is too complex. Palm oil too is regulated by the Round Table on Sustainable Palm-Oil, although investigations by the Forest Peoples Programme has revealed widespread illegality and violence within the industry (MacInnes, 2021). There is clearly a long way to go when powerful companies employ ruthless subsidiaries to corrupt due process, but voluntary agencies like Oritain are now promoting forensic interrogation of supply chains.

While the certification processes must be clarified, further steps are needed for consumers to exercise informed influence. Some of the more responsible corporates such as Unilever have announced their intention to provide carbon footprint data on all food items (Cohen, 2021), ignoring claims that their pursuit of responsible policies amounts to 'ludicrous championing of fashionable causes'. In theory, a standardized Digital Product Passport could now be developed incorporating a wide range of environmental information, including levels of chemical pollutants, expressed as a QR digital code read by mobile phone. Existing apps such as Evocco assess the carbon footprint direct from a grocery receipt to influence consumers directly. At present, a compensatory 'carbon offset' of tree-planting is calculated and passed on to a replanting start-up, but a more comprehensive 'biodiversity offset' supporting wider restoration schemes could be envisaged. The resulting effects of such schemes on consumer choice may bring about the most rapid changes to corporate behavior as experience suggests it is by directly affecting the bottom line that change is most rapidly promoted.

Greenwashing

Responsible business leaders and politicians are already aware that, in the end, 'greenwashing' does not work. Instead, it is authenticity that counts – to customers, staff and, increasingly, investors, previously taken to be a very conservative group. The Norwegian investment group Storebrand has spearheaded the Investors Policy Dialogue on Deforestation, engaging directly with the Brazilian government, although, so far, to little effect. The Norwegian government was the first in the world to ban deforestation throughout its territory, while parts of the Swedish timber industry have shown that, with enlightened management, it is possible to operate commercially and improve biodiversity through sensitive field practice and the restoration of degraded areas. The ensuing reputational gain aids both recruitment and staff retention.

The potential for civil society groups, including independent media, to promote improved environmental performance cannot be underestimated. In India, the Delhi-based Centre for Science and Environment has produced an annual *Citizen's Report on India's Environment* since 1982, most recently including reports on biodiversity. At the same time, the Honey Bee Network in Ahmedabad has promoted environmental innovation for over thirty years. The Blue Marine Foundation campaigns to achieve protection for 30 percent of the world's oceans by 2030, and organizations such as Amazon Watch (2018) monitor environmental abuse and lawbreaking. Working closely with the UN, the Society for Ecological Restoration has defined best restorative practice and encouraged net gain for various ecosystems, as part of the UN Decade on Ecosystem Restoration.

Increasingly, some civil society groups feel that official wheels grind too slowly, or not at all, and direct action is called for. Frustrated at government inaction to curtail bottom trawling even within so-called Marine Protected Zones, Greenpeace volunteers recently took the initiative of dropping enormous boulders in shallow ocean waters on the Dogger Banks in the North Sea, to prevent further vandalism by industrial trawlers. The lack of firmer action on clear-cut conservation issues is an open invitation to civil society groups to question damaging business-as-usual. In free societies, groups of citizens increasingly see themselves as part of the solution, pressurizing politicians and businesses to change tack, offering an opportunity for responsible leadership to anticipate shifts in conventional wisdom and forge a new consensus. Some influential figures suggest that when the invisible hand of the market can't fight climate change, intervention is needed (Rowley, 2021) and that governments urgently need to step up their regulation of businesses (Carney, 2021). What is certain is that saving the planet is no longer a fringe issue – different voices must be heard, new leadership encouraged, and policy choices revisited.

Crime and corruption

At the other end of the scale, crime and corruption, as well as business-as-usual by governments hell-bent on promoting grandiose 'development' projects like roads, tourism schemes and new cities, all continue to cause environmental damage and biodiversity loss on an industrial scale. A forestry adviser in Papua New Guinea pointed out to me some difficulties with his work: "International timber companies that come here have the resources to corrupt the entire political system from village headmen to the Cabinet. In remote areas they even send local intermediaries with suitcases full of banknotes to bribe local chiefs" (Milner, 1994). Reporting for

Channel Four TV in the United Kingdom, I have watched operatives from a timber subsidiary of the giant Hyundai Corporation which prides itself on its high 'ethical standards' devastating forests in the Solomon Islands – ignoring local land rights, polluting streams and compromising offshore coral reefs. As in many countries, there is an excellent Forest Code in the Solomons, just no political will or the means to enforce it. The local government is aware of what is being destroyed, but their ambition is apparently limited to the depiction of the territory's unique biodiversity on ceremonial postage stamps.

In many countries, politicians see personal financial gain as the legitimate reward for electoral success – however achieved (Wrong, 2009). Corruption affecting biodiversity appears to be widespread; myriad corrupt practices in the wildlife trade have been uncovered, often involving shell companies and offshore financial centers. The World Wildlife Fund (2015) offers a primer in strategies to combat such illegal activities. The exposure of illegality by investigative journalists is violently suppressed in many countries, while environmental activists and their supporters are regularly harassed and even murdered, with 212 such deaths worldwide reported in 2020 alone (Global Witness, 2021). Most of these crimes are scarcely investigated, and the powerful instigators – political and commercial – go unpunished. World Press Freedom has warned that the free press is under threat in at least 130 countries. Transparency International is demanding that the UN General Assembly take action against corruption worldwide, including action on offshore tax havens that give cover to criminals. Bellingcat, the innovative 'people's intelligence agency', has yet to tackle environmental crimes, but their approach to citizen-organized policing enables environmental damage even in remote regions to be reported immediately (Higgins, 2020).

Conclusion

The world's biodiversity will continue to be exploited in an unsustainable way unless, as IPBES has urged, protecting biodiversity is promoted at the same time as efforts to cut carbon emissions. The common good must be put ahead of profit maximization if ecosystem collapse is not to bring about the 'ghastly future' predicted by leading scientists (Bradshaw et al., 2021). On a finite planet, unrestrained pursuit of profit and growth becomes dangerous; we need a new paradigm for economic activity, such as 'wellbeing economics' (Club of Rome, 2021), which inform the transformation of societal futures as envisaged by the SDGs.

The word 'biodiversity' explicitly appears only once in the UN SDGs – namely, in 'protecting biodiversity and natural habitats' on land – but it arguably should be part of the thinking about all of them. Somehow the harmful impact of the human footprint has to be reduced. Responsible leadership means not only encouraging new initiatives but strengthening and enforcing regulations and urgently curtailing damaging activities. The commitment to end deforestation by 2030 agreed at

COP26 seems hopelessly inadequate when major new roads, mines, agricultural and tourism projects are still being pushed forward into virgin territories. At some point soon, we need to reach not just peak coal but peak deforestation – as well as peak soya and peak beef – if the natural world is to be respected. As envisaged in the UN SDGs, this means involving all parties – governments, business, indigenous people and civil society – to guide decision-making based on scientific, cultural and social criteria with long-term and inclusive aims. For responsible leadership, the future of a habitable planet must be the first priority.

Over the past few decades, the giant panda as a global conservation icon has surely failed as the promotion of one iconic species has not prevented catastrophic environmental decline elsewhere. We need a new symbol for a different age – a fragile tiny chameleon perhaps, like *brookesia nana*, the world's smallest and most recently discovered new species, together with its entire forest ecosystem. As Greta Thunberg (2019) has famously said: 'No one is too small to make a difference.'

References

Amazon Watch (2018) 'Complicity in destruction: How Northern consumers and financiers sustain the assault on the Brazilian Amazon and its Peoples', *Amazon Watch*, 11 September. Available at: https://amazonwatch.org/news/2018/0911-complicity-in-destruction

Attenborough, D. (2020) *A Life on Our Planet: My Witness Statement and Vision for the Future*, London: Witness Books.

Azoulay, A. et al. (2021) 'Our survival depends on treating nature with more respect', *eScience News*, 24 March. Available at: https://escience.news/opinion-our-survival-depends-on-treating-nature-with-more-respect

Bradshaw, C. J. A. et al. (2021) 'Underestimating the challenges of avoiding a ghastly future', *Frontiers in Conservation Science*, 13 January. Available at: https://www.frontiersin.org/articles/10.3389/fcosc.2020.615419/full

Bullett, J. (2021) 'Why a Global Ocean Treaty is the best hope for saving our seas', *Greenpeace*, 18 May. Available at: https://www.greenpeace.org.uk/news/global-ocean-treaty-hope-saving-seas

Carney, M. (2021) 'Regulate business to tackle climate crisis, urges Mark Carney', *The Guardian*, 17 July. Available at: https://www.theguardian.com/environment/2021/jul/17/regulate-business-to-tackle-climate-crisis-urges-mark-carney

Carson, R. (1962) *Silent Spring*, Boston, MA: Houghton Mifflin Co.

Caufield, C. (1985) *In the Rainforest*, London: William Heinemann.

Club of Rome (2021) 'The Club of Rome calls on the EU to adopt wellbeing economics instead of growth at all costs'. Available at: https://www.clubofrome.org/impact-hubs/reframing-economics/wellbeing/

Cohen, D. (2021) 'Unilever: Breakthrough as food industry giant introduces carbon footprint labels on food', *The Independent*, 15 July. Available at: https://www.independent.co.uk/climate-change/news/unilever-carbon-footprint-labels-food-b1882697

Dasgupta, P. (2021) *The Economics of Biodiversity: The Dasgupta Review*, London: HM Treasury.

De Rugy, V. (2021) 'Is corporate wokeness here to stay?', *National Review*, 10 June. Available at: https://www.nationalreview.com/magazine/2021/07/01/is-corporate-wokeness-here-to-stay

Dhara, C. and Singh, V. (2021) 'The delusion of infinite economic growth', *Scientific American*, 20 June. Available at: https://www.scientificamerican.com/article/the-delusion-of-infinite-economic-growth

Diaz, S. et al. (2020) 'Set ambitious goals for biodiversity and sustainability', *Science* 370(6515): 411–13.

European Food Standards Agency (2018) 'Neonicotinoids: Risks to bees confirmed', EFSA. Available at: https://www.efsa.europa.eu/en/press/news/180228

Farnham, K. (2021) 'Escalating TCFD on your Board's ESG agenda', *Diligent*, 4 February. Available from: https://insights.diligent.com/esg/tcfd-importance-for-boards-esg-agenda

Food and Agriculture Organization (2021) 'Forest governance by indigenous and tribal peoples', Rome: FAO. Available at: http://www.fao.org/americas/publicaciones-audio-video/forest-gov-by-indigenous/en

Global Canopy (2022) 'A climate wake-up: But business failing to hear the alarm on deforestation', Oxford: Forest 500.

Global Reporting Initiative (2016) *GRI-304: Biodiversity. Global Reporting Initiative*, Amsterdam: GSSB.

Global Witness (2020) 'Beef, banks and the Brazilian Amazon'. Available at: https://www.globalwitness.org/en/campaigns/forests/beef-banks-and-brazilian-amazon/

Global Witness (2021) 'Enemies of the state?'. Available at: https://www.globalwitness.org/en/campaigns/environmental-activists/enemies-state

Hickel, J. (2018) 'Why growth can't be green', *Resilience*, 19 September. Available at: https://www.resilience.org/stories/2018-09-19/why-growth-cant-be-green/

Higgins, E. (2020) *We are Bellingcat: An Intelligence Agency for the People*, London: Bloomsbury.

Hopkins, M. (2003) *The Planetary Bargain: Corporate Social Responsibility Matters*, London: Earthscan Publications.

Hung, C-M. et al. (2014) 'Drastic population fluctuations explain the rapid extinction of the passenger pigeon', *Proceedings of the National Academy of Sciences* 111(29). Available at: https://doi.org/10.1073/pnas.1401526111

Intergovernmental Science-Policy Platform on Biodiversity and Ecosystem Services (2019) *Global Assessment Report on Biodiversity and Ecosystem Services*, Geneva: IPBES.

Kimmerer, R. W. (2020) *Braiding Sweetgrass*, New edition, London: Penguin Books.

Kotchen, M. J. (2021) 'The producer benefits of implicit fossil fuel subsidies in the United States', *Proceedings of the National Academy of Sciences* 118(14). Available at: https://resources.environment.yale.edu/kotchen/pubs/FFsubsidies.pdf

Lundquist, E. (2021) 'International partners collaborate to end illegal, unreported and unregulated fishing', *Seapower*, 10 September. Available at: https://seapowermagazine.org/international-partners-collaborate-to-end-illegal-unreported-and-unregulated-fishing/

MacInnes, A. (2021) 'New investigation reveals oil palm industry's use of shadow companies to circumvent social and environmental commitments in Indonesia', Press release, 4 February. Available at: https://www.forestpeoples.org/en/indonesia-investigation-oil-palm-shadow-companies

Mahdawi, A. (2020) 'Most plastic will never be recycled – and the manufacturers couldn't care less', *The Guardian*, 15 September. Available at: https://www.theguardian.com/commentisfree/2020/sep/15/most-plastic-will-never-be-recycled-and-the-manufacturers-couldnt-care-less

Meadows, D. H., Meadows, D. L., Randers, J. and Behrens III, W. W. (1972) *Limits to Growth*, New York: Universe Books.

Milner, J. E. (1994) 'Chainsaw threat in logging protest', *New Straits Times*, Kuala Lumpur.

Osborn. F. (1948) *Our Plundered Planet*, Boston, MA: Little, Brown & Co.

Piperno, D. R. et al. (2021) 'A 5,000-year vegetation and fire history for tierra firme forests in the Medio Putamayo-Algodon watersheds, northeastern Peru', *Proceedings of the National Academy of Sciences* 118(40). Available at: https://doi.org/10.1073/pnas.2022213118

Raworth, K. (2017) *Doughnut Economics: Seven Ways to Think Like a 21st-Century Economist*, London: Penguin Books.

Reich, R. (2021) 'Why Corporate Social Responsibility is BS', *The Guardian*, 26 September. Available at: https://www.theguardian.com/commentisfree/2021/sep/26/why-corporate-social-responsibility-is-bs

Ripple, W. J. (2017) 'World scientists' warning to humanity: A second notice', *BioScience* 67(12): 1026–28.

Rockefeller Foundation (2021) *True Cost of Food*, Washington, DC: Rockefeller Foundation.

Rockstrom, J. et al. (2009) 'A safe operating space for humanity', *Nature* 461: 472–75.

Rowley, A. (2021) 'When the invisible hand of the market can't fight climate change, intervention is needed', *South China Morning Post*, 30 August. Available from: https://www.scmp.com/comment/opinion/article/3146499/when-invisible-hand-market-cant-fight-climate-change-intervention

Rubiano, M. P. (2021) 'After decades of waiting, Indigenous Peoples are finally getting a say in global conservation policy', *Grist*, 27 August. Available at: https://grist.org/accountability/after-decades-of-waiting-indigenous-peoples-are-finally-getting-a-say-in-global-conservation-policy

Schumacher, E. F. (1973) *Small is Beautiful*, London: Sphere Books.

Smith, N. J. H., Williams, J. T., Plucknett, D. L. and Talbot, J. P. (1992) *Tropical Forests and their Crops*, Ithaca, NY: Cornell University Press.

Swiss Re Institute (2020) *Biodiversity and Ecosystem Services: A Business Case*, Zurich: SRI.

Thunberg, G. (2019) *No One is too Small to Make a Difference*, London: Penguin Books.

United Nations (1987) *Our Common Future: The World Commission on Environment and Development*, Geneva: UN.

United Nations (2015) *Transforming Our World: The 2030 Agenda for Sustainable Development*, Geneva: UN.

United Nations (2017) 'Benchmarking Brazil program', Geneva: UN. Available at: https://sustainabledevelopment.un.org/partnership/?p=22525

University of Helsinki (2021) 'Large-scale commodity farming accelerating climate change in the Amazon', *PhysOrg*, 9 February. Available at: https://phys.org/pdf532080315.pdf

Vogtlin, C. (2017) 'What is responsible leadership?', *Manage Magazine*, 26 February. Available at: https://managemagazine.com/article-bank/leadership/what-responsible-leadership

Von Mises, L. (1944) *Bureaucracy*, New Haven, CT: Yale University Press.

Webster, B. (2021) 'Museum gagged by sponsorship deal with Shell', *The Times*, 30 July. Available at: https://www.thetimes.co.uk/article/science-museum-gagged-by-sponsorship-deal-with-shell-58dt00kgr

White, L. (1967) 'The historical roots of our ecological crisis', *Science* 155: 1203–11.

World Resources Institute (2021) 'Forest Pulse: The latest on the world's forests'. Available at: https://research.wri.org/gfr/forest-pulse

World Wildlife Fund (2015) *Strategies for Fighting Corruption in Wildlife Conservation: A Primer*, Washington, DC: World Wildlife Fund.

World Wildlife Fund (2020) *Living Planet Report*, Washington, DC: World Wildlife Fund.

Wrong, M. (2009) *It's Our Turn to Eat*, London: Fourth Estate.

Part VII

Diversity, Challenge and Change

Chapter 18

Responsible Leadership Development

Gender, Diversity and the Route to the Top

Mahima Mitra, Andromachi Athanasopoulou, Sue Dopson and Michael Smets

Introduction

Responsible leadership is a cornerstone of addressing the grand challenges of our time, whether it is in a political office, corporate function or grassroots movement. At its core, a responsible leader's task is "*to weave a web of inclusion* where the leader engages himself among equals" using a combination of emotional, relational and ethical intelligence (Maak and Pless, 2006: 104, emphasis in text). The Sustainable Development Goals (SDGs) of the United Nations (UN) (2015) present leaders with compelling calls to action in pursuit of a more livable, equitable and sustainable global society. To fulfill SDGs relating to, for example, good health and well-being, quality education, gender equality and decent work and economic growth, responsible leaders must "exercise . . . personal influence [for] accomplishing shared objectives in a way that is personally satisfying to those involved" (Nirenberg, 2004: 845–46). These ambitions pose a tremendous opportunity yet also a formidable challenge. The opportunity lies in being able to meet the most pressing needs of the global populace through concerted collaborative action. The challenge, however,

DOI: 10.4324/9781003129189-25

relates to implementing change in an inclusive manner and being willing to listen to the diverse voices of those whose interests the SDGs aim to fulfill.

To rise to this challenge, responsible leaders not only need to tackle world-scale issues but also enable the development of more responsible leaders – for the present, and for the future. This is critical for the creation of an inclusive society in an increasingly global and interconnected world. Efforts to make organizations more purposeful and meaningful for a greater plurality of individuals directly address goals relating to equality and socio-economic progress. Developing a more diverse cohort of leaders, however, is bound to enhance the quality of leadership – and thereby progress a larger group of SDGs.

This chapter addresses the need to create a more representative and diverse group of leaders. It addresses the barriers that inhibit the progress of potential leaders who have to date been under-represented in the upper echelons due to their gender or ethnicity – two key dimensions of diversity. Specifically, this chapter starts by outlining the context of gender and ethnic diversity in leadership. It draws on evidence from aspiring and established leaders across a variety of sectors and organizational contexts to expose institutional and individual barriers to their leadership development. The chapter concludes by utilizing the evidence on barriers to generate a selection of principles for responsible leadership development in organizations.

Gender and other forms of diversity in leadership

Since the 1980s, socio-economic changes have prompted an increasing number of organizations to recruit, promote and retain high-potential females to join the top management ranks (Vinkenburg, Jansen and Koopman, 2000). Yet, in 2018, women still made up only 22.5 percent of the Board of Directors in Fortune 500 companies, with women of color in an even starker minority, at 4.6 percent (DiversityInc, 2020). The picture looks bleaker when it comes to other forms of diversity. For example, in the United Kingdom (UK) there are only 6 ethnic minority Chairs or CEOs across the UK's FTSE 100 (Parker and The Parker Review Committee, 2017). Looking at the public sector, only 6 percent of Chairs in England's National Health Service are from a Black and Minority Ethnic (BAME) background (NHS Confederation, 2019). Similarly, heads of academic institutions with a disability also only stood at 3.1 percent, and a similar absence of leaders with disabilities has also been reported for other organizations (Roulstone and Williams, 2014). The current landscape of leadership is thus only sparsely diverse. Developing a more diverse cohort of leaders is a pressing priority.

Several studies highlight why diversity in leadership is important beyond simply creating a more inclusive work environment. Eagly (2013), for example, found that greater representation of women in senior leadership positions positively affected companies' financial performance, in a study linking their specific leadership style to the high performance of management teams in organizational contexts of innovation. Higher numbers of female leaders have also been found to enhance companies' corporate social performance, which is benefited through the enactment of 'soft' traits such as empathy, care and a generally sensitive disposition (Boulouta, 2013). Additionally, diversity in public leadership can enable those with power and authority to promote the interests of those they represent (Breslin, Pandey and Riccucci, 2017). As such, facilitating diversity at all levels of the leadership pipeline is as important as maintaining it in the upper echelons of organizations.

The multitude of ways in which diversity in leadership is conceptualized and consequently implemented has been highlighted by Ely and Thomas (2001) in the form of three paradigms. According to the authors, despite the – often – good intentions, the first two paradigms can have potential pitfalls. The *discrimination-and-fairness* paradigm recognizes that discrimination is wrong but may end up idealizing assimilation, leading to diversity conformism. The *access-and-legitimacy* paradigm embraces diversity by celebrating differences as a way to access a more diverse customer base but may lead to marginalization or exploitation of certain groups. For Ely and Thomas, a third paradigm overcomes these pitfalls. Specifically, the *integration-and-learning* paradigm aims for integration by promoting a plurality of work perspectives and tapping into the differences in the organizational membership to generate creative ideas and enhance organizational effectiveness. This range of paradigms reflects the complexities associated with understanding and designing diversity policies, let alone implementing them.

The persistent lack, or poor implementation, of diversity policies illustrated in the examples above reflects that under-represented groups are confronted with multiple barriers on their pathways to leadership (Eagly and Carli, 2007). We examine these barriers by applying an intersectional lens. 'Intersectionality' refers to the "idea that social identities such as race, class, and gender interact to form qualitatively different meanings and experiences" for individuals than when considered in isolation (Warner, 2008: 454). Applying an intersectional lens, therefore, enables us to develop a more granular understanding of the multiple levels at which inequalities manifest in individuals' leadership journeys. For the purpose of this chapter, we elucidate these barriers by focusing on two attributes – gender and ethnicity – and how they interact with other forms of diversity to impact individuals' advancement to leadership positions.

Barriers to leadership development among women and ethnic minorities

According to Ibarra, Snook and Guillen Ramo (2010a: 663–64), leadership describes "a type of work or activity rather than a formal position or . . . authority", and leadership development describes the change in "a person's capacity to exercise interpersonal influence to move and shape complex social systems". As such, it is a form of identity development whereby individuals incorporate novel elements into their existing self-concept and cement them as an integral component of their selfhood as leaders. Responsible leadership development, therefore, must nurture the individual identity of aspiring leaders such that it resonates with their preferred self-concept – and helps overcome the barriers that challenge its development. Indeed, the evidence indicates that women leaders, for instance, often get 'trapped' in some form of identity conflict due to behavioral expectations, which obstruct their leadership development (Ibarra and Petriglieri, 2007). The same is also true of ethnic minorities, who struggle with being authentic because of conflicts between cultural expectations, on the one hand, and the identity traits that they are expected to nurture to be a successful leader, on the other (Chin, Desormeaux and Sawyer, 2016). Generally, such barriers operate at two levels – the institutional and the individual – which will now be discussed.

Institutional barriers

Numerous scholars have examined the institutional barriers that slow down the leadership progression of women and ethnic minorities. They found that these primarily encompass structural barriers, gender role stereotypes and cultural impediments.

Structural barriers

One type of structural barrier reported includes the over-mentoring but under-sponsoring of women, which makes them not only less likely than men to be appointed to top roles but also more reluctant to apply in the first place (Ibarra, Carter and Silva, 2010b). Such a lack of sponsorship is also a barrier for ethnic minorities (Arday, 2018) in both the public and private sectors (Key et al., 2012). There is path dependency for female and ethnic minority leadership talent reflected in lack of access to opportunities for career promotion. A related barrier is the lack of leadership training and mentorship or support for career growth, promotions and development (Bhopal and Brown, 2016). This means that such employees may end up being less equipped with skills that would enable them to compete for more senior leadership roles in their organization.

A second structural barrier impeding women and ethnic minorities' leadership development relates to their access to resources such as role models, networks and sponsors (Arday, 2018; Ely, Ibarra and Kolb, 2011), which could give them access to more opportunities to test and prove their leadership potential. A further structural barrier reported particularly among ethnic minorities on corporate boards is the limited organizational willingness to enact diversity initiatives or the belief that there is insufficient diverse talent available (Parker and The Parker Review Committee,

2017). Moreover, "the interplay of race and gender", which reflects the "lived realities of intersectionality" (Oikelome, 2017: 29), functions as a 'double jeopardy' (Key et al., 2012) that greatly impacts the leadership journeys of women of color in particular. This paints the picture of an institutional context where diverse talent is not appreciated to the extent it deserves.

Gender role stereotypes

A further category of barriers for women's leadership development is gender role stereotypes. Examples include describing a typical 'good manager' in masculine terms, assuming women to be less effective, or expecting women to forego their career to have a family (Vinkenburg, Jansen and Koopman, 2000). As Ryan and Haslam (2007) point out, since stereotypes are often culture- or industry-specific, it is important to consider contextual variations. A female's ethnic background and upbringing or her working in male-dominated industries may render such stereotypes more difficult to navigate. Evidence suggests that even subtle forms of gender bias in societal or organizational culture interfere with the identity work of women leaders. Additionally, second-generation bias, which is predominantly unconscious and does not entail a deliberate intention to exclude or cause harm, is particularly powerful in impeding women's leadership progression by creating work structures and practices that prevent women from reaching their full potential (Ely, Ibarra and Kolb, 2011). As a result, both overt and covert discrimination practices triggered by gender and minority role stereotypes impede female and ethnic minority leadership talent from realizing their potential.

Stereotypes have been found to pose barriers for ethnic minorities in several ways, not least in the form of negative perceptions and biases that affect performance evaluations and career outcomes (Bhopal and Brown, 2016; Greer and Virick, 2008). For instance, stereotypes govern assumptions about personality traits that are seen to be incompatible with being a 'good' leader (Marquardt, Brown and Casper, 2018). Thus, Chinese individuals are presumed to be quiet and non-confrontational, while BAME individuals are perceived to be too direct in their communication. Generally, those that do not fit the leadership prototype tend to be disliked or unaccepted (Showunmi, Atewologun and Bebbington, 2016). As such, ethnic minorities find it difficult to be accepted if some presumed aspect of their identity does not fit their professional work.

From an intersectional perspective, biases and stereotypes continue to cause the leadership capabilities of female ethnic minorities to be both questioned and limited (Smith et al., 2019). Black women experience racial biases and have their performance measured against overly harsh standards (Oikelome, 2017; Rosette et al., 2016). In their evaluations, they are often negatively differentiated from White women to create 'a distinct social location' in organizations (Parker, 1996). They also do not get sufficient developmental feedback because of the 'angry black woman' stereotype (Smith et al., 2019). Asian-American women are assumed to be demure and thus penalized for showing dominant behavior (Rosette et al., 2016). Such biases undermine women's authority, especially for ethnic minority women, and prevent their accomplishments from being acknowledged or recognized.

Cultural factors

Finally, leadership development is also impeded by cultural factors that manifest as covert and overt forms of discrimination where minorities struggle to fit the majority culture. For women, such barriers often arise when organizations are gendered, for example, in the corporate practices they promote (Oakley, 2000) or the career paths they offer (Ely et al., 2011). Examples of this include job adverts designed to attract male applicants or new leadership opportunities created which female employees, who may be already struggling to balance work and family obligations, are unable to accommodate and hence are self-excluded from applying. Similarly, the gender ratio of their industry impacts women's leadership style, stress levels and mental health (Gardiner and Tiggemann, 1999). Specifically, barriers to women's ascent to senior management positions include "stereotyping, tokenism, power, preferred leadership styles, and the psychodynamics of male/female relations" (Oakley 2000: 322).

Arday (2018) observes that, for ethnic minorities, cultural barriers take the form of challenges to their authority, excessive scrutiny or surveillance, poor appraisals, missed-out promotions and hindered progression overall. Similarly, being from 'outsider groups' creates the assumption that ethnic minorities 'lack the 'right stuff' for leadership (Eagly and Chin, 2010). Simultaneously, homosociability (where, for example, panels recruit individuals similar to themselves) (Coleman, 2012) and homophily (where, for instance, leaders are rated positively based on the similarity with oneself) (Ospina and Foldy, 2009) further intensify these barriers when cultural biases impact leader appointment decisions and where institutions are reluctant to factor 'race' into decision-making (Arday, 2018).

From an intersectional perspective, the 'double jeopardy' of gender and race continues to manifest in cultural barriers. This can be illustrated when ethnic minority women confront concerns over how they can fit into a White male organization (Oikelome, 2017) and report having their authority undermined and ability to be themselves marred (Showunmi, Atewologun and Bebbington, 2016). They consequently face 'everyday microaggressions' in the workplace, including racism, sexism and discrimination. They also feel 'marginalized and tokenized' (Ospina and Foldy, 2009), and are expected to 'leave their culture at the door' if they want to progress within the organization (Showunmi, Atewologun and Bebbington, 2016). In addition, cultural differences prevent minorities from understanding 'political capital and gamesmanship', which leaves their accomplishments unacknowledged and them personally "unrecognized or doubted as professionals" (Smith et al., 2019: 1721). This means that the environment within which gender and ethnic minority leadership talent operates often tends to neither celebrate their accomplishments nor nurture a space where their successes can be visible.

Individual barriers

Viewing leadership development as a process of identity transition (Ibarra, Snook and Guillen Ramo, 2010a) helps conceptualize individual-level barriers as challenges to the personal self-concept. Such challenges can manifest in two ways – as detrimental emotional states and as self-presentation dilemmas.

Detrimental emotional states

A key individual barrier reported by women is a sense of strife in relation to personal versus managerial roles. As Ruderman and colleagues (2002) note, this can be a source of guilt and exhaustion and impact leadership practice. Another barrier relates to women's (in)visibility, which is prompted by a lack of female role models and maintained through deep-seated organizational processes, practices and power relations (Stead, 2013). Ethnic minorities also report a range of emotional states – such as inferiority, incompetence, insecurity and vulnerability – that impede their leadership journey insofar as they undermine their confidence, influence and ability to network or communicate ideas (Bhopal and Brown, 2016). In 'dominant White spaces', these phenomena are experienced as 'internalized problems' (Arday, 2018) and often attributed to 'lack of pro-activism' (Bhopal and Brown, 2016) and negative expectations held by others (Chin, Desormeaux and Sawyer, 2016).

Self-presentation dilemmas

Ibarra and Petriglieri (2007: 14) have commented that, especially during career transitions, women also engage in 'protective' self-presentation characterized by modesty, reluctance to actively and freely interact with others, and a "propensity towards neutral, uncertain and qualified expressions of judgment" such that the impression conveyed is "unassailable". This is in direct contrast to men, who engage in 'acquisitive' self-presentation to signal credibility and display confidence. Interestingly, the same workplace behaviors that bring positive outcomes to males are largely unsuccessful for females (Budworth and Mann, 2010). Concerns with self-presentation equally pose a barrier for ethnic minorities, who experience difficulties determining which behaviors suit different contexts (Bhopal and Brown, 2016) and internal conflicts between preferred and expected leadership behaviors (Chin, Desormeaux and Sawyer, 2016). They also feel pressured to fulfill diversity-related duties to uphold others' expectations and report being subjected to higher standards at work to be seen as worthy (Ospina and Foldy, 2009).

Examining the intersectional effects of gender and ethnicity reveals that Black women feel the pressure to be "twice as good" as others (Smith et al., 2019: 1719). BAME women feel compelled to maintain a highly professional persona and do not ask for adjustments relating to family life, fearing to appear uncommitted

(Bhopal, 2014). Evidence indicates that they feel constantly challenged as leaders (Showunmi, Atewologun and Bebbington, 2016) – as though "others are waiting for [them] to make a mistake" (Fitzgerald, 2006: 208).

Breaking the barriers: Principles for responsible leadership development

Our review of the barriers to leadership development among women, ethnic minorities and those at the intersection of these two groups helps to identify a set of key principles that can foster the development of responsible leaders of the future. These center on defining success, overcoming biases, increasing representation, recognizing the positive effects of multiple roles, and providing organizational support. To achieve these principles, the current generation of leaders must play multiple roles aimed at bringing together various stakeholders across the personal, organizational and community ecosystems. In doing so, they must demonstrate personal traits that enable them to act as a steward, citizen, servant and visionary for change. Additionally, they must also display the relational characteristics that help them act as architects, change agents, storytellers and coaches (Maak and Pless, 2006). We now consider each of the key principles in turn.

Define success

Responsible leadership development must recognize and respect the cultural differences and values that shape individuals' ideas of success and frame their leadership identity. For example, women's definitions of success and achievement depend on personal criteria such as "a sense of contribution, personal fulfillment and integrity, as well as external tangible measures such as compensation and title" (Hopkins and O'Neil, 2007: 134). Among ethnic minorities, maintaining a sense of personal authenticity is seen as a sign of success (Chin, Desormeaux and Sawyer, 2016), as is hard work and perseverance (Bhopal and Brown, 2016). Female BAMEs rank competence and capability as key to being successful (Oikelome, 2017). It is important to both acknowledge and validate such criteria when appointing and appraising leaders. Current leaders can also facilitate the development of organizational cultures and discourses that both promote and celebrate the diversity of values considered important by individuals.

Yet another measure of success is self-acceptance. Irrespective of their background, highly successful females report a moment of self-acceptance early on in their careers at the outset of their leadership journey. Self-acceptance as potential leaders allows them to take active ownership of their careers, steer their leadership journey with more confidence and look for sources of support within themselves and their environment (Athanasopoulou et al., 2018). Responsible leaders can foster self-acceptance among emerging leaders by providing formal opportunities for coaching and mentoring, as well as through the creation of safe organizational spaces that enable conversation on self-awareness and self-worth in relation to leader identity development. Showcasing the personal identity journeys of emerging leaders can enable responsible leaders to play a pivotal role in redefining what leadership success means in organizations.

Overcome biases and increase representation

Chen and Van Velsor (1996: 299) observe that: "To develop diverse individuals, the leader has to first create an environment that allows different individuals to excel differently". This requires leaders to overcome biases not only at a personal level but also facilitate the development of a bias-free organizational culture and a diverse leadership pipeline. Several measures can be put in place in this regard, such as using a wide breadth of advertising mechanisms to ensure a diverse candidate pool, offering unconscious bias training for recruitment panels (Equality Challenge Unit and Leadership Foundation for Higher Education, 2009) and performance evaluations (Marquardt, Brown and Casper, 2018), as well as overcoming any 'similarity bias' during succession planning (Greer and Virick, 2008). These steps allow the removal of significant barriers for female and ethnic minority leadership talent, paving the way to the top – hence, potentially leading even to the senior executive office.

There are additional sets of measures that can increase diversity in senior leadership roles. These can take the form of affirmative action through statutory quotas or mandated candidate diversity at the shortlisting stage of the leadership appointment process (Arday, 2018), 'positive discrimination' via BAME quotas within senior ranks, or 'softer' measures including mentoring, shadowing or coaching with Board members (Parker and The Parker Review Committee, 2017). Other actions include offering remuneration for board roles to encourage diverse membership for individuals who cannot afford *pro bono* board work (Equality Challenge Unit and Leadership Foundation for Higher Education, 2009), modifying hiring practices by relaxing requirements for diverse candidates or focusing on relevant skills instead of experience in a similar role (Equality Challenge Unit, 2015). In this regard, continuous monitoring of diversity statistics against measurable goals is critical for sustainable outcomes. It is important to note, though, that the establishment of the above 'hard' measures for reducing bias must be accompanied by 'softer' mechanisms that promote an organizational culture of sensitivity, empathy and awareness. Indeed, a responsible leader needs to play a more significant role in this regard at both the personal level, through the practice of reflexive leadership, as well as in their role as trailblazers of diversity at organizational level.

Recognize the positive effects of multiple roles and provide organizational support

Responsible leadership development should recognize the value of incorporating an individual's multiple personal roles in their leadership *persona*. For instance, unlike common assumptions about the negative effects of work-life balance tensions, the roles women play in their personal lives also produce several positive effects in their work lives, including psychological well-being, enriched interpersonal skills and improved leadership effectiveness (Ruderman et al., 2002). Among BAME leaders, effectiveness appears to be linked to their utilization of both personal and social identity, specifically drawing from lived experiences to practice leadership based on cultural values such as consensus and collaboration over competition, and family values and relationships over business (Chin, Desormeaux and Sawyer, 2016). A central aspect of promoting and valuing multiple roles is to stop fitting leaders into 'cookie-cutter' molds and instead conceptualize them in the myriad ways that promote a diversity of leader images to emerge.

Organizations can promote the positive effects of multiple roles by providing organizational support that goes beyond the minimum statutory requirements to embed diversity in their overall organizational strategy (Parker and The Parker Review Committee, 2017). Building mentoring and networking skills among women and ethnic minorities is key in this regard (Athanasopoulou et al., 2018; Coleman, 2012). Those mentoring aspiring ethnic minority leaders should receive relevant leadership training to deliver mentorship within a safe climate (Bhopal and Brown, 2016; Greer and Virick, 2008), act as organizational sponsors for mentees, and help them develop the skills to take on and navigate their leadership roles (Chin, Desormeaux and Sawyer, 2016). Relatedly, responsible leaders must enable the creation of high-visibility assignments that provide the skills, confidence and learning opportunities for women and ethnic minorities to hold a leadership position (Chen and Van Velsor, 1996). This entails not only embracing leadership development interventions but also creating an organizational environment that genuinely values the distinctive leadership style of women and ethnic minorities – one in which they can feel comfortable and authentic to reach their full potential (Athanasopoulou et al., 2018; Chin, Desormeaux and Sawyer, 2016).

Conclusion

This chapter has sought to provide an evidence-based discussion of the challenges faced by under-represented groups as well as the range of interventions possible to enable these groups to become responsible leaders of the future. These opportunities exist conjointly, at the individual, organizational and institutional levels. They help to foster individuals' diverse potential, enable organizations to embrace individual differences, and facilitate institutional environments that celebrate and realize the benefits of having a diverse leadership. It is now incumbent on our current generation of leaders, within the constraints of their contexts, to create the conditions for greater diversity to inform the decision-making and change processes required to translate the UN SDGs into action.

This form of responsible leadership requires leaders to shift away from hierarchical practices and, instead, nurture 'relationships, conversation and shared purpose' (Stokes and Dopson, 2020) that enable diverse leadership talent to emerge, experiment and learn. Another formidable task is for leaders to nudge existing contexts to "cultivate the [organizational] ecosystem and build internal connection and collaboration" (Stokes and Dopson, 2020: 14). As such, the creation of a psychologically safe culture that fosters accountability and learning remains a key aspiration of the responsible leadership that we consider critical for diversity to flourish.

References

Arday, J. (2018) 'Understanding race and educational leadership in higher education: Exploring the Black and ethnic minority (BME) experience', *Management in Education* 32(4): 192–200.

Athanasopoulou, A., Moss Cowan, A., Smets, M. and Morris, T. (2018) 'Claiming the corner office: Female CEO careers and implications for leadership development', *Human Resource Management* 57(2): 617–39.

Bhopal, K. (2014) 'The experiences of BME academics in higher education: Aspirations in the face of inequality', *Leadership Foundation for Higher Education Stimulus Papers*, London: Leadership Foundation for Higher Education.

Bhopal, K. and Brown, H. (2016) *Black and Minority Ethnic Leaders: Support Networks and Strategies for Success in Higher Education*, London: Leadership Foundation for Higher Education.

Boulouta, I. (2013) 'Hidden connections: The link between board gender diversity and corporate social performance', *Journal of Business Ethics* 113(2): 185–97.

Breslin, R. A., Pandey, S. and Riccucci, N. M. (2017) 'Intersectionality in public leadership research: A review and future research agenda', *Review of Public Personnel Administration* 37(2): 160–82.

Budworth, M. and Mann, S. L. (2010) 'Becoming a leader: The challenge of modesty for women', *Journal of Management Development* 29(2): 177–86.

Chen, C. C. and van Velsor, E. (1996) 'New directions for research and practice in diversity leadership', *The Leadership Quarterly* 7(2): 285–302.

Chin, J. L., Desormeaux, L. and Sawyer, K. (2016) 'Making way for paradigms of diversity leadership', *Consulting Psychology Journal: Practice and Research* 68(1): 49–71.

Coleman, M. (2012) 'Leadership and diversity', *Educational Management Administration and Leadership* 40(5): 592–609.

DiversityInc (2020) *2020 Top 50 Facts and Figures*. Available at: https://www.diversityinc.com/facts-figures/

Eagly, A. H. (2013) 'Women as leaders: Leadership style versus leaders' values and attitudes', presentation to Harvard Business School Research Symposium on Gender and Work: Challenging Conventional Wisdom, February.

Eagly, A. H. and Carli, L. (2007) *Through the Labyrinth: The Truth About How Women Become Leaders*, Boston, MA: Harvard Business School Press.

Eagly, A. H. and Chin, J. L. (2010) 'Diversity and leadership in a changing world', *American Psychologist* 65(3): 216–24.

Ely, R. J., Ibarra, H. and Kolb, D. M. (2011) 'Taking gender into account: Theory and design for Women's leadership development programs', *Academy of Management Learning and Education* 10(3): 474–93.

Ely, R. J. and Thomas, D. A. (2001) 'Cultural diversity at work: The effects of diversity perspectives on work group processes and outcomes', *Administrative Science Quarterly* 46(2): 229–73.

Equality Challenge Unit (2015) *Governing Bodies, Equality and Diversity in Scottish Higher Education Institutions: Research Report*, London: Equality Challenge Unit.

Equality Challenge Unit and Leadership Foundation for Higher Education (2009) *Governing Bodies, Equality and Diversity: A Handbook for Governors of Higher Education Institutions*, London: Equality and Diversity Unit.

Fitzgerald, T. (2006) 'Walking between two worlds: Indigenous women and educational leadership', *Educational Management Administration and Leadership* 34(2): 201–13.

Gardiner, M. and Tiggemann, M. (1999) 'Gender differences in leadership style, job stress and mental health in male-and female-dominated industries', *Journal of Occupational and Organizational Psychology* 72(3): 301–15.

Greer, C. R. and Virick, M. (2008) 'Diverse succession planning: Lessons from the industry leaders', *Human Resource Management* 47(2): 351–67.

Hopkins, M. M. and O'Neil, D. A. (2007) 'Women and success: Dilemmas and opportunities', in Bilimoria, D. and Piderit, S. K. (eds) *Handbook on Women in Business and Management*, Cheltenham: Edward Elgar.

Ibarra, H. and Petriglieri, J. (2007) Impossible selves: Image strategies and identity threat in professional women's career transitions', *INSEAD Working Papers Collection* 69: 1–35.

Ibarra, H., Carter, N. M. and Silva, C. (2010b) 'Why men still get more promotions than women', *Harvard Business Review* 88(9): 80–86.

Ibarra, H., Snook, S. and Guillen Ramo, L. (2010a) 'Identity-based leader development', in Nohria, N. and Khurana, R. (eds) *Handbook of Leadership Theory and Practice*, Boston, MA: Harvard University Press.

Key, S., Popkin, S., Munchus, G., Wech, B., Hill, V. and Tanner, J. (2012) 'An exploration of leadership experiences among white women and women of color', *Journal of Organizational Change Management* 25(3): 392–404.

Maak, T. and Pless, N. M. (2006) 'Responsible leadership in a stakeholder society: A relational perspective', *Journal of Business Ethics* 66(1): 99–115.

Marquardt, D. J., Brown, L. W. and Casper, W. J. (2018) 'Ethical leadership perceptions: Does it matter if you're black or white?', *Journal of Business Ethics* 151(3): 599–612.

NHS Confederation (2019) *Chairs and Non-executives in the NHS: The Need for Diverse Leadership*, London: NHS Confederation. Available at: https://www.nhsconfed.org/-/media/Confederation/Files/Publications/Chairs-and-non-executives-in-the-NHS.pdf

Nirenberg, J. (2004) 'Leadership effectiveness', in Goethals, G. R., Sorenson, G. J. and Burns, J. M. (eds) *Encyclopedia of Leadership*, Volume I, London: Sage.

Oakley, J. G. (2000) 'Gender-based barriers to senior management positions: Understanding the scarcity of female CEOs', *Journal of Business Ethics 27*(4): 321–34.

Oikelome, G. (2017) 'Pathway to the presidency: The perceived impact of identity structures on the journey experiences of women college presidents', *International Journal of Multicultural Education* 19(3): 23–40.

Ospina, S. and Foldy, E. (2009) 'A critical review of race and ethnicity in the leadership literature: Surfacing context, power and the collective dimensions of leadership', *Leadership Quarterly* 20(6): 876–96.

Parker, J. and The Parker Review Committee (2017) *A Report into the Ethnic Diversity of UK Boards*, London: EY and Linklaters. Available at: https://assets.ey.com/content/dam/ey-sites/ey-com/en_uk/news/2020/02/ey-parker-review-2017-report-final.pdf

Parker, P. S. (1996) 'Gender, culture, and leadership: Toward a culturally distinct model of African-American women executives' leadership strategies', *Leadership Quarterly* 7(2): 189–214.

Rosette, A. S., Koval, C. Z., Ma, A. and Livingston, R. (2016) 'Race matters for women leaders: Intersectional effects on agentic deficiencies and penalties', *Leadership Quarterly* 27(3): 429–45.

Roulstone, A. and Williams, J. (2014) 'Being disabled, being a manager: "Glass partitions" and conditional identities in the contemporary workplace', *Disability and Society* 29(1): 16–29.

Ruderman, M. N., Ohlott, P. J., Panzer, K., and King, S. N. (2002) 'Benefits of multiple roles for managerial women', *Academy of Management Journal* 45(2): 369–86.

Ryan, M. K. and Haslam, S. (2007) 'The glass cliff: Exploring the dynamics surrounding the appointment of women to precarious leadership positions', *Academy of Management Review* 32(2): 549–72.

Showunmi, V., Atewologun, D. and Bebbington, D. (2016) 'Ethnic, gender and class intersections in British women's leadership experiences', *Educational Management Administration and Leadership* 44(6): 917–35.

Smith, A. N., Watkins, M. B., Ladge, J. J. and Carlton, P. (2019) 'Making the invisible visible: Paradoxical effects of intersectional invisibility on the career experiences of executive Black women', *Academy of Management Journal* 62(6): 1705–34.

Stead, V. (2013) 'Learning to deploy (in)visibility: An examination of women leaders' lived experiences', *Management Learning* 44(1): 63–79.

Stokes, J. and Dopson, S. (2020) *From Ego to Eco: Leadership for the Fourth Industrial Revolution*, Oxford: Saïd Business School.

United Nations (2015) *Transforming Our World: The 2030 Agenda for Sustainable Development*, Geneva: UN.

Vinkenburg, C. J., Jansen, P. G. W. and Koopman, P. L. (2000) 'Feminine leadership: A review of gender differences in managerial behaviour and effectiveness', in Davidson, M. J. and Burke, R. J. (eds) *Women in Management: Current Research Issue*, Volume II, London: Sage.

Warner, L. R. (2008) 'A best practices guide to intersectional approaches in psychological research', *Sex Roles* 59(5): 454–63.

Chapter 19

Human Trafficking and Responsible Leadership

Louise Shelley

Introduction

Leadership in combatting human trafficking has for two decades been in the hands of international, national and local law enforcement and multinational organizations such as the United Nations (UN) and the Organization for Security and Co-operation in Europe (OSCE). Often their activities are supported by many diverse and active civil society organizations. Yet the corporate world has until recently not assumed a significant role in combatting the diverse forms of human trafficking even though technology, transport and the hospitality industry have important roles in facilitating human trafficking. To address this problem requires much more responsible leadership from many sectors of the business community that the public do not traditionally associate with the crime of human trafficking. Yet Leary (2019) has suggested – now as in the past – legitimate corporations have benefited much from the trade in human beings, providing a disincentive to action. This flies in the face of various UN (2015) SDGs – not least empowering women and girls, promoting decent work, making cities safe and creating just societies.

The prioritization of a law enforcement response resulted from the origin of the global legislative framework for human trafficking. In 2000, the UN Office on Drugs and Crime introduced the Convention against Transnational Organized Crime and its associated protocols on human trafficking and smuggling. The UN Protocol to Prevent, Suppress and Punish Trafficking in Persons came into force

DOI: 10.4324/9781003129189-26

in 2003 with a focus on the criminalization of the phenomenon, the prevention of victimization, and the protection of victims (United Nations General Assembly, 2003). This approach is hardly surprising considering that the legislation was developed by the UN Office on Drugs and Crime in conjunction with international law enforcement personnel. However, the Protocol does not address the enabling and facilitating role of legitimate companies in human trafficking – instead focusing on criminal perpetrators.

Since the Protocol was introduced, the operation and logistics of human traffickers have changed dramatically. The business practices of human traffickers have evolved as have their counterparts in the licit economy. No longer is human trafficking a phenomenon primarily associated with the criminal world. Traffickers have modified their business practices, being early adapters and significant users of online platforms, apps and social media to recruit and sell those they traffic. This observation is especially valid in the developed world, yet it is also true in the developing world, as billions are connected through web and social media platforms, facilitating the recruitment of victims for labor and sex trafficking as well as child sexual exploitation.

These new technologies facilitate human trafficking in other ways. Smart phones and social media can allow traffickers to make transport reservations for planes, car-sharing services and hotels. Moreover, the sharing economy that has recently emerged, often accessed through the Internet and phones, plays a key role in facilitating human trafficking. Ride-sharing services such as Uber and apartment sharing such as Airbnb have been exploited by traffickers to their advantage (Marchildon, 2018). Only in recent years have these companies begun to initiate training and oversight to ensure they are not being misused by traffickers. Diverse online services also allow traffickers to access wire transfers, banks and more recently cryptocurrencies to move their operational funds and dispose of the profits of human trafficking and child exploitation without ready detection (Redfern and Lee, 2021).

The financial community has taken a lead in addressing their facilitating role, and banks in particular have been proactive in identifying indicators of human trafficking amongst their billions of financial records. The adage of many criminal investigators, 'to follow the money', has been harnessed by the business community to locate child exploitation and human trafficking. The insights of financial institutions which have partnered with law enforcement have been effective in countering human trafficking. This public-private partnership has been key not only in locating traffickers and trafficking networks that could evade notice but also in reducing the human resources needed to locate and gather evidence on human traffickers.

This proactive behavior and leadership shown by the financial sector, however, has not been replicated by many other key corporate sectors facilitating human trafficking. As will be seen, the hotel sector has done far too little for too long in establishing guidelines to prevent and identify human trafficking and is now facing numerous suits by victims in the United States (US) seeking reparations. And while the air transport industry has responded, this corporate initiative has been a response to the major steps taken by employees to combat human trafficking rather than a sign of corporate leadership.

Most disturbing has been the role of many key corporate actors in the technology sector who have not only failed to respond to human trafficking but have even significantly profited from facilitating it. Legal and computer specialists have pointed out the large sums made by Google and You Tube from monetizing online videos of the exploitation of underage girls (Leary, 2019). Moreover, the enormous power, influence and wealth of the tech community has sometimes been harnessed to deflect attention from their role in this very serious crime, as tech companies lobbied the US Congress not to regulate their activities and change the key legal provision – Section 230 of the Commercial Code – that for a long time protected them from responsibility in facilitating human trafficking (Leary, 2019).

This chapter will overview the response of the different corporate sectors to human trafficking, in relation to both labor trafficking and sexual exploitation. It will argue that there has been too little corporate leadership in combating human trafficking. Moreover, this leadership has been most deficient in the areas where corporations play the most important role as facilitators – in the technology and hospitality industry. Now civil society, legislators, courts and victims are forcing action on companies that have failed to assume leadership voluntarily in combating this crime, violating the human rights of many millions worldwide.

The analysis in this chapter draws on many years of study and a broad multidisciplinary literature base on human trafficking and corporate social responsibility. I have drawn on diverse sources for my insights – from court cases and published work to attendance at academic and professional conferences on law enforcement and other issues, including internationally with the UN and the OSCE, and at a regional and national level. I have also met many corporate actors through my long-time work on human trafficking with the World Economic Forum (Bain and Shelley, 2015). My research has also involved numerous meetings and discussions with law enforcement professionals, civil society, individuals in technology and other sectors of the corporate world, transport, finance and the hospitality industry.

In addition, I have interviewed and worked with people in the Defense Advanced Research Projects Agency (DARPA) (https://www.darpa.mil/) on human trafficking, which is aimed at using advanced data tools to unmask criminal networks operating online (Greenemeier, 2015). More recently, I have read the case files of many human trafficking prosecutions and investigations by the US Congress and other bodies and examined the suits filed by victims against hotels where they were abused. Although these sources are predominantly US based, the phenomenon is global, and American influence in technology and multinational corporations allows a broad window on the global situation.

Corporate responsibility in human trafficking

Over a decade ago, laws were adopted in the US criminalizing financial benefit from human trafficking (Shavers, 2012). These were enacted because those responding to human trafficking increasingly realized that this was not just a crime in the shadows and was exclusively linked to the criminal world. Lawmakers understood that the legitimate economy had a significant role in facilitating this criminal activity. The 2008 Reauthorization of the Trafficking Victims Protection Act introduced provisions to hold specific entities and individuals liable for civil damages, such as motels and hotels as well as "massage parlors, restaurants, and even online platforms, that facilitate or financially benefit from a trafficking enterprise" (Sagduyu, 2017). This law applies to all forms of human trafficking, encompassing both sexual and labor trafficking. American corporations engaged in human trafficking – for example, by using trafficked laborers – run the risk of losing government contracts (Shavers, 2012). These new human trafficking provisions could also lead to liability for companies that abuse migrant and seasonal workers in agricultural labor. Yet American law was very slowly applied against corporations – although in 2017, there were six times as many federal civil trafficking cases filed than in 2004 (Levy, 2018).

Corporations addressing their responsibility in human trafficking have focused primarily on trafficked labor in supply chains rather than on online platforms, social media, hotels/motels and transport companies in the facilitation of sex and labor trafficking. Moreover, human trafficking analysts mainly choose to concentrate on the few companies behaving responsibly as opposed to the very significant number of corporations failing to address their role in human trafficking (Bigio and Vogelstein, 2021).

Corporate action on human trafficking sometimes develops as a response to employee pressure from below rather than policy changes from the top. This is most evident in the airline industry, where flight attendants have responded to their personal exposure and identification of human trafficking victims (Metropolitan Airport News, 2021). At the top of the list of mobilization from below has been the Association of Flight Attendants-CWA (n.d.), which has developed and implemented its own training programs to identify and stop human trafficking, resulting in the rescue of some victims and the identification of their traffickers (Airline Ambassadors International, n.d.). With such initiative from their own personnel, companies such as Delta and United have responded with more proactive corporate policies (Sturken, 2019). These efforts have impacted human trafficking not just in the US but globally because of their large international footprint.

Key leadership has been provided by many in the financial sector who have found ways to use the existing databases of banks and financial service firms to locate human trafficking by identifying key indicators within their large data sets. This started in 2010 with employees of JPMorgan and Chase in New York and was then picked up by other banks that cooperated in the area (Bain and Shelley, 2015). Similar cooperation occurred on the regional level, especially at the time of large sporting events (Sparks, 2019), before going international. Project Shadow, a public-private partnership against child exploitation online, was initiated in Canada (Mari, 2020), and the Finance Against Slavery and Trafficking (FAST) Initiative, also referred to as the Liechtenstein Initiative, has operated under the framework of the UN (Embassy of the Principality of Liechtenstein, n.d.).

Labor trafficking and supply chains

In the US, for the last twenty years the vast preponderance of prosecutions are for sex trafficking. The year 2020 was no exception – when only 6 percent of active trafficking cases involved labor trafficking (Feehs and Currier Wheeler, 2021). Unfortunately, the US is not unique in its failure to pursue cases of labor exploitation (Bracy, Lul, and Roe-Sepowitz, 2021). More attention, however, has been paid to the exploitation of workers overseas and the need for corporations to act responsibly regarding international supply chains lest the products they sell are produced by trafficked laborers (Ciliberti, Pontrandolfo and Scozzi, 2008; Schumann, 2019). Unpacking the supply chains for a particular product can be difficult, as many companies engage in subcontracting to save money, and it is hard to determine the people involved in the production of a particular item. Concern about supply chains is much needed because agricultural products, extracted natural resources, fish, and textiles are far too often produced with exploited labor. However, companies have been forced to more carefully scrutinize their supply chains as a result of journalistic exposés (Balch, 2021) and pressure from citizens (Freedom United, n.d.), consumers and investors (Know the Chain, 2015).

Legislation to promote greater accountability in supply chains is of recent origin. In 2010, the California Transparency in Supply Chains Act was enacted, coming into effect in 2012. It was the first legislation of its kind to address modern slavery in supply chains through transparency and reporting obligations (Know the Chain, 2015). This Act was followed by legislation in the United Kingdom (UK), such as the UK Modern Slavery Act in 2015, with Europe also legally requiring greater company diligence over human rights concerns (Bullock, Neil and Romanelli, 2021; Bullock et al., 2021). European legal action is not as direct as in the US and UK, but the focus on human rights has resulted in more attention being given to problematic supply chains. Some European legislative measures and covenants are tied to the supply chain of particular industries, such as textile producers. These are usually a response to human tragedies such as factory accidents or the factory fires in Bangladesh in which many textile workers perished (Dickson and Warren, 2020).

The California Transparency in Supply Chains Act requires companies doing business in California with gross receipts of $100 million worldwide to eradicate human trafficking and slavery from their supply chains. The potential impact of the California Supply Chain Act is significant because California is the most populous state in the US, and few large international companies would seek to be excluded from this market. However, the Supply Chain Act has not been as transformational as anticipated. It requires that companies make disclosures about their actions on their websites to verify that their product supply chains are free of trafficked labor. But California has rarely responded to violations of its supply chain law with legal action, and federal measures to address the problem at the national level have unfortunately not been passed. Fortunately, though, US and UK laws have prompted some companies to proactively seek outside expertise to ensure that their supply chains are free of exploited laborers – even if the UK law on Modern Slavery, like its California counterpart, has also not prevented many global companies from still having slave labor within their supply chains (Steiner-Dicks, 2019). It is not surprising, therefore, that a group of twenty Non-Governmental Organizations (NGOs) recently wrote to the leadership of the G7 calling for member states to prioritize eliminating forced labor from their supply chains (Thulander, 2021).

Social media and online platforms

Human trafficking has transformed in recent decades with the widespread use of the Internet and social media by billions of people. Access to information, greater connectivity across the globe and the increasing speed of communications have benefited many. Yet one of the greatest costs has been the growth of human trafficking and online child sexual exploitation. Many of the most known technology firms in the world are key hubs in the supply chains for human trafficking. The increasing vulnerability of individuals online was noticed in the mid-1990s by the US Customs Service, as most of the world's Internet Service Providers (ISPs) then traversed the Washington DC area. This meant that they could chart the rising presence of child sexual exploitation material online (Shelley, 1998) as online sexual advertisements proliferated – many for trafficked minors (Senate Permanent Subcommittee on Investigations, 2017). The corporate response to the massive misuse of the new technologies was limited, although the Financial Coalition Against Child Sexual Exploitation was established in 2006, with dozens of leading banks, credit card payments, electronic payment networks and Internet service companies seeking to stem the problem. More recently, cryptocurrency payment processing has been added. However, the focus of this financial coalition on the dissemination and sale of images rather than the victims of sex trafficking should be noted (International Centre for Missing and Exploited Children, n.d.).

Encouragingly, DARPA, a branch of the US Department of Defense that helped develop the Internet, allocated years of labor power and over $60 million to understand the use and abuse of online platforms by human traffickers (Pellerin, 2017). Their research revealed the very significant size of this market – about $250 million was spent by traffickers within a two-year period posting more than 60 million advertisements internationally for commercial sexual services (Greenemeier, 2015).

Although the research was carried out in the US, it revealed global networks of human trafficking. In one Canadian-American criminal case that resulted from the network analysis, an operator in China was running trafficking networks with victims in over fifty cities in the US, Canada and Australia (United States v. Chen, 2018; United States Department of Justice, 2019). But the dependence on online advertisements for the trafficking business does not just occur in the developing world. As an in-depth analysis of human trafficking in Malaysia revealed, online advertisements are key to the exploitation of women there as well (Mahalingam and Sidhu, 2020).

Traffickers could not expand their businesses so significantly without being able to post advertisements so easily online at low cost, a dissemination strategy facilitated by the legitimate economy. Such facilitators evaded criminal responsibility for a long time because of a specific provision of Section 230 of the Communication Decency Act of the Telecommunication Act of 1996, in which platforms were exempted from responsibility for the user content they hosted, even if they included explicit sexual content facilitating human trafficking. The rationale was that it aided the growth of the Internet by affording "protection from civil liability to internet providers that host content created by a third party" (Carney, 2019: 360). One of the consequences was the ability to sell individuals, particularly minors, for sexual exploitation without accountability.

Traffickers placed advertisements with some of the largest online advertisers catering to customers who wanted to buy sexual services. Two American-based companies, first Craig's List and then Backpage.com, were major purveyors of advertisements for paid sexual services, which accounted for the vast majority of the profits of these two online businesses. In 2010, the 'erotic services' section of Craig's List was shut down by law enforcement (Saletan, 2010), and then some of these advertisements migrated to the sales platform of Backpage. Both of these companies began in the US, but traffickers around the world bought advertisements. At its height, Craig's List was operating in over 70 countries, and Backpage was present in 97 countries and 943 locales worldwide (Senate Permanent Subcommittee on Investigations, 2017). Neither Craig's List nor Backpage, despite intense law enforcement pressure, chose to leave the business of online sexual advertisements because they made so much money. The founders of Backpage had made $135 million in 2014 with 82 percent profitability, primarily from posting online sexual advertisements. Each of the founders of Backpage received a $10 million bonus in 2014 (Savage and Williams, 2018). Moreover, companies hosting Craig's List and Backpage did not remove these advertisements from their platforms. There was an absence of corporate social responsibility therefore in the companies directly marketing sexual services and in the hosting companies allowing these advertisers to operate – even after law enforcement investigations revealed the criminal activity facilitated by these online advertisements.

In 2018, one of the founders of Backpage.com pleaded guilty in three states to charges of money laundering and the facilitation of prostitution (Jackman, 2018).

Backpage was ultimately shutdown in 2018 after an indictment in which it was alleged that the company had laundered $500 million since initiating its online advertising in 2004 and several young girls who responded to online advertisements had been murdered (Jackman and Berman, 2018). In response, legislation was proposed in the US Congress to lift the protections afforded by provision 230 of the Commercial Code. In Spring 2018, the Stop Enabling Sex Traffickers Act (SESTA) and Allow States and Victims to Fight Online Sex Trafficking Act (FOSTA) legislation was passed with wide bi-partisan support, now known as the FOSTA-SESTA legislation. The adoption of these laws followed intense corporate lobbying. Google and Alphabet along with other tech companies spent millions lobbying against changes in provision 230, but they eventually relented given the tide of public opinion for the removal of the protections concerned (Leary, 2019).

As the Allow States and Victims to Fight Online Sex Trafficking Act of 2017 stated, the "Communications Decency Act of 1996 was never intended to provide legal protection to websites that unlawfully promote and facilitate prostitution and websites that facilitate traffickers in advertising the sale of unlawful sex acts with sex trafficking victims". The ensuing legislation removed the protections for web hosting services, ISPs, and social media sites for the crime of human trafficking. The legislation further provided penalties for someone who "owns, manages, or operates an interactive computer service (or attempts or conspires to do so) to promote or facilitate the prostitution of another person". Those found guilty can face up to ten years in prison and hefty fines. This law consequently expected a higher standard of responsibility from the ISPs (Balfour, 2019).

The US Congress, after forcing American companies to behave responsibly, had not solved the problem of online advertisements. Within a month of the passage of the FOSTA-SESTA legislation and the shutdown of Backpage in early 2018, advertisements for commercial sex in the US plummeted by 82 percent. After four months, however, the numbers of advertisements jumped back to 75 percent of their daily volume before Backpage was closed and FOSTA-SESTA was passed into law (Tarinelli, 2018). There is evidence that the geographic locations of the servers hosting sexual content shifted abroad to platforms hosted outside the reach of the US and not subject to the new legislation. Some 90 percent of global images of child abuse are hosted by servers in Europe, where The Netherlands is the hub of websites hosting images of child sex abuse because of Internet regulatory failure there (Gibbons, 2020). The problem of corporate responsibility in hosting and contributing to sexual abuse is therefore not confined to a single country but shifts location depending on national regulation and enforcement.

The FOSTA-SESTA law has also recently been applied to social media companies such as Facebook, which has been identified as a key facilitator of human trafficking (Scheck, Purnell and Horwitz, 2021). The problem of social media platforms as trafficking facilitators is not confined to the US. Instagram has also reputedly been used to recruit women from Africa and Asia who are exploited in domestic servitude in the Gulf. Upon arrival in the Middle East, Instagram has apparently also been used to advertise their availability and then distribute them (McQue, 2021).

According to the Human Trafficking Institute's analysis of US federal criminal cases, Facebook was the most common platform for child recruitment in 2020 based on active child sex trafficking cases; it has been alleged that 59 percent of child victims were recruited on social media through Facebook, a pattern also identified in 2019 (Feehs and Currier Wheeler, 2021) – despite teens not being the population usually using Facebook. Instagram and Snapchat seem to be the next most used forms of recruitment of child victims of sex trafficking, and they are also owned by Facebook. In early 2021, Facebook reported that it had identified over 20 million images of child sexual exploitation on its platform (Porter, 2021). Facebook asserts that its corporate policy is to address human trafficking online and its identification of millions of child exploitation images reveals that its algorithms are having success in online identification. However, the prominence of Facebook and its social media platforms in federal cases related to the recruitment of identified trafficking victims suggests that it is not allocating enough resources to address this. Moreover, the push by Facebook to have full end-to-end encryption (Hutchinson, 2021) promises to reduce the possibility of identifying images of child sex exploitation online and targeting the recruiters of youthful victims. This has prompted concern at the highest levels of the US Department of Justice (McCabe, Isaac and Benner, 2019).

In late June 2021, the Texas Supreme Court ruled against Facebook on behalf of plaintiffs who alleged they had been recruited by pimps through Facebook and Instagram. The mother of one of the minors recruited by a trafficker through Instagram reported this problem to Facebook but received no response. Facebook argued that Section 230 of the Communications Decency Act exempted them from responsibility. The Texas Supreme Court denied Facebook's motion and stated that Section 230 "does not 'create a lawless no-man's-land on the Internet'" (Johnson, 2021). In another case involving the federal courts in Texas, victims were allowed to sue Salesforce, which provided Backpage with the software to advertise individuals who subsequently became victims of sex trafficking. According to the suit (*A.B. v. Salesforce.com*, 2020), Salesforce was knowingly and directly facilitating the sex trafficking of Backpage.

Human trafficking and hotels

Hotels figure prominently in human trafficking; they are key elements of the supply chains of human trafficking. The 2020 Trafficking in Persons Report issued by the US State Department named hotels in many countries as sites where trafficking victims are exploited. Examples from individual country reports identify this problem in Asia, Europe, Africa, the Caribbean, Central America and the Middle East. Training programs have been initiated in many countries to warn victims and incentivize hotel staff to report human trafficking, but much still needs to be done to address this pervasive problem (United States Department of State, 2020). The misused role of hotels and resorts may be particularly pronounced in some countries dependent on tourism but is by no means confined to these.

Too little attention has been paid in the research literature to the role of hotels in facilitating human trafficking for both sexual and labor exploitation. The problem has been rarely discussed in Europe (Paraskevas and Brookes, 2018) and very infrequently analyzed in the US until recently. Most of the analysis occurs in civil society and government research reports rather than by those within the academic community. The impression therefore remains in much of the literature that human trafficking is confined to the illicit (or shadow) economy and does not intersect with the legitimate economy. Hotels, though, provide an important case, along with the tech industry, where a legitimate business is an important facilitator of human trafficking. Moreover, the two legitimate sectors are connected because many hotel reservations are made online to arrange for clients to meet human trafficking victims, thereby limiting insights into the identity of individuals who rent hotel rooms (Anthony, 2018)

The human trafficking hotline in the US run by the Polaris project has identified hotels as key locales for both labor and sexual exploitation. According to their multi-year hotline data, there were 3,596 reported cases occurring at hotels (Anthony, 2018). Hotels also figure significantly in prosecuted cases of human trafficking. In recent years, the Human Trafficking Institute noted that hotels were cited as places of exploitation in the overwhelming preponderance of federal cases. In 2020, the percentage was 73 percent as against the comparable figure for 2019 of 80 percent (Feehs and Currier Wheeler, 2020). The same chains of hotels consistently figure prominently as the sites of exploitation of victims of sex trafficking. In 2019, federal cases revealed that most sex trafficking occurred in small chain or non-chain hotels followed by Motel 6, Super 8, Days Inn and Red Roof (Feehs and Currier Wheeler, 2020). Although many of these are low-end hotels, middle to high-end chains such as Hilton, Marriott and Wyndham are allegedly also sites of exploitation according to examined cases and civil suits filed by trafficking victims (Ramey, 2020).

The original intent of the human trafficking law in the US was to establish criminal penalties for human trafficking. But in the Trafficking Victims Protection Act (TVPA) Reauthorization of 2008, an important civil dimension was added to the approach towards human trafficking that expanded the capacity of victims to seek damage from entities such as hotels where they were exploited. Under this law, expanded civil liability applies to individuals or companies who 'knowingly benefit' from what they knew or should have known was a trafficking enterprise (Sagduyu, 2017). While this ability to sue hotels has existed for over a decade now, it has only been used in the last few years as a significant tool by trafficking victims seeking damages from corporate entities that have facilitated their exploitation. Case numbers of victims suing hotels grew to at least 125 in 2019 (Adams and Mashelkar,

2020). These suits make allegations about the diverse ways in which hotels help facilitate sexual trafficking, including employees serving as police lookouts and taking cash bribes from traffickers, reserving a top floor of a hotel for traffickers for an extra cash fee, and hotel managers and other employees paying a trafficker to have sex with the victim being held at the hotel concerned.

Hotels have been so central to human trafficking because they provide such convenience for clients of the trafficked women and so much anonymity for the traffickers through online reservations. Most hotel chains and franchises have not established guidelines and adequate training for employees, and few hotels have publicly committed to eliminating human trafficking from their facilities. In fact, my discussions with some global hotel chains have indicated that attempting to limit prostitution and human trafficking in their hotels in the Middle East and Asia would be 'bad for business'. End Child Prostitution and Trafficking (ECPAT), an NGO that fights child sexual exploitation, has developed a partnership with the tourism sector to try and foster better behavior and greater awareness of human trafficking. Companies which endorse the Tourism Child-Protection Code of Conduct, a joint venture between the private hospitality industry and ECPAT known as 'The Code', are expected to uphold six criteria, including establishing policy and procedure against sexual exploitation of children, training employees on prevention and reporting, providing information to travelers on children's rights and exploitation, and developing annual reports on the implementation of these criteria (End Child Prostitution and Trafficking-USA, n.d.). However, the data available on their websites reveal that the few hotel chains partnering with ECPAT have not fully lived up to the obligations of this partnership – many companies fail to provide sufficient training as well as an annual report on Code criteria (The Code, 2021).

Conclusion

Two decades have passed since the UN Protocol to Prevent, Suppress and Punish Trafficking in Persons was introduced in 2003. Whereas some anti-trafficking advocates focus on the possibility of eliminating human trafficking, analysis of the phenomenon reveals that the problem is growing rather than contracting. New technologies, complex global supply chains and greater anonymity have allowed human trafficking – especially the exploitation of vulnerable minors in sex trafficking – and the presence of labor trafficking in many diverse sectors of the global economy. Although the Protocol places the problem of trafficking firmly within the sphere of criminal activity, it does not recognize the very central role that legitimate businesses play in the supply chains for human trafficking.

Only now the role of facilitators in crime and corruption has become a topic that has emerged from the shadows and is beginning to command the policy attention it deserves (Vogl, 2021). Those seeking to address human trafficking must focus more on the facilitating role of legitimate companies in human trafficking. This analysis has shown that far too few companies have addressed human trafficking within their supply chains, and many have done too little to eliminate human trafficking from their hotels, their online platforms or social media. The absence of corporate social responsibility and leadership, except in the financial sector, is striking. In some cases, registered companies have deliberately persevered in enabling human trafficking because of the vast profits that can be achieved, and others have failed to invest the resources needed to address the issue. As Leary (2019) points out, there are historical precedents for this in the history of slavery, and legitimate companies then and now have made significant profits from the trade in human beings. This insight suggests that the absence of corporate leadership is not unexpected. Moreover, the focus on human trafficking as an organized and transnational crime problem results in a failure to appreciate the role of the legitimate economy in perpetuating the trade.

The slave trade was ended in the nineteenth century as a result of civic activism (Shelley, 2018). This, as well as citizen mobilization, is key in forcing greater corporate responsibility in line with the UN SDGs. As in the past, religious groups today play a key role in pressing for changes in the business community and forcing them to recognize and address diverse forms of human trafficking. Yet it is also other elements of civil society that are forcing change. Employees of airlines have forced their employers to be more responsive to human trafficking. Survivors, often with the aid of *pro bono* legal counsel, are filing suits against corporations such as hotels and ISPs demanding shifts in corporate behavior and reparations for their role in facilitating their abuse. In demanding more transparent and responsible supply chains by corporations, shareholder and consumer activism have done much to produce more responsible supply (Freedom United, n.d). More responsible corporate behavior must be initiated within all types of businesses and should not merely result from external pressure.

References

A.B. v. Salesforce.com (2020) No. 4:20-cv-01254, State Department of Texas. Available at: https://regmedia.co.uk/2021/03/26/pacer_ab_v_salesforce.pdf

Adams, E. and Mashelkar, S. (2020) 'Human Trafficking Lawsuits and the Hotel Industry', *Hotel Business*, 11 August. Available at: https://www.hotelbusiness.com/human-trafficking-lawsuits-and-the-hotel-industry/

Airline Ambassadors International (n.d.) *Human Trafficking*. Available at: https://airlineamb.org/human-trafficking/

Anthony, B. (2018) *On-ramps, Intersections and Exit Routes: A Roadmap for Systems and Industries to Prevent and Disrupt Human Trafficking: Hotels and Motels*, Polaris. Available at: https://polarisproject.org/wp-content/uploads/2018/08/A-Roadmap-for-Systems-and-Industries-to-Prevent-and-Disrupt-Human-Trafficking-Hotels-and-Motels.pdf

Association of Flight Attendants-CWA (n.d.) 'Stop human trafficking'. Available at: https://www.afacwa.org/stop_human_trafficking

Bain, C. and Shelley, L. (2015) 'Hedging risk by combating human trafficking: Insights from the private sector', Geneva: World Economic Forum.

Balch, O. (2021) 'Mars, Nestlé and Hershey to face child slavery lawsuit in US', *The Guardian* (US edition), 12 February. Available at: https://www.theguardian.com/global-development/2021/feb/12/mars-nestle-and-hershey-to-face-landmark-child-slavery-lawsuit-in-us

Balfour, A. W. (2019) 'Where one marketplace closes, (hopefully) another won't open: In defense of FOSTA', *Boston College Law Review* 60(8): 2475–2509.

Bigio, J. and Vogelstein, R. (2021) *Ending Human Trafficking in the Twenty-first Century*, New York: Council on Foreign Relations.

Bracy, K., Lul, B. and Roe-Sepowitz, D. (2021) 'A four-year analysis of labor trafficking cases in the United States: Exploring characteristics and labor trafficking patterns', *Journal of Human Trafficking* 7(1): 35–52.

Bullock, S., Fender, P., Jura, P., Welch, O. and Zeidler, F. (2021) 'Gibson Dunn discusses mandatory corporate human rights due diligence', *The CLS Blue Skye Blog*. Available at: https://clsbluesky.law.columbia.edu/2021/03/24/gibson-dunn-discusses-mandatory-corporate-human-rights-due-diligence/

Bullock, S., Neil, A. and Romanelli, A. (2021) 'Gibson Dunn discusses EU developments in corporate human rights due diligence', *The CLS Blue Sky Blog*. Available at: https://clsbluesky.law.columbia.edu/2021/02/15/gibson-dunn-discusses-eu-developments-in-corporate-human-rights-due-diligence/

Carney, E. (2019) 'Protecting internet freedom at the expense of facilitating online child sex trafficking? An explanation as to why CDA's Section 230 has no place in a new NAFTA', *Catholic University Law Review* 68(2): 353–78.

Ciliberti, F., Pontrandolfo, P. and Scozzi, B. (2008) 'Investigating corporate social responsibility in supply chains: A SME perspective', *Journal of Cleaner Production* 16(15): 79–88.

Dickson, M. and Warren, H. (2020) 'A look at labor issues in the manufacturing of fashion through the perspective of human trafficking and modern-day slavery', in Marcketti, S. B. and Karpova, E. E. (eds) *The Dangers of Fashion: Towards Ethical and Sustainable Solutions*, London: Bloomsbury Visual Arts.

Embassy of the Principality of Liechtenstein (n.d.) 'Liechtenstein initiative launches Finance Against Slavery and Trafficking (FAST)'. Available at: https://www.liechtensteinusa.org/article/liechtenstein-initiative-launches-finance-against-slavery-and-trafficking-fast

End Child Prostitution and Trafficking-USA (n.d.) 'The tourism-child protection code of conduct "The Code"'. Available at: https://www.ecpatusa.org/code

Feehs, K. and Currier Wheeler, A. (2021) *2020 Federal Human Trafficking Report*, Fairfax, VA.

Freedom United (n.d) 'Urge Monster to investigate slavery risk in its drinks'. Available at: https://www.freedomunited.org/advocate/monster-slavery/

Gibbons, K. (2020) '71% of child sex abuse images are from the Netherlands', *The Times*, 27 April. Available at: https://www.thetimes.co.uk/article/71-of-child-sex-abuse-images-are-from-netherlands-rx9s5c69n

Greenemeier, L. (2015) 'Human traffickers caught on hidden internet', *Scientific American*, 8 February. Available at: https://www.scientificamerican.com/article/human-traffickers-caught-on-hidden-internet/

Hutchinson, A. (2021) 'Facebook pushes ahead with plans for full end-to-end encryption of its messaging tools', *Social Media Today*, 30 April. Available at: https://www.socialmediatoday.com/news/facebook-pushes-ahead-with-plans-for-full-end-to-end-encryption-of-its-mess/599397/

International Centre for Missing and Exploited Children (n.d.) 'U.S. financial coalition against child exploitation'. Available at: https://www.icmec.org/fcacse/

Jackman, T. (2018) 'Backpage CEO Carl Ferrer pleads guilty in three states, agrees to testify against other website officials', *Washington Post*, 13 April. Available at: https://www.washingtonpost.com/news/true-crime/wp/2018/04/13/backpage-ceo-carl-ferrer-pleads-guilty-in-three-states-agrees-to-testify-against-other-website-officials/

Jackman, T. and Berman, M. (2018) 'Top officials at Backpage.com indicted after classifieds site taken offline', *Washington Post*, 9 April. Available at: https://www.washington post.com/local/public-safety/top-officials-at-backpagecom-indicted-after-classifieds-site-taken-offline/2018/04/09/0b646f36–39db-11e8–9c0a-85d477d9a226_story.html

Johnson, H. (2021) 'Texas Supreme Court rules that Facebook can be sued for sex trafficking', *Jurist*, 28 June. Available at: https://www.jurist.org/news/2021/06/texas-supreme-court-rules-facebook-can-be-sued-for-sex-trafficking/

Know the Chain (2015) *Insights brief: Five Years of the California Transparency in Supply Chains Act*. Available at: https://knowthechain.org/wp-content/uploads/2015/10/KnowTheChain_InsightsBrief_093015.pdf

Leary, M. G. (2019) 'History repeats itself: Some new faces behind sex trafficking are more familiar than you think', *Emory Law Journal Online* 68: 1083–1108.

Levy, A. (2018) *Human Trafficking Civil Litigation: 15 Years of the Private Right of Legal Action*, Human Trafficking Legal Center. Available at: https://www.htlegalcenter.org/wp-content/uploads/Federal-Human-Trafficking-Civil-Litigation-1.pdf

Mahalingam, R. and Sidhu, J. S. (2020) 'Inside the crime of sex trafficking in Sabah, Malaysia', *Journal of Human Trafficking* 7(3): 308–24.

Marchildon, J. (2018) 'Airbnb rentals are increasingly being used for human trafficking, police say', *Global Citizen*, 23 February. Available at: https://www.globalcitizen.org/fr/content/airbnb-human-trafficking/?template=next

Mari, J. (2020) 'Project Shadow: AML investigations into online child sexual exploitation', *ACAMS Today*. Available at: https://www.acamstoday.org/project-shadow-aml-investi gations-into-online-child-sexual-exploitation/

McCabe, D., Isaac, M. and Benner, K. (2019) 'Facebook and Barr escalate standoff over encrypted messages', *New York Times*, 10 December. Available at: https://www.nytimes.com/2019/12/10/technology/whatsapp-barr-encryption.html

McQue, K. (2021) 'Instagram fuels rise of black-market sales of maids into Persian Gulf servitude', *Washington Post*, 4 May. Available at: https://www.washingtonpost.com/world/middle_east/gulf-uae-migrant-workers-instagram/2021/05/04/3a767564-a44d-11eb-b314-2e993bd83e31_story.html

Metropolitan Airport News (2021) 'Flight attendant prevents human trafficking on Alaska Airlines', 22 January. Available at: https://metroairportnews.com/flight-attendant-prevents-human-trafficking-on-alaska-airlines/

Paraskevas, A. and Brookes, M. (2018) 'Human trafficking in hotels: An "invisible" threat for a vulnerable industry', *International Journal of Contemporary Hospitality Management* 30(3): 1996–2014.

Pellerin, C. (2017) 'DARPA program helps to fight human trafficking', *US Department of Defense News*, 4 January. Available at: https://dod.defense.gov/News/Article/Article/1041509/darpa-program-helps-to-fight-human-trafficking/

Porter, T. (2021) 'Facebook reported more than 20 million child sex abuse images in 2020, more than any other company', *Business Insider*, 26 February. Available at: https://www.businessinsider.com/facebook-instagram-report-20-million-child-sexual-abuse-im ages-2021-2

Ramey, C. (2020) 'Lawsuits accuse big hotel chains of allowing sex trafficking', *Wall Street Journal*, 4 March. Available at: https://www.wsj.com/articles/lawsuits-accuse-big-hotel-chains-of-allowing-sex-trafficking-11583317800

Redfern, C. and Lee, S. (2021) 'Sex criminals use Bitcoin. So do the police', *Foreign Policy*, 30 January. Available at: https://foreignpolicy.com/2021/01/30/sex-criminals-use-bitcoin-so-do-the-police/

Sagduyu, C. (2017) 'Nightmare in Shangri-La: Consequences likely for entities who benefit from human trafficking', *Trafficking Matters*, 5 April. Available at: https://www.traffickingmatters.com/nightmare-in-shangri-la-consequences-likely-for-entities-who-benefit-from-human-trafficking/

Saletan, W. (2010) 'Pimp Mobile: Craigslist shuts its "adult" section. Where will the sex ads go now?', *Slate*, 7 September. Available at: https://slate.com/news-and-politics/2010/09/craigslist-shuts-its-adult-section-where-will-sex-ads-go-now.html

Savage, C. and Williams, T. (2018) 'U.S. seizes Backpage.com, a site accused of enabling prostitution', *New York Times*, 7 April. Available at: https://www.nytimes.com/2018/04/07/us/politics/backpage-prostitution-classified.html

Scheck, J., Purnell, N. and Horwitz, J. (2021) 'Facebook employees flag drug cartels and human traffickers. The company's response is weak, documents show', *Wall Street Journal*, 16 September. Available at: https://www.wsj.com/articles/facebook-drug-cartels-human-traffickers-response-is-weak-documents-11631812953

Schumann, S. (2019) 'Corporate criminal liability on human trafficking', in Winterdyk, J. and Jones, J. (eds), *The Palgrave International Handbook of Human Trafficking*, London: Palgrave Macmillan.

Senate Permanent Subcommittee on Investigations (2017) *Backpage.com's Knowing Facilitation of Online Child Sex Trafficking*. Available at: https://www.hsgac.senate.gov/imo/media/doc/Backpage%20Report%202017.01.10%20FINAL.pdf

Shavers, A. W. (2012) 'Human trafficking, the rule of law, and corporate social responsibility', *South Carolina Journal of International Law and Business* 9(1): 39–88.

Shelley, L. (1998) 'Crime and corruption in the digital age', *Journal of International Affairs* 51(2): 605–620.

Shelley, L. (2018) *Dark Commerce: How a New Illicit Economy is Threatening our Future*, Princeton, NJ: Princeton University Press.

Sparks, E. (2019) 'At Super Bowl, U.S. bank tackles human trafficking', *ABA Banking Journal*, 30 January. Available at: https://bankingjournal.aba.com/2019/01/at-super-bowl-u-s-bank-tackles-human-trafficking/

Steiner-Dicks, K. (2019) 'We know most global companies have modern slavery in their supply chains', *Reuters Events*, 6 August. Available at: https://www.reutersevents.com/sustainability/we-know-most-global-companies-have-modern-slavery-their-supply-chains

Sturken, C. (2019) 'What airlines are doing to combat human trafficking', *Northstar Meetings Group*, 7 May. Available at: https://www.northstarmeetingsgroup.com/News/Industry/Airlines-Human-Trafficking-Efforts

Tarinelli, R. (2018) 'Online sex ads rebound, months after shutdown of Backpage', *AP News*, 29 November. Available at: https://apnews.com/article/159434f052eb40dd87b9dd9b65da53f5

The Code (2021) *Our Members*. Available at: http://thecode.org/ourmembers/

Thulander, S. (2021) 'G7 nations should create a race to the top to eliminate forced labor: Our letter to global leaders', *Global Fund to End Modern Slavery*, 7 June. Available at: https://www.gfems.org/news/2021/6/7/g7-nations-should-create-a-race-to-the-top-to-eliminate-forced-labor-our-letter-to-global-leaders

United Nations (2015) *Transforming Our World: The 2030 Agenda for Sustainable Development*, Geneva: UN.

United Nations General Assembly (2003) *Protocol to Prevent, Suppress, and Punish Trafficking in Persons, Especially Women and Children, Supplementing the United Nations Convention against Transnational Organized Crime*. Available at: https://undocs.org/en/A/Res/55/25

United States v. Chen (2018) No. 3:18-CR-00559, District of Oregon. Available at: https://www.justice.gov/usao-or/press-release/file/1124296/download

United States Department of Justice (2019) 'Nationwide sting operation targets illegal Asian brothels, six indicted for racketeering', 16 January. Available at: https://www.justice.gov/usao-or/pr/nationwide-sting-operation-targets-illegal-asian-brothels-six-indicted-racketeering

United States Department of State (2020) *Trafficking in Persons Report*, 20th Edition. Available at: https://www.state.gov/wp-content/uploads/2020/06/2020-TIP-Report-Complete-062420-FINAL.pdf

Vogl, F. (2021) *The Enablers: How the West Supports Kleptocrats and Corruption – Endangering our Democracy*, London: Rowman & Littlefield.

Acknowledgments

The author acknowledges the support of the National Science Foundation (Award #1837881) for her research on A New Multi-Layered Network Approach for Improving the Detection of Human Trafficking.

Chapter 20

Youth, Social Media and Responsible Leadership

Sebastian Hofbauer

Introduction

Picture a youth leader. Chances are that you are thinking about Greta Thunberg and Malala Yousafzai and the great things they have achieved in the areas of climate change and female education, respectively. It is far less likely that Felix Kjellberg or Charli D'Amelio come to mind. More likely than not, you have not even heard of them. Meanwhile, the videos of Felix Kjellberg (age 31) on YouTube have been viewed over 27 billion times. And in just two years, Charli D'Amelio (age 17) has reached over 246 million views. Granted, even if you go ahead and Google their names now you will be hard pressed to see how their work links to youth leadership. Indeed, on the surface it probably does not. But it could. And it should.

Greta Thunberg and Malala Yousafzai and their incredible work, including in the latter case being the youngest Nobel Peace Prize winning laureate, are indeed great examples of youth leadership. Yet, in the 2020s, they are only the tip of the youth leadership iceberg. Today, youth leadership happens largely online – and this space is firmly occupied by youth leaders who are rarely acknowledged as such: young social media influencers. Their posts and endorsements, whether informative or entertaining, have a significant impact on their followers. And, in a world that is increasingly shaped by social media, their societal importance – for better or for worse – is rising. Both Greta Thunberg and Malala Yousafzai will fulfill whatever definition of responsible youth leadership we come up with. While we spend time pondering

DOI: 10.4324/9781003129189-27

what exactly youth leadership is, they are doing just fine and are impacting the world in tangible ways. They do not need anyone's help in leading responsibly. Social media influencers on the other hand? While it is arguably clear that they are leaders, it is more questionable if they are *responsible* leaders. And they could certainly use some guidance on how to transition into a more responsible leadership. At the same time, we have a lot to learn from them.

It is this very consideration that makes them such a fascinating topic to explore in a book about responsible leadership and sustainable development. After all, social media influencers reach audiences – both in terms of numbers and demographics – that many large organizations can only dream of attaining. Their potential is already well understood and utilized for marketing purposes. You will frequently see young influencers partner with cosmetic brands or promote new headphones or a travel company. Unfortunately, several cases also highlight the capacity for potential influencers to misinform. That they might not be responsible leaders today does not mean that they cannot be tomorrow. By leveraging their outreach in a responsible manner, young online leaders could be much more than vehicles to promote yet another product. Responsible young influencers – or online leaders – could have a considerable impact for good.

Yet today, these same young online leaders are rarely recognized as the *leaders* they are. Their potential is often wasted, or in the worst of cases, their practices aggravate social issues because they do not act responsibly. Fueled by the recent urgency of the COVID-19 pandemic, now is the right time to embrace young social media influencers as leaders and to help them lead responsibly.

The rise of social media and the democratizing of leadership

Let us make one thing clear: youth are *not* the future. It is about time we stopped talking about the young generation as mere symbols of futuristic hope. They are actors of the present that need and deserve to be actively included in society. A key driving factor behind this development is how the Internet has broken, and continues to break down, knowledge monopolies. The growth of the Internet, in particular the explosion of social media usage, have revolutionized the way we interact, communicate and engage. For many, social media platforms play a central role in all aspects of their lives.

This development has clearly also revolutionized and democratized the way we lead. Just think about how different election campaigns are conducted today compared to 15 years ago. In a similar manner, youth leadership has been transformed through the new opportunities opened by social media. Going back to Greta Thunberg, it is not likely that she would have become a global symbol for the fight against the climate emergency without a strong online engagement campaign. Being just 17 years old at the time, Avi Schiffmann built what would become one of the world's most popular coronavirus tracking sites, which has received praise from Dr Fauci and other scientists and government health agencies around the world (World Wide Web Foundation, 2021). Similarly, 13-year-old Samaira Mehta's board game is teaching young kids how to code every day (Rich, 2021). The impact young people are having is tangible, it is real, and it is happening now.

With the Internet at their fingertips, the young generation, as digital natives, has started to take a front seat. True leaders are emerging by seizing the new opportunities of their age. Gone are the days in which youth were a symbol of futuristic hope and, at best, seen as benefactors of programs aimed at their inclusion. In the age of online youth leadership, it is not youth who are the benefactors. It is society that can benefit from online youth leadership – if it is responsible. And this brings us back to young influencers and their role as youth leaders.

The rise of a new kind of youth leader

Understanding that youth leadership happens in large parts online is the first step. The second step is acknowledging that online youth leaders are not necessarily the most obvious ones. While there are youth leaders that are easily identified and acknowledged as such, there are countless others. Some of them are reaching tens of thousands or even hundreds of thousands every day. As we will explore later, these young online leaders clearly have a large impact on their followers and also society at large. Yet, by nature of their work, they are not necessarily leading for a good cause and may even be seen as having a negative impact.

The Internet has enabled anyone to voice their opinion and to launch initiatives, campaigns or products without access to many resources. The rise of social media in particular goes hand in hand with the rise of this new kind of youth leader, commonly referred to as *social media influencers* (SMIs). SMIs are defined as "people who built a large network of followers and are regarded as trusted tastemakers in one or several niches" (De Veirman, Cauberghe and Hudders, 2017: 1). Anyone can be a SMI, from a university professor to a high-school student. It is no coincidence, however, that the young generation is particularly heavily represented in this field. Young people are not only characterized by their ability to innovate and think outside the box, but they also grew up with the Internet literally in their pockets. As digital natives, youth typically understand how to interact online in ways that may be hard to grasp for those that grew up with television, radio and the telephone as the main modes of communication and entertainment. In 2019, the International Telecommunication Union (2019) found that 69 percent of youth worldwide are using the Internet compared to 51 percent of the total population. While this, unfortunately, leaves a considerable number of youth offline, they are much more likely to be connected than older generations.

Social media as a tool to gather information has rapidly gained in importance over the last decade. It has replaced the more traditional channels of mass communication, such as television, radio and newspapers, as the most dominant and efficient sources of information (Lou and Yuan, 2019). Social media as a medium has a large influence on young people. It provides access to information and enables them to communicate with their peers, but it also gives them opportunities to express their beliefs and opinions far outside their social circles. Within these new channels, SMIs have established themselves as a most important and effective source of information. This position makes them extremely valuable actors in the social media age. As Vulkko (2021: 11) puts it: "a good example of a young opinion leader is a young social media influencer who, due to relatability and trustworthiness, has a large impact on their followers". Young SMIs are the youth leaders of the Internet.

The influencers' influence

If young SMIs can be considered leaders, it is because of the effect they have on their followers. They have been shown to have a similar effect on people's opinions as traditional opinion leaders (Uzunoğlu, 2014). In order to understand how young online leaders shape the digital world, it is worth taking a look at their measured impact on consumers. This marketing lens is useful, given that it is a field that first and foremost deals with shaping opinions and behavior of people. Indeed, marketeers have long understood the potential that lies with SMIs to sway opinions and change behaviors.

As our dependence on social media is rising by the day, SMIs are more and more emerging in worldwide advertising space as key players (Sehgal and Sabharwal, 2021). A study by McKinsey in India revealed that "up to 80 percent of consumers will consider a new brand based on the recommendation of a key influencer" (Agarwal et al., 2019: 7). And a report by Insider Intelligence (2021) on marketing during COVID-19 found that influencers are on track to be a $15 billion business by 2022, nearly double the $9 billion they generated in 2019.

What makes SMIs good marketing partners? They have managed to position themselves as trusted and important sources of information for their followers. It is well understood that people often seek to reinforce their opinion before making a decision. This reinforcement can be achieved through benchmarking against an opinion leader (Rogers and Cartano, 1962). In today's world, this is often done through SMIs. They have great power to influence purchase decisions through their platforms, and this has led to influencer marketing becoming one of the most powerful forms of marketing (Sehgal and Sabharwal, 2021).

Research by Tran and Strutton (2014) has shown that people have a positive attitude toward endorsed brands, perceive influencers to be trustworthy, have a strong social presence and feel envious. They also found that consumers connect strongly to influencers, who are regarded as authentic (Stefanone, Lackaff and Rosen, 2010). SMIs are seen as more accessible, believable, intimate and easy to relate to (Abidin, 2016). According to one study, 6 out of 10 teenagers are more likely to follow advice from social media influencers over celebrities due to a strong and more personal relationship with the former (Ipsos Connect, 2015). Findings of another study presented at the European Congress on Obesity in 2018 showed that children who saw YouTube stars consuming unhealthy snacks went on to consume over one quarter more calories than children exposed to non-food products (BBC, 2018).

Influencers clearly have the potential to be strong opinion leaders in social media. More than 'traditional' celebrities, they are perceived as real, which results in a feeling of deeper connectedness because consumers personally identify with them and try to imitate them (Tran and Strutton, 2014). Frequently, SMIs offer their audiences an insight into their personal lives (De Veirman, Cauberghe and Hudders, 2017). The sharing of content that includes everyday challenges and thoughts makes SMIs appear more relatable and trustworthy – and helps build a relationship between the SMI and the follower. All in all, SMIs can connect with their audience on a deeper level and influence them more than if they were to see an advert on television (Wahl, 2019).

Their potential to connect with their audience in a trusted way makes young influencers true opinion leaders on the most important platforms of the Internet. The question then is: if they can be considered 'leaders' in the traditional sense, are they what we would consider *responsible* leaders? How can we leverage the potential of young online leaders for positive social impact? Let us now turn to discuss this.

Not every leader is a responsible leader

Over the last decade, several cases exemplify what happens when influencers do not act responsibly. Unlike traditional leaders, the barrier to become an influencer is much lower. In principle, the role is open to anyone. In addition, many influencers do not build their platforms around social causes. Instead, their position emerges from selling a lifestyle or beauty trend, or travel tips. Here they differ clearly from traditional youth leaders, such as the three examples given at the beginning of this chapter. Greta Thunberg is leading the fight against the climate emergency. Avi Schiffmann helped to track the spread of the coronavirus when the world was just starting to wake up to its danger. And Samaira Mehta is giving kids new perspectives by teaching them how to code. These clearly are noble causes that result in positive impacts on our society. All three built their platforms around a social cause – responsibility is deeply ingrained into their business model. They grow and nurture their position by continuing to act responsibly.

Although there are other examples of social media being used to advance the social good (see, for example, Hamblin, 2015), the same cannot typically be said about all influencers. They operate more like businesses aiming to make a profit. Their large following on social media platforms translates into outreach which attracts advertising business. The more followers they have, and the more engaged these followers are, the higher the potential business value. They are tasked to continuously grow the business value by attracting more followers and by keeping them engaged through posting the right content. The separate goals of creating cash value and acting responsibly can clash. Influencers are not governed by any specific set of rules. This means that their power to influence opinions and behaviors has the potential to mislead or misinform (The Finery Report, 2020). Considering the increasing importance of influencers, concern about this potential and their responsibility are not misplaced (Pham, 2021).

In light of the large amount of money flowing into this relatively new and largely unregulated market, it is not surprising that several issues have emerged over time. The Finery Report (2020) mentions one example where a number of influencers have been investigated over endorsement deals for a business that stole and misused their customers' credit card information. Owens (2019) reports that influencers have tried to extort businesses by threatening to talk badly about a product or simply ignore it. There is also a big issue with honesty and transparency. In 2018, the *New York Times* published an exhaustive investigation titled 'The follower factory'. The story unveils how wannabe influencers used social media bots to inflate their importance online when negotiating sponsored posts (Confessore et al., 2018). Additionally, paid posts are frequently not labelled as such. In some cases, influencers endorsing a brand or product showcase it as if they were giving a personal or expert opinion, when they are being paid to promote it (The Finery Report, 2020).

Another noteworthy case happened in 2019. A number of famous YouTubers shared stories about their struggles with depression and burnout, which sparked many stories about issues those seeking online fame face. The practice of sharing struggles was openly welcomed by the community. The mood soon changed when it became apparent that these YouTubers ended their videos by promoting an online therapy service. Instead of genuinely sharing valid concerns about mental health and well-being, they were accused of cynically exploiting the issue for profit (Owens, 2019). Just like with businesses, when the separate goals of creating cash value and acting sustainably clash, there is a clear need to ensure that this does not happen.

Current efforts to regulate are not enough

Cases such the ones mentioned earlier have already led to calls for more regulation. Some countries have started to introduce regulations to that effect. In Norway, for example, influencers are now legally obligated to disclose if a post is a paid promotion (Chiu, 2021). In India, the Bombay High Court decided that influencers cannot make statements with the same freedom available to an ordinary person, indicating that the courts are beginning to recognize the need for regulation, considering the power influencers wield in particular over the young generation (Sehgal and Sabharwal, 2021).

On the tech side, the major social media platforms are also starting to take influencer fraud more seriously. Some of them have put policies in place that aim to regulate influencers within their own ecosystems. Both Facebook and YouTube, for example, introduced disclosure guidelines for posts containing branded, paid-for content. And, on the corporate side, major brands have begun to tighten the rules around how they engage with influencers, introducing new ways to identify campaigns to reduce the risk of fraud (Owens, 2019).

As the importance of social media as a primary source of information is rising, so is its potential to mislead. Influencers, with their large power in that space to shape narratives, sway opinions, and influence decisions, can become sources of misinformation. States, courts, social media platforms and businesses have started putting counter-measures in place. According to Owens (2019), current efforts are not enough; a Cambridge Analytica moment could shake up the industry in a serious way, leading to increased scrutiny and coordination, as well as the adoption of more drastic measures to counter fraud and bad practices.

Since the Internet and the work of online leaders embedded in it transcend the governance of nation states, there are gaps in global governance related to their work. These deficits offer opportunities for online leaders to act in ways that are not responsible, with detrimental effects on society. On the other hand, the resulting increased scrutiny by industry and governments also poses a threat even to more responsible influencers, who may be losing out on business opportunities or be faced with tougher rules. Negative connotations associated with influencing also risks that brands will struggle to identify trustworthy influencers with which to partner. This is particularly challenging for social impact organizations with a primary mission to serve societal needs – such as the United Nations (UN) or non-profits. There is clearly a need here for responsible online leadership.

In the corporate world, governance gaps surrounding negative business externalities on a global level are nothing new, as illustrated by the 2008 financial crisis (Saks and Muzio, 2018). In the business world, some frameworks exist to mitigate these effects and facilitate trusted partnerships with social impact organizations, but these are not watertight – as illustrated by the case of international professional service firms, which operate largely outside the formal regulation applied within national bounds (Saks, 2021). Similarly, a proportionate regulatory framework for responsible online leadership could be a scalable solution for the industry.

Towards responsible online youth leadership

In trying to identify how such a framework for engaging young SMIs might look like, we can turn to the UN and how this organization works with the private sector.

Around the turn of the last century, a change occurred with the UN. A lack of funding from UN member states resulted in a serious financial crisis. At the same time, ideological shifts towards a more neo-liberal approach led to the UN seeing itself as less of a regulator and more of a partner of business organizations. These developments opened the door for new partnerships between the UN and private sector corporations (Vasavada and Kim, 2017). From the viewpoint of the UN, there was one problem: how to partner with a sector that, arguably, has such different objectives – worldviews even – from those of the UN?

This issue is hardly solved today. But there are workable approaches that have facilitated these public-private partnerships. In 1999, then UN Secretary-General Kofi Anan addressed leaders at the World Economic Forum Annual Meeting in Davos, Switzerland. In his speech, he called for dialogue with business and moving the UN towards a more proactive role that regards business as part of the solution to global problems. The speech is credited with the birth of what would become the UN Global Compact (UNGC) (Voegtlin and Pless, 2014).

Self-regulatory initiatives addressing governance gaps on the global level through Corporate Social Responsibility (CSR) have become an important part of doing business, including through SMIs (Cheng, Chen and Hung-Baesecke, 2021). The UNGC is the most prominent of what can be seen as CSR-facing business practices (Abbott and Snidal, 2010; Waddock, 2008). It mainly has two objectives:

- to invite the private sector to embrace, support and carry out a set of core values in the areas of human rights, labor, environment and anti-corruption within the business world to encourage corporate citizenship
- to provide a common place that facilitates cooperation among the various economic and social actors in the global arena to promote UN values (Therien and Pouliot, 2006).

Those advocating for the UNGC say it effectively facilitates dialogue between social impact organizations and the private sector, achieving a broad consensus on global ethical standards. The argument is that the mere exposure of corporations to CSR principles and their public display leads to outside pressure and organizational learning. There is ongoing debate whether or not the UNGC is successful in achieving this. Voegtlin and Pless (2014) provide an overview of the main arguments about the purpose, achievements and critique of the UNGC.

The UNGC clearly is successful in one metric – the number of organizations that have joined it. Since it was created in 2000, the initiative has witnessed strong growth. Today, more than 17,000 organizational participants from business and civil society form part of its network (United Nations, 2021). The UNGC clearly meets a need – the creation of trusted partnerships between the UN and the private sector. Its underlying principles are listed below in Box 20.1. Can a similar mechanism for responsible online youth leadership help to facilitate a new kind of partnership between SMIs and social impact organizations, unlocking their outreach potential for positive change?

Box 20.1 The ten principles of the UN Global Compact

Human Rights

1. Businesses should support and respect the protection of internationally proclaimed human rights; and
2. Make sure that they are not complicit in human rights abuses.

Labour

3. Businesses should uphold the *freedom of association* and the effective recognition of the right to *collective bargaining*;
4. The elimination of all forms of forced and compulsory labour;
5. The effective abolition of child labour; and
6. The elimination of discrimination in respect of employment and occupation.

Environment

7. Businesses should support a precautionary approach to environmental challenges;
8. Undertake initiatives to promote greater environmental responsibility; and
9. Encourage the development and diffusion of environmentally friendly technologies.

Anti-corruption

10. Businesses should work against corruption in all its forms, including extortion and bribery.

Source: United Nations (2021) *United Nations Global Compact*, Geneva: UN.

What could influencer social responsibility look like?

Influencer social responsibility (ISR), in particular targeting young SMIs, could be a self-regulating business model that helps SMIs to be socially accountable – to themselves, their stakeholders and the public. By practicing ISR, influencers would be conscious of the kind of impact they are having on all aspects of society, including the economic, social and environmental dimensions. Engaging in ISR would mean that, in the ordinary course of business, an influencer works in a way that enhances society, instead of contributing negatively to it. Meanwhile, just like CSR, ISR would not be about charity or philanthropy. It would need to be positioned and designed in a way to put the creation of additional value front and center.

Regulation from social media platforms, governments and business increasingly puts pressure on influencers to act responsibly. This can be a challenge as they aim to comply with a set of new and ever-changing rules, in particular for the large group of young SMIs, who may not be well-versed in this. From a societal perspective, it is unlikely that such regulations will be enough to mitigate the adverse effects of social media influencing, let alone unlock its potential for social good. However, ISR could help influencers to recognize the impact they have on society and to align their business model accordingly. As a self-regulating model, it could help these online leaders to reduce risk by aligning their business model with values that are likely to be in line with present and future regulations.

The ISR may also help to unlock additional value by opening up new business opportunities with sustainability-minded consumers and companies, as well as social impact organizations. A key barrier for social impact organizations in leveraging the outreach potential of SMIs is a lack of trust. In the past, influencers, including those who are young, have been associated with topics that are often not directly related to good causes or even practices that run counter to them. Establishing trust between social impact organizations and SMIs is therefore key if partnerships are to be built between them to unlock this potential. In youth leadership, a field that receives much attention, this potential is a largely untapped resource that should be capitalized upon.

Conclusion

To sum up, in the age of social media, we need to rethink what a youth leader is. Youth are not the future. They are actors of the present. Youth leaders are forging ahead with new thinking about pressing issues such as the climate emergency and social injustice. Young influencers have established themselves among the primary opinion leaders on social media. Their unique position is already being leveraged by marketing departments, but irresponsible leadership practices stand in the way of unlocking their potential for social good.

There plainly exists a need to mitigate the adverse effects of influencing and to leverage its potential for good. The UN Global Compact has succeeded in facilitating partnerships between social impact organizations and the private sector. Its functioning as a self-regulating model with a set of principles establishes trust between the actors concerned. ISR may be a useful model for social media as we aim to reduce the adverse effects of its influence, and, more than that, to salvage its potential for social good.

Selected initiatives have already been launched, but the field is plagued by a lack of trust between the actors concerned, fueled by common cases of irresponsible behavior. Inspired by CSR, ISR could guide influencers as they aim to lead responsibly, thereby unlocking value on several fronts. Influencers could reduce business risk and open new markets. Social impact organizations could benefit from influencers' outreach. Reducing the negative effects of influencing and unlocking its positive potential would benefit society as a whole – not least in terms of helping to achieve the UN (2015) Sustainable Development Goals.

References

Abbott, K. W. and Snidal, D. (2010) 'International regulation without international government: Improving IO performance through orchestration', *Review of International Organizations* 5(3): 315–44.

Abidin, C. (2016) '"Aren't these just young, rich women doing vain things online?": Influencer selfies as subversive frivolity', *Social Media + Society* 2(2): 1–17.

Agarwal, A., Brar, J., Elzinga, D. and Tyagi, A. (2019) 'Marketing consumer durables in India: A journey into the minds of digital-age consumers', *McKinsey*, 30 July. Available at: Marketing-consumer-durables-in-India-A-journey-into-the-minds-of-digital-age-consumers.ashx (mckinsey.com)

BBC (2018) 'YouTube stars "might encourage kids to eat more calories"', BBC, 26 May. Available at: https://www.bbc.co.uk/news/health-44258509

Cheng, Y., Chen, Y.-R. R. and Hung-Baesecke, C.-J. F. (2021) 'Social media influencers in CSR endorsement: The effect of consumer mimicry on CSR behaviors and consumer relationships', *Social Science Computer Review* 39(4): 744–61.

Chiu, A. (2021) 'Why experts say Norway's retouched photo law won't help fight body image issues', *Washington Post*, 8 July. Available at: https://www.washingtonpost.com/lifestyle/wellness/photo-edit-social-media-norway/2021/07/08/f30d59ca-df2c-11eb-ae31-6b7c5c34f0d6_story.html

Confessore, N., Dance, G. J. X., Harris, R. and Hansen, M. (2018) 'The follower factory', *New York Times*, 27 January. Available at: https://www.nytimes.com/interactive/2018/01/27/technology/social-media-bots.html

De Veirman, M., Cauberghe, V. and Hudders, L. (2017) 'Marketing through Instagram influencers: The impact of the number of followers and product divergence on brand attitude', *International Journal of Advertising* 36(5): 798–828.

Hamblin, J. (2015) 'The food babe: Enemy of chemicals', *The Atlantic*, 11 February. Available at: https://www.theatlantic.com/health/archive/2015/02/the-food-babe-enemy-of-chemicals/385301/

Insider Intelligence (2021) 'Influencer marketing: Social media influencer market stats and research for 2021', *Insider Intelligence*, 27 July. Available at: https://www.insiderintelligence.com/insights/influencer-marketing-report/

International Telecommunication Union (2019) 'Measuring digital development: Facts and figures 2020'. Available at: https://www.itu.int/en/ITU-D/Statistics/Documents/facts/FactsFigures2020.pdf

Ipsos Connect (2015) *The YouTube Generation Study*, Ipsos Connect.

Lou, C. and Yuan, S. (2019) 'Influencer marketing: How message value and credibility affect consumer trust of branded content on social media', *Journal of Interactive Advertising* 19(1): 1–45.

Owens, S. (2019) 'Is it time to regulate social media influencers?', *Intelligencer*, 17 January. Available at: https://nymag.com/intelligencer/2019/01/is-it-time-to-regulate-social-media-influencers.html

Pham, B. (2021) 'What is the social responsibility of social media influencers?', *The Post and Courier*, 3 March. Available at: https://www.postandcourier.com/free-times/food/what-is-the-social-responsibility-of-social-media-influencers/article_77175896-7ab6-11eb-9740–3ffb16469284.html

Rich, G. (2021) 'Samaira Mehta shows other kids the fun of coding by inventing board games', *Washington Post*, 9 February. Available at: https://www.washingtonpost.com/lifestyle/kidspost/early-on-samaira-mehta-learned-coding-is-fun-now-shes-spreading-the-word/2021/02/08/093ce42e-6000–11eb-9061–07abcc1f9229_story.html

Rogers, E. and Cartano, D. (1962) 'Methods of measuring opinion leadership', *Public Opinion Quarterly* 26(3): 435–41.

Saks, M. (2021) *Professions: A Key Idea for Business and Society*, London: Routledge.

Saks, M. and Muzio, D. (2018) (eds) *Professions and Professional Service Firms: Private and Public Sector Enterprises in the Global Economy*, London: Routledge.

Sehgal, V. and Sabharwal, A. (2021) 'Social media influencers and the need for responsible advertising', Chadha and Chadha Intellectual Property Law Firm.

Stefanone, M., Lackaff, D. and Rosen, D. (2010) 'The relationship between traditional mass media and "social media": Reality television as a model for social network site behavior', *Journal of Broadcasting and Electronic Media* 54(3): 508–25.

The Finery Report (2020) 'Should we regulate influencers?', 3 December. Available at: https://www.thefineryreport.com/latestupdate/eng

Therien, J-P. and Pouliot, V. (2006) 'The Global Compact: Shifting the politics of international development', *Global Governance* 12(1): 55–75.

Tran, G. and Strutton, D. (2014) 'Has reality television come of age as a promotional platform? Modelling the endorsement effectiveness of celebreality and reality stars', *Psychology and Marketing* 31(4): 294–305.

United Nations (2015) *Transforming Our World: The 2030 Agenda for Sustainable Development*, Geneva: UN.

United Nations (2021) *United Nations Global Compact*, Geneva: UN. Available at: https://www.unglobalcompact.org/what-is-gc/participants

Uzunoğlu, E. (2014) 'Brand communication through digital influencers: Leveraging blogger engagement', *International Journal of Information Management* 34(5). Available at: https://doi.org/10.1016/j.ijinfomgt.2014.04.007

Vasavada, T. and Kim, S. (2017) 'Corporate Social Responsibility and the United Nations Global Compact Initiative', in Hasan, S. (ed) *Corporate Social Responsibility and the Three Sectors in Asia*, New York: Springer.

Voegtlin, C. and Pless, N. M. (2014) 'Global governance: CSR and the Role of the UN Global Compact', *Journal of Business Ethics* 122(2): 179–91.

Vulkko, V. (2021) 'Social media influencers and their social responsibility: Factors that affect micro influencers' decisions to collaborate with a company', Helsinki Metropolia University of Applied Sciences.

Waddock, S. (2008) 'Building a new institutional infrastructure for corporate responsibility', *Academy of Management Perspectives* 22(3): 87–108.

Wahl, R. (2019) Where does influencer responsibility begin and end?', *Better Marketing*, 18 July.

World Wide Web Foundation (2021) World Wide Web Foundation. Available at: https://webfoundation.org/2021/03/web-champion-avi/

Author Index

Subject Index